UNIVERSITY OF MARY HARDIN-BAYLOR
3 4637 002 164 118

D1274731

TRINITY, TIME, AND CHURCH

Robert W. Jenson

Trinity, Time, and Church

A Response to the Theology of Robert W. Jenson

Edited by

Colin E. Gunton

William B. Eerdmans Publishing Company
Grand Rapids, Michigan / Cambridge, U.K.

Wm. B. Eerdmans Publishing Company
255 Jefferson Ave. S.E., Grand Rapids, Michigan 49503 /
P.O. Box 163, Cambridge CB3 9PU U.K.

Printed in the United States of America

05 04 03 02 01 00 7 6 5 4 3 2 1

Library of Congress Cataloging-in-Publication Data

Trinity, time, and church: a response to the theology of Robert W. Jenson /
edited by Colin E. Gunton.
p. cm.
Includes bibliographical references.
ISBN 0-8028-3899-5 (hardcover)
1. Jenson, Robert W. I. Jenson, Robert W. II. Gunton, Colin E.

BX8080.J44 T75 2000
230′.41′092 — dc21

00-41734

www.eerdmans.com

For Blanche also

Contents

CONTENTS

Robert William Jenson — A Personal Memoir

CARL E. BRAATEN

Introduction

In his capacity as the editor of this *Festschrift,* Professor Colin Gunton asked me to write a personal memoir in honor of my friend and colleague, Robert W. Jenson. How could I refuse? I have enjoyed a close working relationship with Jens since our graduate student days at Heidelberg University in 1957-58. Incredible! That's over forty years. Together with our spouses and families we have shared many things beyond our intellectual interests, professional careers, and theological projects. A travelogue recounting the occasions we have lived or traveled together would have to include — in addition to Heidelberg — Oxford, Cuernavaca, Acapulco, Rome, Athens, and Istanbul, not to mention the many visits to each other's homes in Decorah, Maywood, Chicago, Flossmoor, Gettysburg, Sun City West, Northfield, and Princeton. All the good food that Blanche and LaVonne prepared and served to the four of us, and all the good wine that we have taken turns pouring at each other's tables — this memoir will hardly be able to give an account of all that wonderful and unforgettable family history. Instead, it will restrict itself to the ideas, developments, and commitments that have providentially linked our respective theological journeys. That also means that this account of Jenson's theological biography will not be able to delve into his childhood and youth, nor say anything about his life in a Lutheran parsonage or his student days at Luther

College — all of which would undoubtedly shed light on what makes Jens tick as a person, or gets him ticked off as a theologian.

Classmates at Luther Seminary

Jens began his studies at Luther Seminary in St. Paul, Minnesota, in 1951. We should have entered the same year, but I took a detour to Paris as a Fulbright Scholar in philosophy at the Sorbonne. My first year at the seminary I recall listening in on a fierce theological controversy taking place among upperclassmen outside the library. Little did I know then that this was the controversy that defined the battle positions throughout the faculty and the student body. Seeing that I was only listening and not saying anything, one of the antagonists turned to me and asked, "Well, where do you stand? Whose side are you on?" I didn't know anything about the matter. Later, when some friends clued me in on what the controversy was all about, I knew where I stood and whose side I was on, and that was exactly opposite where Robert Jenson was known to stand.

At that time we called him Bill Jenson; why, I don't know. Some who knew him from college called him Billie Bob. To me he was Bill Jenson, the brains on the other side of the issue, representing what was then variously referred to as the Luther College position, the more orthodox party. Midwest Lutherans were involved in what was classically known as the "election controversy." At issue in the controversy was the role of faith and its relationship to God's foreknowledge and predestination. When Norwegian American Lutheran Synods merged in 1917, they agreed to tolerate two forms of mutually incompatible teaching on election that have coexisted among Lutherans ever since the sixteenth century and that the *Formula of Concord* failed to resolve.

Reduced to its simplest terms, the question is whether God elects those whom he foresees will come to faith, or whether God's election is inherently decisive in effecting faith. There is a significant difference between "foreseeing" something that will happen and "seeing to it." The orthodox side stressed the preeminent priority and efficacy of divine grace; the pietist party stressed the role of free will and the necessity of human decision.

The old election controversy was being replayed on the campus of Luther Seminary, headed up by two professors bitterly at odds. On the one side was Professor George Aus, representing a mixture of pietism, biblicism, and revivalism; on the other side was Professor Herman Preus, representing Lutheran orthodoxy, confessionalism, and the catholic liturgy as reformed by Luther. They did not agree to tolerate each other's position. One was right, the other was wrong. Yet perhaps more important was the battle for the hearts and minds of the students. Professor Aus seemed to be winning hands down. Most of the seminarians came from the tradition of Lutheran pietism and were thus always suspicious of the doctrines of "dead orthodoxy." Jens was decidedly on the side of Preus; in fact, he became Preus's assistant and trustworthy defender.

At St. Olaf College I had majored in philosophy, read Kierkegaard's writings under Howard Hong, studied Sartre's existentialism at the Sorbonne, and was thus predisposed to the position of pietistic Lutheranism. After all, Kierkegaard was a pietist. After a long internal struggle of soul and mind, I switched sides. Jens did not know it then, but during my senior year I was won over to the side of Herman Preus and confessional Lutheran theology. The professor who persuaded me was a refugee theologian from Latvia, Edmund Smits; he was the first to teach me that orthodoxy was a vision worth claiming, and that the intention of classical Lutheranism was to maintain continuity with catholic teaching.

Graduate Study at Heidelberg University

After graduation from Luther Seminary Robert Jenson was called to teach in the religion department at Luther College. He was widely recognized as the most promising young theologian to carry on the tradition of the founding fathers of the college. He was there the two years (1955-57) during which I was studying under Paul Tillich at Harvard Divinity School. In the summer of 1957, while attending an assembly of the Lutheran World Federation in Minneapolis, I learned that Robert Jenson and his wife Blanche were going to Heidelberg, Germany. And so were we. Blanche loves to tell the story — we have rehearsed it many times — how we first encountered each other in Heidelberg. The two couples were both walking down Hauptstrasse from opposite ends of the street. We saw them; they saw us. I said to LaVonne, "Let's cross over to the other side." I wanted to avoid the encounter. Jens apparently felt the same way, but Blanche had a different idea in mind. So they just kept coming our way, until the meeting was unavoidable. That broke the ice. They invited us to their apartment, initiating a year of exchanging hospitality from house to house.

Robert Jenson flourished in the setting of Heidelberg University, which had assembled the greatest theological faculty of the post–World War II era. The names that immediately come to mind are Gerhard von Rad, Günther Bornkamm, Freiherr von Campenhausen, Heinrich Bornkamm, Peter Brunner, Edmund Schlink, and Wolfhart Pannenberg. Peter Brunner became Jens' doctor-father, to whom Jens has dedicated two of his books. Our year together in Heidelberg was memorable for three reasons, as I reflect on it (Jens might offer a different account). (1) There we listened to lectures by professors who were impressive models of teaching dogmatic and systematic theology in the grand style; (2) we encountered and responded to the challenge of Rudolf Bultmann's program of demythologizing the New Testament and his existentialist interpretation of the gospel; and (3) we learned that the way to influence the theology of the church and its ministry, in addition to classroom teaching and churchwide lecturing, is through writing books, articles, and even founding a theological journal to express our ideas.

Teaching at Luther College

Robert Jenson returned to Luther College to teach theology with a doctorate in hand. He wrote his dissertation on the theology of Karl Barth, not surprisingly on Barth's doctrine of election and related topics, from the kind of critical Lutheran perspective shared by Brunner and Schlink. Jens published a revised version of his dissertation under the title, *Alpha and Omega, A Study in the Theology of Karl Barth* (Thomas Nelson & Sons, 1963). Later, when Barth was once asked to comment on the reception of his theology in America, he made reference to a certain young American who had rightly grasped and interpreted his theology. Jens has since always been a Barthian with a sharp Lutheran cutting edge, but increasingly less so the more he has engaged the thought of Catholic (Joseph Ratzinger and Hans Urs von Balthasar) and Orthodox (John Zizioulas and Vladimir Lossky) theologians.

I will mention briefly only one episode of his Luther College years. As one could expect, Jens taught what he knew and believed with impassioned vigor and uncompromising integrity. That included the new hermeneutics of biblical interpretation, new dogmatics based on rereading the texts of the classical tradition, and serious engagement with the great thinkers of German Protestantism — Immanuel Kant, Georg Hegel, and Friedrich Schleiermacher. In Jens' teaching it all came out sounding emphatically different from what Luther College had come to expect from its religion department. I don't recall the details, if I ever knew them, but the upshot was that other members of the department began to accuse Jens of teaching false doctrine. They demanded that the college president get rid of the heretic. The president did not accept the charge of heresy and stood firm in his support of the young professor. The leading members of the department threatened to resign if the president did not fire the new teacher of theology. The president called their bluff, and all went looking for new jobs.

Jens began his career as a prolific author of theological works while at Luther College. The first book he wrote following the publication of his doctoral thesis carried a Barthian-sounding title, *A Religion Against Itself* (John Knox Press, 1966). In the spirit of Barth's *Epistle to the Romans* it carried the attack against religion in the name of the gospel of God's revelation in Jesus Christ. Some of Jenson's distinctive and enduring ideas surfaced in this book: "It is time to let the gospel tell us what we shall do and say, if we are not to be religious. . . . Our judgment upon the religion of our time is an attempt to interpret that religion by the story of Jesus."

Jens and I met Roy Harrisville at a conference for international students in Bonn in 1957. Three years later over lunch at the Harrisvilles the three of us — it was the summer of 1960 — reflected on our respective encounters with German academic theology. Jens was teaching at Luther College, Roy at Luther Seminary, and I was a parish pastor in North Minneapolis. Suddenly the thought occurred to all three of us: let us do as German theologians often do and start our own theological journal. We sensed that something was astir in Midwest Lutheranism and that the time was ripe for it to break out of its ethnic cocoon and to become engaged fully in the various currents of contemporary theology on the frontline of American culture. So, we started a quarterly journal of theology and called it *dialog,* intermittently editing it until we resigned in 1991 to start a new journal, *Pro Ecclesia — A Journal of Catholic and Evangelical Theology,* more in harmony with our progressive ecumenical convictions and commitment to the renewal of classical Christianity.

Dean and Tutor of Lutheran Students, Mansfield College, Oxford University

Jens weathered the storm at Luther College. There he had already established himself as one of the "promising young theologians," to use a phrase current at the time. In recognition of his growing stature Robert Jenson was invited to become the Dean and Tutor of Lutheran Students at Mansfield College, Oxford University. The three years at Oxford marked a creative period in Jenson's work as a theologian. He wrote two major books, *The Knowledge of Things Hoped For* (Oxford University Press, 1969), and *God after God: The God of the Past and the God of the Future, Seen in the Work of Karl Barth* (The Bobbs-Merrill Company, 1969). In these two books Jenson staked out his own positions in critical conversation with the great Christian thinkers of the past (e.g., Origen and Thomas Aquinas) and the leading trends of contemporary theology — language analysis, radical theology, process metaphysics, new hermeneutics, theology of hope, and so forth. In particular he brought the insights of the then regnant Oxbridge linguistic philosophers (e.g., Ludwig Wittgenstein, John Wisdom, J. L. Austin) to explore the meaning of the statements of Christian eschatology, which were being newly affirmed by the theologians of hope (Jürgen Moltmann and Wolfhart Pannenberg).

The academic year 1967-68 was especially significant in further deepening our partnership in theological work. I was fortunate to receive a Guggenheim Fellowship to do postdoctoral research at Oxford University while Jens was in his last year at Mansfield College. Virtually every week throughout the year we discussed every new theological idea in relation to our own research and writing projects, and in the process we enjoyed not only the camaraderie but the discovery of a lot of overlapping ground. That was also the year in which the fabric of American culture was being ripped apart at the seams — the Vietnam War, the urban riots, the assassination of Martin Luther King, Jr. and Robert Kennedy. We were both "radicalized" by these events and returned to America on the side of the antiwar movement. A few years later our two families went for a stint of summer school teaching in Cuernavaca, Mexico, at the institute founded by the Jesuit guru, Ivan Illich, a congenial meeting place for a lot of similarly radicalized spirits experiencing alienation from their mother country then engaged in an unjust war.

The Gettysburg Years

Robert Jenson received a call to join the faculty at the Lutheran Seminary in Gettysburg, Pennsylvania. He also felt a commitment to return to Luther College, where he and Blanche had many friends, and where Jens had flourished in his first years of teaching. From England he wrote me for my opinion — Luther or Gettysburg? I pulled out all the stops in arguing that a seminary would provide a more stimulating context for doing churchly theology than a church college. "Can you think of a single theologian who operates out of a college religion department? None! You must do theology for the church and its ministry." That was my conviction then. Today my judgment would be qualified by the capitulation of most (all?) seminaries to political correctness, with its accompanying ideology of quotas, inclusivity, and multiculturalism, which have wreaked havoc on the quality of theological education. Jens chose to go to Gettysburg Seminary, where he taught theology for twenty productive years.

At Gettysburg Jenson became a front-ranking ecumenical theologian of the Lutheran tradition. He was a participant in the Lutheran-Episcopal Dialogue and a consultant to the International Roman Catholic-Lutheran Dialogue. Out of this experience he wrote a book very few critics have managed to understand, *Unbaptized God: The Basic Flaw in Ecumenical Theology* (Fortress Press, 1992). His writing at the Lutheran Seminary in Gettysburg was multifaceted. In 1973 he published what has since become a classic, *Story and Promise: A Brief Theology of the Gospel about Jesus* (Fortress Press, 1973). He also wrote several books on specifically Lutheran topics, one coauthored with Eric Gritsch on *Lutheranism,* dealing with its beginnings, history, and theology, and another a commentary on Luther's Large Catechism. It was during this period that he became recognized as a major figure in the renewal of Trinitarian theology, writing a monograph on *The Triune Identity* (Fortress Press, 1982) and contributing to and co-editing with me a two-volume work titled *Christian Dogmatics,* writing the chapters on the Trinity, the Holy Spirit, and the Sacraments.

In the late 1980s Jenson wrote a book on Jonathan Edwards, entitled *America's Theologian* (Oxford University Press, 1988). This is the only interpretation of Edwards' theology I have found appealing. The Edwards I learned about from church history was the one preaching about "sinners in the hands of an angry God," hell fire and damnation, and so forth. Jenson made a creative and I think novel contribution to the Edwards renaissance by stressing his radical Christological interpretation of God, more in line with the Alexandrian Lutheran type of Christology than one normally expects of a Calvinist.

A Decade at St. Olaf College (1988-98)

Robert Jenson began a decade of teaching in the religion department of St. Olaf College in 1988. Three years later LaVonne and I pulled up stakes after thirty years of life and work together in Chicago and joined the Jensons in Northfield, Minnesota to found the Center for Catholic and Evangelical Theology. There we, together with our spouses, worked for seven years. We launched a new theological journal, *Pro Ecclesia,* which many readers and authors tell us is their favorite theological journal. We have organized no less than sixteen theological conferences and have published eight books with Eerdmans Publishing Company.[1] We have sponsored colloquia and seminars for theological reflection and conversation on a variety of special topics. It was also during our time together in Northfield that we completed a work begun years before, *A Map of Twentieth Century Theology: Readings from Karl Barth to Radical Pluralism* (Fortress Press, 1995).

Undoubtedly the crowning fulfillment of Jens's career is the recent publication of a two-volume systematic theology. He wrote both volumes while teaching at St. Olaf College. But when he is asked, "How long did it take you to write it?" his answer is, "The last forty years." Volume one is entitled, *The Triune God,* and volume two, *The Works of God,* both published by Oxford University Press. The chapters in this *Festschrift* offer eloquent tribute to the significance of this remarkable achievement of writing on dogmatics for the whole church in an ecumenical key.

1. The titles are: *Either/Or: The Gospel or Neopaganism* (1995); *Reclaiming the Bible for the Church* (1995); *The Catholicity of the Reformation* (1996); *The Two Cities of God: The Church's Responsibility for the Earthly City* (1997); *Marks of the Body of Christ* (1998); *Union with Christ: The New Finnish Interpretation of Luther* (1998); *Sin, Death, and the Devil* (1999); and *Church Unity and the Papal Office* (2000).

Center of Theological Inquiry, Princeton (1998-)

This is an unfinished memoir. Jens and Blanche left Northfield for Princeton in 1998. There Jens is the Senior Scholar for Research at the Center of Theological Inquiry. He is starting a new chapter in his long and prolific career. LaVonne and I have also left Northfield, to continue the work of the Center for Catholic and Evangelical Theology in warmer weather, Sun City West, Arizona. We don't see the Jensons as often as before, but thanks to air travel, telephone, fax and e-mail, we are in constant communication and have not skipped a beat in directing the Center and planning its future activities.

Persons of Norwegian heritage are notoriously given to hiding their feelings, not letting it all hang out, as they say. My words have merely skimmed the surface of more than forty years of collaboration and can scarcely convey the full depth of personal friendship and bonhomie that characterize what happens when the Jensons and Braatens get together. If I were to choose an epitaph that expresses the deep foundation and enduring quality of our theological commitment and ecumenical vision, it would embrace what is said about Christian unity in Ephesians 4:4-6: "There is one body and one Spirit, just as you were called to the one hope of your calling, one Lord, one faith, one baptism, one God and Father of all, who is above all and through all and in all."

Intimacy: The Character of Robert Jenson's Theology

JAMES J. BUCKLEY

I. On Not Confusing Theology and Theologians

That Robert Jenson is a character, and has character, no one who knows him will doubt. That his or any theology has a "character" in a sufficiently analogous sense to make the question of *its* character useful may be doubted. For example, at the beginning of both volumes of his *Systematic Theology,* Jenson remarks that "[i]t is the fate of every theological system to be dismembered and have its fragments bandied in an ongoing debate."[1] He admits this fate applies to his own theology, in two ways: his theology "dismembers its predecessors and uses the fragments in strange ways"; and he offers his own system as a predecessor for comparable treatment by others. Here Jenson is partly warding off the wrath of those who object to his theology primarily by way of disputing his reading of Thomas Aquinas or Gregory Palamas, Martin Luther or Karl Barth — those who think that showing mistakes in Jenson's reading of other theologians dismembers his theology. However, he can also be heard expressing skepticism with what I am calling "the character" of his theology, for one might wonder whether

1. *Systematic Theology,* vol. I: *The Triune God* (Oxford: Oxford University Press, 1997), p. 18; *Systematic Theology,* vol. II, *The Works of God* (Oxford: Oxford University Press, 1999), p. vi. Hereafter abbreviated *ST,* by volume and page. Italics in quotations are Jenson's.

an inevitably dismembered system can or should have its own "character." Thus, the first thing to be said about any interest in the character of Robert Jenson's theology (or, according to Jenson's theology, any theology) is that it may well be misplaced — a confusion (as Pascal once put it) of theology and theologians.[2]

Here is another way to state the confusion. Jenson's magnum opus to date is his *Systematic Theology,* and I will draw my remarks on the character of his theology largely from this gold mine. Yet one of the risks of "systematic theology" is that it will create a kind of attention to itself that will confuse theology and theologians. This is surely one reason Jenson begins his own systematic theology with a chapter on "what systematic theology is about." It turns out that theology can be "about" in more than one way. To put it in my own grammatical terms, if we think of "about" as a preposition, it must have an object — as when medieval Catholic theology spoke of God as the "subject matter" of theology. "What is theology about? God." Theology is, in this case, a "speculative" discipline — not abstract but concrete speculation, "looking" toward God. However, if we think of "about" as an adverb, it must modify a verb — the practice of faith in God, as Evangelical theology came to think of it. "What is theology about? Reflecting on faith in God." Theology is, in this case, a "practical" discipline — once again, not in the abstract but as a guide to faith's practices.

The temptation of the first answer is that we will think "theologians occupy some third-person vantage from which to view and describe the affair between God and his people." The temptation of the second answer is that theology will make as gospel whatever "value the theologian finds her- or himself affirming," as when a nineteenth-century theologian said, "I, the Christian, am the object of knowledge for me, the theologian." The notion of theologians' standing above the relationship between God and God's people or being paradigms of that relationship is, of course, hilarious or ludicrous — except that it happens, and not just to theologians. In both cases, theology is confused with the theologian (*ST* I, x, 11-12).

What, then, is the alternative to such dismemberment and strange use of a theology? Theology must be both speculative and practical, and this will require revising what we mean by both. For starters, in the case of both "abouts," theology is not primarily or secondarily about theologians.

2. Blaise Pascal, *The Provincial Letters,* trans. A. J. Krailsheimer (New York: Penguin Books, 1967), third letter, p. 60.

First, theology is the church's "continuing discourse about her individuating and carrying communal purpose" (*ST* I, 3). Part of the alternative to dismemberment and strange use is locating theologians amid the purpose and purposes of the communion of saints — for example, the way Dante locates theologians and their ilk at various points amid his journey in the *Divine Comedy.* In this way, the character of Jenson's theology is inseparable from the character of the church — a divided and therefore self-contradicting church that Jenson is out to contradict (*ST* I, vii). It has not always been true that Jenson's theology is characterized "ecumenically," as "Catholic and Evangelical" (to use the subtitle of the journal he and Carl Braaten edit).[3] Yet this focus of his *Systematic Theology* makes it the most important synthesis of its kind at the end of the twentieth century.

It also raises a question. If theology is about the task of guiding the church's practice, and if the church's practice is divided against itself, whence the leverage to contradict the self-contradiction (other than the humorous whim of the autonomous theologian)? This is where theology's second "about" comes into play. The church's "individuating and carrying communal purpose" is not the trigrammaton, "god," but the Gospel-God of Israel who raised Jesus of Nazareth from the dead for us all (*ST* I, 4-6). This is the triune God of Jenson's *Systematic Theology.* The character of Jenson's theology is inseparable not only from the divided communion of saints but also from the identity and character of the triune God, who is the beginning and middle and telos of human and cosmic life.

Thus, Jenson's theology is centrally about the identification of this God (*ST* I, chap. 3). How so? "God himself is identified by and with the particular plotted sequence of events that make the narrative of Israel and her Christ" (*ST* I, 60). Jenson calls the move from God's identification *by* such events to his identification *with* those events the move on which "the whole argument of the work depends" (*ST* I, 59). How so? To simply say that God identified himself and is identified "by" the narrative of Israel and her Christ may make us wonder whether this is who God "really" is. Is God's character in the biblical story who God really is, or is God's character a role he abandons once the play is over? We could also ask the opposite

3. I will not here deal with the fact that the character of Jenson's theology (like all theologies and all characters) has changed in some ways. In a theologian like Jenson, the place to start plotting such changes to his theology would be the footnotes and other places where he himself tells the reader where he has changed.

question. If God is identified "with" those events, does God have an "identity" beyond or besides the events characterized as the creation and election of Israel, the incarnation, death, and resurrection of Jesus, and the Pentecostal Spirit alive in the church and her saints today?

We avoid confusing theology and theologians by holding apart and together the practical and speculative objects of theology. We do this by learning to hold apart and together the way God is "by and with" this plotted sequence of events. "Apart and together" I have said, twice. There is a clear direction to Jenson's theology — toward the intimate togetherness of God and the world, even in the face of our efforts to dismember that deep communion. If there is a central shock to a frequently shocking theology, it is Jenson's insistence on this promised intimacy. In still other words, "church" and "Gospel" "mutually determine each other" (*ST* I, 5). The divided church (the church whose practices constitute the context of theology) is and will be saved by the Gospel-God who is identified by and with the very events that are the church. If we deny this mutual determination, we will dismember Jenson's theology; if we figure out how to re-member it, we will succeed in not confusing Jenson the theologian with Jenson's theology. How?

II. Three Characteristics of Jenson's Theology

In the rest of this essay, I can only begin to suggest how to answer this question. I will propose three characteristics of the theology Jenson engages in for the sake of explicating the mutual relations between church and gospel, between the ways God is identified "by and with" the temporal events of our world, between our practical and speculative objects. They will not claim to comprehensively summarize "the character" of Jenson's theology but only to "characterize" ways he tries to hold together and apart — gospel and church, the speculative and practical objects and aims of theology, the two ways theology is "about." I think that Jenson does not always succeed, but my focus will be on the way the flaws are internal to his theology rather than external. I do not intend to dismember his theology and use the members in strange ways, but this may in fact be the end result. It is good to be absolved, in advance.

A. The Biblical Drama

First, Jenson's theology is characterized by attention to the identification of the triune God in the biblical narrative, or drama. Thus, the first connection between the ways God is identified "by and with" the plotted events of our history is a narrative one. What does this mean? The categories of narrative, drama, and story have long been central to Jenson's theology — before Hans Urs von Balthasar's *Theodrama* came on the scene, before Hans Frei's classic story of the eclipse of specifically biblical narrative, before more generalized "narrative theologies" made their appearance.[4] The biblical narrative provides us with proper names and descriptions of specific temporal actions that cumulatively identify the God who raised Jesus from the dead as the God of Israel and all creation. God is identified *by* a proper name (YHWH) and *by* such descriptions; thus, "Father and Son and Spirit" is both a personal name for God and a compressed telling of a story (*ST* I, 46). God is *not* identified *by* this name and description in the sense that there is a trigrammaton (God) behind the tetragrammaton, or triune name — as if the way God is identified is extrinsic to the identity God has. That is, God is also identified *with* this name and such descriptions in the sense that there is no other god (perhaps the real one) behind this name and temporal description. Yet God is *not* identified *with* this name and description in the sense that God had no other possible name and could do no other acts, for this would mean that God is not free. We must say that God is identified *both by and with* (both, somehow, together) the temporal events displayed in the biblical narrative.

Jenson's unpacks this "somehow" in the first place by explicating, or

4. For "drama" in some of Jenson's earlier writings, see *God after God: The God of the Past and the God of the Future, Seen in the Work of Karl Barth* (Indianapolis and New York: The Bobbs-Merrill Company, 1969) and *The Knowledge of Things Hoped For: The Sense of Theological Discourse* (New York: Oxford University Press, 1969), passim. On my other allusions, see Hans Urs von Balthasar, *Theodrama,* 4 vols. (Einsiedeln: Johannes Verlag, 1973-83 [English translation in five volumes from Ignatius Press, 1988-98]); Hans Frei, *The Eclipse of Biblical Narrative* (New Haven and London: Yale University Press, 1974); and Stanley Hauerwas and L. Gregory Jones, eds., *Why Narrative? Readings in Narrative Theology* (Grand Rapids: Eerdmans, 1989). I will not here unpack differences and even oppositions between characterizing large sections of the Bible as narrative, drama, or story. This would require a careful look at the biblical narrative in the light of Aristotle's *Poetics* and Hegel's *Aesthetics* — Jenson more often making explicit use of the former than the latter.

presuming explication, of this biblical drama. For example, God's identity, Jenson says, "is constituted in *dramatic coherence*." Israel's story displays "Israel's ability to conceive a continuity of her own history through the discontinuities of her fate, and, for centuries, to interpret and re-interpret that history theologically to produce the Scripture the church received . . ." (*ST* I, 64). Diverse and sometimes conflicting narratives of election and rejection, of Exodus covenant and apostasy, of kingdoms come and gone are held together by the "repeatedly rewon conviction" that JHWH was and is and will be their God. Further, on Jenson's reading, "[a]t the chief dramatic peripety within the story told by Israel's Bible, the Exile, the Lord explicitly puts his self-identity at narrative risk" (*ST* I, 65) — prefiguring "[t]he crisis of the total biblical narrative": Jesus' crucifixion. The church "resolves an antinomy at the heart of Israel's hope," an event on the way to the fulfillment of God's promises to Israel (*ST* II, 170, 178). Dramatic coherence also means, however, that God's self-identity "is established not from the beginning but from the end, not at birth but at death, not in *persistence* but in *anticipation*" (*ST* I, 66). The telos of the drama is God's life with us and our life with God, variously described. God's identity, then, is constituted in the continuities and discontinuities of the story of Israel and Jesus, even unto their deaths but also anticipating their final telos. The continuities prevail. God has fully invested his life in promised intimacy with Israel and all the nations. Indeed, the seven days of the first chapter of Genesis tell the story of "a total dramatically unified divine action" from beginning to end — an action unified by and with being plotted (*ST* II, 14).

That God is identified by and with the biblical narrative makes for a circular relation between the two. "The biblical narrative" is one narrative only as it is about the one God — and God's oneness is the oneness of the narrated Father, Son, and Spirit. The circle, Jenson says, is benign. "We will follow the one biblical narrative to identify the one biblical God, only as we read the Bible by the purpose for which the church assembled this book in the first place, to be in its entirety and all its parts witness to Jesus' Resurrection and so to a particular God" (*ST* I, 58). We note, then, that the circle here is one version of the mutual determination of gospel and church we earlier said was central to the character of Jenson's theology. It is important that it is only one version, not *the* version. To read the Bible "by the purpose for which the church assembled this book in the first place" is to read it with the purpose for which the church reads, heeds, and preaches this book today — especially in the liturgy that provides a context for the church's Scripture, creed, and office (*ST* I, 24, 189-90; II, 279).

The best way, then, to grasp Jenson's version of the biblical drama is to follow him as he summarizes and explores it, although following Jenson's explication of the biblical narrative is not always easy. He often presumes explication of the narrative as he performs it. For example, Jenson's Christology is nested in "a sort of general sketch of Jesus' identity" (a sketch, he says, that will vary from theologian to theologian) rather than a synopsis of the canonical narrative or research into the historical Jesus (*ST* II, 175-76). Again, his doctrine of creation and creatures is commentary on the first chapters of Genesis, but he presumes readers familiar with the drama (*ST* II, 5-6). Thus, we do not have Karl Barth's wonderfully detailed explication of the Genesis or Gospel narratives. Of course, it is also true that Jenson actually finished a systematic theology and Barth did not — and theological anxiety about thick redescription of the biblical drama may mask anxiety about the way the church rather than theology alone bears the gospel. Yet why does Jenson as often presume explication of the narrative as perform it?

Jenson once characterizes his *Systematic Theology* as "highly abstracted theology" (*ST* II, 275). By this he means, in context, that it is often abstracted from the irreplaceable biblical narrative. His point is that even such theologies cannot help but rely on the privileged language of Scripture.[5] Jenson knows the disadvantages of such a theology: "The discourse of systematic theology — as that of 'philosophy' — too easily elides the [dramatic, we might also say] sensuousness of human being" (*ST* II, 183). To avoid eliding the sensuousness of Jenson's theology, we need to presume that he is dealing with one or another of the issues raised by one or more problems in the dramatic coherence of Scripture, precisely at the points where his theology becomes most "abstracted." Then, I think, we need to recognize that he is reading this gospel drama with a particular is-

5. This is not the place to pursue the important question of what it means "to abstract" in the abstract, or outside the passage here cited. For example, we could rightly say something is "abstract" if it takes leave of the way things were, are, or will be — "contrary to fact" questions (e.g., What would the world be like if God has not created us for union with his life of love?). Jenson does raise such questions, more regularly than most theologians dare, but he (again) raises them precisely because they are periodically generated by the biblical story itself (e.g., *ST* I, 46-50).

sue in mind — namely, showing how Israel (called and liberated and exiled) and Jesus Christ (living and teaching, crucified and risen) are the ones by whom and with whom God is self-identified.

B. Revisionary (Gospel-normed) Metaphysics

Why, then, the "highly abstracted" character? Jenson's sketch (see above) of the dramatic coherence of God raises two questions — versions of the question Jenson has put about God's "by and with." First, how does God's *dramatic* character have a *coherent* identity as the creator God who elects Israel and is incarnate in Jesus and sends the Pentecostal Spirit on the church? Second, how can God's *identity* have this dramatic *character* and still be, coherently, God?[6] Questions like these cannot be answered by simply repeating the narrative, any more than they could be asked without the biblical drama. Thus, besides narrative identification, a second way Jenson holds together and apart God's triune identification by and with our tensed world is by a "metaphysics" normed by the gospel, by a "*universal* hermeneutics," or by a "universal grammar" that is not determined by foundational philosophy (*ST* I, 20-21). I restrict myself here to some remarks about the metaphysics (rather than the hermeneutics or grammar). Even though this metaphysics will not be foundational to the gospel drama and will always be "metaphysically revisionary," it also does this in a language inherited from history (*ST* II, 65 n. 50). Gospel-normed metaphysics (or "metaphysics") is always engaged, constructively as well as critically, with an antecedent metaphysics of the culture.[7] How so?

Jenson speaks of "the metaphysics that this work has bit by bit proposed" (*ST* II, 150). On the one hand, Jenson's gospel-normed metaphysics is proposed "bit by bit" — one bit in his prolegomena, another in his theology of God's identity and character, another in his theology of creation and church and final telos. In this sense, his metaphysics is (to use a lexi-

6. So volume 1, part I is on God's "identity," and part II is on God's "character," the point of both sections being that God has this identity by and with this character. As Jenson points out in volume II, however, the church could as well have been treated in volume I as the anticipation of the Spirit's kingdom (*ST* II, 167).

7. The antecedent culture is not always Hellenistic, or Western. Jenson's metaphysics of speech arises out of the metaphysics of Israel's wisdom literature (*ST* II, 157-59).

con Jenson does not) very occasion-specific,[8] difficult to dismember from the specific issue at stake — whether that be temporality or language, evil or the *hypostatic union.* Furthermore, as far as I can see, every church doctrine that could plausibly be called "metaphysical" has been very occasion-specific, whether it be Nicaea's *homoousion* or Lateran IV's pre-Nietzschean truism that "truth cannot contradict truth."[9] Jenson also aims to follow in the footsteps of Karl Barth, who is read as "the first major system of Western metaphysics since the collapse of Hegelianism" (*ST* II, 21).[10] Here Jenson sounds as if the accumulated occasion-specific bits amount to something more occasion-comprehensive — although he also says that theology can get along without "a comprehensive metaphysics," at least for the moment.[11] So let's say Jenson is perched between an occasion-specific and a comprehensive metaphysics — a good place, I should say, to perch. How so? "It is the metaphysically fundamental fact of Israel's and the church's faith that its God is freely but, just so, truly self-identified by, and so with, contingent created temporal events" (*ST* I, 47-48). How does this metaphysics normed by the gospel drama (or "metaphysics") contribute to holding God's "by and with" together?

Consider *the* traditional precedent.[12] When Christians came in contact with antecedent culture, they developed (Jenson says) three main re-

8. On occasion-specificity and occasion-comprehensiveness (both in contrast to topic-comprehensiveness), see William A. Christian, Sr., *Doctrines of Religious Communities: A Philosophical Study* (New Haven and London: Yale University Press, 1987), pp. 186ff. and 225ff.

9. I take Jenson to be part of an ecumenical consensus that occasion-specific claims have unfortunately been frequently confused with occasion-comprehensive ones, so that Nicaea is thought to agree with rather than transform *ousia,* or the law of noncontradiction is thought to give us the power to pick and choose only the putatively noncontradictory things from the biblical drama. Reversible metaphysical claims (see n. 12 below) are confused with irreversible ones, with deadly results.

10. I tend to follow Frei rather than Jenson on this particular issue: Barth's metaphysics was (to use the lexicon I began to use at n. 8) occasion-specific rather than occasion-comprehensive. This can be confused with being anti-metaphysical, as Jenson does not do with Barth but he does do with Frei (*ST* II, 277 n. 24).

11. Robert Jenson, *Essays in "Theology of Culture"* (Grand Rapids: Eerdmans, 1995), pp. 77, 82.

12. This is the point to merely note that the covenant drama is not exclusively biblical. Some postbiblical church decisions are "*dramatically* necessary" contingently but really necessary for the sake of the gospel and irreversible in the light of the Spirit's future (*ST* II, 238-40).

sponses to Hellenism's questions about God's *ousia.* They could accept the concept but only allow it partly to apply to God: God has being but is also somehow "above" it — a belief typical in Eastern Orthodoxy. Or they could accept the concept for everything else but deny its application to God, as is the belief in rabbinic Judaism and among some Christian Heideggerians, risking the confusion of God's nonbeing with violence. Or they could "reinterpret being to accommodate the gospel," as did Thomas Aquinas and Gregory of Nyssa — and as does Jenson (*ST* I, 211-12). To say that metaphysics is accommodated to the gospel is, in the first place, to say that it is normed by the biblical drama of God we saw above.

The way this reinterpretation of being occurred is that the culture's "immutable being" was "inwardly subverted" by Nicaea's confession that Jesus is God from God, *homoousion* with the Father, as well as by the Cappadocians' theology of Trinitarian hypostases as different subsisting relations. However, this revisionary reinterpretation of being was incomplete, or flawed. For example, impassible being continued to be presumed (except by neo-Chalcedonians), God's *Logos* was understood as possession rather than communication, and the eschatological character of God's history and therefore the Spirit were suppressed (*ST* I, 108). Jenson's metaphysics aims to say how God is identified by and with the temporal world by completing the traditional inward subversion of *ousia,* now in relation to the modern reinterpretation of being as history, or time. "[T]he one unavoidable metaphysical fact" is our temporality (*ST* I, 89). This is not a metaphysical fact supposedly abstracted from the gospel drama. In the context of glossing the drama of Genesis 1, Jenson says that "God does not create a world that thereupon has a history; he creates a history that is a world, in that it is purposive and so makes a whole," with temporal-spatial objects as "an endlessly complicated web of mutually appropriate relations" (*ST* II, 14, 41, 46). Still further, "[t]he great metaphysical question on the border between the gospel and our culture's antecedent theology" is whether the order of a good story toward the future (as we saw in the biblical drama) "may be regarded as its own kind of causality . . . ," so that things go, as the gospel drama says, "from the end" (*ST* I, 159).

In such a world, the alternatives, we might say, are not much different than they were for revisionary efforts on *ousia.* We might say that God is in time but also (somehow) above it — God is identified "by" and "with" but not "by *and* with"; that God has no relations with the temporal world — that God is identified neither "by" nor "with" our world; or that the gospel drama's God defines time, rather than the reverse. Jenson chooses the last. If God is (as Jenson has said the gospel drama shows) identified by and with the temporal world, then God must be "by and with" God: "the Father begets the Son and freely breathes his Spirit; the Spirit liberates the Father for the Son and the Son from and for the Father; the Son is begotten and liberated, and so reconciles the Father with the future his Spirit is." Thus, "the dynamism of God's life is a narrative causation in and so of God" (*ST* I, 160-61). Indeed, in the future "each of the divine identities arrives at new relations to the others" (*ST* II, 339). Yet God's way of being temporal is not our way — if it was, God would be identified "with" our world but not "by" it. The triune event is "temporal infinity." God in Christ is (here follow Gregory of Nyssa's own words) "infinite over the past and infinite over the future," and (here is God's futurological asymmetry) "the mark of deity is endless futurity" (*ST* I, 216-17). This is God's time, "taking 'time' as an analogous concept" (*ST* II, 35).[13]

This is a novel theological proposal: an assertion of God's infinite temporality, tied to a theology of the triune God arising from the biblical drama. Most theologies of divine temporality have been tied to denying or ignoring the triune God and/or the biblical drama. Jenson claims to do neither. Indeed, the claim is that this metaphysics of the matter is normed by that God and that liturgically embedded drama. It is a metaphysics in the service of God's intimate communion with us, embedded in God's ever-greater triune intimacy.

Some have asked and others will surely ask: Is God's identification "with" us at the expense of God's identification "by" us?[14] Answering this question would depend on what we think of Jenson's gospel-normed metaphysics. But my question is different: What sort of claim is Jenson making at this point? Insofar as it is the claim of what I earlier called a "comprehensive metaphysics" (or at least a metaphysics on the way to being such), the odds that any emerging Catholic and Evangelical *internationale* will agree on such are slim indeed. Yet insofar as it is an occasion-specific claim, it is tied to a comprehensive narrative of the church's history (including what is reversible

13. Jenson admits he does not always succeed at this point. For example, he once planned to conclude *Unbaptized God* (Minneapolis: Fortress, 1992) with the chapter on time, until it dawned on him that this was a version of the very mistake with which he was charging traditional theology (p. 108).

14. See, for example, Bruce Marshall, "The Trinity," in *The Blackwell Companion to Theology* (Oxford: Blackwells, forthcoming), n. 23.

and irreversible about that story), and the odds are slim that the emerging Catholic and Evangelical *internationale* will agree on such a narrative. Which claims of Jenson's (admittedly) gospel-normed metaphysics should be church claims (dogmas) and which should be subject to the disputes of Jenson's theological schools (*ST* I, 17)? On which features of his gospel-normed metaphysics is Jenson asking the church to agree, and which can or should be left to disputes with his fellow theologians?

C. A Liturgical Test

The best way to try to answer this question may be to test this highly abstracted question back on dramatic ground. Certainly one of *the* spaces of contestation would be sin, evil, and suffering. There is no room here to conduct even a partial test, but, against the background of the ways I have characterized Jenson's theology, it is clear how the test would go. For example, what about the fact that we are and live in a world that either does not care whether God is identified by and with us and our world or offers alternative gods (i.e., no gods)? We could take this as a question of apologetics (e.g., How do we respond to a world caught between polemic against and indifference to the gospel and the church?). If we did, then Jenson's theology might take the question to be a challenge of nihilism — the story that things amount to nothing, from which we can abstract a metaphysics focused on "the awaited advent of nothingness" (*ST* I, ix).[15] To focus in more than occasional ways on this challenge would be to avoid another: that the key challenge to God's identification by and with the temporal world is not the evil others do but that which we do, our sin.[16]

15. This is the context in which Jenson notes that his systematic theology is not "apologetics." I take it that Jenson agrees with Barth that all apologetics must be "supplementary, incidental, and implicit" to the dogmatic task (*Church Dogmatics,* trans. Rev. T. H. L. Parker et al. [Edinburgh: T. & T. Clark, 1957], vol. 2, pt. 1, p. 8), and this is why Jenson's theology of culture is "brazenly trinitarian and churchly" (*Essays,* p. ix). Aquinas might say that apologetics is in a position analogous to Aristotle, when his sophistic (nihilist?) irritant denies the law of noncontradiction (*Summa Theologiae* Ia, 1, 8) — the response must be "ad hoc apologetics" (as Hans Frei might have said).

16. As in the case of Israel, "the biblical critique of religion recoils primarily on the devotees of biblical religion" (*ST* I, 52). "To the question 'Who crucified Jesus?' *only the church* is able to say, 'We did.' The race in general must, in justice, say, 'We were not there,' and just go its way" (*ST* I, 192).

Even here we must be careful if we are not to subtly undercut the biblical drama and its metaphysics. Jenson says he could have omitted his chapter on sin "since all its matter appears elsewhere in the work." But he does not want to be accused, "as sometimes I rightly have been," of "sharing the modern aversion to the whole subject" (*ST* II, 133 n. 3). A separate chapter on sin abstracts from the biblical drama what Jenson presumes or explicates throughout. We might then treat our sin — our idolatry, lust, injustice, and despair — as if God was "by and with" us, except for such sin. Yet, as we have seen, stories of sin and death are a crucial part of the gospel drama — and the gospel-normed metaphysics of triune infinity creates the space for the Lamb of God to take away the sins of the world. There is no space here to test how this is done with the sin of creation, of crucifixion, of the justified in the church, and even possibly with sin at the final judgment. Jenson will sometimes go so far as to speak of the actual life of God as "conflicted and twisting." "Since this drama is God's, its conflict is infinite, the conflict of death and life" (*ST* II, 23). We could ask of this what we asked of Jenson's metaphysics above: How much is church doctrine, and how much theological opinion — or, how much is church theology and how much that of a theological school?

It would dismember Jenson's theology to end here. All this, Jenson insists, is no theodicy (*ST* II, 23). In fact, he twice repeats that the resolution of such questions about sin and evil cannot, at least for now, be "from the conceptual outside; but it can be liturgically inhabited," especially in the Triduum (*ST* II, 24; cp. *ST* I, 190). So, one final time, the way Gospel-God is by and with us in full intimacy is inseparable from our intimacy with each other as the church's sacramental anticipation of our final telos. I know of no other contemporary theology that performs this intimacy so well in both its speculative heights and practical depths, calling us to both God's story and the metaphysics thereof, challenging us to do it better — whether bit by bit, or more comprehensively.

Handing Over the Name: Christian Reflection on the Divine Name YHWH

C. R. SEITZ

In this essay I investigate what it means for Christians to have possession of an Old Testament Scripture where the name of God is central to its highest theological claims.[1] Yet that name is not sounded in either the New Testament or common Christian practice. Instead, it is referenced by means of various conventions.

I offer this essay in tribute to Professor Jenson, who has labored to speak of the name of the God of Israel as he who "raised Israel from the dead."[2] This effort at equivalence with Christian claims, namely, that God is he who "raised Jesus from the dead," goes a long way toward highlighting

1. See my essays, "The Call of Moses and the 'Revelation' of the Divine Name" and "The Divine Name in Christian Scripture," in *Word Without End: The Old Testament as Abiding Theological Witness* (Grand Rapids: Eerdmans, 1998). See also Michael Wyschogrod, *The Body of Faith: God in the People of Israel* (San Francisco: Harper & Row, 1983). "*The God of Israel has a proper name.* There is no fact in Jewish theology more significant than this" (*Body of Faith,* p. 91; quoted from R. Jenson, *Systematic Theology,* vol. I: *The Triune God* [Oxford: Oxford University Press, 1997], p. 43, n. 10). Hereafter abbreviated *ST,* by volume and page. Italics in quotations are Jenson's.

2. As Jenson puts it, "Asked who God is, Israel's answer is, 'Whoever rescued us from Egypt'" and "Thus 'the one who rescued Israel from Egypt' is confirmed as an identification of *God* in that it is continued 'as he thereupon rescued the Israelite Jesus from the dead'" (*ST* I, 44).

for Christians the delicate matter of identity in speaking of God's person. God's identity in Christ must be situated in relationship to God's identity with and to Israel.

I. The Problem: Conventions

A. The L*ORD*

The most widely adopted convention for speaking of the God of Israel by name is based upon the translation practice in place when the Scriptures were prepared for Greek speakers, and it is the one with which we are most familiar. The named God of Israel is referred to as "the LORD" *(kyrios).* That the earliest renderings also preserve other conventions need not bother us here.[3] It should remind us, however, that the situation was fluid from the very beginning and the production of a major, large-scale translation meant that the inherited fluidity was being constrained and interpreted through the very nature of the undertaking. The Hebrew text of the Old Testament was likely already evidencing similar conventions within its own field of expression (see, e.g., the use of *'adonay* before YHWH in Isa. 50:3-9). I will say more about that in due course.

Even to speak aloud the convention, "the LORD," points to a fundamental problem. It is impossible to differentiate, in public speech, between a common use of the English word "lord" or even "the Lord" and this very specific convention (LORD), whereby a personal name has been glossed out of reverence, fear of misuse, or for other reasons. Capitalization in the convention (LORD) cannot be orally reproduced.[4]

This situation can be helpfully illustrated with a modern example. Celebrating the twenty-fifth anniversary of the (then illegal) ordination of women in the Episcopal Church in Philadelphia last July, the worshipers

3. These include the special orthographic rendering of the tetragrammaton in Hebrew script.

4. Jenson says of the practical problem of using a convention, "It is unlikely that the text of this work will often be read aloud, but to cover the eventuality, where it seems desirable to use JHWH in the text, the name will be spelled in that fashion, with only the consonants" (*ST* I, 44 n. 12). If his text were read aloud, the reader would have to use another convention for oral delivery, like "the LORD," thus illustrating what is at issue.

were not to have to hear the phrase "the Lord" in their prayers since it was a male-oriented, oppressive term. The logic of the complaint is by now familiar, and in certain circles unimpeachable.

Yet at what is the umbrage directed? At a metaphor ("lord"), at a person who is called that in scriptural texts (Jesus, "my Lord"), at the naming practice itself (by disciples, the church, etc.), or at the convention here under discussion, whereby Israel's properly named God is referred to, for dense historical reasons, as the Lord? Ironically, an act intended to guard a personal name, with corollary, indeed massive, implications for what it means to address Jesus this way, has at the end of our era been heard as an act of oppression. The most charitable thing to say is that those who feel oppressed have forgotten, if they ever knew, that the practice of referring to God's personal name by this convention coincided with the joy and bracing confession of seeing in Jesus of Nazareth the very face of God, the Lord, the Maker of Heaven and Earth.[5]

What this illustrates, however, is the far more banal problem of asking a convention to carry the weight of its own clarification, which it does not. Moreover, there is no good way to speak the convention aloud and stipulate thereby that the God who raised Jesus from the dead is intended (the Lord), and not the Raised One himself (e.g., "my Lord and my God"). Traditionally, context has been relied upon to provide the clarification, and added to this, a certain basic knowledge of Christian or Jewish faith, but these are the two things precisely under negotiation at present. It is likely no coincidence that repudiation of the name of God under the cover of liberating us from oppression in reality means detaching Jesus as Lord from convictions about the One who raised him, the Lord. Instead of the Named One (YHWH) the Philadelphia worshipers invoked a god they

5. Jenson's rhetorical power is on display as he makes this point in another context: "Precisely being able to turn from their gods to the true God occasioned 'the joy' with which the apostles' gentile converts 'received the word.' In the act of faith, gentile believers recognize themselves as those who have worshiped or might worship Moloch the baby-killer or Astarte the universal whore or *Deutsches Blut* or the Free Market or the Dialectic of History or the Metaphor of our gender or ethnic ressentiment, and on through an endless list of tyrants. Only a naiveté impossible for the apostolic church, which fully inhabited the religious maelstrom of late antiquity, can think that religion as such is a good thing or that gods are necessarily beneficent" (*ST* I, 50-51). What is said here of "religion as such" applies *a fortiori* to language for God cut loose from connection with Israel's Lord, who raised Israel and Jesus from the dead.

called "Sophia." Here we have a strange turnabout. A common Greek word for wisdom is meant to stand as a personal name, allegedly because it points to a deity or a deifiable Hebrew reality, which of course has no personal name in the manner that Israel's God does. This is a perfect inversion of the state of affairs proclaimed by the Old Testament and Christian theology. A personal name has become a Greek concept that has become a deity invoked to offset the offense of "lordliness." "They know not what they do" one might generously infer, but that is far from clear.

B. The "Yahweh" Convention

I have written in other places about the problem of actually presenting us with what purports to be a true or proximate vocalization of the personal name of God,[6] but I want to go over more of that ground here. Parenthetically, I saw a livery service at a major airport in the United States called "Yahweh's Transportation Service," or something to that effect. I doubt scholars responsible for this learned production of the name would have anticipated the success of their efforts along these lines.

While it is not possible to police motivations, it is possible to conjecture about the reasons for this modern practice having taken such hold. First, there was the recognition that an older practice of calling God "Jehovah" and meaning thereby to state his personal name was based upon a mistake (I use the term with caution). That is, the vowels supplied for the name were drawn from its ancient gloss (*e, o, a* from *'adonay*) and not from the name proper. This conflation produced a perfectly presentable, suitably sonorous name for God, "Jehovah," and it gives one pause to consider how many people, how many hymns, and how much praying went on under the influence of the King James Bible's rendering. Indeed, simply in the realm of linguistic aesthetics (not to mention livery service advertising) I think one could make the argument that the name "Jehovah" is in fact a decent rival for "Yahweh." In the light of the Philadelphia example

6. See n. 1 above. Jenson notes, "We probably will never be quite sure what JHWH originally meant; since historical Israel did not either, the theological loss cannot be great" (*ST* I, 43 n. 9). This likely overstates the matter. Israel probably knew that the name had to do with God "being who he is in the events he shares with Israel in deliverance from Egypt," but only Hebrew speakers living within the nexus of the scripturally attested universe of discourse could be expected to feel the force of this.

above, we ought not to forget that knowledge and custom are two different things and spin on different orbits. The custom of speaking of Yahweh instead of Jehovah is now largely independent of any knowledge of the reasons why we have these two alternatives in the first place.

Second, and related to this ethos of "scholarly correction," was the conviction that we actually were in a better position to vocalize the name properly than we were before, based upon our knowledge of Hebrew, cognate languages, and other matters. This confidence was part and parcel of a general mood of enthusiasm ushered in with the rise of historical criticism, among its manifold practitioners. A quick look at Frank Cross's *Canaanite Myth and Hebrew Epic* will show a confident discussion of the divine name with arguments for the vocalization adopted based upon internal and comparative linguistic investigations.[7]

Third, it was thought that we could somehow de-Christianize the Old Testament if we could speak the name of God unsullied by later conventions, and this was judged a good thing. The hunt for origins and the atavism that hovered all around encouraged us to "get at the true picture of things" without later contaminations or missteps. The Jerusalem Bible adopted the convention of referring to the personal name "Yahweh" directly, not as Jehovah or through a glossing convention, and many popular lectionaries and preaching aids went along with this too. Far from being a scholarly move only, all church people could hope that with the proper name available for pronunciation, we would be getting a truer picture, would be capturing the God of the Old Testament on God's own terms, and would be standing alongside Moses and Miriam, not just Paul or Peter or on later church practices.[8]

A fourth reason for this comes with specific ecumenical concern. At a conference on prayer I recently attended one prominent New Testament scholar defended his use of "Yahweh" in his writing and in his speaking, quite passionately, by connecting that usage with his sensitivity for honor-

7. "The discussion of the meaning and origin of the name Yahweh constitutes a monumental witness to the industry and ingenuity of biblical scholars" is the way Frank M. Cross opens his own treatment; it is unclear as one reads on whether he was being ironic or not (*Canaanite Myth and Hebrew Epic: Essays in the History of the Religion of Israel* [Cambridge: Harvard University Press], 60ff.).

8. Interestingly, this extrusion of "Yahweh" into common parlance was soon followed by "Hebrew Bible" as preferable to Old Testament or Tanak. See my discussion in *Word Without End* (pp. 61-74) and *Pro Ecclesia* 6 (1997): 136-40.

ing the "Jewish context" of Jesus. Since most people do not understand the function of the convention "the LORD" and its connection to a personal name, it was argued that the use of "Yahweh" will remedy that and will assure that the historicity of the New Testament remains in the forefront. It does not matter, in the logic of this concern, whether those of New Testament times were more familiar with a convention *(kyrios)* than with an alleged vocalization ("Yahweh"). Reproducing the vocalization in our day will jog us into a more historically oriented mode and will release, it is hoped, the historical character of the New Testament in a theologically appropriate way. Using the name "Yahweh," in other words, serves the purpose of putting us on notice that God has a personal name, and that act of putting on notice is the critical thing, indeed, possibly more critical than the actual name itself. Therein, to my mind, lies a major part of the problem. Are we honoring the name by vocalizing it or honoring historical contextualization as theologically necessary?

At this juncture it would be appropriate to suggest what is wrong with these several rationales for vocalizing God's personal name as "Yahweh." First, the scholarly production of the name is just that. That is, it does not belong to any genuine historical usage in the life of the church or in wider culture in the manner recent scholars mean. Indeed, that is its appeal! As a scholarly finding, in other words, it turns on special knowledge that is in turn open to debate and scrutiny only within a fairly circumscribed realm. What if, for example, someone were to argue that the proper vocalization of the name of God was "Yehweh"? In practical terms, would a new Bible version have to appear with all references to God's personal name spelled this way? Would the precise inflection have to be policed? Who would be in a position to judge which vocalization was accurate?

Let us be clear. In a matter as important as God's name, it would certainly be possible (and indeed it has happened) for scholars to produce a different, equally precise vocalization. Why would "Yahweh" then remain in currency? Probably for all sorts of reasons that have nothing whatsoever to do with scholarship, a fact that shows that "Yahweh" is not in a position to lay claim to any scholarly lock on accuracy; *the term has simply become its own kind of convention.* The Old Testament did not preserve for us one precise vocalization; in the form we have it, it has left the true name of God hidden and therefore lost to the ages. What does it mean, then, to recover or discover the vocalization? It is nothing more than the reassertion of a convention under the guise of learning and accuracy.

Second, it is helpful to be clear about what we are doing when we purport to be pronouncing the name of God, "Yahweh." I suspect the practice of saying "Jehovah" is different now because when scholars reproduced this name in Bibles they clearly did not assume that they had recovered or discovered the "real" name of God. The reproduction of the name was innocent and genuinely naïve and likely had more to do with respect than learning. The return to primary sources meant that the name was there for translation, and even translators of the Hebrew into a daughter tongue did not try to do other translators one better.

The desire for sympathetic participation in the life of Israel, or with some New Testament version of that, can only with difficulty be squared with the practice of actually speaking the word "Yahweh" and meaning thereby "the personal God of Israel who raised Jesus from the dead." "Yahweh" is, after all, a transliteration extruding into the daughter translation. It does not exist with any possible cognation in the English language, except of course as an exception, as a "marked word," in the same way "Moshe" or "fatwa" are marked.

The effects of this on sympathetic participation are twofold and massive. First, the word will of necessity be "foreign," and that runs counter in the nature of the thing to wonted intimacy and participation. How much personal prayer addressed to "Yahweh" actually takes place? Second, and this is far more critical, we are told that the name, when it is explained to us in Exodus 3, has something to do with the verb "to be" *(hyh)*. God's personal name conveys something about him personally, and that something entails being or becoming. Stated differently, those who spoke the name of God heard therein a reference to God being or becoming something, and that resonance existed within the framework of the Hebrew language. It cannot, by definition, exist in another language. Moreover, the name of God is related to a specific act of being or becoming that is riveted to Israel's own historical experience and memory: God's *being who he would dramatically and really be,* in deliverance from Egypt and revelation at Sinai, acts that are themselves demonstrations that YHWH is Lord, the Maker of Heaven and Earth.[9]

It is simply false to believe that pronouncing the phonemes *yahweh*

9. "Israel's and the church's God is thus identified by specific temporal actions and is known within certain temporal communities by personal names and identifying descriptions thereby provided" (*ST* I, 46).

in English will produce anything like the same sets of associations and identifications that existed among those who heard God's name when he revealed it and thereby said something crucial about it and about himself. "Then you shall know that I am the LORD" is the way YHWH puts it through his various servants, Moses, Ezekiel, or Isaiah the latter.

C. YHWH and Kindred Conventions

Here we confront the opposite problem as with the convention, "The LORD." Certain conventions for handling the divine name work only in texts, not in speech, and indeed their rationale is thereby disclosed. By leaving the vowels out, we send a signal that pronunciation and signification are different things. Saying aloud, "The LORD," can lead to the Philadelphia confusion mentioned above, while adopting the convention of vowelless signing solves the problem but at the cost of leaving unresolved what we are meant to say. William F. Albright is said to have argued that whenever an obscurity in Hebrew declared itself in the text, the wisest translation practice was simply to indicate by dots an ellipsis and leave the text untranslated. This is an example of how the phrase "merely academic" is not a compliment. Ellipsis invites us to defer to a mother text, but silence in speech is still silence and not genuine communication of the sort most seek when they wait to hear the Bible's word.

In any event, this sort of textualized convention is restricted in the nature of the thing and does not move us very far along in how to handle the problem of the divine name. What it does suggest, just the same, is that many conventions have their home in quite specific settings. The practice of referring to God's name as "the name" *(hashem)* or with a substitute acclamation, "the Eternal" *(haʿolam)*, went on within circles that knew full well that God has a personal name, and they were not offering thereby new substitutes or learned corrections but were ranging their practice alongside the Bible's own interior logic.[10]

10. Again, Jenson captures this nicely in his compact sentences: "Asked about her access to this God, Israel's answer is, 'We are permitted to call on him by name' — just so, the name was eventually felt too holy for regular utterance aloud and was replaced by stated euphemisms, in reading Scripture by *Adonai,* 'the Lord.' The name does not thereby lose its power; on the contrary, in rabbinic discourse the phrase *Hashem,* 'the Name,' is often used instead of 'God'" (*ST* I, 44).

This is particularly true in the case of *hashem,* "the name." Throughout the psalms, for example, we are bidden to praise God's name. God's name is worthy of honor, we are told, and that statement is made and can be made without the tetragrammaton ever appearing, though usually a parallelism asserts this. In other words, in the Psalms it is the reverence held for Israel's God, known by reference to his revealed name and self, which leads to the practice of holding up the name while not mentioning it as such. "Bless the LORD, O my soul, and all that is within me, bless his holy name" will become in time, "Bless the Name, O my soul."

Karl Barth once said that all Christian theology is commentary on the phrase, YHWH-*kyrios.* The practical problem remains of how to speak of the God of Israel by his personal name.[11]

D. New Testament

It cannot be our task here to sort out the various social and historical reasons for the withdrawal of God's name from the sort of general speech and use we see throughout the Old Testament.[12] One thing that is clear is that the New Testament presents no exception to this picture and, if anything, confirms it. At most we see allusions to the divine name, or evocations of it. The "I am" statements of Jesus in John's Gospel and his statement that "before Abraham was, I am" appear to direct us to the "I am who I will be" divine (first-person) explanation for the name, as this is found in Exodus 3:14. John is insistent both that the Father is greater and that Jesus and the Father are one. The "I am" statements assert through the simple force of their declaration what later theologians sought in the term "of one substance" *(homoousia)* to describe the relationship between Jesus and the LORD, the God of Israel, Maker of Heaven and Earth.[13]

11. See the discussion by Kendall Soulen, "YHWH the Triune God," *Modern Theology* 15 (1999): 25-54.

12. One explanation may entail Israel's extrusion into the Gentile world and the attendant fear of breaking the decalogue's commandment regarding the keeping holy of God's name.

13. See the fine treatment by David Yeago, "The New Testament and Nicene Dogma: A Contribution to the Recovery of Theological Exegesis," *Pro Ecclesia* 3 (1994): 152-64.

Otherwise, what we find throughout the New Testament is not the personal name, but conventions for referring to YHWH, or attributions that point to him. Again, there is not space here to demonstrate all of these, but two can be filed by title (a third I will look at in detail below). First, "the God who made the world and everything in it, he who is Lord of heaven and earth" is Paul's language in Athens before his non-Jewish audience (Acts 17:24). "The Lord of heaven and earth" is doubtless an unambiguous reference to YHWH and should not be thought of as Paul's effort at genericizing deity on behalf of his audience; indeed, it is more likely that here Paul uses a formal convention already well established in his own Jewish context. The only referent he intends by this is YHWH, making Paul's use of the phrase before those who worship other gods, including an unknown one, confessional by its mere utterance.

Second, in the book of Revelation, alongside the very high Christology associated with the Lamb, the Son of God, we hear in the opening chapter a self-declaration that could otherwise appear in the Old Testament without further ado. Isaiah 44 and Exodus 3 (and doubtless other texts) combine to announce in a new spirit of inspiration, "I am the Alpha and the Omega, says the Lord God, who is and was and who is to come, the Almighty" (Rev. 1:8).

In both of these cases, reference to YHWH by specific attribution or convention stands on its own, and we must wait to see how Christological statements are correlated with it. Here is Christian theology at its most basic and crucial form, as commentary on the divine name YHWH-*kyrios.*

E. Holy Trinity, One God

In the last decades, there has been a Trinitarian revival of sorts. Jürgen Moltmann's *Crucified God* was an effort to detach discussion of God in Christ from a conceptual framework overly indebted to metaphysics and Hegelianism.[14] This meant greater attention to the literal sense of the New Testament and especially the passionate and nonpropositional character of its depiction, which never fit well in certain metaphysical discussions. The language, "crucified God," was selected so as to drive home the outlandish

14. Jürgen Moltmann, *The Crucified God: The Cross of Christ as the Foundation and Criticism of Christian Theology* (New York: Harper & Row, 1974).

potential of Christian God talk. This also obliged Moltmann to be clear about God talk in respect of God the Father, since the crucified God was God the Son. At this point it was not clear he had escaped the gravitational pull of previous metaphysical systems, and I shall have more to say about this in constructive proposals to follow.[15]

Alongside this, there has been a wider effort to speak in more personal terms about the Trinity. Here again, the blame is assigned to a metaphysics more interested in substance or being, and coherency, than in personal language true to God's personal character. Sometimes the appeal has nothing to do with Scripture's *sensus literalis,* or defense of its specific, personal language over against philosophical systems. Who would not want a personal deity, dancing and celebrating, within his or her own self? The problem, however, is the introduction of yet another more friendly or participatory Trinitarian concept without any genuine anchorage in Christian Scripture as a whole, Old Testament or New Testament. Swapping philosophical systems is not what Paul was about at Athens, at any rate.

One can see how a special burden is here carried by the name in the Old Testament and in Christian theology. Is it not the self-revelation of God, in his name, that stands at the very center of the Old Testament? It is hard to imagine a more personal form of disclosure. It is the word "God" that opens itself to abstraction and depersonalizing manipulation. The word "God" *('elohim)* in the Old Testament carries with it this and other problematics, including the capacity for natural existence within polytheism, idolatry, and syncretism. The sentence "I am the LORD your God," is a dense confession, combining two things: the personal and the sovereign. This rules out any genericizing or universalizing from anthropological insight, and rules in jealousy as the decisive complement to holiness and righteousness in God's personal character.[16] He will be as he is quite truly, in the disclosure of himself to a people he loves and holds accountable for that love, with jealousy and holiness. It is this solemn disclosure that grounds the personal character of God and shows his name to be the critical lens on himself, without which history

15. See my remarks on this in the review of Richard Bauckham's *God Crucified: Monotheism and Christology in the New Testament* (Carlisle: Paternoster, 1998) in the *International Journal of Systematic Theology* 2 (2000): 112-16.

16. "In the Scriptures . . . it is first among the Lord's attributes that he is 'a *jealous* God'," Jenson writes with reference to Exod. 34:14 (*ST* I, 47).

reveals nothing and "acts of God" make no sense at all except as conjuring tricks of the wise or crafty.

II. The Name in the Old Testament

I have at other places sought to establish the centrality of God's personal name for any theological account of the Old Testament. In this I am following where others have led the way (e.g., Walter Zimmerli). I will only summarize and abridge here, since I wish to return to the question of Trinitarian talk and the practical need for personal language about the God of Israel, the LORD, Maker of Heaven and Earth.[17]

In the revelation of God's name in the book of Exodus several things are going on at once. Only narrative is in a position to carry the weight of establishing theological truth when so much is at stake and when the issues are so complicated. Propositions or religious empiricism falls short.[18]

First, there is the revelation of God's name to Moses. Moses asks to know God's name because he does not know it and assumes that when he appears before the people of Israel, commissioned by God for them, they will know the name and will expect him to know it as well. How else could they verify that the God of Israel, and not someone else, had sent him? God reveals his name to Moses in response to his request.

Second, the revelation of the name gathers to itself a set of other concerns, over and above validating Moses should such an inquiry arise from the people of Israel. Before the solemn declaration of God's name, hints are given that God's name will involve the verb to be or to become. The phrase "say to them, 'I will be has sent me to you'" (Exod. 3:14) harks back to the response of God to Moses at verse 12 about his own adequacy ("I will be with you") before the formal explanation is given at verse 14.

Third, this explanation of God's name is meant to say something to Moses and to the Israelites, who otherwise know the name, as well as to the reader, and the full import of this is not shared until Exodus 6. At this juncture Moses has joined the Israelites and has himself been joined by

17. See my several essays in *Word Without End.* Zimmerli begins his Old Testament theology with a discussion of the name of God (*Old Testament Theology in Outline* [Atlanta: John Knox, 1978]).

18. The theological case for this has been made, e.g., by Hans Frei and George Lindbeck.

Aaron. An audience with Pharaoh has, as God indicated it would, demonstrated Pharaoh's resistance. Exodus 6 then explains to a complaining Moses that the resistance is part of God's design, that a protracted encounter will eventually mean a dramatic deliverance, and that "then you will know that I am the LORD your God, who brought you out from under the yoke of the Egyptians" (Exod. 3:6). Knowing the name is one thing, and knowing God as he means to be known is another thing, and this latter knowledge will come after trial and testing, so that all the world may know as well that the LORD is God.[19]

The importance of the name is also underscored in the context of sin and forfeit in the affair of the golden calf. Assurance that God, and not a surrogate, will accompany a sinful people comes to Moses by God's speaking forth his name, "The LORD, the LORD, the compassionate and gracious God" (Exod. 34:6). The name is presence and testimony to a specific shared history that will continue with this people.

III. Being and Person in Exodus 3:14

Understood in this way, it is clear that the name of God in the Exodus narratives is as personal a disclosure as God can make. God's name is himself; God's name expresses his promise and his faithfulness to that promise, to his elected people.

As is well known, the Greek rendering of Exodus 3:14 produced a different nuance, and the reason for this has been sought within different conceptual priorities. The English translation, "I am who I am," especially when heard in isolation from the narrative movement of Exodus 3–14 and its governing logic revealed at 6:7 (an isolation now assisted by talking about discrete sources in the Pentateuch), could almost be heard as pointing to the Hebrew *'ani 'asher 'ani*, "what I am I am." Or, encroach no further. Then we would be in the realm not of disclosure but of its opposite, the stuff of Rudolph Otto's *hin und her* (fascination/dread).

Yet the rendering of the Hebrew behind "I am who I am" was picked up differently in the LXX, as a statement involving God's being (so also

19. For a full treatment of the argument summarized here, see "The Call of Moses and the 'Revelation' of the Divine Name," in *Theological Exegesis: Essays in Honor of Brevard S. Childs* (Grand Rapids: Eerdmans, 1998), pp. 145-61.

Maimonides).[20] "I am the One who is" *(egō eimi ho ōn)* is the daughter rendering into Greek. It was this nuance, arguably different from the narrative direction of Exodus, which in turn influenced certain New Testament and subsequent theological statements and which focused on being rather than personality. It is a very small leap to see how *ousia* dominated the options for Trinitarian confession. In my judgment, later Trinitarian statements would be wrongly judged antiexegetical or philosophical, rather than scriptural. Instead, their scriptural location was either detached or obscured, given the climate of exchange, or the Hebrew tradition in place in Exodus was wrongly assessed to begin with due to the LXX rendering. In the case of Exodus 3:14 we are not learning something about God's substance or essence but something about a personal identity and history he is about to make good on at Sea and Sinai.

IV. Handing over the Name

In recent years, scholars have paid special attention to the role of the holy name in Christological coordination and have focused their attention quite rightly on the confession of Philippians 2:6-11. David Yeago and Richard Bauckham have drawn important attention to this hymn. Yeago does so to underscore that a divide between the church's theological speech and exegesis is a false one, and that even the phrase *homoousia* ("of one substance") in Nicene confession is exegesis, not desire for extrabiblical coherency.[21]

The argument is as follows. Chapters 40–48 of Isaiah speak quite frequently about the Lord being God alone, and they also insist that the nations come to discover this reality and confess it: "Surely God is with you, and there is no other; there is no other god" (45:14). At 45:23 God swears by himself "a word that will not be revoked" that "before me every knee shall bow; and by me every tongue shall swear." The content of their pledge

20. "This is, therefore, the expression of the idea that God exists, but not in the ordinary sense of the term; or, in other words, He is 'the existing Being which is the existing Being,' that is to say, the Being whose existence is absolute" (Moses Maimonides, *The Guide for the Perplexed*, 2nd ed., trans. M. Friedlander [London: Routledge & Kegan Paul, 1904], p. 95).

21. Yeago, "The New Testament and Nicene Dogma"; Bauckham, *God Crucified.*

is given in 45:24: "They will say of me, in the LORD alone are righteousness and strength."

What is contemplated here? It is nothing less than that all creation will give honor to God, know his name, speak forth his name, and give honor to the LORD, in whom alone are righteousness and strength. That is, what has been true of Israel's experience of God, in name and in holy presence, will according to God be true for all creation, with God's righteousness and his election of a people affirmed (45:25). This promise is sealed by an oath that cannot be revoked. It is sworn by God in his own name. The name of God, as revealed to Israel, will be known throughout all creation. (Jehovah's Witnesses, for obvious reasons, take this text quite literally and quite seriously.)

In Philippians 2:6-11 we have a hymn to Christ, whom Christians are told to imitate. Then language of condescension is used. Christ was of the form of God, he relinquished this, and he died on a cross. Therefore, the text says, "God gave him the name that is above every name," and reference is made to every knee bowing "in heaven and on earth and under the earth," and every tongue confessing "that Jesus Christ is Lord, to the glory of God the Father" (2:9-11).

The intratextual connection to Isaiah 45 is unmistakable. The name above every name, to which every knee shall bow and every tongue confess, is the holy name, YHWH. So what are we to make of the literal sense in Philippians, and how does what it says inform our speech about God, our understanding of God's personal name, subsequent credal confessions, and a proper conception of God as three in one?

We begin with the reality of Christian speech about God, which is the topic of this essay. Christians do not name the name of God as was true in Israel, as the Old Testament reveals God was known and worshiped. The Old Testament promises that as God was known in Israel, by his name and in himself, all nations will also know God, and for that give praise. This promise takes the form of a solemn oath.

What has happened to this oath that will not be revoked? It is not the case that all nations know God by name, and those who in Christ claim to know him do not use his name nor know his name in the strict sense in which Israel knew his name. Has the oath fallen to the ground? In the case of the first question, Christians have answered with the production of Christian eschatology. The promises of God remain irrevocable, and Christ's raising by God is a firstfruit of a larger harvest he remains committed to, and it is under his sovereignty that we must live now by faith in Christ.[22]

The second question is answered by Philippians in the terse transition of 2:10, "that at the name of Jesus," not at the personal name of the LORD, the promises sworn by himself are being fulfilled. This is made explicit in the final verse of the hymn. The confession is that Jesus Christ is Lord. The name of Jesus Christ stands where the promise had said that the name of the LORD would stand. This has taken place to the glory of God the Father.

V. Conclusions

The implications of this hymn for Christian talk are hard to overemphasize. I will begin with the most obvious ones and will assume that the works mentioned above provide additional elaboration.

First, the hymn clarifies the silence over the explicit mention of God's name in ongoing Christian practice. The New Testament speaks of YHWH in ways that we have discussed already, but it never seeks to imitate in its literal sense the exact practice of the Old Testament. Neither are there any efforts to reconnect with Israel's experience of God through the name by means of vocalizations of Hebrew, such as Jehovah or Yahweh.

Second, the hymn is quite clear that a delivery of something is taking place. It is not the case that the text seeks to conflate the name of Jesus and the name of "the LORD." The name of Jesus is not a vocalization of YHWH! God has a name, and it is the name above every name. He gives this name to Jesus. In so doing, the personal character of the exchange is preserved. It is not that we are discovering a deeper intention or a secret lying below the plain sense promises of God in the Old Testament. God really did swear by himself that his name would be confessed throughout creation; he was not being indirect or subtle.

Third, the giving of the name affects Jesus, but it also affects God. The giving of the name to Jesus is a complete vindication by God of Jesus, an acknowledgment that he has been perfect in his obedience and in his

22. See my treatment, "Creed, Scripture and 'Historical Jesus,'" in E. Radner and G. Sumner, eds., *The Rule of Faith: Scripture, Canon, and Creed in a Critical Age* (Harrisburg, PA: Morehouse Publishing, 1998), pp. 126-35.

complete congruence with God's will. The way this congruence is underscored is the only way to make this absolutely clear, on the terms of the Old Testament's governing center. The name of God is God's very self, and by giving it to Jesus, maximal identity is affirmed. Jesus Christ is Lord. He who will be as he is is this One raised by God.

How does this affect God? Here we return to the Trinitarian revival mentioned above. It should be clear that whatever else the Philippian hymn is, it is *not* a philosophical effort to coordinate abstract Trinitarian concepts. The intimate connection with the Old Testament's language insures that we are talking about a personal God and his personal Son. This is clarified once one sees the centrality of the name in the Old Testament and its transfer here.[23] There is an actual transaction taking place, and it could not be more personal than it is. Jesus gives up his life with God and in so doing becomes nothing, even to the extent of dying on a cross. The Trinitarian revival has done a good job focusing on Jesus the dereliction given utterance to and the love it bespeaks within the eternal life of God. When trying to maintain a commitment to *perichoresis* at the moment of death and nothingness, we have been asked to imagine the suffering of the Father, who truly loses his Son, and in that loss has his own unique, differentiated personal life within the Godhead.

The hymn from Philippians, understood against the backdrop of the divine name, gives us another alternative. The condescension of Jesus has its counterpart in the giving over of the name. God surrenders his name and himself to his Son and his name, *that at the name of Jesus* every knee shall bow. The identification is two-way, of Jesus with YHWH and of YHWH with Jesus. The hymn concludes, however, that this identification of Jesus with YHWH is "to the glory of God the Father."

To be given a glimpse at the life of YHWH through the lens of Jesus is to see God from within, from inside the relationship, from the standpoint of

23. Sadly, it must be regarded as a particularly Christian temptation to underestimate the significance of God's giving to Jesus the "name which is above every name," because that Name (YHWH) was not universally available, existing within the bosom of Israel and her faith. Gentile Christians (as in Philadelphia) may not even recognize access to the LORD through naming the name of Jesus; rather, "lord" is a term of oppression to be improved upon by address to "Sophia." Something has gone dreadfully wrong here. The root of the problem lies with a failure to understand the self-disclosure by God of himself, in Israel, in the name above every name, and hence a failure to understand what it means to call Jesus anything at all.

the Son. The consequence of this is to call God Father and mean by that YHWH, as seen from the standpoint of his Son, to whom has been given the name above every name. To name the holy name is for Christians to name the name of Jesus, but this happens to the glory of God the Father. The "loss of the divine name" is what it means for God, the LORD, the Maker of Heaven and Earth, to share himself with those outside Israel in the person of his Son. This constitutes the sacrifice of the Father in obedience to his own name and oath, as delivered to Israel, on behalf of all creation. It is a sacrifice with its own integrity, as God allows his forsaking of Jesus to be a truthful statement of his wrath, without thereby diminishing his own sacrificial act of love in sending the Son. By giving the Son his name we see the Father express in the most intimate way possible his identification with Jesus Christ the Lord, an identification that involves what the Greek Fathers called *taxis,* the ordered life within God's personal self. This ordering is as much about obedience and sacrifice as it is about triumph and joy, for in God's holy self, mercy and truth have kissed each other.

It belongs to the most mature Christian confession that the name of God has been given to Jesus. Efforts therefore to reinstate the name run up against the likelihood of misunderstanding and miscommunicating this confession and the implications of it for our understanding of God: the Father, the Son, and the Holy Spirit. The effort should be made, instead, to reinstate the heart of the Trinitarian life as that which is worthy of our praise and obedience, which has been shared with us out of Israel and her Scriptures, for all God's creation, to the glory of the Father, the LORD, the Maker of Heaven and Earth.

In practical terms, the identification of YHWH with Jesus means not that the attributes of God as rendered by the literal sense of the Old Testament have become lost in some transfer. Holiness, righteousness, justice, mercy, compassion, and jealousy, as these describe YHWH in the Old Testament, remain true of God in his essence, and *perichoresis* means they are true of the Son and the Holy Spirit in their eternal life as well. They have not been "handed over." For this reason, it will be important in Christian talk about God to retain meaningful links to God as he has been described in the Old Testament, in ways other than by his sacred name (YHWH). The traditional ways of speaking of God as God Almighty, Father, Lord God of Hosts, should be complemented and enriched, not corrected or abridged in the name of some false modality, whereby God's "mode" in Jesus is truer or more worthy of Christian talk.

If the concern expressed by efforts to vocalize God's name is to be addressed, then let the Old Testament lead the way with its own rich stock of terms. Nothing prevents the Christian community from addressing God as "Holy One" (so Isaiah), or Lord Most High, or God Almighty, or Maker of Heaven and Earth, alongside the predominantly Christological "Father." In this way it will be made clear that we are speaking of God in the same way as the Israel of old spoke to him in his holy name, now confessed by Christian tongues through the power of the Holy Spirit, "Jesus Christ, Lord, to the glory of God the Father."

Theology and Philosophy: An Exchange with Robert Jenson

DAVID NOVAK

I

My friendship with Robert Jenson over the past twelve years or so has been a blessing in my life and a benefit to my own work as a Jewish theologian. The blessing and the benefit are inextricably mixed in that Jenson's theology is very much the work of "Jens" the man, and that "Jens" is the man he is in large part because of the theology of Jenson the Christian theologian. This has been acutely brought to mind in reading volume one of his *Systematic Theology: The Triune God.* It is truly a systematic presentation of many insights his friends have been hearing over the years in conversations both official and spontaneous. Accordingly, reading the book is not so much déjà vu as it is a chance once more to pick up a conversation with Jens that has never really ended since it deals with those matters, which, in traditional Jewish parlance, "stand at the height of the very cosmos."[1]

From my perspective, the conversation with Jens has been so good not only because of Jens's great intelligence and deeply engaging personality but much more so because the conversation has been essentially theo-

1. Parts of this paper were first presented at the Dulles Colloquium, an ongoing forum of the Institute of Religion and Public Life in New York, which includes Catholic, Evangelical, and Jewish theologians, and in which Robert Jenson and I have been colleagues from its inception.

logical, even when we are only engaging in "small talk." What could be of greater importance to theologians than theology? Perhaps more than any other discipline, theology calls for the passion of its practitioners. Theology has provided our conversation enough commonality to make it possible. Furthermore, that theological commonality is not just about any "god" (the *theos* in "theology") — a point we would have in common with "theists" outside Judaism or Christianity — it is about the Lord (YHWH), who has named himself as "the God of Abraham, the God of Isaac, and the God of Jacob" (Exod. 3:15).

Theology also provides enough of a difference to make our conversation a genuine dialogue and not an antiphonal monologue. The theological difference is that as a Christian and a Jew, Jens and I are existentially dedicated to faith assertions (i.e., willing to die for them if need be) about the truest relationship with God available in this world, which are undeniably not just distinctive but mutually exclusive head-on. Which is the best way to and from the Lord God of Israel: the Torah or Christ? (Conversely, Jews, Christians, and Muslims commonly worship the God of Abraham, but that commonality is not nearly as specific and concrete as the common Jewish-Christian worship of the Lord God of Israel since it is not made over the proper interpretation of the same Scripture and does not involve a dispute over the nature of the community covenanted with this God.)[2]

A further commonality between Jens and myself is that we are both theologians in regular touch with philosophy; indeed, we could not do our work without that contact. This point of contact, both with each other and with the philosophers, is where I would like to conduct this exchange with Jens. Yet instead of directly commenting on Jens's thoughts on the relation of theology and philosophy, I would like to present some of my own thoughts on the subject and intersperse them with some of Jens's thoughts. My thoughts will have a necessarily Jewish cast to them. As Jens's great teacher Karl Barth said somewhere, "I cannot see with eyes other than my own." Hopefully, this exchange will give readers of this volume a sense of the flavor of our ongoing conversation that, God willing, will continue for many years to come. If nothing else, it might give readers a sense of what I

2. For the view that Judaism has more in common with Islam than with Christianity because of monotheism, see L. E. Goodman, *God of Abraham* (New York: Oxford University Press, 1996), pp. 34-35. This is a question that has been debated ever since the early Middle Ages.

have learned from Jens and with Jens over the years. (In this paper, when his written work is being formally cited, he is called "Jenson.")

II

Of late, some Jewish thinkers have attempted to designate themselves "Jewish philosophers" who are engaged in a discipline called "Jewish philosophy." It is even suggested that Jews "do Jewish philosophy" whereas Christians "do Christian theology." As I shall argue here, however, there is no discipline of "Jewish philosophy," that is, one that can be cogently defined, even though it is used now more than ever. I do believe, however, that there is a discipline of "Jewish theology," which has enough concerns in common with Christian theology for them both to be called "theology." There is also a discipline of "philosophy," which functions independently of theology. As such, I think the term "Jewish philosophy" only makes sense when it speaks of the relation of Judaism *and* philosophy in much the same way "Christian philosophy" speaks of the relation of Christianity *and* philosophy. The question is whether this relation is a positive correlation or a negative dissonance.

Most modern philosophers, having a decided prejudice against any theology, especially when it is Jewish or Christian, would accordingly ask: Aren't philosophy and theology antithetical? Isn't philosophy the product of reason, which can be universally validated? Isn't theology the product of faith, whose validation comes from a revelation to a particular historical community, and which is preserved by their tradition?

Since it is assumed by most philosophers, following Plato, that the universal should fully include the particular, whereas the particular cannot include the universal, it would seem that any interrelation of philosophy and theology would have to be on philosophy's terms.[3] That is how, most impressively, Georg W. F. Hegel interrelated the two in his "philosophy of religion," which in effect was his "philosophical religion."[4] This is where philosophy has presented itself as metaphysics, whereby it attempts to sub-

3. Nevertheless, Plato had to admit the universal never does include all particulars; see *Timaeus,* 49D-E.

4. See G. W. F. Hegel, *Lectures on the Philosophy of Religion,* trans. R. F. Brown, P. C. Hodgson, and J. M. Stewart (Berkeley: University of California Press, 1988), pp. 401-2.

sume theology into its own operations by denying theology its own foundations in revelation and thereby substituting its own, supposedly more universal, foundations for them. Of course, no self-respecting theologian could possibly accept that since no faithful Jew or Christian could accept such theological surrender. The Lord God of Israel does not tolerate a pantheon, let alone a pantheon in which he is subordinate to a larger "divine" order, even if it is a pantheon where he is the first person. He is very much a jealous God, before whom no other gods may be acknowledged, even secondarily.[5]

The way to counter this type of philosophical capture of revelation (about which theology speaks), is to deny the universal claims of philosophy as metaphysics. As Robert Jenson writes, "the West's Mediterranean-pagan religious heritage — truly no more anchored in universal humanity than any other — was elevated to be the judge of its biblical heritage."[6] Soon thereafter, he notes that "Greek philosophy was simply the theology of the historically particular Olympian-Parmenidean religion, later shared with the wider Mediterranean cultic world" (*ST* I, 10). Thus, he makes the point, "what must not continue is only the Enlightenment's elevation of the Greek element of our thinking to be the unilateral judge of the whole" (*ST* I, 9). What I learn from this is that the question between philosophy and theology is not which is more universal and which is more particular. At the ontological level, both philosophy and theology are universal inasmuch as they both make assertions about the entire cosmos. Both are also particular inasmuch as they both stem from the constructions of cosmic reality by particular cultures, cultures that locate their origins in a revelation given to them. Each, then, is universal in principle, but particular in fact.[7]

At this level, it would seem that theology, which is more explicit about its roots in a revelation than is philosophy, has a decided edge. That is because a devotion to the truth that characterizes metaphysics can

5. See *de-ba-Hodesh,* chap. 8 on Exod. 20:3, in *Mekilta de-Rabbi Ishmael,* vol. 2, trans. J. Z. Lauterbach (Philadelphia: Jewish Publication Society of America, 1934), pp. 262-63.

6. R. Jenson, *Systematic Theology,* vol. I: *The Triune God* (Oxford: Oxford University Press, 1997), p. 8. Hereafter abbreviated *ST,* by volume and page. Italics in quotations are Jenson's.

7. Along these lines, see Alasdair MacIntyre, *Whose Justice? Which Rationality?* (Notre Dame, Ind.: University of Notre Dame Press, 1987), chap. 1.

hardly be separated from the sociality that is essential to human nature. The religions of revelation — Judaism, Christianity, and Islam — have ontologically constituted coherent communities, which have locations in space and duration in time (traditions). Greek religion's enunciation as philosophy can now claim only scattered individual adherents. That might well explain why in the West it has been easier for theologians to incorporate philosophy into their work than it has been for philosophers to incorporate theology into their work. This itself is an aspect of the way the religions of revelation all accept converts, who themselves were previously pagan. Even though, for Jews and Christians, conversion is being "born again," these former pagans are encouraged to bring the best of their former culture with them into the new religion.[8] Indeed, some theologians see the best of the pagan culture as the basis for seeking the revelation of the (for them) new God of Israel. The search for the unknown God there can lead to the God who begins to make himself known here and now.

III

My assumption that there is such a discipline as "Jewish theology" has hardly gone unchallenged, however. There are many who would question its possibility, let alone its cogent presence. For them, following Baruch Spinoza, Moses Mendelssohn, and, especially, Immanuel Kant, Judaism is essentially law.[9] However, despite all its obviously legal content, doesn't Judaism claim that its law is the law of God? Isn't the very assertion of a "law of God" a theological assertion? Certainly, the legal claims of Judaism *(halakah)* rest squarely on theological foundations. Furthermore, these theological foundations not only undergird the Jewish legal system, they permeate it as well, especially in discussions of the "reasons of the commandments" *(ta'amei ha-mitsvot)*. As for the nonlegal aspects of Judaism known as *haggadah* (literally, "narrative"), a good part of it consists of "God-talk," which is the literal definition of *theo-logy*. Thus the separation of law and theology in Judaism is formal not substantial. One could look

8. See *b. Yebam.* 22a. Cf. John 3:3-7.

9. For a critique of this view, whether held by non-Jews or by Jews themselves, see Abraham Joshua Heschel, *God in Search of Man* (New York: Farrar, Straus, and Cudahy, 1955), pp. 320-35.

upon *halakah* as the practical pole of Judaism, *haggadah* as the theoretical pole, and the Jewish life of the commandments *(mitsvot)* as being conducted within these two poles. Sometimes that life is closer to one, sometimes it is closer to the other, but never is it so close to one that the other can be totally ignored.[10] In the area of esoteric Jewish thought known as Kabbalah, God-talk is ubiquitous; there is nothing else there.

Jewish theology is possible for any kind of Jewish thought that is not legalistic per se, that is, Jewish thought concerned with the ontological origins of Judaism. Jewish theology can engage philosophy when it can recognize the phenomenological independence of the world, since philosophy comes from the world. Revelation, conversely, comes to the world.[11] As we have also seen, however, especially as taught to us by Jenson, theology cannot be systematically connected, with integrity, to any metaphysics a priori. The most it can do ontologically is to selectively incorporate some insights of philosophically constituted metaphysics that help explicate points already found in the theological tradition itself. That is inevitable since, as Jenson notes, "[t]heologians of Western Christianity [one could just as easily say 'Western Judaism'] must indeed converse with the philosophers because and insofar as both are engaged in the same sort of exercise" (*ST* I, 10). Thus Jenson speaks of the theological error of "finding the 'right' metaphysics among those offered by officially designated philosophers" (*ST* I, 21). He notes in this regard that, contrary to the usual designation of Thomas Aquinas as an "Aristotelian," this is "exactly what Thomas did not do. He *conversed* with Aristotle, and in the conversations was stimulated and helped to his own metaphysical positions" (*ST* I, 21). Among Jewish theologians, one could say the same about Philo in relation to Plato, or Maimonides in relation to Aristotle, or Franz Rosenzweig in relation to Georg W. F. Hegel, or Abraham Joshua Heschel in relation to Max Scheler.

It would seem, then, that the best a Jewish or Christian theologian can do with religious integrity is to *use* philosophical methods to better understand Judaism or Christianity. However, it must always be explicit that Judaism or Christianity is the irreducible datum present (best named

10. See D. Novak, *Law and Theology in Judaism*, vol. 1 (New York: KTAV, 1974), chap. 1.

11. That is why the denial of the dogma "the Torah is from God" has been designated the first Jewish heresy. See *m. Sanh.* 10.1.

by the German *das Urphaenomen*). This is, of course, the function of philosophy when taken to be the "handmaiden of theology" *(ancilla theologiae)*, a concept that was a staple of medieval theology.[12] One can see this use of philosophical method when Jewish theology is called "a philosophy of Judaism." Indeed, this was how one of the greatest Jewish theologians of this century, my late revered teacher Abraham Joshua Heschel, subtitled his central work, *God in Search of Man.* Heschel seemed rather unconcerned with there being any real distinction between a philosophy *of* Judaism and Jewish theology per se. In fact, he also called his own philosophy of Judaism presented in this same book "depth theology."[13] In using the word "depth," Heschel wanted to distinguish his foundational approach from a kind of dogmatism that takes the theological statements of the past and treats them as if they were legally mandated norms simply to be clarified and applied rather than to be critically examined in the light of the entire phenomenon of revelation and the subsequent tradition that preserves its content.

IV

This seeming reduction of Jewish philosophy to philosophy of Judaism and hence to Jewish theology does raise an important question for philosophers. Just why does any philosopher choose to direct his or her own attention and interest (what is called *Sorge* in German) to one phenomenon rather than to another? The notion of a philosophy *of* anything presupposes that philosophy itself does not provide its own object for itself but, rather, that philosophy is a method for understanding the phenomenon already there before one. Philosophers will quickly recognize such a presupposition as that of phenomenology.

As Plato had Parmenides point out to Socrates, and as his critics pointed out to Edmund Husserl, just *any* phenomenon will not do.[14] For a philosopher to be able to truly, that is, philosophically, sustain his or her attention and interest in the object before him or her, that object has to be

12. For the history of this concept, see H. A. Wolfson, *Philo,* vol. 1 (Cambridge, Mass.: Harvard University Press, 1947), pp. 145-47.

13. Heschel, *God in Search of Man,* pp. 7-8.

14. See Plato, *Parmenides,* 130B-D; Martin Heidegger, *Being and Time,* trans. J. Stambaugh (Albany, N.Y.: SUNY Press, 1996), pp. 32-34 (sec. 7).

supremely worthy of such profound attention and interest. Yet if a philosopher accepts this great challenge, then isn't he or she veering very close to theology? Theologians explicitly deal with an object whose very name must minimally mean "that than which nothing greater can be conceived."[15] If the philosophical quest for the highest truth intends an object of *ultimate concern,* to use the term employed most famously by Paul Tillich, doesn't that object immediately mean the object theologians designate "God"?[16] Could anyone be ultimately concerned with anything else?

This applies to the God of Abraham, Isaac, and Jacob as well as it applies to the God of Aristotle (the "God of the philosophers" par excellence, to borrow from Blaise Pascal). Weren't Aristotle and Hegel, to cite two God-centered philosophers, in effect functioning as theologians? Isn't Aristotle's metaphysics a type of Greek theology, and isn't Hegel's metaphysics modeled after Aristotle's, albeit with a large detour through a certain type of scholastic theology?[17] Could either thinker have discovered the "God" of whom they respectively speak if they had not uttered a name they had already heard and which their hearers and readers had already heard? Wasn't René Descartes right when he insisted that the very notion of God as absolute had to have been presented to the mind rather than be taken as something constructed by it, even if he wrongly assumed that this notion need not be mediated by a specific historical tradition?[18] Could Aristotle and Hegel have truly invented the God each constituted philosophically? Didn't they differ from the theologians of their own *polis,* Aristotle from those in Athens and Hegel from those in Berlin, only by virtue of the fact that their respective theologies are more coherent and more comprehen-

15. See Karl Barth, *Fides Quaerens Intellectum,* trans. I. W. Robertson (London: SCM Press, 1960), pp. 74-75.

16. See Tillich, *Systematic Theology,* vol. 1 (Chicago: University of Chicago Press, 1951), pp. 12-14; also, Thomas Aquinas, *Summa Theologiae* 1, q.2, a.3.

17. See G. W. F. Hegel, *Phenomenology of Spirit,* trans. A. V. Miller (Oxford: Oxford University Press, 1977), p. 12 (preface). Let it not be forgotten how Aristotle begins his discussion about God as the supreme cosmic *telos,* "thought thinking thought," namely, "A tradition has been handed down *(paradidotai)* by the ancient thinkers of very early times, and bequeathed to posterity in the form of a myth, . . . that the heavenly bodies are gods and that the Divine pervades the whole of nature" (*Metaphysics,* trans. H. Tredennick [Cambridge, Mass.: Harvard University Press, 1935], pp. 162-63 [1074b1-3]). See also Plato, *Laws,* 966E-967A.

18. René Descartes, *Meditations* 3, trans. A. Wollaston (Baltimore, Md.: Penguin Books, 1960), p. 127.

sive than those of their fellow theologians, those having less intelligence and imagination than they? (In this sense, Kant to my mind was more radical theologically than either Aristotle or Hegel since he constituted a God who is clearly not the absolute.[19] With Kant as with Alfred North Whitehead, we are back to a demiurge like that of Plato, that is, a god who mediates between the ultimate and what lies below it.)[20] When metaphysics forgets its theological origins, does it not in effect assume all the pitfalls Ludwig Wittgenstein saw in any "private language," which is a language in which the current speaker presents himself or herself as the first speaker, the founder of his or her own speech acts?[21]

Ontology (of which "metaphysics" is but one kind) always veers so close to theology that it becomes in the end a more articulate form of some theology or other. The challenge, then, to philosophers unwilling to make such ontological commitments is just what is distinctive about what they are doing. Thus, for example, what distinguishes a philosopher of law from a methodologically reflective jurist, or a philosopher of science from a methodologically reflective scientist, or a biomedical ethicist (most of whom now see themselves as philosophers) from a methodologically reflective physician, or a philosopher of language from a methodologically reflective linguist? In other words, what distinguishes philosophy from weltanschauung, as Hegel asked?[22] The very refusal to deal with this question, it seems to me, constitutes the very positivism that Plato so well saw as the death knell of philosophy itself.[23] (Let it be remembered that Plato sought to reform Greek theology from within, not to eliminate it altogether.)[24] This is also a chal-

19. For the attempt to overcome Kant's inadequate notion of God, by a Jewish philosopher most heavily influenced by Kant, see Hermann Cohen, *Ethik des reinen Willens,* 4th ed. (Berlin: Bruno Cassirer, 1923), pp. 455-70; also, D. Novak, *The Election of Israel* (Cambridge: Cambridge University Press, 1995), pp. 54-64.

20. See A. N. Whitehead, *Process and Reality* (New York: Macmillan, 1929), p. 112. Cf. Plato, *Timaeus,* 29E-30D. For an attempt to constitute *Transzendenz* as what is beyond God, which also represents a Platonic-like theology, see Karl Jaspers, *Philosophy,* vol. 1, trans. E. B. Ashton (Chicago: University of Chicago Press, 1969), pp. 87-89.

21. See Ludwig Wittgenstein, *Philosophical Investigations,* 2nd ed., trans. G. E. M. Anscombe (New York: Macmillan, 1958), pp. 88-89 (1.240-46).

22. See Hegel, *Phenomenology of Spirit,* pp. 41-42 (preface); also, Emil L. Fackenheim, *The Religious Dimension in Hegel's Thought* (Bloomington and London: Indiana University Press, 1967), pp. 16-17.

23. See Plato, *Republic,* 511B-C.

24. See Plato, *Republic,* 379A-E.

lenge made to philosophy by Pope John Paul II in his recent encyclical, *Fides et Ratio,* where he warns how trivial, even insipid, philosophy becomes when it loses its historical contact with theology.[25] Here again, Jenson's point about the earliest philosophers having been theologians themselves is most apt.[26]

V

So, is there a relation between philosophy and theology? The question assumes that there is enough that distinguishes the two for such a relation to be possible. However, is there a relation that does not reduce theology to philosophy or philosophy to theology? Haven't both reductions failed?

Let me suggest that there is a third model, which can be presented as preferable to the two that I have been examining above. I would call this model "philosophical theology," or more accurately, "philosophically informed theology." One can well think of Robert Jenson as a model practitioner of this kind of philosophically informed theology in his own work.

To assume that there can be a *philosophical* theology also assumes that the word "philosophical" functions as an adjective modifying the noun "theology." This also implies that there are other forms of theology that are minimally nonphilosophical, and maximally antiphilosophical. What, then, distinguishes philosophical theology from nonphilosophical theology? I propose that the difference between philosophical and nonphilosophical

25. See *Fides et Ratio,* chap. 5.

26. The late Leo Strauss (d. 1973) made much of the chasm between philosophy and theology, insisting that philosophers do not accept arguments from traditional authority as theologians do. However, Strauss cites as his main sources Plato and Aristotle, both of whom were theologians. See Strauss, *Natural Right and History* (Chicago: University of Chicago Press, 1953), chap. 3. For a critique of Strauss's attempt to make philosophy ahistorical, see Hans-Georg Gadamer, *Truth and Method,* trans. G. Barden and J. Cumming (New York: Crossroad, 1982), pp. 482-90. Perhaps, contra Strauss, one can say that just as Augustine and Anselm could propose *credo ut intelligam* as a way of directly apprehending revealed truth *after* having indirectly received it through tradition and its authority, so Plato and Aristotle were attempting to do the same with what had been revealed to Greek culture by their gods. See Plato, *Republic,* 499B; *Laws,* 747E. Cf. Augustine, *De Libero Arbitrio,* 2.2.5-6 re Isa. 7:9; also, Novak, *Law and Theology in Judaism,* chap. 15.

theology lies in the theological constitution of the world. By "the world" I mean that which appears outside the realm of revelation.

In Judaism, this difference has most often been located in the question of creation. Creation both precedes revelation in time (it happened first) and exceeds revelation in space (it happens to everything). Jenson explains this quite clearly when he writes, "Israel knew that her beginning had a date within history, and thus Israel acknowledged a history of humankind and of her God before there was an Israel. Therefore Israel had . . . to acknowledge a Creation not identical with her own origin" (*ST* I, 48). (Hence creation and revelation are only finally reconciled in redemption, a point most insightfully made and theologically developed among Jewish thinkers by Franz Rosenzweig.)[27]

To follow this line of thought, it might be well to infer the positive from the negative, that is, to begin by looking at what could be considered *the* most antiphilosophical Jewish theology possible: Kabbalah. I say that Kabbalah is not just nonphilosophical but antiphilosophical because, as Gershom Scholem suggested in many of his great historical studies, Kabbalah very much involves the rejection of the philosophical theology of earlier Jewish theologians like Saadiah and Maimonides.[28] A main point that distinguishes this new theology from the older theology is the prominence of the doctrine of creation in the older theology and its near absence in the newer theology. In Kabbalah, God's relation to the world is not through creation *(beri'ah)* but, rather, through *atsilut* (literally, "approximation"), what we usually call "emanation."[29] The reality and meaning of the world lies totally in its being some aspect or other of the Godhead *('elohut)*. The world is not externally related to the creator God; it is, rather, a mediated participation in the larger substantial reality. Even the most mundane aspects of the world are taken to be symbolic manifestations *(sefirot)* of the one and only reality, which is divine. Such a radically panentheistic theology becomes just as radically acosmic.

Whereas in pantheism God and the world are interchangeable, namely, *deus sive natura,* in kabbalistic theology, unlike Spinoza, there is

27. See Franz Rosenzweig, *The Star of Redemption,* trans. W. W. Hallo (New York: Holt, Rinehart, and Winston, 1970), pp. 380-92.

28. See Gershom Scholem, *Major Trends in Jewish Mysticism* (New York: Schocken, 1946), pp. 23-25.

29. See Gershom Scholem, *On the Kabbalah and Its Symbolism,* trans. R. Manheim (New York: Schocken, 1969), pp. 66-77.

only *natura naturans* (that is, nature as person); there is no *natura naturata* (that is, nature as a system of distinct entities).[30] True *science* here can only be revealed and received, that is, it must be *kabbalah* (literally, "what has been received" and "how it has been received"); hence no truth can be derived from any nonrevealed source. Anything taken to be substantially separate from God, what the kabbalists call "the other side" *(sitra ahra)*, is by definition unintelligible, indeed, demonic.[31] In short, our experience of the world, outside of revelation, in truth has nothing in common with revelation at all. This world is but an illusion.

Both the kabbalists and the philosophical theologians like Saadiah and Maimonides attempted to avoid the type of dualism that characterizes much of what could be called nonphilosophical Jewish theology. Historically speaking, this type of theology is usually prephilosophical, that is, it has been conducted by thinkers who have never been confronted with systematically impressive philosophy. (This turns out to be what the rabbis called *hokhmah yevanit,* "Greek wisdom.")[32] In this type of theology, the Torah and the world become separate realms, at least as regards the methods formulated to understand each realm. Here, theology simply speaks about its own particular tradition much like the discourse of positive law. Such theology is ontologically naïve. However, such a methodological dualism seems to entail a type of ontological dualism that is ultimately foreign to the Pharisaic project (from which all subsequent Judaisms stem) of bringing the Torah to bear on everything experienced in the world. As the Mishnah states about the Torah, "everything is in it."[33] Thus to avoid this dualism, both epistemological and ontological, the kabbalists see the method for knowing everything and anything, all of which is real only within the life of the Godhead, as being innate within the Torah itself. The Torah for them is not "from God" *(min ha-shamayim)* but is itself the various permutations of the divine name per se.[34] The Torah itself is uncreated since it is essentially divine. There is no external world since there is noth-

30. Cf. Spinoza, *Ethics* 1, prop. 29.

31. See Gershom Scholem, *The Messianic Idea in Judaism* (New York: Schocken, 1971), p. 187.

32. For the origin of this term, see *b. B. Qam.* 83a; also, Saul Lieberman, *Hellenism in Jewish Palestine,* 2nd ed. (New York: Jewish Theological Seminary of America, 1962), pp. 100-114.

33. *m. 'Abot* 5.22.

34. See Scholem, *On the Kabbalah and Its Symbolism,* pp. 36-45.

ing else to talk about. All relations are inner relations, which makes creation a lesser form of emanation at best.

For the philosophical theologians, conversely, for whom creation is an extradivine event, a transitive, effective act of God, the world that is independent of but related to God must provide its own intelligibility, at least prima facie. Since creation precedes revelation, the method for understanding the Torah itself must come from the world itself. This is so, as Maimonides insisted, because the Torah, like the world, is a creation *by* God.[35] The Torah itself, though, is not divine. Because the Torah is a more specific creation by God than is the world as a whole, the methodology for understanding the more general created entity, the world, must be applied to the understanding of the more specific created entity, the Torah, even if the Torah is taken to be the ultimate form of all creation.[36] As Maimonides (who is inevitably *the* methodological model — even when he is not the ontological model — for every subsequent Jewish philosophical theologian) well put it, "although the Torah itself is not natural [that is, from the world], it enters into nature."[37] One might say, it is *in* the world not *of* it, that is, not *from* it.

In a legal responsum, when he is asked about the liturgical appropriateness of praising God as "the teacher of the Torah *(ha-melamed torah)* to his people Israel," Maimonides rules against it for explicitly theological reasons. (A Jewish version, no doubt, of *lex orandi est lex credendi.*) Although God is the giver of the Torah *(noten ha-torah)*, expressed liturgically in a way Maimonides can endorse, it is humans, not God, who teach the Torah to themselves — as they similarly teach themselves about the world that God gives them as the created order.[38] That is why Maimonides and others like him are so fond of the rabbinic dictum, "the Torah speaks in human language" *(dibrah torah ke-lashon benei 'adam)*.[39] That is, the Torah is given to humans in the world of which they are already part and from which they have already derived their powers of speech and understanding.

35. See Maimonides, *Guide of the Perplexed,* 1.65.

36. See *m. Gen. Rab.* 1.1.

37. Maimonides, *Guide of the Perplexed,* 2.40.

38. Maimonides, *Teshuvot ha-Rambam,* ed. J. Blau (Jerusalem: Miqitsei Nirdamim, 1960), p. 333 (2, no. 182).

39. See Maimonides, *Guide of the Perplexed,* 1.26. For the much different earlier meaning of this term in rabbinic literature, see J. M. Harris, *How Do We Know This?* (Albany, N.Y.: SUNY Press, 1995), pp. 71-72.

VI

This approach, which attempts to learn from philosophy how there is an opening for revelation in the created world, is quite consistent with the whole covenantal thrust of the Jewish tradition. This is especially so with what theologians can learn from political philosophy, which might well be seen as the social construction of reality.

Both the record of Scripture itself and the findings of modern historical-critical scholarship indicate that the primary Jewish polity, the covenant *(berit),* of which the Torah (biblical and traditional) is the constitution (what in German would be called its *Rechtsordnung*), is not something the Torah itself introduced into the world. It was already present in the world as a form of relationship between a sovereign and his subordinates. These subordinates were given a certain amount of self-rule, which was more for the sake of the relationship *with* the sovereign than it was simply an application of law *from* him. The covenant derives its initial form from what scholars call the "suzerainty treaty."[40] What the Torah introduced to the world socially constructed is a direct relationship in history (hence temporally and spatially finite), one that is located between the creator God and a singular human community. Since the Torah addresses itself to created human nature per se, and since it anticipates God's redemption of the whole world, which is the ultimate reconciliation of God and creation, the covenantal Torah is of cosmic significance.[41] The point of contact with the world and its worldly wisdom — philosophy — is located in the quest for the truth that law per se teaches. Indeed, it is no accident that the translation of the Torah into another language, Greek, rendered the Hebrew *torah* as *nomos.*

Contrary to much misunderstanding, this emphasis of law is not where a Jewish theologian and a Christian theologian like Jenson — especially a Lutheran Christian theologian — have to part theological company and end the discussion as a draw. The question of law is not an antinomy forming an impasse between Jewish theology and Christian theology. The question is not whether or not law is central to the God-human relationship *(quod sit lex?)* but, rather, where is the exact locus of the law of God here and

40. See D. R. Hillers, *Covenant* (Baltimore, Md.: Johns Hopkins University Press, 1969).

41. See *b. Pesaḥ.* 68b re Jer. 33:25.

now for the covenant *(quid est lex?)*. Christianity is no more antinomian (that is, without law) than Judaism is legalistic (that is, nothing but law). When Paul saw Christ as superseding "the law" *(ho nomos)*, he meant that Christ himself had superseded the Mosaic law (and its Pharisaic-rabbinic tradition) as the covenantal norm per se.[42] It is to this question, not to a Christian rejection of law per se, that Jews have said no. Moreover, only the parts of that law historically contingent on pre-Christian events have been superseded; the more general theological and moral norms remain authoritative. To assert otherwise would be to succumb to Marcionism, the first heresy the church had to repudiate.

This point, it seems to me, comes out in Jenson's dispute with his fellow Lutheran theologian, George Lindbeck. Heavily influenced by Ludwig Wittgenstein's later philosophy of language, Lindbeck has proposed that theology is the grammar of the language-form religion.[43] Although accepting the lawlike character of grammar for theology, Jenson criticizes Lindbeck's grammatical definition of theology for two reasons. One, it seems to reduce theology to a descriptive role: tracing what is already there rather than prescribing what is to be. He writes, "if Christian theology is grammar, then it is prescriptive grammar. . . . Secular modernity has supposed that grammar cannot prescribe usage but can only describe it, because secular modernity could acknowledge no one to give the prescriptions. . . . Speakers of Christianese need not share this privation, not having lost their king" (*ST* I, 20). Two, Lindbeck seems to be willing to leave theological grammar at the level of semiotics, that is, internal references within a linguistic field. Yet Jenson insists that "[t]heological propositions seem, however, never actually to appear as pure grammatical rules . . . [they] say something not just about language but also about an extralinguistic entity . . . and the drafters and promulgators of the doctrine would certainly have denied that it could accomplish its grammatical task except just as it has this descriptive force."[44]

These two departures from Lindbeck are very much connected since prescription and "extralinguistic entity" can be correlated. This can be

42. See Rom. 10:2-4; also, E. P. Sanders, *Paul and Palestinian Judaism* (Philadelphia: Westminster Press, 1977), pp. 550-51.

43. George Lindbeck, *The Nature of Doctrine* (Philadelphia: Westminster Press, 1984), pp. 79-84.

44. *ST* I, 18. See *ST* I, 19 n. 45 for his sharpest criticism of Lindbeck, where he says that "Lindbeck may not have shaken off positivist prejudgments."

done, I think, by enlisting the help of philosophy, in this case Kant's philosophical notion of the-thing-in-itself *(Ding an sich).*

Despite the fact that Kant confines all of our knowledge of the world to the conceptualization of our perception of phenomena, he nevertheless posits that behind these phenomena, as it were, there lies an entity that is more than just the subject matter of our phenomenal experience. He posits its existence *(an sit)* but not its essence *(quid est).* He, moreover, calls this entity *noumenon,* namely, an entity having an intelligibility known to a mind that knows it far more intimately than we humans can with our limited phenomenal equipment.[45] In the realm of theoretical or speculative reason, Kant simply leaves the matter at that existential level. (Thus it is no wonder that post-Kantian philosophers, such as Georg W. F. Hegel and Hermann Cohen, who moved in an idealistic direction, sought to eliminate this surd altogether from philosophical consideration.)[46] However, at the level of practical or moral reason, Kant sees the *noumenon* in the self-consciousness of the acting being, the being who can command itself and others by analogy to do the good.[47] Such a being is *autonomous:* it can make law for itself and any other rational being in similar circumstances. Thus unlike theoretical reason, the knower here is a creator, not just a spectator. Really and not just retroactively, this knower knows a priori and not just a posteriori: before the fact and not after it. In this real sense, only a maker can know his own work in advance, that is, when he intends its being.

If one sees Kant's notion of the autonomous moral being as being a colossal deconstruction of the biblical God, namely, the transfer of unique divine attributes to human reason, then it is theologically quite useful to deconstruct his deconstruction and set the world right again.[48] That is, we

45. See I. Kant, *Critique of Pure Reason,* B306-8.

46. See G. W. F. Hegel, *The Encyclopedia Logic,* trans. T. F. Geraets, W. A. Suchting, and H. S. Harris (Indianapolis and Cambridge: Hackett, 1991), p. 194 (sec. 125); H. Cohen, *Logik der reinen Erkenntnis,* 3rd ed. (Berlin: Bruno Cassirer, 1922), pp. 271, 376-77. This rejection seems to be followed by Edmund Husserl in his notion of "bracketing" *(epochē)* of the question of being; see *Ideas,* trans. W. R. Boyce Gibson (New York and London: Collier, 1962), pp. 99-100 (sec. 32).

47. See I. Kant, *Groundwork of the Metaphysic of Morals,* trans. H. J. Paton (New York: Harper and Row, 1964), pp. 104-15.

48. See I. Kant, *Religion within the Limits of Reason Alone,* trans. T. M. Greene and H. H. Hudson (New York: Harper and Brothers, 1960), p. 157 and note.

can restore to talk about God what Kant misplaced in his talk about man. In the case of Jenson's critique of Lindbeck, we can learn from this deconstruction of Kant's deconstruction of traditional Jewish and Christian creation theology and revelation theology. What we can learn is that whereas descriptive grammar cannot carry us to a point where a truly extralinguistic entity appears, prescriptive grammar can carry us to such a point. How? Prescription itself requires a person behind the commanding voice, *someone* whose will is being enunciated, and someone who cannot be reduced to an internal function of the prescription itself in the way that a cause can be reduced to an internal function of a phenomenal field for Kant.[49] As such, the extralinguistic entity that theological grammar intends is not the being lying *beyond* it as an object like the self-knowing *telos* in Aristotle's metaphysics.[50] Instead, God is the subject who stands *behind* us, whose commandment is addressed to us: the voice from heaven *who* reaches *down* to us on earth. What we know of God is from the commandments he as prime Subject addresses to us as privileged objects. We do not know God as the supreme Object whom our own subjective consciousness intends and who transcends our own projections because it is more than an ideal. For biblically based Judaism and Christianity, God is the "I" and we are the "thou," not vice versa.[51] Speaking to God about God is possible only because God has spoken to us about himself first; indeed, it is not only possible, it is necessary for those who listen to God (see *ST* I, 80). As I have heard Jens say on several occasions, "we are involved in a conversation in which God is the first speaker." Any speaker, and certainly the first speaker, by the very act of speaking to us makes a demand that we listen to him. The task of such direct address is to persuade the listeners that what is being proposed is for our own good, that it gives us the objects of our deepest strivings. To acknowledge the extralinguistic character of the commanding voice, a voice that can choose to speak or be silent, is necessary and not arbitrary for us.

49. See Kant, *Critique of Pure Reason,* B280.

50. See Aristotle, *Metaphysics,* 1074b1-35.

51. See Abraham Joshua Heschel, *Man Is Not Alone* (Philadelphia: Jewish Publication Society of America, 1951), pp. 125-29.

VII

The ontological relation of the Torah and the world, which the methodological relation of theology and philosophy enunciates, can be seen on two levels. The one level is the attempt to apply the teaching of the Torah *to* the world in which it is to function. The second level is the attempt to see how the world allows the Torah to enter *into* it, even before it actually transforms it.

At the level of application, the more general the phenomenon being addressed by the Torah, the more appropriate a philosophical perspective becomes in and for that application. Thus in the area of civil and criminal law, for example, where the subject matter is not uniquely Jewish at all, philosophical questions concerning political rights and duties come to the forefront. Because of greater interaction between Jewish and non-Jewish thinkers today, especially when political-ethical questions are at hand, even the normative study of Jewish law is becoming more and more philosophically oriented. Even the discussion of more intimately Jewish matters such as marriage and divorce is involving more and more philosophical reflection on such general issues as embodiment, gender, and reproduction.[52]

Indeed, those Jewish thinkers, especially those Jewish legal scholars who are either nonphilosophical or antiphilosophical, when having to deal with questions of principle over and above questions of specific norms per se, inevitably introduce what can only be designated unexamined prejudices in place of the rigorous examination philosophical reflection entails. Such prejudices almost always boil down to rather crude arguments from personal authority. These prejudices can be faulted on legal grounds, especially that aspect of the law that deals with judicial procedures. Yet it is that aspect of the law that leads one rather quickly into both theological and philosophical questions. The greater worldly involvement of even very traditional Jewish legal scholars (who are now called by the neologism "halakists") inevitably requires that a more philosophical perspective be employed in dealing with many questions of law, which are themselves informed and transformed by this growing worldliness.

At the level of what might be termed presuppositions of theology,

52. See, e.g., D. Novak, *Jewish Social Ethics* (New York: Oxford University Press, 1992), chap. 4.

the question of the relation of the Torah and the world becomes the question of how the world's self-limitation can make entry of the Torah into it possible — but not necessary. (If it were necessary, then the Torah could be derived from the world itself instead of being brought to it.)[53] This requires what I would call a Kantian-critical move, one conducted methodologically but not one that accepts Kant's ontology.

Kant's project required him to constitute and limit the range of speculative reason in order to make room for the authentic exercise of practical reason, where alone the rational person can be noumenally constituted.[54] Similarly, Jewish and Christian philosophical theology must make close alliances with those philosophies that allow a transcendent horizon for the world and which do not present any rationally constructed totalizing structure in and for the world. In my view, those close alliances, which are always partial and never surrenders, are best formed now with phenomenology and those types of analytic philosophy closest to the concerns of the later Ludwig Wittgenstein.[55]

At the ethical level, the presuppositional status of the world constituted by philosophy takes on great significance. Here the highest ethical standard philosophy can propose in the world, which is the standard of justice, becomes the *conditio sine qua non* for the proper interpretation of the Torah's norms governing interhuman relationships. This function is best expressed by the talmudic principle, "nothing prohibited to humans in general is permitted to Jews specifically."[56] This principle and its corollaries have provided a powerful critical limit on all sorts of fanatical and chauvinistic interpretations of Jewish law. That has been the case essentially when it has been assumed that what is prohibited to humans in general is determined by human reason's discovery of natural law in the world, namely, the adequacy of *inclinatio rationalis* to *inclinatio naturalis.*

Here is where philosophy is most important to theology, for the dis-

53. See D. Novak, *Natural Law in Judaism* (Cambridge: Cambridge University Press, 1998), pp. 142-48.

54. See Kant, *Critique of Pure Reason,* B823-24. This is quite similar to what Heidegger called *Seinlassen;* see *Being and Time,* pp. 78-79 (sec. 18); also, *Kant and the Problem of Metaphysics,* trans. J. S. Churchill (Bloomington and London: Indiana University Press, 1962), pp. 30-31.

55. For this selective use of philosophy, both positively and negatively, see *ST* I, 19, 120-21.

56. *b. Sanh.* 59a.

covery of standards of justice in the world involves us in the simultaneous discovery of the worthiness of human nature for justice, however unworthy most human action really is. Only a prior appreciation of the worthiness of human nature, which even human sin cannot destroy, enables us to see why God's address to humankind and God's redemption of humankind are possible for and desirable by human persons. Philosophy at its best helps us to appreciate what our nature is capable of. I hope this is a role for philosophy that is consistent with the great theological project of Robert Jenson.

Eternity, Time, and the Trinitarian God

WOLFHART PANNENBERG

What is time? "When nobody is asking me, I know what it is, but when I try to explain it to somebody who asks me, then I don't know." Thus Augustine opened his famous investigation of the nature of time in his *Confessions* (XI.14.17). His perplexity was due to the fact that in each moment of time the past is already nonexistent, and the future is not yet; the present, however, is past before we are able to fix our attention upon it. If the present would not pass over into the past but always remain present, it would no longer be temporal, but eternal (XI.14.17), since in eternity nothing passes away, but everything remains present (XI.11.13). Our present, however, passes away. It does not have duration (*nullum habet spatium,* XI.15.20). It is hardly more than the point of demarcation between past and future, and yet we intuit the present moment, remember the past, and anticipate the future (XI.20.26). How is that possible? Augustine's answer was that it is the nature of the soul to extend into past and future (XI.26.33). The soul does so by the power of its attention (XI.28.37ff.). Our attention anticipates the future and remembers the past. Thus we perceive the whole of a melody that we just started to sing, and we continue to perceive the whole of that melody while we continue to sing. Otherwise, we could neither sing a song nor speak a sentence, the words of which are passing away while we are speaking. To a certain extent, then, the soul achieves a kind of enduring presence while it moves through the flux of time, always remembering the past and anticipating the future. The soul does so by distending its floating presence over past and future. Therefore, Augustine called time the distention of the soul, *distentio animi.* The perception of duration in time has a certain resemblance to the divine eternity, where nothing passes away and where the future is present already. Yet the eternal God is not in need of keeping the past present to himself by way of memory because our memory is but a substitution for the continuing actual presence of the past, while in God's eternity the past itself remains present to God. Similarly the future is not just anticipated but is itself present to God. Therefore, the way we experience a piece of music as a whole with the help of memory and anticipation is but a faint analogy of the divine eternity, where all things are present to God in their actuality (XI.31.41).

Augustine conceived of eternity as timeless. In his exposition of the book of Genesis he affirmed that God is without change and consequently timeless.[1] In contrast to the Platonic philosophy of his period, which was otherwise very influential in his thought, Augustine did not conceive of eternity in terms of the whole of time[2] or, rather, in terms of the whole of life, which in our experience is lost because it is divided up into a succession of momentary events. This was the idea of eternity in Plotinus: the whole of life in simultaneous presence.[3] In this conception, time and eternity were not simply opposed to each other, but eternity was conceived in terms of the simultaneous whole of life that according to Plotinus is constitutive of time itself, constitutive of the cohesiveness of temporal processes in the transition from one moment to the next. This continuity in the flow of time could not be explained except for the presence of the eternal whole within the succession of separate moments. The separation of succeeding moments in the flow of time is due, according to Plotinus, to a "fall" of the soul from the original unity, and yet that unity is still present and effective in the sequence of temporal moments, and the temporal realities strive to reobtain that original wholeness from the future of time. In the case of Augustine time did not come into existence by a "fall" but by the divine act of creation. Time is the form of creaturely existence. Yet in the case of the human creature the temporal dispersion of its life also indicates the loss of unity and a loss of its center in consequence of sin. It is not clear whether Augustine even knew and read Plotinus's treatise on time

1. Augustine, *De Genesi ad litt.*, IV.155; cf. 159 (CSEL 28.1). See K. H. Manzke, *Ewigkeit und Zeitlichkeit: Aspekte für eine theologische Deutung der Zeit* (Göttingen: Vandenhoeck & Ruprecht, 1992), p. 351.

2. Manzke, *Ewigkeit und Zeitlichkeit,* p. 363.

3. Plotinus, *Enn.* III.7.3 and 4. See W. Beierwaltes, *Plotin über Ewigkeit und Zeit (Enneade III,7)* (Frankfurt: Klostermann, 1967; 3rd ed., 1981), pp. 98-101.

and eternity, but if he had done so, his focusing on the sinful disruption of the unity of our life might explain why he emphasized the contrast of time to eternity rather than their positive connection through the wholeness of life.

Augustine was convinced that his concept of eternity was based on the biblical witness to the one and eternal God. He found this idea particularly in some of the psalms: When Psalm 102 says of God that his years "last throughout all generations" (v. 24), Augustine found in these words an expression of God's eternity. In his exposition of the psalms this phrase provided the occasion for explaining the concept of eternity, which is no less than the very substance of God *(ipsa Dei substantia est),* since there is nothing changeable, no past that is no longer, and no future that is not yet, but only being, in accordance with Exodus 3:14, where God says of himself: "I am who I am" *(ego sum qui sum).* Our contemporary exegesis, of course, tells us to read that phrase "I shall be who I shall be." This changes the point and deprives Augustine's argument of its most important evidence. There is future to God, then, and he will show himself to be what he will be. In other words, he is free and unrestricted in his actions. This is a far cry from the timeless identity of "I am who I am." Thus in his reference to Exodus 3:14 Augustine was mistaken, because he used a misleading translation. In his comment on Psalm 102:24, however, he was not completely wrong. The psalm says indeed that God exists forever, and it continues to affirm that God remains the same, while everything else passes away (Ps. 102:27). So God is indeed unchanging in his identity, God "from everlasting to everlasting" (Ps. 90:2). This need not import timelessness, however, only faithfulness through the changes of time and history, faithfulness in identity with himself and therefore in relation to his creatures, too. The psalm also says that in God's life time does not pass in the same way as it does in our human experience: "a thousand years in thy sight are but as yesterday, when it is past" (Ps. 90:4). Time does not pass away from the presence of God, but he looks at the whole of time as we do when a period is complete.[4] This is also to be kept in mind when God is called everlasting (Isa. 40:28). That not only means that his existence continues

4. Therefore it is not enough to say that "God's deity is temporal infinity" (Robert W. Jenson, *Systematic Theology,* vol. I: *The Triune God* [Oxford: Oxford University Press, 1997], pp. 216-17). *Systematic Theology* is hereafter abbreviated *ST,* by volume and page. Italics in quotations are Jenson's. His deity not only is continuing without end but also means wholeness of life.

through time; it also implies his continuous identity, undisturbed by the process of time (Isa. 41:4).

Augustine's concept of eternity deviates from the biblical view of God's everlasting identity in one point: the idea of timelessness. The God who will be whosoever he will be is not a God to whom time does not matter. Therefore, the biblical view of God's everlasting existence is more similar to the Plotinian concept of eternity than to that of Augustine. In Plotinus's idea there virtually is a positive relationship between eternity and time, because eternity means the wholeness of life that in our case is disrupted in the temporal process but is still present in the temporal sequence and even forms the aim of an endeavor of temporal beings to reobtain that wholeness of life in the future. Yet the similarity between the Plotinian concept of eternity and the biblical view is limited. A first limitation is that in Plotinus's thought there is no real eschatology. The striving of temporal beings to obtain the wholeness of their life from the future is in vain, according to this philosopher. Therefore, self-abnegation in the experience of mystical union is the only way to participation in the One, according to Plotinus, while in the biblical view the future of God's kingdom comprises the promise of salvation for his creatures.

A second limitation of the similarity between the Plotinian concept of eternity and the biblical view of God's everlasting life is that the future is thought to be constitutive of the wholeness of life only in the creatures, but not in the case of God. Although eternity is said to be simultaneous possession of the wholeness of life, that life does not have a future, nor is its wholeness constituted by such a future. Yet if the whole of life is structured by the future source of its completion, which is also the source of the new that happens in the course of that life, then even the simultaneous possession of that life should be expected to be structured correspondingly. Regarding the biblical God we have no word that precisely states the importance of the future for himself. When he calls himself the God "who will be who he will be" (Exod. 3:14), however, his future action seems to constitute his identity. In addition, it seems there will be something new in connection with God's future or rather issuing from his future.

There is another biblical idea suggesting a constitutive importance of the future concerning God's own identity: the expectation of the kingdom of God to come. In the last day, the prophet Zechariah says that God will be king of the whole earth (Zech. 14:9). The same expectation is expressed in Obadiah (21) and in Zephaniah (3:15), while in Second Isaiah the event of God's accession to the throne is seen to have just occurred and is proclaimed by the messengers who announce to the Jewish people their liberation (Isa. 52:8). The event may have been envisioned by the prophet, however, as a future one, though it is described as having occurred already. This proclamation of God's kingdom recurs in Jesus' teaching. It is the central issue of the "gospel" Jesus proclaimed (Mark 1:14): The kingdom of God is close at hand, and indeed, its advent becomes a present reality already (Luke 11:20). On the other hand, in the Old Testament God is called the eternal king (Jer. 10:18; Exod. 15:18; Ps. 10:16). Similarly, in the New Testament, the one God is called the eternal king (*basileus tōn aiōnōn*, 1 Tim. 1:17), everlasting and invisible.

How are those predications to be reconciled? On the one hand, God's kingdom is eternal; on the other, it is still to come. Is it only in human experience that God's kingdom is still future, while in itself it is always the same? Yet then it would make no difference in God whether or not he is recognized to be king by his creatures. Can he be king without such recognition? That seems hardly possible. Even if he could rule over his creatures without their awareness, the fact of resistance to his rule and of open rebellion cannot be disregarded and can hardly be said to make no difference. The problem is sharpened when we consider that God's kingship over his creation is not something accidental with regard to his own identity as being God. It is inseparable from his divine nature. Thus, with the manifestation and recognition of his kingship his divine nature itself is at stake.

The tension among the biblical pronouncements on the kingdom of God epitomizes the problem of how the eternal God is related to time or, more precisely, of what is the impact, if any, of temporal events and of the outcome of the process of history upon his eternal identity.

In Christian theology this problem is also posed, and most sharply so, by the Christian faith in the incarnation of the eternal Son of God in the person of Jesus Christ. The incarnation certainly cannot be thought of as making no difference to the eternal life of the one God. This was the insight that prompted Karl Rahner to develop his now famous thesis that the immanent Trinity and the economic Trinity are one.[5] The reason is that

5. K. Rahner, "Bemerkungen zum dogmatischen Traktat 'De Trinitate'," *Schriften zur Theologie* 4 (1961): 103-33, 115; "Der dreifaltige Gott als transzendenter Urgrund der Heilsgeschichte," in *Mysterium Salutis*, vol. 2 (Solothurn: Benziger, 1967), pp. 317-401, 328.

the incarnation as well as the salvation of humankind and the final, eschatological consummation of the world belong to the divine economy. If, however, the incarnation also belongs to the immanent Trinitarian life of God, then the immanent Trinitarian life and the divine economy must be one. That need not mean that their unity is without differentiation and consequently that the immanent Trinity would be dissolved into the process of the divine economy in the history of creation, beginning with the act of creation of the world and completed in the eschatological consummation by the Spirit. Karl Rahner himself emphasized the need for distinguishing the immanent Trinity from God's economic self-communication in the history of salvation: Self-communication presupposes the self that is to be communicated.[6] Furthermore, the immanent Trinity functions as condition of the freedom of God's economic self-communication.[7] Yet how are we to conceive the eternal identity of the triune God as conditioned by events in time like the incarnation and the future consummation of his creation without dissolving itself into the process of that history?

The eternal identity of God belongs first of all to the Father, who is the God of Israel. The Father is prior to the Son and to his mission into the flesh that issues in the event of his incarnation. Yet the kingdom of the Father is not only proclaimed by Jesus Christ but also established on earth by the risen Lord and will be consummated by the action of the Spirit. The apparent contradiction between these affirmations can be avoided if the divine identity of the Father is conceived in terms of the power of his future, which is the very source of new events in history, including the incarnation of his Son and the consummation of all creation by the power of his Spirit. God the Father was always the future of the world, even in the act of its creation and again in the act of sending his Son, as well as in the future achievement of the consummation of all creation by participation in his own glory. The identity of God as the power of the future constitutes the "dramatic coherence of his eventful actuality." It is true that "God is one with himself" in that "eventful actuality" (*ST* I, 64). He is also prior to the eventful actuality of his economy in the history of salvation, since he is the power of the future from which that eventful actuality originates. If that were not so, the "dramatic coherence" of the narrative sequence of those events as well as the identity of those events themselves would be lost. God is also present in the course of that narrative se-

6. Rahner, *Mysterium Salutis,* pp. 382-83.
7. Rahner, *Mysterium Salutis,* p. 384 n. 21.

quence, and he is so present by the actions of his Son and of his Spirit. The Christian confession that Jesus Christ is the eternal Son of the Father ascertains that God himself, the eternal Father, is present in history through his Son. The "eventful actuality" of that history is not something accidental to the eternal identity of God the Father. Yet the Father is prior to that eventful actuality, and therefore the Son is also prior to his involvement in that dramatic history. Otherwise he could not be of one essence with the eternal Father. His incarnation is the result of his "mission" by the Father, but that mission presupposes his existence as Son in communion with the Father before he was sent into the flesh (Rom. 8:3). It is true that according to the Gospel of John the Son was already involved in the creation of the world. He has been the divine word of the Father, through whom everything has been created, but that involvement with creation was not the same as in his incarnation. There was, then, the divine logos before he became flesh, the *logos asarkos.*[8] This logos, the eternal Son of God, was always to become incarnate, *filius Dei incarnandus,* and therefore his incarnation was not accidental to his eternal identity as Logos and Son of the Father. Conversely, the Father was always about to send his Son into the flesh when "the time is fulfilled" (Gal. 4:4). The sending of the Son belongs to the eternal identity of the Father, if the Father is seen as determined from eternity to complete his creation.[9] This is to understand the eternity of God from the point of view of his future action in time, in the completion of his creation.

Thomas Aquinas expressed the divine actuality of being, which is not "a" being but the act of being itself, *esse subsistens,* in his formula *Deus est suum esse,* that is, God is nothing but the actuality of being. Similarly, I wrote twenty years ago that God is his own future. The meaning is a little different from the dictum of Thomas Aquinas, since future is of course not

8. If the precedence of the eternal birth of the Son from the Father over his temporal history is admitted, as Jenson does (*ST* I, 138ff.), it is difficult to see how the notion of *logos asarkos* can still be rejected (as on p. 141 n. 85).

9. That the incarnation belongs to the original design of God's creation of humanity without regard to Adam's fall was perhaps implicit already in the theology of Irenaeus and explicitly affirmed by John Duns Scotus. If the alternative way to conceive of the incarnation as an "emergency repair" of the accident of Adam's fall is rejected, as Jenson does (*ST* I, 72-73), the possibility of an incarnation "apart from sin" can be avoided (as Jenson wants) only if sin is conceived as preordained by God. The doctrine of Duns Scotus preserves the distinction that the incarnation belongs to the original intention of the creator, while sin does not.

the definition of the divine essence, but God is his own future in the sense that he has no future beyond himself. Otherwise, he could not be the one God but would be dependent on something else or even succeeded by something else. If God is his own future, however, the consequence is that the future cannot occur to his present in the same way as it happens in our human experience. God is not subject to the march of time. God's future constitutes his present, but it is not distinct from his presence as we experience our future as contingent upon the present reality of our lives. Robert Jenson objected to this thesis that God's future is not distinct from his presence, as if it would fall back upon the old idea of eternity as timeless presence (*ST* I, 218 n. 61). Yet the presence of God is different, since it is no other than his future. Furthermore, it is important that this statement refers to the Trinitarian God as a unity, not to the three persons in their distinctiveness, except as they participate in the one divine essence. Concerning their mutual relationships it may be said that the Son is the future of the Father, because it is the Son who establishes the kingdom of the Father on earth. Similarly, the Spirit is the future of the Son since it is the Spirit who raises Jesus from the dead. Again, the Father is the future of both, the Son and the Spirit, since it is the Father's kingdom they bring about by their joint activities. As they all share in the communion of the one living God, however, they share in his eternal life that has no future outside and beyond itself to occur to it. The Trinitarian God has eternal life within himself.

This is true in the first place of the Father. The Father is the God of Israel whose eternity the Psalms and Deutero-Isaiah praise. The Son, however, by his obedience to the Father participates in the eternal life of the Father. "For as the Father has life in himself, so he has granted the Son also to have life in himself" (John 5:26). Thus the Son shares the divine essence of the Father. He does not share it in the way believers share in his eternal life because it is said of the Son only that he like the Father has life in himself. Believers do not have eternal life in and of themselves, but only "in Christ." He, the Son, has life in himself like the Father. The Son is not the Father, but he shares the same eternal life, and the same applies to the Spirit. Therefore it is necessary to distinguish the one divine essence from the three persons who share the one and same eternal life. If that distinction were not admitted, there would be no way to account for the Christian affirmation that the Father, the Son, and the Spirit — all three of them — are God, and only one God. "God" is, of course, a predicate (*ST* I, 214 following Gregory of Nyssa), not a substance subsisting by itself without the three persons. The divine, eternal life has concrete reality only in the three persons, first in the Father, but also in the Son and in the Spirit. The Father has eternal life in himself, but not without the Son. The Father possesses that life precisely in sharing it with the Son through the Spirit. In their mutual relations they are the one living God. The eternal life they have in common is their one divine essence, but it would become a timeless abstraction except for the interrelatedness of the persons. Only in that interrelatedness is the one God a living God. The one divine essence taken by itself, without the persons, is not personal,[10] not the one personal God. Otherwise it would have to count as a fourth person in addition to Father, Son, and Spirit. In each of the three persons as well as in their interrelatedness the one God is personal and as such he is eternal life, in full and simultaneous possession of the wholeness of his life.

In the Trinitarian life of the one God, then, the Plotinian definition of eternity is fully realized: simultaneous presence of life as a whole. Yet that life admits of internal distinctions of presence and future, as I tried to argue before, and also of presence and past, if we consider the descent of Son and Spirit from the Father. Even so, however, in the Trinitarian life the present is never separated from the future and the past because of the unity of the eternal life they share. If we imagine the simultaneous possession of life as a whole in a solitary subject, all temporal distinction would evaporate, and together with that the quality of life itself. Therefore it is only in the Trinitarian life of the one God that the Plotinian description of eternity in terms of wholeness of life is realized.

The divine economy that manifests the activities of Father, Son, and Spirit includes the temporal distinctions between creation, incarnation, and the final consummation of the world. The unity of immanent and economic Trinity secures these distinctions to be significant within the eternal life of the immanent Trinity. Conversely, however, the same unity of the divine economy and the immanent life of the Trinity guarantees the wholeness in the "eventful actuality" of the divine economy. It does not get separated in the course of time, but it overcomes the separateness of our temporal experience and of our finite life in such a way as to let it participate in the wholeness of God's eternal life.

10. Contrary to Jenson (*ST* I, 116); see also p. 122, where it is affirmed that the Trinity is "a person."

Jenson on Time

DOUGLAS KNIGHT

Robert Jenson is a pioneer of the strong ecclesiology. He has put Israel in her proper place as the object of the election of God and established the Trinity as the tool that keeps theology Christian. He is a champion of talk of temporality and exploring the notion that God has time for us. This has involved him in demythologizing the modern notion that time is single, worldwide, and culture independent, and that time is forward, in a direction given by an orientation and cosmology never made explicit. Though the edge may be off the optimism, and we are now too sophisticated to use the word, the idea of progress is as constitutive of us now as it ever was. Time is not a concept that the West has among others; rather, the West is nothing more than the idea of time, constituted by the set of mental-corporal bad habits that can conveniently be given this name.

Vanquishing God's Shadow is the subtitle of a book by Brian Ingraffia.[1] God's shadow is what time is, as time is nothing but time toward what or who else but God. When time as God's shadow has been vanquished, it becomes Man's shadow, *imago hominis,* and man is no longer man with all the dignity of the creature of God, but "Man" in capital letters, the incubus not under his own or any other control. Neither modern nor postmodern thought makes this distinction between man as creature, and under control, and man as under his own control, and therefore under no control. Inasmuch as the Man postmodern thinkers want to deconstruct is a usurper god,

1. Brian D. Ingraffia, *Postmodern Theory and Biblical Theology: Vanquishing God's Shadow* (Cambridge: Cambridge University Press, 1997).

who stands in God's place without being able to perform any of his functions, their project is worthwhile, though of course it is not one they can carry out. The order of man in God's place is a parasitic antiorder, and, no matter how reduced, no version of man can survive under it.

Time relates not to substance or quality, but to direction. It relates therefore to relationship, that specific relationship that allows it to be time for one another. On the modern view we steadily increase our distance from the events of Jesus Christ and leave the church behind just as the church left Israel.[2] Robert Jenson insists however that Israel is not back there, but here; the actual presence of the Jewish people is the theological datum. Her survival is evidence of God's faithfulness, and the guarantee of this redefinition of this time as the specific joint time of Israel and God, into which we are also called and gathered.[3]

The history of the West is the history of the supplanting of the election of this people, the specific people of God's choosing, with a generalized version of the same by which all are indifferently chosen, the concept of God's choosing abstracted to meaninglessness. When, in the seventeenth century, election was reduced to providence, history became a flow in a single direction, a flow out of the past and away from it. However, toward what does this time flow, and what space does it flow through? Without an answer here, we can hardly maintain that time is a single stream moving in one direction: it would simply be flux, flowing in all directions and no direction, which

2. R. Jenson, "The Religious Power of Scripture," *Scottish Journal of Theology* 52 (1999): 95: "It is a specific and defining character of modernity to experience the stretch of time between ourselves and eg, Socrates' life and teaching as distance, though of course it might be experienced as connection, and for most of human history has been."

3. R. Jenson, *Systematic Theology,* vol. II: *The Works of God* (Oxford: Oxford University Press, 1999), p. 336: "Thus until the Last Judgement and our resurrection, Christ has not yet come in the way that fully consummates Israel's history." A more critical assessment of Jenson's position comes from Kendall R. Soulen, "YHWH the Triune God," *Modern Theology* 15.1 (1999): 25-54. On p. 44 Soulen states: "In Jenson's eagerness to underscore the claim that the Trinity is the *distinctively Christian way* of identifying God (up to the claim that Father, Son and Holy Spirit constitute God's *proper name*) Jenson fails to give the name YHWH the significance that it achieved in Barth's thought. Jenson stoutly defends the thesis that 'YHWH is the triune God,' but he does so in a way that historicizes the God of Israel on the one hand, and turns it into the instantiation of a metaphysical truth on the other." Eugene F. Rogers, Jr. concludes the opposite, preferring Jenson to Barth on this issue ("Supplementing Barth on Jews and Gender," *Modern Theology* 14.1 [1998]: 43-81).

would make it as pre-Socratic as postmodern. Platonism is a handy label for the idea that time flows from an origin with God out to us, and that eventually this tide turns and flows back to him. To speak theologically, however, we must get rid of both these ideas, that time is flowing out of God to humanity, and that humanity is being borne from the human past toward the future where God is. We must not make the assumption that of past or future one is more divine and the other more human.

If we refuse to acknowledge this people as the elect people, we cannot make a coherent claim on the concept of time, without which there can also hardly be any concept of freedom. The idea of progress was the beginning of the reduction of the people of Israel to the *idea* of Israel, and the turning of the idea *against* Israel to oust her.[4] According to the idea of progress we are borne along, forward. Yet this movement can be said to be forward only in relation to something other than ourselves. Indeed our movement can be described as such only retrospectively, inasmuch as God takes it to correspond to his movement to us. Only in relation to the intentions of this mover, in the sense of his determination toward meeting and agreement, can we think of our movement as forward, or time as single and unified.

God on the Trinitarian conception is not only agent but guarantor and host of the agency of many agents, and the conception includes that action and hospitality that God and Israel come to have for each other. Time could then serve to name the movement by which God and Israel grow into the room each has for the other.

We cannot talk about time without having to say whose time, or without this becoming talk about space, and then having to say whose space. This is the question Robert Jenson asks and answers by talking about the Eucharist and the location of Christ's body.[5] His argument is that, when we have discussed the action of God, for centuries we have been content with the wrong metaphor, that of the Ptolemaic universe, in which we sit in the middle and God is on the edge, as though it were we who gave

4. Rogers, "Supplementing Barth." Yirmiyahu Yovel (*Dark Riddle: Hegel, Nietzsche and the Jews* [Oxford: Polity, 1998]) believes Kant appreciated the strength of Moses Mendelssohn's account of Judaism as a system of universal reason, and in *Religion within the Bounds of Reason Alone,* turned what he had plundered from Mendelssohn against him, to present Judaism as the single obstacle to the reign of Reason.

5. R. Jenson, *Systematic Theology,* vol. I: *The Triune God* (Oxford: Oxford University Press, 1997), pp. 201-6. Hereafter abbreviated *ST,* by volume and page. Italics in quotations are Jenson's.

him place, and on the "outside" is where we place him. Jenson uses the sixteenth-century Lutherans of Swabia to deconstruct this idea, which makes it so difficult to say how God is in heaven and is the bread on the altar, is both here and there, divided between two places. Is God divided by place, or is place not rather united and divided by God? The world is not a container, and our concept of place that places God outside must therefore be said to be wrong.

Yet, and here begins my attempt to go beyond Jenson, the concept of a "container," and of the Ptolemaic world system, is not quite wrong. It is rather God who holds us in this place: it contains us; it does not exclude him. It means not that we are in an envelope of space evacuated by him, but in the place which is his place for us and in which he really can be with us. The fall was not a free fall through empty space, but a falling and being caught and placed in a particular God-determined time and place, a soft place within which, though we are sin-damaged, sin is effectively limited by death and cannot make an end of us. Sin and death are theological, not publicly given, concepts. Death is not its own master, but is confined to this world container, placed from the beginning by God, for God's purposes. So within this death-delimited place of our falling and landing is the world that, because it is the world of God's working, has enough give and flexibility in it to allow for us and to withstand the whole excess and deficiency that sin represents.

Jenson has been challenged on whether God must then establish himself against death, whether the resurrection is *ontologically* constitutive of the being of God.[6] This becomes a crisis only if we do not submit the concept of death to the proper process of interpretation. We should say that these concepts — death, murder, and sin — are the exclusive fruit of Israel's thoroughly theological, God-tutored understanding; they are what Israel has identified and turned away from, or even what Israel *is* the turning away from.[7] Israel defines all the various paths of the divergent times

6. Douglas Farrow, "Robert Jenson's *Systematic Theology,* Three Responses," *International Journal of Systematic Theology* 1.1 (1999): 89-104: "It is an imposition on the biblical narrative, as on dogmatic tradition, to suggest that the God who has decided not to be God without us is therefore only God by being God with us" (91).

7. Emanuel Feldman (*Biblical and Post-Biblical Defilement and Mourning: Law as Theology* [New York: Yeshiva University, 1977]) argues that Israel is concerned demonstrably not to do what the pagans do, to propitiate and expiate the forces of the dead. "Death" is Israel's name for the demands of other people's ancestors.

of the world as nondirections, as "death," and defines death as what will never be. She is the new form of life that puts death away — not in a place outside, but in a no-place, no-hypostasis. The resurrection reveals that sin is not constitutive. Death is then merely the name of the "goneness" of what does not correspond to the creation of God, and Israel is the only one who can fully and correctly name it as such. Thus the concept "death" is a prohibition of certain forms of nonlife, and it is the announcement and command of the freedom of God and Israel.[8] The resurrection is not simply a reversal of the crucifixion, it is the transformation of the cross from our estimation of it to the Father's estimation of it — as work, satisfaction, and triumph, and thus as the reversing and bouleversement of our cosmology and orientation.

God is therefore in place — his own place — in a more solid sense than we are. He is "here," though this "here" is not a here available to us — we cannot say where it is. We are entirely present to him, the function of his making and holding us to him; but we are neither properly present to each other, nor, other than by eucharistic epiclesis, using one particular name, is he accessible to us. In this world we so insouciantly take for our own, we are not yet what he determines we will be: of ourselves, we have neither time nor space for each other. We inhabit this territory not as an established human species but only as myriad competing organisms and forms of behavior, beings as yet without means of occupying place or of being free in it. We are not yet in place such that we can return his place and praise to him — for we do not have the skill by which to co-constitute and articulate place, by taking it from him to share it with him. Yet these competing territories and forms of life will become — for they have no other telos by which they could resist becoming — humanity, the species that is free and that occupies and combines the single territory of heaven and earth.

We may not set on one side Israel the nation and on another Israel the Son. We must not distinguish the many generations of this people from Jesus Christ, the one instantiation of this people, who sits fully

8. *ST* I, 73: "Usual assumptions about the content of God's eternal will, about his relation to sin and evil, and about the relation between creaturehood and death must be rethought. . . . it will suffice to say that something like Barth's teaching must be true: the goal of God's path is just what does in fact happen with Jesus Christ, and sin and evil belong to God's intent precisely — but *only* — as they do appear in Christ's victory over them."

clothed in his flesh on the right hand of the Father, and by which this whole people stands before God, and is with God, holy and complete. A distinction between this One and this Many is not a distinction God allows. He sees "from the future," and the future is what his seeing calls into place. His time is complete and perfect, and it both measures against this standard and works and transforms everything up to this standard. So we are in no position to declare that the people of Israel are not yet the work and presence of God, or to place Israel here with us as human and God somewhere else as divine. God is with the creature of his creation and the incarnation is the present and ongoing state of his being with his creature. God's single and definitive assessment of the creation is the future he crafts for it.

Definitions of place and of time that contrast humanity and divinity are not adequately theological. These concepts must receive their reference from the work of the Creator who puts his creatures before him and is with them. They are a function of the doctrine of creation, which is about the course and destination of the world as the work of God. The creature is not in a position to tell God that God may not be with his creatures. Createdness or creatureliness may not determine the impossibility of the God-Man or decide that God may not be one creature among others. God has not acted in such a way as by his action to lose his freedom: his economy and work do not prejudice his being or his freedom, or his freedom for his creature.

We are placed by and contained within the Ptolemaic container of God's working, and it is by this same working that this container is broken open. This container is the single work of God's placing us before him, placed and closed by the crucifixion, and placed and opened by the resurrection. On this basis Jenson rightly maintains that God affirms his identity as Israel's God against death, as this death brings to nothing the many alternative creations and projections of the Gentiles, and so brings to nothing the threats to the oneness of the creation of God. We could inelegantly say that "death" is the being-brought-to-nothing of the alternative creations of the Gentiles.

Jenson combines language and bodiliness into a single concept of "availability," or being an object.[9] Perhaps his concern is that Christ's being

9. *ST* I, 155. And R. Jenson, "The Body of God's Presence: A Trinitarian Theory," in R. McKinney, ed., *Creation, Christ and Culture: Studies in Honor of T. F. Torrance*

in some specific (fleshly) character in one place would militate against his being in some other, necessarily lesser, because less fleshly, place in any or all other places. He is determined that the answer to the question Where is Jesus now? also be the answer to the question of whence our real being is arriving. The new body of the resurrected Many must not be seen to be weakened or made ambiguous by a separate consideration of the fleshly body of Jesus post tomb. Language is the ongoing activity of bodies' "bodiment" to each other and of each other, and an overdrawn distinction between body and language would be the return of a matter-spirit dichotomy, opening a gap between God and his work, between a statically conceived divinity and humanity each threatening to make the other redundant.

From the ascended Man in heaven the Spirit issues flesh to us, formatting us into the whole relatedness of the kingdom of God, in behavior, in language, and in place. Language is just something that flesh does; the whole idiom of bodily being is linguistic. Language is the event in which obedient speech becomes obedient practices and forms of life, actualized as human persons. The answer to the question of where our future being is is not "Some way further in the direction in which we are headed," but "In the hands of a craftsman"; for it is the Holy Spirit who has put the God-Man here before us and formatted around him a place for the many who will join him. His "hereness" is eucharistically made known and mediated to us not as presence but as the to-us ongoing absence of the God-Man. By his eucharistic exercise of us, the Spirit teaches us that "He is coming," and therefore that "He is not here"; the Son is not in any place where he is accessible to us, but now immediately accessible to him, we come to take up his flesh in that same place the Son has with the Father.

The concepts of body and of place are more pliable than those of presence and absence. Place is not an absence in general, but a specific, informed absence, that relates to the specific body that is not there yet, and so it is also a readiness for it, the result of training and preparation. It is being in its place that makes a body irreducible, for every place is the work of the many bodies that open it up and give it its character. This Son is given

---

(Edinburgh: T. & T. Clark, 1976), p. 88: "God's Body. (1) God is Word eternally in himself. 'If he chooses to have himself as an object that is also our object, that is how it is.' (2) To say God has a body is to say God transcends himself. God has himself as what he is free from, and just so free for."

this place by the Father: it is the place that has put him out of reach of our placing him.

It is never easy to get just the necessary amount of dualism into the right place, but Trinitarian grammar does allow us to make occasional resort to two discourses at once. Since time is the occasioning of persons, it is plural and does not always fit into a single account or unit of measurement. He *is* the end, and he works *from* the end. God has a time that is now perfect and complete, and he has a time that is now *working* perfection and completeness. He has the finished object, and finishing the object is what he is now doing. It is properly called time when it has come to fruition, which is when time itself produces time. Time thus means both the fullness of time and the coming to be of that fullness; this fullness will be the situation when all persons are adequate to constitute time enough for each other.

The God-Man is that specific language speaker who is placed by the Spirit at the right hand of the Father. He and the Father share a single speech and language. Just as this place of theirs is able to situate all places within it, this speech of theirs is able to transform all linguistic and bodily being into one conversation with themselves. No speech is capable of resisting the place held out for it by the conversation of God. The Spirit supplies the God-Man to us as many ways of life and speech, and the body of Christ takes delivery of them. The language that we learn from listening in at the Eucharist, or which inveigles its way into us from there, is the already spoken and lived experience of the Father and Son. Though it is speech, it is not detachable from them; it *is* their presence and availability, one word for which is "flesh." "What bodies really are, is *availabilities* that enable *freedom.* It is tempting to say that the space occupied by the bread and cup, and by the space-occupying aspects of the church's sacraments and life generally, is God's place in his creation . . . saying this would redefine heaven christologically: heaven would exist only in that the incarnation occurs, only in that God *incarnationally* occupies space in his creation."[10]

The Eucharist is that effect of the act and speech of Father and Son by which the various divergent trajectories that together we call "the world" are interrupted and prevented from bringing the world to any end of its own. Though the world continually issues error messages and at-

10. R. Jenson, "You Wonder Where the Body Went," in *Essays in Theology of Culture* (Grand Rapids: Eerdmans, 1995), p. 221.

tempts to close itself down, from the community gathered in this world by the Eucharist the Spirit speaks a continuous override message. The Eucharist resituates all the language of the world, putting it in a new place in the conversation of God. The conversation of the world is returned, by the Holy Spirit, to the Father, and returned not just as language but as newly become actuality. Language does not displace flesh but is what flesh does.[11] God's word goes out from him as speech, but it comes home to him as the actualized being of his creatures.

I have suggested that talk about time is always talk about space, and we must not assume that the concepts of time and space are irretrievably lost to some sub-Christian cosmology that is never given a name, but that we can and should refer them to the gospel events for transformative reinterpretation. I have suggested that we can usefully distinguish space and place.[12] I have impertinently suggested that the argument would be stronger if bodies are understood to be in places, and that as place is not synonymous with space, place is the work and effect of persons, and so is linguistically — and that means eucharistically — mediated. Israel is the guarantee of the future and eschatological redefinition of this time as the time of God and man, Jesus and his church.

11. Herbert McCabe (*Law, Love and Language* [London: Sheed & Ward, 1979]) connects language and Eucharist and provides a Wittgensteinian exploration how sublinguistic beings may be drawn into a shared and greater space and become free without becoming less bodily.

12. For a prolonged development, or rather recovery, of this distinction, see Edward S. Casey, *The Fate of Place* (Berkeley and Los Angeles: University of California Press, 1997).

Creation and Mediation in the Theology of Robert W. Jenson: An Encounter and a Convergence

COLIN GUNTON

I. Mediation

"The first proposition [of a doctrine of creation]: that God creates means that there is other reality than God and that it is really other than he."[1] That lapidary statement of one of the fundamentals of the Christian faith introduces our question, for if God and the world are ontologically other, some account of their relation — some theology of *mediation* — is indispensable.[2] Specifically, the notion is necessary because Christian theology is devoted to the articulation of a gospel involving divine action in and toward the world. It could be said that mediation broadly conceived has been crucial for Robert Jenson's theology from the very beginning, for he has always brought into contrast two ways in which the gospel has been conceived to be mediated. The matter can be put culturally, from the point of

1. Robert W. Jenson, *Systematic Theology,* vol. II: *The Works of God* (Oxford: Oxford University Press, 1999), p. 5. See also vol. I: *The Triune God* (Oxford: Oxford University Press, 1997). Hereafter abbreviated *ST,* by volume and page. Italics in quotations are Jenson's unless otherwise noted.

2. From such a generalization, indeed, further generalizations follow: that the differences among the so-called theistic religions and, indeed, the differences within the varieties of Christian theology consist at least in part of differences of mediation.

view of his self-understanding as a consciously American theologian. What is America's theological weakness today? It is that, having rejected a robust view of the divine ordering of history — as, for example, it is represented in Jonathan Edwards's predestinarian theology of providence — it has opted instead for what Jenson calls "religion," by which is meant a form of mediation opposed to that given in the gospel.[3] In that it is an attempt to escape "outward" from time into a timeless eternity it denies the affirmation of created time made real in the incarnation of the Word. In this form, religion is a concept appropriated from the early Karl Barth and employed in a searching diagnosis of the American condition. "Religion" is America's fate and problem, the stumbling block before its acceptance of the gospel, and has its basis in the Greek contribution to the complicated fabric of Western thought. It is the attempt of the soul to transcend its temporal framework to a timeless realm above and beyond.

The beginnings of Jenson's theological authorship — about the time when I had the privilege of being set by him on the route at once of postgraduate research and Barth scholarship — were developed in engagement with Barth, and especially with his understanding of mediation as it emerged in his various treatments of the relation of eternal God and temporal world. Barth's Christological and Trinitarian conception of mediation generates an affirmation of created reality in contradiction of Hellenism's tendency to its implicit relativization by timeless eternity.[4] Yet both of Jenson's books devoted to Barth's theology uncover tendencies in him that work against the project. In Barth's Christology, there is a danger that Jesus Christ will become less a concrete historical reality than a timeless Platonic form;[5] in his view of the Trinity, divine timelessness threatens to subvert the doctrine of divine eternity as representing the affirmation of created time.[6] The problem is that the shape of a doctrine of God's eternity may threaten the very media of revelation

3. Robert W. Jenson, *America's Theologian: A Recommendation of Jonathan Edwards* (Oxford: Oxford University Press, 1988).

4. What is the student, as yet unacquainted with Robert Jenson, to expect from an entry in the 1967 Oxford University lecture list entitled, "The Trinity as an Anti-Religious Doctrine"? Not what turned out to be the case!

5. Robert W. Jenson, *Alpha and Omega: A Study in the Theology of Karl Barth* (New York: Thomas Nelson, 1963).

6. Robert W. Jenson, *God After God: The God of the Past and the God of the Future, Seen in the Work of Karl Barth* (Indianapolis and New York: Bobbs Merrill, 1969).

from which Barth's starting point was derived. In that respect, if not in others, Barth is classically Augustinian, and something that can only be mentioned here is that Jenson is one of the several seminal theologians of our time who have pointed to the importance of the Cappadocian Fathers as sources for the reappropriation of Trinitarian insights that the West has for the most part neglected.[7]

That a concern for the true being of the creation in relation to God has been a continuing interest is indicated by the fact that it reappears in more recent writings also, for example, in connection with Jenson's query to Edwards's theology of creation. "[T]o say that 'God himself, in the immediate exercise of his power' is the creatures' sole support and coherence, were we to take the proposition without trinitarian differentiation, would surely threaten the distinct reality of creation" (*ST* II, 41). The reason is that an authentically Christian theology must make two affirmations that so easily slip into contradiction of one another: that, first, God is the sole creator, and indeed, sole lord of what happens within that creation's history subsequent to its creation; and that, second, as creator and redeemer he is at the same time the one who gives to that creation its proper *Selbständigkeit* or relative independence, a subsistence that it receives from its relation to God. That is apparently to want to have one's cake and eat it too. Are the two claims incompatible? One reason for the modern world's rejection of the gospel is that it has come to the conclusion that this is indeed the case. To affirm the world, and especially to establish the freedom of the human agent within that world, it has been thought that it is necessary to deny God. That is almost an axiom of modern atheism, and indeed of much that affects to be a Christian response to it. Yet the fall into Arminianism that characterizes both American culture and much of the church's response to the apparent dilemma leads Jenson to take precisely the wrong route out of the morass. Effectively, it is atheism, for it denies divine lordship, and therefore the reality of the Bible's God.

7. Robert W. Jenson, *The Triune Identity: God According to the Gospel* (Philadelphia: Fortress Press, 1982).

II. Christology

As has already been suggested, Jenson's approach to the situation is firmly Trinitarian, and his is a Trinitarianism predicated on the claim, developed from Barth, that in Jesus Christ we meet God, and that Jesus is the only eternal Son that there is. This is not, as some have taken it to be, a denial of an eternal or "immanent" Trinity. Indeed, the fact that some commentators accuse him of denying that reality,[8] others of conceding too much to traditional doctrines of divine eternity,[9] is indication of the fact that here we encounter a more careful revision of the tradition than meets some eyes. The crucial focus is Christological: that there is to be no positing of a "logos asarkos," a kind of double of the incarnate Christ who provides a route back into timeless eternity — a God behind God, in some way undetermined by the triune shape he takes in history. "What in eternity precedes the Son's birth to Mary is not an unincarnate state of the Son, but a pattern of movement within the event of the incarnation, the movement to incarnation, as itself a pattern of God's triune life" (*ST* I, 141).

What has caused the most widespread dissent from this position is its essentially Lutheran character, which is in an interesting way parallel to the later Dietrich Bonhoeffer's movement beyond the Christology of his teacher. It is no accident that the sharpest disagreement has come from commentators aligned to a more Reformed conception, whose tradition of the so-called "Calvinist extra" — which seems to me in essence also Athanasius's position[10] — necessarily drives them, if not to a stronger affirmation of a "logos asarkos," at least to a sharper distinction between the states of being of the eternal Son and the incarnate Lord. That I share in the dissent — as Jenson has himself commented, confessional disagreements continue to mark the way in which the problems take form for all of us — will I hope make possible some clarification of what is at stake. What is agreed between us is that a Trinitarian mediation of creation is indispensable to a Christian systematic theology. What is not is the form that the Christological center should take. Let us then review Jenson's Christology as it appears in his recent *Systematic Theology.*

8. Ellen T. Charry, *By the Renewing of Your Minds: The Pastoral Function of Christian Doctrine* (Oxford: Oxford University Press, 1997), pp. 124-25.

9. Ted Peters, *God as Trinity: Relationality and Temporality in Divine Life* (Louisville, Ky.: Westminster/John Knox Press, 1993), pp. 144-45.

10. Athanasius, *On the Incarnation of the Word,* 17.

Immediately apparent is that this takes a more monophysite than dyophysite interpretation of Chalcedon, after the tradition of Luther himself. Indeed, Jenson would have wished that "from two natures" had been preferred by the Council to "in two natures" (*ST* I, 131-32). The reason is that the substance of the new relation to God achieved by the incarnation can be conveyed only by stressing the one hypostasis in a way precluded by the typical usage of later Western Christology with its dangerously dualistic separation of the "natures." Jenson's sympathy with certain Eastern trends is clear:

> Cyril's followers who remained within the imperial church went on to produce an interpretation of Chalcedon that made it say what, in their view, it should have said. By a strong version of the communion of attributes, they made the one hypostasis to be the "synthetic" agent of the whole gospel narrative, both of what is divine in it and of what is human in it, and they identified the eternal *Logos* as himself this hypostasis. (*ST* I, 133)

The continuities with later Lutheranism are clear: "The incarnation given, what we call the humanity of Christ and the deity of Christ are only actual as one sole person, so that where the deity of the Son is, there must be Jesus' humanity, unabridged as soul and body" (*ST* I, 203).

But must there? While the doctrine of the communion of attributes does not necessarily lead to Feuerbach — although historically it did — it does have grave consequences for the doctrine of the humanity of Christ. It must be conceded that almost anything is to be preferred to the double agency encouraged by the formulation of the *Tome of Leo* according to which Jesus performed some acts as human, others as divine — anticipated as that is, it must be recalled, also in the writings of the Eastern Fathers before Cyril[11] — so that surely Jenson is right to deny house room to the suggestion that "the 'natures' may, in context of the total document, be taken as each a distinct agent of its part of the gospel narrative" (*ST* I, 132). Yet a strong version of the communion of attributes would seem inevitably to offend against Chalcedon's "without confusion." Given the asymmetry of the relation between creator and creature, the communication of attri-

11. See, for example, Athanasius's attempt to show that as man Jesus was ignorant and as the divine Word he was omniscient (*Against the Arians,* 3.42ff.).

butes is likely to eventuate in the effective submerging of the human Jesus in the action of the divine, as is also unavoidably the case with the application of *perichoresis* to the two natures.[12] If Christology is to provide a matrix for an understanding of the relation between creator and creature, must not more be done to ensure the distinct reality of Jesus' humanity as the eternal Son become incarnate? If Jesus is a *creature* — to be sure, not in an Arian sense, but as *verus homo*[13] — must not an account of his humanity contain something more than an assertion that this is a function of the one hypostasis? I am not suggesting that there is none given in *Systematic Theology*, but that its tendency is to downplay the necessary otherness of Jesus and the Father by overstressing their identity. In other words, while it can be conceded that "the idea of the *Logos's* human nature speaking on its own has a rather too Antiochene ring" (*ST* II, 159), may it not yet be objected that more effort should be devoted to demonstrating that the Logos speaks *as human?*

Considerations similar to those pertaining to the *incarnate* apply also in the account of the *incarnation.* If there is too strong an *identification* of the incarnate with what, however unsatisfactorily, we call the preincarnate Word — and here the argument hangs in part on the relation of John 8:58 ("before Abraham was, I am") and that Gospel's prologue ("the Word became flesh") (*ST* I, 139) — once again the "space" of Jesus' humanity is in danger of being invaded. Jenson here cites a crucial passage from Irenaeus: "The Word of God, who is the Saviour of all and the ruler of heaven and earth, *who is Jesus,* who assumed flesh and was anointed by the Father with the Spirit, *was made to be Jesus* Christ [emphases added]."[14] As with the Fourth Gospel, much depends on how the apparent tension in the two statements — of identity ("who is Jesus") and temporal realization ("was made to be Jesus") — is to be resolved. We shall return to Irenaeus when we come to discuss the mediation of creation.

The point of all this is that differences between Christologies generate differences in the conception of the mediation of creation. Yet here I

12. What is appropriate for the three equal persons of the Trinity is far less satisfactory when applied to the asymmetrical relation between God and man. See Leonard Prestige, "PERIXŌREŌ and PERIXŌRĒSIS in the Fathers," *Journal of Theological Studies* 29 (1928): 242-52.

13. Colin E. Gunton, *Christ and Creation: The 1990 Didsbury Lectures* (Carlisle: Paternoster; Grand Rapids: Eerdmans, 1993), lecture 2.

14. *ST* I, 140, citing Irenaeus, *Against the Heresies,* 2.4.3.

want to emphasize that these Christological questions are the sharpest I want to ask of Robert Jenson's theology in this paper, because after the antithesis between a "Lutheran" and a "Reformed" approach, I shall hope to move not to an easy synthesis, but to an attempt to relativize the differences between us in an account that will allow the large amount of common ground to be revealed. By thus beginning with our greatest difference, I shall hope to move into a positive conversation — aided by an actual oral one at a recent conference that has helped me to see where the heart of the matter of mediation is to be found. It is encapsulated in the question Jenson himself asked of Barth, "You wonder where the Spirit went?"[15] The humanity of the Word is most satisfactorily articulated where attention is given to his relation to his Father as it is mediated by the Spirit, and this plays little part in the *Systematic Theology*.[16] My contention is this: when in his account of mediation Jenson makes room for pneumatology, there the differences between us begin to be relativized.

III. Creation

In a summary of a recent paper by Robert Jenson on the doctrine of creation, I wrote as follows:

> Professor Jenson articulates the main affirmations of the doctrine [of creation] in a number of points. . . . [They] together guarantee what some theologies . . . do not always adequately safeguard, that what we are concerned with in the doctrine of creation is not a timeless relation between God and the world but one which requires a notion of the relation

15. Robert W. Jenson, "You Wonder Where the Spirit Went," *Pro Ecclesia* 2 (1993): 296-304.

16. This has been achieved in Reformed theology without conceding to Antiochene dualism. I do not wish to repeat here accounts of the way in which John Owen and his successors, within a fundamentally Calvinist Christological framework, have sought to ensure, pneumatologically, a stronger doctrine of Christ's humanity. However, their historical context is worth indicating. Owen's work was written in the face of Socinian charges that Christological dogma effectively abolished the humanity of Jesus, and these cannot be answered unless more effort is put into showing that, while Jesus is the eternal Word, he is so only as fully human, like us in all things sin apart. See Alan Spence, "Inspiration and Incarnation: John Owen and the Coherence of Christology," *King's Theological Review* 12 (1989): 52-55.

> between the eternal and time that better guarantees the reality and importance of the latter.[17]

That takes us to the place where this paper began, Jenson's assault on the divine timelessness that is characteristic of religion. What is distinctive, however, about his formulation of the doctrine emerges in two passages from the paper being introduced:

> I can now jump to my central assertion, which is merely the converse of these considerations: for God to create is for him to open place in his triune life for others than the three whose mutual life he is. John of Damascus again: "God is . . . his own place." In that place, he *makes room,* and that act is the event of creation.[18]

It follows that

> the triune God is precisely not a sheer point of Presence, not even the one at the center of the turning circle from which all things are equally present. And therefore, whether we want to talk about God's "time" or not, creation is not a problem for God and the posit of time imposes no strain on the character of being. God is roomy; he can make room in himself if he chooses; if he so chooses the room he makes we call time; and that he creates means that he so chooses.[19]

The complexities of our topic are to be found in the fact that we are here in the realm not simply of the relation of eternity and time, but also of infinity and space. We are, furthermore, in the realm of metaphor, which, to repeat what should not, but does, require repeating, is in no way to suggest that we are in the realm of mere construction or projection. Metaphors are the necessary means of our interaction with the world, the necessary means of our widening our grasp of what it is to be a creature of the good God in the world he has created and redeemed. In that respect, some are

17. Colin E. Gunton, "Introduction," in Colin E. Gunton, ed., *The Doctrine of Creation* (Edinburgh: T. & T. Clark, 1997), pp. 1-15, on 6.

18. Robert W. Jenson, "Aspects of a Doctrine of Creation," in Gunton, *The Doctrine of Creation,* p. 24, citing John of Damascus, *The Catholic Faith,* 13.9-11. Much of this exposition reappears in *ST* II, 25-28.

19. Jenson, "Aspects of a Doctrine of Creation," p. 27.

true and some false, and in this particular context, the truth of the metaphor of roominess consists, at least in part, in its counteracting of the dogma, amounting for much of the tradition almost to an axiom, that the creator of space is necessarily nonspatial. Barth, as is well known, was among the first in this particular field of combat. "God is spatial as the One who loves in freedom, and therefore as Himself . . . God possesses His space. He is in Himself as in a space. He creates space."[20] Because God lives in a dynamic order of Trinitarian space, he is able to create a world that has space to be the world.

In this light, let us explore how the notion of God's "roominess" is articulated in a Trinitarian way in the *Systematic Theology.* Our chief question concerns the way in which it is made to imply that creation takes place in some way *within* the being of God. Of particular moment is the relation between pneumatology and freedom. "The Spirit is *Spiritus Creator* as he frees the Father from retaining all being with himself, and so frees what the Father initiates from being the mere emanation it would have been were the Father God by himself" (*ST* II, 26). The work of the Son in this is that "he mediates between the Father's originating and the Spirit's liberating" (*ST* II, 26-27, cf. p. 45) "thereby to *hold open* the creatures' space in being" (*ST* II, 27). In this way, a notion of creation not only as taking place within God but also as externalization begins to make an appearance. While I do not want to suggest that this in any way subverts the notion of creation as the opening up of space for creatures within the divine being, that "withinness" is carefully qualified, as a juxtaposition of the following passages suggests:

> God makes narrative room in his triune life for others than himself. . . . Thus as we "live and move and have our being" in him, the "distention" within which we do this is an order *external* to us, which therefore can provide a metric that is objective for us. . . . (*ST* II, 34, my italics)

And:

> To be a creature in specific relation to the Father is to be a motif in the orchestration that occurs when God's musicality opens *ad extra.* (*ST* II, 39)

20. Karl Barth, *Church Dogmatics,* trans. and ed. G. W. Bromiley and T. F. Torrance (Edinburgh: T. & T. Clark, 1957-75), vol. 2/1, p. 470.

> God opens otherness between himself and us, and so there is present room for us. (*ST* II, 47)

The *ad extra* is significant. May we not here cautiously draw a parallel with a point made by a commentator on George Berkeley's teaching that ideas (that is to say in our context, created things) exist only *in* the mind of God and the minds of finite beings, to the effect that the "in" should not be taken literally?[21] We must be cautious because of the insistence on creation as in some sense within God's being. Yet the balance between internality and otherness is well summarized in this fine passage:

> The Father's love of the Son is, we have seen, the possibility of creation. Insofar as to be a creature is to be other than God, we may say that the Father's love of the Son as other than himself is the possibility of creation's otherness from God. . . . Moreover, we now also see why we had to say that time was the "room" God made for us in his life: did not God set us other than himself, did he not make space between him and us, all time would just be *his* time and there would be no "accommodation" in him. . . . "That place is called God's place that more fully participates in his energy and grace."[22]

The question is this: Is there a difference between saying, as Barth tends to say, that there is an analogy between God's spatiality and that of the world he creates, and saying with Jenson that created space is in some way within God? The answer to that is, we have just seen, not necessarily. In his argument with the Gnostics, Irenaeus argued that anything that God does not contain must necessarily contain God, and so be God itself.[23] Yet must not the metaphorical containing also allow for an element of externality, in the sense of an otherness that is established by God so that the creature shall be authentically itself? The necessity is to express the relation so as to be true to Athanasius's principle that "a work is external to

21. "The phrase 'in the mind' should not be taken in the literal sense — as, for instance, 'the apples are in the basket'; it should be taken more in the sense of 'I shall keep you in mind.'" David Berman, *George Berkeley: Idealism and the Man* (Oxford: Clarendon Press, 1994), p. 39.

22. *ST* II, 48, citing John of Damascus, *The Orthodox Faith,* I.13.17-18.

23. Irenaeus, *Against the Heresies,* 2.1.2.

the nature, but a son is the proper offspring of the essence."[24] So, we are ready for the limning of possible convergences.

IV. Convergences?

At stake in all this is the way in which we shall conceive the relation of God and the world realistically but — to use the politically correct, questionable, but here useful, jargon — nonoppressively. It is agreed between our representative "Lutheran" and "Reformed" positions that the Trinity is the indispensable key. We probably also accept Samuel Coleridge's argument that in the end there are only two theological possibilities, pantheism or Trinitarian theism, with only the latter allowing that "space" between the creator and the creation that insures at once the *Selbständigkeit* of the created order and its continuing dependence upon God for everything that is and takes place. Where we differ in this conversation is to be found in the different ways, shaped or determined by different Christologies, of construing the spatial metaphors with the help of which the God-world relation is conceived. The one doctrine mediated in a Trinitarian way takes different forms because the Christologies are different.

As we have seen, Jenson expresses the matter in the spatial language of "withinness." What I have identified as a Lutheran Christology has a tendency to stress the divine Christ, so that to say that God creates "in" Christ is to suggest that what happens "in Christ" must also be said to happen "within" God. One could speculate here about the extent of Hegelian influence in modern Lutheran Christology, Jenson's and Wolfhart Pannenberg's alike. To go the whole way with Hegel is to push the "withinness" in a pantheist direction, and this both Jenson and Pannenberg, with their less realized eschatology, remain well short of committing.[25] Yet it remains a permanent danger of the language of within, as the history of theology shows only too well. How can what is within God, it is asked, fail to be part of God? We have seen something of Jenson's answer, and we must retain in mind the fact

24. Athanasius, *Against the Arians,* 1.29.

25. The reference to Hegel, though seriously meant, is also designed to enable me to cite my favorite Jenson footnote, repeatedly quoted to students to this day. "Hegel's only real fault was that he confused himself with the last judge; but that is quite a fault" (Robert W. Jenson, *The Knowledge of Things Hoped For: The Sense of Theological Discourse* [Oxford: Oxford University Press, 1969], p. 233).

that we are here in the realm of a metaphor in terms of which the continuing relatedness of the creation to God is being construed.

On the other side, the stress in the Calvinist tradition — Barth interestingly excepted — is on a greater distinction between the divine and the human in Christ, and so a tendency to conceive creation as externalization, as God's creation of something "outside" himself, and so with a stress on its otherness. The danger here is that without a strong pneumatology the outcome will be the excessive separation of God and the world, corresponding to Nestorianism, that in fact came to be deism. One can be over schematic, but perhaps it is not too much of a simplification to say that each tendency seeks to conceive the relation-in-otherness of God and the world, the first stressing the relation, the second the otherness — again, in parallel with their corresponding Christological emphases.

However, the important feature held in common is that on both sides of the divide a genuinely Trinitarian conception of mediation is being sought. Here we return to the question of "religion." At the beginning of the paper, I suggested that Jenson is opposing one form of mediation, that of what we might call the revealed gospel — and here the points made in David Novak's contribution to this volume are highly relevant — to the conception implicit in religion of the creature's autonomous movement into eternity, "from below." The point may be made more sharply. The religion that began, at least so far as our culture is concerned, in Greece — and indeed may be a form of that which is universal apart from those places where the Bible's God has made his presence felt — is more a quest for immediacy than a form of mediation; indeed, it is a denial of the necessity of mediation. Søren Kierkegaard's attack on Georg Hegel is in this respect a defense of the necessity of Christological mediation against the immediacy that would make the human in some way continuous with, perhaps ultimately identical with, the divine.

In that light, the seriousness of the differences between the two conceptions of Trinitarian mediation that I have been comparing can at least be mitigated. So long, on the one hand, as the being of creation "within God" is not construed as implying continuity; and so long, on the other hand, as creation as externalization is not conceived in such a way as to rule out the continuing presence to, and capacity of God for immanence within, the created order, both traditions are aiming at the same outcome. Yet how best is the relation between immanence and transcendence to be preserved? My preference would be to say that the creation takes place within *Christ,* rather than within God *simpliciter.* To confine the spatial metaphor to Christ is to take up a hint from Colossians 1:16 in order to make the point that the place where the relation between God and the world is both realized and understood is the person of him who is the externalization in the world of the one who mediates all the Father's creating and redeeming action. This, it must be stressed, is not a matter of proof texting but of attempting to ensure that the general relation between God and the world is focused in the particular place where their relation takes paradigmatic and determinative form.[26]

The outcome of this account of the differences between a Lutheran and a Reformed orientation on the doctrine of creation is that we are enabled to see that in certain respects the two traditions are seeking to reach the same kind of conclusion. This is not to recommend the sentimental modern relativism that all routes lead to the same place, but to suggest that shared — credal rather than confessional! — interests in some way lead us, because of our different historical and ecclesial formation, to different conclusions that, although they cannot be left undiscussed, should not be the occasion of personal or ecclesial alienation either. There are, and there will continue to be, ways of conceiving the same problem that can, but ought not to be allowed to, appear as antithetical, as leading to accusations, respectively, of pantheism and deism. That his former pupil[27] should in this manner recommend a model of interconfessional relationships somewhere near the Leuenberg pattern of reconciled diversity may, ironically, manifest another fairly important difference between us. It is not only in the theology of creation that Jenson has a stronger unifying drive than seems to me acceptable, as the discussions of ecclesiology in this volume will make all too clear. Yet are not the most fruitful encounters often between those whose fundamental commitment to the God and Father of our Lord Jesus Christ allows wide scope for differences even in things sometimes thought essential?[28] Is this not an eschatologically oriented ap-

26. For this conception, and its background in Athanasius, see Colin E. Gunton, *The Triune Creator: A Historical and Systematic Study* (Edinburgh: Edinburgh University Press; Grand Rapids: Eerdmans, 1998), pp. 142-43.

27. And more than that. Our Research Institute in Systematic Theology at King's College, London, owes a deep debt to Jens's continuing interest and participation in our theological *koinonia.*

28. It is, to give a personal example, a blessing for research students to have a supervisor whose theology is different enough to keep them on their intellectual toes.

proach of the kind of which Jenson might approve? Whatever the answer to that, and I am not predicting its outcome, we can surely agree on one characteristically Reformed principle: *Soli deo gloria.*[29]

29. I am most grateful to Shirley Martin, who read an earlier draft of this paper and made some important queries and suggestions, to its considerable improvement.

The Lutheran *Capax* Lives

GABRIEL FACKRE

On a memorable 1968 evening in Oxford, two theologians who knew and loved the theology of Karl Barth locked horns in a sabbatical living room.[1] Paul van Buren trumpeted the secularity of Christ in a version of the then-current death of God theology.[2] Wasn't this the logic of Barth's distancing of deity from human doings? Robert Jenson thought otherwise. Trivializing Barth! Emptying the story of its central character! Why can't you see the God among us in Jesus Christ? Barth's God . . . in *solidarity* with us, not in flight from us.

Taking part in the evening's fray, this participant discovered a kindred spirit and wanted to know more. Here was uncompromising Christological clarity. Here too, with host Carl Braaten, were the notes of an evangelical catholicity that sounded much like my own "Mercersburg theology."[3] So a thirty-year theological exchange began, and continues to this day in board meetings of the Center for Catholic and Evangelical Theology.

1. Carl Braaten was the host.

2. So Paul Van Buren, *The Secular Meaning of the Gospel* (New York: The Macmillan Co., 1963). The conversation is echoed in the writer's treatment of the subject in *Humiliation and Celebration: Post-Radical Themes in Doctrine, Morality and Mission* (New York: Sheed and Ward, 1969), pp. 28-52, 91-122.

3. An evangelical catholic movement in the nineteenth-century German Reformed Church in North America with leadership coming from Philip Schaff and John Williamson Nevin, faculty members of the Reformed seminary in Mercersburg, Pennsylvania. See, for example, Nevin's *The Mystical Presence and Other Writings on the Eucharist*, ed. Bard Thompson and George H. Bricker (Philadelphia: United Church Press, 1966).

The "exchange" includes some differences, ones reflected in the comments to follow. They surfaced in our disagreements on the North American Lutheran-Reformed Conversation, set out in diverging opinion pieces in the first issue of *Pro Ecclesia,* the journal of the Center.[4] They have to do with a very old debate between two major streams of Reformation thought: Lutheran and Reformed views on the difference between *finitum capax infiniti* and *finitum non capax infiniti.* Indeed, a case could be made that Jenson used the Lutheran *capax* in refuting the reductionist conclusions van Buren drew from his own reading of the Reformed *non capax* in Barth. Do not send your distant deity to a point of no return!

My contention is that whatever else shapes Jenson's theology, the Lutheran *capax* plays a vital role. His recent two-volume systematics is the most current evidence of it, although the refrain appears throughout his writings, notably so in *Unbaptized God.*[5] I'll confine myself here to references from his *Systematic Theology* and argue that it is a gift Jenson and his Lutheran heritage bring to the rest of us, without which both the church and the faith are impoverished. Yet the Lutheran charism, while necessary, is not sufficient; it is part of the body of sound doctrine, but not the whole of it. Thus Lutherans have a word to hear from their long-time Reformed interlocutor. As befits a Corinthian catholicity in the Mercersburg tradition, neither theological limb constitutes the fullness of the body of Christian thought. These comments are an exercise in "mutual affirmation and mutual admonition," the formula of the North American Lutheran-Reformed Covenant of Agreement of 1997 that sought to embody that catholicity.[6]

Ted Peters and Richard Neuhaus in their reviews of volume 1 discern the leitmotif of *Systematic Theology:* the God who "takes time" for us.[7] All

4. Robert W. Jenson, "Comments on *A Common Calling,*" *Pro Ecclesia* 1.1 (Fall 1992): 16-20; Gabriel Fackre, "Call and Catholicity," *Pro Ecclesia* 1.1 (Fall 1992): 20-26.

5. Robert W. Jenson, *Unbaptized God: The Basic Flaw of Ecumenical Theology* (Minneapolis: Fortress Press, 1992). See esp. pp. 119-47.

6. Set forth in Keith F. Nickle and Timothy F. Lull, eds., *A Common Calling: The Witness of Our Reformation Churches in North America Today* (Minneapolis: Augsburg, 1993). See esp. pp. 65-67.

7. Robert W. Jenson, *Systematic Theology,* vol. I: *The Triune God* (Oxford: Oxford University Press, 1997), p. 217. The reviews: Ted Peters, "God Happens: The Timeliness of the Triune God," *The Christian Century* 115.10 (1 April 1998): 342-44, and Richard Neuhaus, "Theology to Pray By," *First Things* 83 (June/July 1998): 67-68.

While respondents to both volumes I and II in *International Journal of Systematic Theology* characterize his work in different ways, they all circle about this leading the good things in Jenson's work flow from it: the narrative reading of Christian faith grounded in the narrative life together of the triune God; the rejection of the teaching of the divine impassibility conjoined to a profound interpretation of the suffering of God; the inseparability of the Christian community from the incarnate Word and thus a "high" doctrine of church, sacraments and ministry; an antisupersessionist view of Israel consonant with an unfolding story; and a thoughtful interpretation of petitionary prayer. Furthermore, in matters of theological authority and interpretation: the assertion of Scripture as *norma normans* and the tradition as its hermeneutical principle, albeit the latter deployed ecumenically in such wise as to honor Roman Catholic and Orthodox traditions and even (noted appreciatively through these Reformed spectacles) the likes of Jonathan Edwards and Karl Barth.

Whence these contributions? In the words of Lutheran theologian Martin Heinicken: "The central issue is . . . that the finite is capable of the infinite."[8] God is in *solidarity* with us in Jesus Christ . . . and, just so, in the body of Christ. This is the "haveability" of God as Dietrich Bonhoeffer describes it in an early critique of Barth.[9] Or as Luther put it graphically:

> It is the honor and glory of our God . . . that giving himself for our sake in deepest condescension, he passes into our flesh, the bread, our hearts,

---

theme. None allude to the functioning of the *capax*. However, where the otherwise appreciative Reformed commentary of Douglas Farrow and David Demson, and the Roman Catholic assessment of J. A. Di Noia, express doubts about Jenson's proposals, they can be understood as a conjoined critique of the hegemony of the *capax* ("Robert Jenson's *Systematic Theology:* Three Responses — Douglas Farrow, David Demson and J. Augustine Di Noia, O.P.," *International Journal of Systematic Theology* 1.1 [March 1999]: 89-104). Jenson himself acknowledges the Reformed/Roman Catholic "specific if polite shared opposition to Lutheran innovations" in the interpretation of the eucharistic Presence (Jenson, *Unbaptized God,* p. 130). I argue elsewhere that the objection has to do with the common Reformed and Roman Catholic stress on the divine sovereignty over us in distinction from the Lutheran accent on the divine solidarity with us (as in its theory of ubiquity). See Gabriel Fackre and Michael Root, *Affirmations and Admonitions* (Grand Rapids: Eerdmans, 1998), pp. 23-24 and passim.

8. Martin J. Heinicken, "Christology, The Lord's Supper and Its Observance in the Church," in Paul C. Empie and James I. McCord, eds., *Marburg Revisited: A Reexamination of Lutheran and Reformed Traditions* (Minneapolis: Augsburg, 1966), p. 90.

9. "God is *there,* which is to say not in eternal non-objectivity . . . [but] 'haveable,' graspable in his Word within the church" (Dietrich Bonhoeffer, *Act and Being,* trans. Bernard Noble [New York: Harper and Brothers, 1961], pp. 90-91).

> our mouths, entrails, and suffers also for our sake that he be dishonorably . . . handled on the altar as on the Cross.[10]

Otherwise stated in a citation of Luther by Jenson:

> The church is the place or people where God dwells to bring us to enter the kingdom of heaven, for it is the gate of heaven.[11]

And again, Jenson on justification from Luther's *Commentary on Galatians:*

> By faith the human person becomes God. . . . Every Christian fills heaven and earth in his faith.[12]

Jenson comments,

> Carried along by the Scripture he is expounding, Luther can go beyond even his radical young followers and make not only Christ but the believer, united with Christ, the subject of a real communion of divine attributes.[13]

Here is Luther's *capax,* and Lutheranism, in one or another way, followed suit. In Christology it invites the interest in Cyril and expresses itself in the teaching of a "communion of attributes." In eucharistic theology, the *capax*'s fighting words are "in, with, and under," with its elaboration in the theory of ubiquity. If Episcopal observer R. R. Reno is right about Jenson on justification, his view presupposes a "carnal" form that means that "the evangelical and catholic theologian must be open, in principle, to the possibility that the historic episcopate may be the soteriological condition of the gospel."[14]

10. Martin Luther, *W.A.* 23.157, quoted by Bonhoeffer, *Act and Being,* p. 81.

11. Robert W. Jenson, *Systematic Theology,* vol. II: *The Works of God* (Oxford: Oxford University Press, 1999), p. 172.

12. Luther in the *Commentary on Galatians* quoted by Jenson, *Systematic Theology* II, pp. 296-97.

13. Jenson, *Systematic Theology* II, p. 296.

14. R. R. Reno, "The Doctrine of Justification: Lutheran Lessons for Anglicans in Search of Confessional Integrity," *Pro Ecclesia* 3.4 (Fall 1994): 474.

What I believe Jenson has done in his systematics (signaled to us in earlier works) is reread with a relentless consistency the classical loci through the lens of the *finitum capax infiniti.* In doing so, he has shown the inconsistencies, or more charitably perhaps, the undeveloped nature, of the thought of those that stand in the Cyrillian tradition. More importantly, whatever criticism Jenson may have of contemporary Lutheranism, and whatever attractions he may have to other ecclesial traditions that appear to steward better the Word of the God who takes time for us (sometimes Constantinople, sometimes Rome), he gives here the Lutheran charism to the church catholic, and we are the better for it. This Lutheran chemistry — the *capax*/communion of attributes/Cyrillian Christology/sacramental realism — does "develop the film," so to speak, of the divine passibility, narrativity, and temporality in ways not done by other chemical baths. We are in Jenson's debt for his work in the darkroom.

Having tracked the current systematics phenomenon in recent years (now with seventy new projects),[15] I believe this two-volume work is done with greater brilliance than most. Though in shorter compass, it certainly ranks with Wolfhart Pannenberg's systematics.

A self-critical and ecumenically committed Reformed perspective can welcome Jenson's gift. To take the most obvious examples of need: (1) the Zwinglian expression of the Reformed tradition has distanced God from the Eucharist, making it into a human visual aid (is van Buren's "secular meaning of the gospel" a cosmic memorialism?); (2) a hyper-Calvinist predestinarianism has no passible God in narrative life among us. Both (1) and (2) are cases of the Reformed *incapax* gone amok. (3) Meanwhile, a Reformed pietism, ironically, has fallen uncritically into the *capax* but has relocated it from the church to the individual soul, and its occasional partner, Reformed biblicism, has fixed it upon a book.

Yet "mutual admonition" goes both ways. I put the counterpoint in the form of some questions. A Reformed query: What is the place in this system for the divine sovereignty? The glory of God that is *not* coextensive with the givens? Thus the Barth of "*Deo soli gloria*" and the "resolute refusal to deify any created thing . . . its *finitum non est capax infiniti*" con-

15. As in my "In Quest of the Comprehensive: The Systematics Revival," *Religious Studies Review* 20.1 (January 1994): 7-12, and "The Revival of Systematic Theology: An Overview," *Interpretation* 49.5 (July 1995): 229-42. See also John Webster, "Editorial," *International Journal of Systematic Theology* 1.1 (March 1999): 1-3.

cludes that while the Reformed have a strong confessional and creedal tradition (one to which he gave minute attention), still

> our fathers had *no* Augsburg Confession authentically interpreting the word of God, *no* Formula of Concord, *no* "Symbolic Books" which might later, like the Lutheran, come to possess an odor of sanctity. . . . It *may* be our doctrinal task to make a careful revision of the theology of Geneva or the Heidelberg Catechism or the Synod of Dort . . . it *may* be our task to draw up a new creed.[16]

The Reformed accent on the divine sovereignty is the warrant for reexamining ever and again the inherited lore of the church. God is beyond our human reach. True, sovereignty, standing alone, is susceptible to a novelism or contextualism lusting after the new and "relevant," disdainful of the doctrinal and textual givens. Hence the need for a Jensonian admonition about the solidarity of God with those givens. But this is a two-way street. The temptation of the solidarity tradition is to domesticate deity. "Leave those givens alone. What a travesty an *altered* Augsburg Confession!" Missing here is openness to the "ever-new light and truth that breaks forth from God's holy Word" — Barth's point as formulated by Pastor John Robinson of Pilgrim polity and theology. The *capax,* standing alone, tempts us to think that the "was" and "is" constitute the "ought." Jenson's argument for the *esse* of the episcopacy fits the picture. Kindred is the number of pages (213) given to the doctrine of the church, the locus of the haveability of God, relative to other sections (e.g., the Christian's justified and sanctified life [26]). Again, the doctrine of the church is discussed in terms of its indicatives not its imperatives, its nature as gift not its mission as command. Indeed, its mission appears to *be* its nature. Another example of the *capax* at work is Jenson's treatment of the atonement. True, there is no dogmatic consensus on the Work comparable to that on the Person of Christ. Thus Jenson reviews the various models — exemplarist, penal, conflict, and victory — and chooses to go another way, one that seeks to avoid this traditional model making and instead argues for an "embodied" communal liturgical living out of "the Three Days" interpreted as "actual atonement." However, this move is really *not* another way,

16. Karl Barth, *The Word of God and the Word of Man,* trans. Douglas Horton (Boston: The Pilgrim Press, 1928), pp. 229, 230.

but rather a model with a long lineage in the Eastern tradition — the incarnation *as* the atonement.[17] The solidarity of God with us, begun in the incarnate Word and announced at his resurrection, is continued in and through church, sacrament and ministry, culminating in deification.

There is another kind of atonement model, with an ecumenical trail that runs through both Eastern and Western traditions but was developed in more detail than most by Calvin, one that attempts to honor and interrelate the partialities of the four standard models in the concept of the "threefold office" — prophet, priest, and king, the Work as carried through by the divine-human Person. As it took four centuries of Christological controversy to arrive at some consensus on the incarnation, one that rejected sundry reductionisms, an equivalent struggle in the church has been going on, one that might eventuate in an ecumenical reading of the atonement that honors and attempts to integrate the contribution of each historic model.[18]

The threefold office is an example of the Reformed quest for something more than the ecclesial givens (*semper reformanda* in doctrine). It's no accident that Barth takes it up and does so in a fresh way. Its value also resides in the place given to the priestly office, indeed, its centrality in any full-orbed understanding of Christ's reconciling work. So both an ecumenical and a Reformed voice must ask Jenson: How in a systematics so focused on the resurrection does the cross get the attention it is due? Indeed, why would not such a theology make the open tomb rather than the cross the central Christian symbol? A related inquiry on matters of subjective soteriology: in a system in which the personal is so important (the personal God answering personal petitionary prayer) — Where is the place for the personal appropriation of the priestly work of Christ in a graced faith that saves persons, and the evangelistic call to preach the Word that is the means of that grace? These matters need development in this systematics.

A related question is posed by Miroslav Volf to a view comparable to Jenson's.[19] He notes the ecclesial implications of John Zizioulas's view of

17. For a discussion of it as a fourth major model, see Gabriel Fackre, *The Christian Story,* 3rd ed. (Grand Rapids: Eerdmans, 1996), pp. 131-33.

18. Anticipated in ecumenical theologian Geoffrey Wainwright's argument for the threefold office in *For Our Salvation: Two Approaches* (London: SPCK, 1997), pp. 97-186.

19. Miroslav Volf, *After Our Likeness: The Church as the Image of the Trinity* (Grand Rapids: Eerdmans, 1998).

the Trinity. Zizioulas's defense of the hierarchical role of the bishop, with a correlative subsidiary role of the laity, is grounded in the Trinitarian asymmetry of the Father vis-à-vis the Son and the Spirit. Volf's alternative concept of the Trinity argues instead for symmetry, for the mutual interdependence of the Persons. Its ecclesial derivative is the priesthood of all believers and thus an interrelationship of ministries in which office holder and people are mutually subordinate. This radical sharing of the charismata is part of the Reformed as well as Volf's evangelical tradition, for in both the Holy Spirit gives personal gifts and graces to all in the family of God.

Jenson's doctrine of the Trinity assigns the Holy Spirit, working from the future to the present and the past, a formative role vis-à-vis Father and Son that appears consonant with Volf's understanding of Trinitarian interchange and symmetry. However, Jenson's view of the structure of the church appears to be, using Volf's terms, "episcopocentric" and "subordinationist," not an interactivity that would reflect the mutualities of the triune Life Together. Indeed, Jenson believes that there can be no *communio* ecclesiology without "a pastor of the universal church."[20] A question must be raised about the consistency of Jenson's Trinitarian and ecclesial teaching.

A question in ethics must also be put by the Reformed tradition. In the Lutheran-Reformed dialogue in this century, it has been commonplace to note the important Lutheran contribution: witness to the persistence of sin in the life of the redeemed and in movements for social change in society, church-promoted or otherwise. This sobriety about simultaneity *(simul iustus et peccator)* is a corrective to Reformed illusions about inordinate possibilities of sanctification in both believer and society. So too in ethics, Lutherans remind us of the givens, as in the stabilities of the orders of creation or the importance of the vocation of the laity within the received economic, social, and political structures (the *capax* at work here as elsewhere).[21]

For all its contributions, the ethics of solidarity cum simultaneity needs as its companion the ethics of sovereignty cum sanctification. Standing alone, the former is tempted to quietism and the defense of the

20. Robert W. Jenson, "The Church as *Communio*," in Carl E. Braaten and Robert W. Jenson, eds., *The Catholicity of the Reformation* (Grand Rapids: Eerdmans, 1996), p. 10.

21. So argued by me in Fackre and Root, *Affirmations and Admonitions*, pp. 1-20.

status quo. A sovereign God calls the givens to account. Further, grace as power in us as well as pardon for us gives reason to hope for advances in both soul and society. Roman Catholic and Reformed traditions steward that latter hope, even as Lutheran and Orthodox have been custodians of solidarity and simultaneity.[22] A full-orbed ethics requires a Corinthian catholicity of charisms.

Lutheran self-criticism on matters of ethics can be seen in Bonhoeffer's concern over "cheap grace." Indeed, his *Letters and Papers from Prison* can be interpreted as a rethinking of the *capax*. There he ruminated about the solidarity of God with us in the *world*, pressing outward his earlier stress on the haveability of God in the church. Now, we are called to keep company with a real Presence — indeed the same crucified One — by participating in the "suffering of God" in the world's agonies, as well as in the bread and wine now relocated to an ecclesial "secret discipline."[23]

Conclusion

A truly catholic theology will include all the charisms of Christian teaching. A great contribution of Jenson's systematics is the portrayal of a fuller body of faith, one with a limb too often otherwise missing, a body with its *capax*. But let it have as well its *incapax*. For "the eye cannot say to the hand, 'I have no need of you'" (1 Cor. 12:21).

22. Fackre and Root, *Affirmations and Admonitions*, pp. 21-41.

23. See especially the letters of 16 July 1944 and 18 July 1944 and the poem "Christians and Pagans," in Dietrich Bonhoeffer, *Letters and Papers from Prison*, ed. Eberhard Bethge (New York: The Macmillan Co., 1972), pp. 348-49, 357-63.

Once Again, Christ and Culture: Remarks on the Christological Bases of a Theology of Culture

CHRISTOPH SCHWÖBEL

The problem of the relationship between Christianity and culture is as old as Christianity itself. However we may define Christianity, it seems clear that every attempt at doing so must refer everything in Christianity to Jesus of Nazareth, whom Christians confess as the Christ, the one in whom the relationship between God, the world, and humanity is definitively disclosed. Furthermore, however we may define culture, it seems clear that every attempt at doing so must focus on the interface between the way we interpret the world and the way we shape the world, the way in which we transform what is given to us in such a way that it conforms with the way we interpret the world. It is therefore not surprising that the main aspects of the problem of the relationship between Christianity and culture can be traced back to central features of the message of Jesus of Nazareth and the manner in which his message and his person are mutually defined. Jesus' message of the coming of the kingdom of God had an equally constructive and critical impact on the culture of his day. It invited his hearers to understand the whole of reality, God, the world, and themselves, in the horizon of the coming of the kingdom, which comes toward us from God in such a way that its transformative power affects not only our future but also our present and our past.

The critical force of this message is rooted in the fact that the coming of the kingdom of God challenges the ways in which reality is ordinarily interpreted and shaped according to such an interpretation. In particular, it questions the claims of all ideas and institutions that function as a focus for the interpretation of reality. In the horizon of the coming of the kingdom their authority is at best relative to the kingdom; it can no longer be understood independently from it. All claims to ultimate authority are denied by the ultimate authority of the coming of the kingdom. The constructive impact of this message is intrinsically related to its critical force. Since the coming of God's kingdom affects all aspects and dimensions of reality, no sphere of reality can be understood apart from it. The whole of reality receives its direction from the coming of God's kingdom, and this requires that it must be treated according to the new direction that is given to it in Jesus' message, practice, and person. The complexity of the interrelationship of the critical and the constructive aspects of Jesus' message becomes clear only if we consider that the coming of the kingdom is not an outstanding event that is totally disconnected to the present. In Jesus' message the coming of the kingdom has already begun in his proclamation and enactment of the message. The transformation of the old order of things has already started in the proclamation of the new order by word and deed in the old order of reality. In one sense, this transformation occurs from without since the coming of God's kingdom is not the product of the intrinsic antecedent conditions of the old order of reality. In another sense, this transformation occurs from within because it does not simply replace or supersede old with new but transforms the material of the old order so that it is redefined and redirected by the new order.

The whole of Jesus' life's witness displays this relationship of the critical and the constructive, of discontinuity and new continuity. He grants forgiveness of sins not by replacing the sinners with righteous persons, but by creating righteousness through forgiving those who have sinned. He heals the sick not by exchanging the sick with the healthy but by transforming their sickness into a new wholeness of the same person. The same pattern is also evident in Jesus' discourse of the kingdom through parables. The kingdom is discontinuous with the history of reality that is defined from the past, but it also establishes a new continuity that goes so far that the matter of the old order, the processes of growth and development, can become a parable for the coming of the kingdom. In the same way the critical impact of Jesus' message for a culture that defines itself from another focus of meaning than the coming of the kingdom becomes its constructive force once the kingdom of God becomes the new focus of meaning through which the universe of existing meaning is not abolished but radically rearranged.

The history of the relationship of Christianity and culture documents many ways of dealing with the problem of Christianity and culture, a rich variety of patterns of critical and constructive aspects, of discontinuity and continuity. Superficially, the history of Western Christianity can be described as one in which a small counter culture, precisely because of its critical stance toward its existing cultural environment, develops such an effect on its surrounding cultures that it becomes the main cultural force integrating within itself all other spheres of culture. In the process cultural institutions to which Christian communities could entertain only external relations were integrated within the framework of Christianity so that they were now internally related. What is often described as the grand synthesis of medieval Christendom seemed to contain, however, tensions that eventually led to a new cultural differentiation. The relationship within one Christian cultural framework of spiritual rule and imperial rule, of *sacerdotium* and imperium, of divine law and human law, of spiritual power and worldly power, of the authority of ecclesiastical doctrine and of reason led to the need to distinguish between them and redefine their relationships by specifying their field of application. The process that began with the medieval reform movements and came to a climax with the Reformation was continued in the Enlightenment in such a way that the synthesis of culture within a Christian framework itself was questioned. Could it be that Christianity, a religion as it was then called in a new sense, provided the overall pattern for the integration of all spheres of culture? Is it not the case that the autonomy of each sphere of culture must be fought for in a battle of emancipation and defended against claims of integration on the part of Christianity? The segmentation of modern culture is the result of this process of radical questioning. Once the Christian synthesis was regarded as an alienating tutelage of culture, all spheres of culture could glory in their newly won sense of independence and autonomy. However, radical autonomy cannot be granted to all spheres of culture if society is to function through the interaction of its different spheres. The age of reason can be understood only if one can appreciate its rhetoric of a universal human reason as supplying both the means of liberation from an alienating religious rule and the means of integrating the now autonomous spheres of cultures. Autonomy was no problem as long as the *nomos* in all spheres of culture was the one universal reason. It is obvious that one should start building altars for the goddess of reason only if it can offer both the freedom of autonomy and the unity of culture.

The current debate on postmodernity shows nothing less than a failure of nerve of the religion of reason. It documents a two-pronged attack on the religion of the Enlightenment. First of all, it questions whether radical autonomy of reason is possible at all. Is it not the case that all claims to autonomy only serve to disguise the way in which reason is conditioned by a variety of pluriform cultural conditions? Second, it questions whether the universality of reason is possible. Is reason not intrinsically particular, embedded in particular modes of thought, basic convictions, social conventions, cultural preferences, and communal interests? Is therefore the appeal to universal reason not an expression of a particular claim to power? If so, what are the universal standards of rationality and justice? Taking refuge in the strategy of claiming that at least the methods and procedures of rationality and justice must be universal appears as the last post for defending the religion of reason, once it becomes clear that the reasons for adopting these methods and subscribing these procedures will be based on particular beliefs and convictions that we hold, so that it is impossible to abstract formal rules of conduct from their material grounds.

Whatever our stances toward the situation of postmodernity, the problem of the relationship between Christianity and culture becomes a complex one in this situation. Whether we see the need for a revival of a Christian cultural synthesis and an attempt to rally the troops with cries of "Christendom awake!" or whether we accept that in such a situation Christians will never exist in any other form than as resident aliens in their cultural contexts will to a large extent depend on our analysis of the way in which the two "entities," Christianity and culture, interact. Many of our inherited ways of formulating the problem (including the one I have sketched here that therefore can claim only superficial status) are themselves the product of a particular perspective of interpretation, inherited from the Enlightenment, tending to contrast the two spheres of "Christianity" and "culture." However, this may not be very helpful in every respect. Views about the relationship between Christianity and culture are not independent of the view of reality we hold, but form an integral part of such a view. If we want to develop a theological view of the relationship between Christianity and culture, it may be misleading to start with the Enlightenment picture of two independent spheres of dealing with reality and then somehow try to fit Christian theology into such a preconceived pattern. If the very essence of Christianity consists in the fact that Christianity does not have an essence of its own but needs to refer to Jesus Christ for the purpose of Christian identity definition, the question of the relationship between Christianity and culture is ultimately a Christological question. Could it be that the problem should not be phrased as the question of the relationship between Christianity and culture but as the problem of Christ and culture? Furthermore, could it be that not only our different proposals for solving this problem but also the very way we perceive the problem depends on our Christology? If so, our reflection could benefit a great deal from once again engaging with the problem of Christ and culture and of seeking guidance from two American theologians for whom this is the heart of the problem of Christianity and culture: H. Richard Niebuhr and Robert W. Jenson.

Christ and Culture: H. Richard Niebuhr's Approach

H. Richard Niebuhr's book on Christ and culture remains one of the most distinguished efforts of twentieth-century theology to bring the problem of Christianity and culture into focus. For Niebuhr the transposition from the question of the relationship between Christianity and culture to the question on Christ and culture indicates an important insight. The question is not just one concerning the relationship between Christianity and other views of life and between Christianity and other cultural spheres; it also concerns Christianity itself, "for Christianity, whether defined as church, creed, ethics or movement of thought moves itself between the poles of Christ and culture. The relation of these two authorities constitutes its problem."[1] In its relations to other cultural spheres Christianity encounters the polarities again that also characterize its own being. Clarifying the relationship between Christ and culture is therefore as much an internal problem for Christianity as it is one of its relations to those outside. Indeed, it seems to be Niebuhr's primary objective "to set forth typical Christian answers to the problem of Christ and culture and so contribute to the mutual understanding of variant and often conflicting groups."[2]

1. H. Richard Niebuhr, *Christ and Culture* (London: Faber & Faber, 1952), p. 26.
2. Niebuhr, *Christ and Culture*, p. 18.

This ecumenical intention, however, is not Niebuhr's final aim since the different Christian replies to the question of Christ and culture will receive their validation only through Christ's answer to the problem: "Christ's answer to the problem of human culture is one thing, Christian answers are another; yet his followers are assured that he uses their various works in accomplishing his own. . . . The belief which lies back of this effort, however, is the conviction that Christ as living Lord is answering the question in the totality of history and life in a fashion which transcends the wisdom of all his interpreters yet employs their partial insights and their necessary conflicts."[3] This is not merely a piece of pious rhetoric for Niebuhr. Rather it points to the reason why he can accept the relativity of all Christian answers to the problem and yet believe that through these relativities Christ is at work in forging his answer to the question.[4] We are here mainly concerned with the way in which Niebuhr sets up the problem of the relationship between Christ and culture, not so much with his attempt at developing a typology of different views of the relationship. It may therefore suffice to focus briefly on the terms that constitute that relationship.

Niebuhr's Christ

As one who has gone through the school of Troeltschian historical relativism, Niebuhr starts with the observation that there is such a great "variety of personal and communal 'belief in Jesus Christ' that the question arises 'whether the Christ of Christianity is indeed one Lord.'"[5] While recognizing the relativity of all images of Christ, he is nevertheless confident that all these images complement and correct one another: "For the Jesus

3. Niebuhr, *Christ and Culture,* p. 18.

4. This is an example of H. Richard Niebuhr's engagement with the problem of historical relativism that he learned from Ernst Troeltsch. Niebuhr writes in the "acknowledgements": "He [Troeltsch] has helped me to accept and to profit by the acceptance of the relativity not only of historical objects but, more, of the historical subject, the observer and interpreter. If I think of my essay as an effort to correct Troeltsch's analyses of the encounters of church and world it is mostly because I try to understand this historical relativism in the light of theological and theo-centric relativism. I believe that it is an aberration of faith as well as of reason to absolutize the finite but that all this relative history of finite men and movements is under the governance of the absolute God" (Niebuhr, *Christ and Culture,* p. 14).

5. Niebuhr, *Christ and Culture,* p. 27.

Christ of the New Testament is in our actual history, in history as we remember and live it, as it shapes our present faith and action. And this Jesus Christ is a definite person, one and the same whether he appears as man of flesh and blood or as risen Lord."[6] This confidence is based on the fact that underlying the different later pictures are the "original portraits with which all later pictures may be compared and by which all caricatures may be corrected. And in these original portraits he is recognizably one and the same. Whatever roles he plays in the varieties of Christian experience, it is the same Christ who exercises these various offices."[7] Although Niebuhr is sure that there is a common reference point for the different pictures of Christ, offering a description of Christ as this common focus means one is involved in the dispute of interpretations. Niebuhr is wise to avoid the all-or-nothing positions that are held both by historical skeptics and representatives of what he calls "biblical positivism." His robust defense of the realist character of partial descriptive interpretations is well worth quoting: "If we cannot say anything adequately, we can say some things inadequately. If we cannot point to the heart and essence of this Christ, we can at least point to some phenomena in which his essence appears. Though every description is an interpretation, it can be an interpretation of the objective reality. Jesus Christ who is the Christian's authority can be described, though every description falls short of completeness and must fail to satisfy others who have encountered him."[8]

Niebuhr's strategy is then to characterize Jesus Christ by taking as a starting point one virtue or characteristic described as the key to his interpretation by different theological schools — love by the liberals, hope by the "eschatologists," obedience by the Christian existentialists, faith by Protestants, humility in the monastic tradition — and to show that in the "original portraits" these "virtues" are radicalized in such a way that they complement one another in a profound theological sense. Thus Niebuhr can agree that love is a central focus in Jesus' message and history. However, this love gains its significance from the fact that it is love of God. "The unity of his person lies in the simplicity and completeness of his direction toward God, whether the relation be one of love or of faith or of fear."[9] The

6. Niebuhr, *Christ and Culture,* p. 28.
7. Niebuhr, *Christ and Culture,* p. 28.
8. Niebuhr, *Christ and Culture,* p. 29.
9. Niebuhr, *Christ and Culture,* p. 31.

"unique nature of the virtue of love in Jesus as based on the single-mindedness of his devotion to God" is not compromised by the fact that Jesus called for love of the neighbor as well as of God. Contrary to the liberal interpretation, love of neighbor is for Niebuhr "not merely an illustration of universal benevolence but a decisive act of divine agape."[10] Niebuhr puts the contrast as sharply as possible:

> His love of God and his love of neighbor are two distinct virtues that have no common quality but only a common source. . . . The love of God is nonpossessive Eros; the love of man pure Agape; the love of God is passion, the love of man, compassion. There is duality here, but not of like-minded interest in two great values, God and Man. It is rather the duality of the Son of Man and Son of God, who loves God as man should love Him, and loves man as only God can love, with powerful pity for those who are foundering.[11]

Starting from the liberal moralist's emphasis on love as the sole virtue that is the focus for the understanding of Jesus Christ, Niebuhr shows the radicalization of this view in the original portraits that, for him, permit no other conclusion than one that is far removed from the liberal hero of love: "There seems then to be no other adequate way to describe Jesus as having the virtue of love than to say that his love was that of the Son of God. It was not love but God that filled his soul."[12] Similarly, Niebuhr can start from the eschatologist's view (exemplified in Albert Schweitzer) that hope is the key to interpreting Jesus only to show that what Jesus hoped in and hoped for was God. Therefore the conclusion must be: "Not eschatology but sonship to God is the key to Jesus' ethics."[13] Again similarly, Niebuhr demonstrates that the existentialist stress on Jesus' obedience underlines an important feature of Jesus' person, but that the way this theme is developed in Rudolf Bultmann becomes anachronistic in the sense that "the ascription to Jesus of this twentieth-century view of freedom results in a caricature of the New Testament Christ."[14] The examination of Jesus' faith or of his humility leads to the same result: "thus any of the virtues of

10. Niebuhr, *Christ and Culture,* pp. 32, 33.
11. Niebuhr, *Christ and Culture,* p. 33.
12. Niebuhr, *Christ and Culture,* p. 34.
13. Niebuhr, *Christ and Culture,* p. 37.
14. Niebuhr, *Christ and Culture,* p. 39.

Jesus may be taken as the key to the understanding of his character and teaching; but each is intelligible in its apparent radicalism only as a relation to God."[15] This relation cannot more precisely be expressed than in saying that Jesus is the Son of God the Father so that in the unity of his person he actualizes the double movement "with men toward God, with God toward men; from the world to the Other, from the Other to the world; from work to Grace, from Grace to work, from time to the Eternal and from the Eternal to the temporal."[16] It is this double movement of Christ the Son of God that shapes the pattern of the Christian relationship to culture. "Belief in him and loyalty to his cause involves men in the double movement from world to God and from God to world. Even when theologies fail to do justice to this fact, Christians living with Christ in their cultures are aware of it. For they are forever challenged to abandon all things for the sake of God; and forever being sent back into the world to teach and practise all the things that have been commanded them."[17]

Niebuhr's Definition of Culture

The other term in the relationship of Christ and culture is by Niebuhr defined "in similarly tenuous fashion."[18] He intends to define the phenomenon of culture at first "without theological" interpretation in order to show in what regard the theological interpretations of culture differ. Therefore Niebuhr rejects all definitions of culture that focus on a specific culture or distinguish culture (in Jakob Burckhardt's manner) too sharply from religion and state, or from civilization. Culture in the broadest possible sense is for Niebuhr, who borrows the expression from Bronislaw Malinowski, "the 'artificial, secondary environment' which man superimposes on the natural. It comprises language, habits, ideas, beliefs, customs, social organization, inherited artifacts, technical processes and values."[19] Culture is therefore always social; it is to be understood as "human achievement" insofar as it reflects "human purposive-

15. Niebuhr, *Christ and Culture,* p. 41.
16. Niebuhr, *Christ and Culture,* p. 43.
17. Niebuhr, *Christ and Culture,* p. 43.
18. Niebuhr, *Christ and Culture,* p. 44.
19. Niebuhr, *Christ and Culture,* p. 46; the quotation is from Bronislaw Malinowski, "Culture," in *Encyclopedia of Social Sciences,* vol. 4, pp. 621ff.

ness and effort."[20] Because of that it is always concerned with the actualization of values that show culture to be the field of human intentionality. According to Niebuhr this inevitably means that cultural values are directed toward the realization of what is "good for man"[21]; that makes culture inevitably an anthropocentric exercise, although this need not be exclusive. Furthermore, culture is always oriented toward the "temporal and material realization of values."[22] Even values that transcend the temporal and material must find expression in time and matter if they are to become part of culture. Interestingly, Niebuhr also takes up Henri Bergson's emphasis on the necessity of the "conservation of values"[23] as a condition for the continued existence of culture. Finally, Niebuhr, as ever an acute observer of the modern situation, emphasizes the "pluralism that is characteristic of all culture."[24] "The values we seek in our societies and find represented in their institutional behaviour are many, disparate and often incomparable, so that these societies are always involved in a more or less laborious effort to hold together in tolerable conflict the many efforts of many men in many groups to achieve and conserve many goods."[25] More than other features this seems to constitute the challenge for Christian faith, because whatever is of supreme importance for faith will in the field of culture be only one factor in the pluralistic situation. "Jesus Christ and God the Father, the gospel, the church and eternal life may find places in the cultural complex, but only as elements in the great pluralism."[26]

Niebuhr's view of culture is extraordinarily perceptive and anticipates much of the discussion that gained a wider forum only with the rise of cultural anthropology. For him the description of the two terms serves as the backdrop of a typology of answers to the problem of the relationship of Christ and culture. The image that Niebuhr employs to explore the relationship of the "two complex realities," Christ and culture, is that of an "infinite dialogue" not so much between Christianity and culture, as "in the Christian conscience and the Christian community": "In his single-

20. Niebuhr, *Christ and Culture,* p. 47.
21. Niebuhr, *Christ and Culture,* p. 48.
22. Niebuhr, *Christ and Culture,* p. 50.
23. Niebuhr, *Christ and Culture,* p. 50.
24. Niebuhr, *Christ and Culture,* p. 51.
25. Niebuhr, *Christ and Culture,* p. 52.
26. Niebuhr, *Christ and Culture,* p. 52.

minded direction toward God, Christ leads men away from the temporality and pluralism of culture. In its concern for the many values of the past, culture rejects the Christ who bids men to rely on grace. Yet the Son of God is himself child of a religious culture, and sends his disciples to tend his lambs and sheep, who cannot be guarded without cultural work. The dialogue proceeds with denials and affirmations, reconstructions, compromises and new denials. Neither individual nor church can come to a stopping-place in the endless search for an answer which will not provoke a new rejoinder."[27]

Yet, this dialogue of the interaction of Christ and culture is for Niebuhr not an amorphous never-ending tale in which all distinctive features are blurred. Rather, he proposes his typology as a way of following the conversation more intelligently, of stopping the flow of interaction from time to time to gain greater understanding. The typology is based on the polarity of two opposing types of answers: the first emphasizes the opposition of Christ and culture, and the second stresses their fundamental agreement. In between these opposing poles there is space for three other types that "agree with each other in seeking to maintain the great differences between the two principles and in undertaking to hold them together in some unity."[28] The third "synthetic" type sees Christ as "the fulfillment of cultural aspirations and the restorer of the institutions of true society." Yet he also transcends culture, so that he becomes "Christ above culture"[29] — a type that is for Niebuhr best exemplified by Thomas Aquinas. The fourth type that shares with the third its "median" character is for Niebuhr characterized by a double standard of obedience. Its representatives "refuse to accommodate the claims of Christ to those of secular society" yet also hold "the conviction that obedience to requires obedience to the institutions of society and loyalty to its members as well as obedience to a Christ who sits in judgement on that society. Hence man is seen as subject of two moralities, and as a citizen of two worlds that are not only discontinuous but largely opposed."[30] This view that tries to hold the "polarity and tension of Christ and culture" together is for Niebuhr represented by Luther — although we shall see that at least one Lutheran dis-

27. Niebuhr, *Christ and Culture,* p. 53.
28. Niebuhr, *Christ and Culture,* p. 55.
29. Niebuhr, *Christ and Culture,* p. 55.
30. Niebuhr, *Christ and Culture,* pp. 55-56.

agrees. The fifth type is characterized by Niebuhr as the "conversionist solution," represented by John Calvin. The opposition between Christ and culture is recognized but is resolved neither in withdrawal from the world nor in the endurance of its tensions: "Christ is seen as the converter of man in his culture and society, not apart from these, for there is no nature without culture and no turning of men from self and idols to God save in society."[31]

Niebuhr does not attempt to present his own solution as a new type resolving all difficulties found in the others. That would for him be an "act of usurpation of the Lordship of Christ which at the same time would involve doing violence to the liberty of Christian men and to the unconcluded history of the church in culture."[32] Short of presuming upon the Lordship of Christ and the end of the world, what is needed is a step from "insight to decision" that is to be taken individually. "Each believer reaches his own 'final' decision."[33] However, everything depends on the "character of the decisions we make in the freedom of faith."[34] For Niebuhr, they are existential as well as relative decisions, but they are not individualistic, since they are decisions of "social men who have no selfhood apart from their relations to other human selves," and moreover they cannot be based on a merely subjectivistic truth. Hence Niebuhr recommends a "social existentialism" as the way in which the freedom of decision is exercised in utter dependence on God's faithfulness. "To make our decisions in faith is to make them in view of the fact that no single man or group or historical time is the church; but that there is a church of faith in which we do our partial, relative work and on which we count. It is to make them in view of the fact that Christ is risen from the dead, and is not only the head of the church but the redeemer of the world. It is to make them in view of the fact that the world of culture — man's achievement — exists within the world of grace — God's Kingdom."[35]

Much needed to be said to give a fair assessment of Niebuhr's answer to the problem of Christ and culture. However, what should interest us here is not so much his answer but the way in which he sets out the question. For him Christ and culture are "two complex realities" that are char-

31. Niebuhr, *Christ and Culture,* p. 56.
32. Niebuhr, *Christ and Culture,* p. 231.
33. Niebuhr, *Christ and Culture,* p. 232.
34. Niebuhr, *Christ and Culture,* p. 233.
35. Niebuhr, *Christ and Culture,* p. 253.

acterized by a polar tension. The "single-minded direction toward God" that constituted the unity of Christ's being leads away from the temporality of pluralism and culture. Yet this direction away from culture is also embedded in culture and, if it is to gain followers, is also dependent on culture. In directing those who believe in him from the world to God, Christ is the challenge of all culture; in "being sent back into the world" believers take part in the movement from grace to work. Conversely, culture rejects the Christ "who bids men to rely on grace" because it is the sphere of human achievement; nevertheless it is also dependent on finding a focus in the pluralism of values that threaten the project of human culture with a self-destructive lack of orientation. Independence from one another and mutual interdependence on one another characterize the interaction of the "two complex realities" that Niebuhr describes. Between the two poles the dialogue must flow in question and answer, counter-question and reply — till kingdom come. Between the two poles Christians must take their decisions, influenced by both — at least sometimes, one suspects, not unlike Buridan's ass. Is this description of the problem of Christ and culture correct? Let us look at another way of perceiving the question.

"You Wonder Where the Body Went": R. W. Jenson's Approach to Christ and Culture

Jenson's modestly entitled book *Essays in Theology of Culture* is, like Niebuhr's, one of the most distinguished efforts in twentieth-century theology to bring the problem of Christianity and culture into focus. However, the strategy employed by these two American theologians could not be more different. Whereas Niebuhr attempts to present a general typology of Christian attitudes toward culture, Jenson reflects on the impact specific insights of the Christian gospel have on particular problems of culture. Many of the essays collected in the book started life as commissioned addresses or essays for particular occasions, occasional writings in the best sense of the word. Yet, their cumulative effect is to present a wide-ranging view of how the Christian gospel pertains to problems that may be raised in particular contexts but that, nevertheless, highlight connected aspects of cultural life at the end of the twentieth century. There is no attempt to forge from these occasional writings a systematic whole, as well befits an author who went on to publish a full-scale systematic theology. However, the connections that appear sometimes produce startling new insights, immensely irritating for our preconceived way of perceiving problems in the relationship of Christianity and culture.

Of the many essays in the book none struck me more than the last one, "Autobiographical Reflections on the Relation of Theology, Science and Philosophy; or, You Wonder Where the Body Went." In the space of eight pages there is a proposal for conceiving of the relation of theology, science, and philosophy that is startling because it is based on an old, and for most systematic theologians rather distanced, debate between the Reformers on the implications of the presence of the risen Christ's body in the Lord's Supper. Yet, it seems to me to underline a way in which Niebuhr's problem is dealt with in an unexpected manner. It has long been known that the theology of the sacraments is the test case for Christology. Tell me what your theology of the sacraments is, and I shall tell you what your Christology is. The interface between the two doctrines is clearly the question of the so-called real presence of Christ in the Lord's Supper. Therefore it is not an exaggeration to say that every Christology contains a (more or less) implicit theology of the sacraments, and every sacramental theology a (more or less) implicit Christology. Because of this interconnection it might not be too audacious to take this brief essay as the starting point for once again looking at the problem of Christ and culture.

In his essay Jenson comes to the Christological question by a circuitous route. He starts with the notion of "heaven." Even if we consider that God "is his own proper place . . . if there are to be creatures, God . . . needs a created place from which to be among them." Therefore: "Heaven is God's pad within his creation."[36] The Ptolemaic mapping of the universe appeared to offer a location for God's heaven on the outermost shell of heavenly spheres surrounding the earth in concentric circles that is both "ontologically different from the rest of the universe, and so suited for God, and spatially related to the universe's other places."[37] On the Ptolemaic worldview it is to this place that the body of the risen Christ ascended. The question that is raised with the Copernican revolution is, of course: "In the universe as mapped by Copernicus, where can the risen

36. Robert W. Jenson, *Essays in Theology of Culture* (Grand Rapids: Eerdmans, 1995), p. 216.

37. Jenson, *Essays in Theology of Culture,* p. 217.

Christ's body be, between his 'comings' to us?"[38] This, of course, raised questions about the presence of the body of the risen Christ in the Lord's Supper. "If heaven is the place just described, it would seem he would have to travel from the one place to the other."[39] If one wanted to avoid the mythic notion of "divine journeyings," as Jenson dubs it, and attempts not to evade the issue by postulating a merely "spiritual" presence, one was committed with the Catholic to regard the bodily presence of Christ in the Lord's Supper as "supernatural" and to find a means of turning the miracle (which could be explained by a theory of transubstantiation) into a "reliable miracle": "The ministry of the church was credited with authorization to petition the presence with absolute assurance that it would occur."[40] The first step, the supernatural interpretation of the bodily presence of Christ in the Lord's Supper, which, in turn, necessitates a theory of transubstantiation, solves the problem of Christ's having to travel from one place to another only by introducing the new mystery of the changing of one substance into another and by calling the bodily reality of the risen Christ into question. How is a supernatural bodily presence to be distinguished from a spiritual bodily presence? The second step is the one the Reformers reacted against in their criticism of the late medieval practice of mass that they accused of conflating divine work and human work in a sense that for them became manifest in the alleged understanding of mass as the repetition of Christ's sacrifice. If, however, the church cannot guarantee a "reliable miracle," how is the presence of Christ in the Lord's Supper to be understood?

Jenson puts the alternative routes taken by the Reformers in stark contrast: "Some reformers denied the eucharistic bodily presence. Luther and some of his younger followers instead denied the traditional understanding of heaven" in the sense "that heaven is any other place than the place of Jesus' sacramental presence to us, that is, that it is 'place' strictly speaking at all."[41] There is no spatial distance to be overcome since there is no space that separates the table of the Lord's Supper and heaven.

In volume I of his *Systematic Theology* Jenson has developed this point, first introduced by Johannes Brenz and the Swabian school of Lu-

38. Jenson, *Essays in Theology of Culture,* p. 217.
39. Jenson, *Essays in Theology of Culture,* p. 218.
40. Jenson, *Essays in Theology of Culture,* p. 218.
41. Jenson, *Essays in Theology of Culture,* p. 218.

theran theologians, further. According to this school God is his own place, but this place is not located at a specific point in space that then needs to be related to other places in creation. For God the whole created universe is one single place so that God can be present to the whole of creation simultaneously in a manner that is not distinguished by the locations of creation but by the modes of divine activity. God's presence to creation is different in the word of the gospel and the sacraments and in the hearts of believers, different again in the creative presence that maintains the being of the whole of creation. However, all these modes of presence are not to be spatially differentiated; they follow the differentiation and relation of God's Trinitarian self-giving as Luther developed it in the Large Catechism. This view of space as defined by the place God is, is combined with the Cyrillian Christology the Lutheran reformers held. The strict view of the unity of the person of Christ forbids thinking of the deity being anywhere without the humanity, because that would immediately lead to the assumption of two persons in the one Christ — a relapse into Nestorianism. If this is to be avoided, there is only one conclusion, which Jenson quotes from Brenz's *De personali unione duarum naturarum in Christo*:[42] "Although it is a property only of the divine nature of Christ to be everywhere and fill all things, nevertheless he possesses this property only in common with his human nature, that he assumed into the one and the same person that he is."[43] Because of the unity of his person the risen Christ participates in his divinity and humanity in the relation of God who is his own place to all other places in creation.

On the basis of this view of "heaven" the challenge of the Copernican revolution could be responded to creatively. No topographic location of heaven was needed that in any case could not be built into the homogeneity of the Copernican cosmos, and no spatial explanation of its relation to the table at the Lord's Supper was required since God's presence to creation and the presence of the risen Christ for the church are not to be conceived spatially. As Jenson says, the whole question had changed: ". . . the question of Christ's bodily presence on the eucharistic altars is not one of

42. Published in Tübingen in 1561. Cf. Johannes Brenz, *Die christologischen Schriften*, ed. Theodor Mahlmann (Tübingen: Mohr Siebeck, 1981). This volume contains both *De personali unione duarum naturarum in Christo* and *De maiestate*, on which Jenson bases his interpretation.

43. Brenz, *De personali unione*, p. 11, cited in Robert W. Jenson, *Systematic Theology*, vol. I: *The Triune God* (Oxford: Oxford University Press, 1997), p. 203.

containment in one set of places instead of another but one of availability to experience in one set of places instead of another."[44]

The conclusions Jenson draws from this insight from a long forgotten school of Lutheran Christology are considerable. In his essay he develops them in two lines of inquiry, one concerning the understanding of "body," the other concerning the notion of "heaven." If body is no longer to be understood in terms of containment in one place, how should it then be understood? To replace the notion of containment as the guiding idea for understanding what a "body" is with availability has for Jenson a twofold corollary. Availability is our becoming present for others and so intending others, but at the same time allowing others to intend us. Both are held together in the understanding of body as availability. This has a surprising implication that Jenson indicates with reference to Georg Hegel's famous section on "Knechtschaft und Herrschaft" in *Die Phänomenologie des Geistes.* Through Christ's bodily presence in the bread and the cup in the Lord's Supper Christ not only intends us as a subject but also "gives himself to be our object."[45] The significance of this can be understood from the reciprocity of the subject-object relation in Hegel's analysis: ". . . were someone to be present to me as subject only and not also as my object in turn, I would just so be that someone's object only and not a subject over against him/her. Thus such a personal presence would enslave me."[46] The disembodied presence of Christ would give believers no recourse to relate to Christ as subjects who can relate to the Christ who gave himself as our subject. Yet since Christ gives himself to us in this way, not only as a subject, but also as an object, not only as a spiritual presence, but also as bodily presence in the bread and the cup, we gain our freedom in relating to Christ's bodily presence in Communion. Through the presence of the body of Christ in Communion we are liberated to be persons in communion. Jenson insists that this revised notion of "body" gained from Christological reflection would also have far-reaching implications for our understanding of the physical universe. Once the traditional concept of body has been rendered highly problematical by the development of quantum mechanics, could not a relational view of bodies as "availabilities that enable freedom" prove "suggestive also to more strictly physical research"?[47]

44. Jenson, *Essays in Theology of Culture,* p. 219.
45. Jenson, *Essays in Theology of Culture,* p. 220.
46. Jenson, *Essays in Theology of Culture,* p. 220.
47. Jenson, *Essays in Theology of Culture,* p. 221.

The second line of inquiry concerns the notion of heaven. Has this notion been rendered obsolete by the theological and scientific critique of heaven as a place in space? The question has important ramifications since the suggestion made by Luther, Brenz, and the Swabian school seems to invite the accusation of pantheism. Or more radically: If God is everywhere, is the distinction between God and the world not sublated in such a way that either pantheism or, indeed, atheism might follow? Jenson suggests that if one "is prepared to be speculatively brazen it is tempting to say that the space occupied by the bread and cup, and by the space-occupying aspects of the church's sacraments and sacramental life, is God's pad in his creation."[48] Jenson does not argue for this view in our essay, but he points to the implications of such a view. It would behoove me to "redefine heaven christologically: Heaven would exist only in that the Incarnation occurs, only in that God incarnationally occupies space in his creation. It would become conceptually impossible to describe the Creator's presence to his creatures without reference to Jesus Christ."[49] Adopting this view would require us not only to affirm that Christ would have come if Adam had not sinned, firmly taking a stand with Athanasius, Scotus, Luther, and Karl Barth, but also to subscribe to the view "that the church was constitutive for the reality of creation; if no church then no big bang."[50]

Some of us might not be "speculatively brazen" enough to agree with this last point without further argument and reflection. However, the conclusion Jenson draws from this exploration that started from the Christological reflection how the body of the risen Christ could be present in the Lord's Supper is highly relevant for our question about the relationship between Christ and culture. For Jenson these reflections that allow free traffic of theological ideas across the borders of several intellectual disciplines are intended to call into question the (in many cases self-imposed) isolation of theological inquiry from other spheres of intellectual engagement following the displacement of theology through the acceptance of a "mechanistic" interpretation of the Newtonian physics — a recurrent theme in his engagement with questions of the theology of culture. He writes: "For two centuries, we have in consequence supposed that Christian talk of God and human destiny must be epistemologically dis-

48. Jenson, *Essays in Theology of Culture,* p. 221.
49. Jenson, *Essays in Theology of Culture,* p. 221.
50. Jenson, *Essays in Theology of Culture,* p. 220.

connected from scientific talk, and that since what science does is describe reality, Christian talk of God and human destiny cannot describe reality, whatever else it may be permitted to do."[51] The attempt at inventing some other "epistemological function for theology" is for Jenson characterized by utter futility that is based on "uncritical acceptance of a — to boot, intrinsically implausible — metaphysical root metaphor." His advice is to give up the search for some other function for theology than that of describing reality since "no subregion of human discourse can be a normative paradigm of any other."[52] That will not remove the difference between different disciplines, but it will commit them to say that insofar as they are making truth-claims they must do so in the arena of one cognitive discourse. Jenson's conclusion lacks neither clarity nor punch: "Do I then say that '$E = mc^2$' and 'The Son proceeds from the Father' work just the same way? I do not think I do. But I do say that insofar as either '$E = mc^2$' or 'The Son proceeds from the Father' is true, insofar as either has any purchase on something other than itself, they depend for this purchase on their situation in one total human cognitive discourse, which has no clear internal epistemological boundaries. To put it from the side that will make the point most offensively plain: if science does not belong to the same discourse as does theology, then science is a play of fictions."[53]

Jenson's proposal for conceiving the relationship between Christianity and culture is markedly different from that of H. Richard Niebuhr. However, they both agree on seeing the perspective from which the question should be perceived and should be dealt with as one of Christology. The primary question is "Christ and culture," and only on the basis of trying to deal with this question can we hope to engage with the question of Christianity and culture. What interests us here is the way in which different Christological emphases shape the way in which the problem is perceived.

Questions for Further Conversations

For Niebuhr Christ and culture confront one another as two complex realities that are both independent from each other and interdependent on

51. Jenson, *Essays in Theology of Culture,* p. 223.
52. Jenson, *Essays in Theology of Culture,* p. 224.
53. Jenson, *Essays in Theology of Culture,* pp. 223-24.

each other. Therefore it makes sense to approach the question by starting from this initial polarity and trying to define the two realities independently of each other, and then to inquire into the different types in which the relationship between the two poles is interpreted. This theological enterprise takes the form of balancing the transcendence of Christ over culture with the immanence of Christ in culture. Ultimately, a resolution of the tension cannot be found on the plane of theological theory, but in the field of action, in the decisions we take in faith in the cultural field.

Jenson offers a corrective of such a view, and he does so for Christological reasons. The insight of the Swabian school of Lutheran theologians on which he builds is that God's realm and creation cannot be related like two places contained in space. The mode of God's presence in and for creation is different from the way in which created entities relate to one another in space. Through the unity of his person, through being the Son of the Father, Christ participates in this mode of presence. However, the incarnation makes a difference because it means that in the mode of God's presence is now included the God-Man. "The Incarnation given, what we call the humanity of Christ and the deity of Christ, are only actual as one sole person, so that where the deity of the Son is, there must be Jesus' humanity, unabridged as soul and body."[54] The mode of God's presence in the incarnation is thus continued through the body of the risen Christ in the Lord's Supper. For Jenson, here going beyond Brenz and his followers, this is the point where Christology and ecclesiology are joined through the theology of the sacraments: "We must learn to say: the entity rightly called the body of Christ is whatever object it is that is Christ's availability to us as subjects; by the promise of Christ, this object is the bread and cup and the gathering of the church around them. There is where creatures can locate him, to respond to his word to them."[55]

The immediate effect this has for a theology of culture is that the notion of "two complex realities" — one is almost tempted to say, two spaces of Christ and culture — is overcome by the image of one reality that is identified and discerned in the Lord's Supper. This becomes abundantly clear when Jenson suggests that we understand the notion of heaven Christologically, so that God "incarnationally occupies space in his creation," which after the resurrection and ascension is Christ's availability to

54. Jenson, *Systematic Theology,* vol. I, p. 203.
55. Jenson, *Systematic Theology,* vol. I, p. 205.

us in the Lord's Supper and the church. There is then no reason to withdraw theological discourse from the field of culture or cultural discourse from theological reflection because the one reality of the incarnate Son of God made available to us in the church and her sacraments is constitutive for the reality of creation. The upshot of this can be seen in Jenson's essays on the theology of culture. There is for him no need to engage in Tillichian exercises of distinguishing and relating cultural form and religious content, or form and substance. The categories that we find in Christology, language as address and response and so conversation, time, body, space, and so forth, are the ones that we can fruitfully employ in the interpretation of culture. The real *Auseinandersetzung* is not between Christianity and culture or theology and the sciences and the arts as if these were self-contained compartments. The real battle of interpretations occurs between the disciples of Christ and the disciples of Socrates, Apollo, or Orpheus; its aim is not to stake a claim on a small portion of reality that remains unchallenged in the hands of theology or the church but to seek the truth.

Jenson's proposal to perceive the problem of a theology of culture has a liberating effect in breaking down — for Christological reasons — the compartmentalized view of culture that we have inherited from the Enlightenment, and it can serve to encourage a theology of culture to pursue its business without undue respect for the intellectual fences that have been erected around different spheres of culture. Yet, theologically Jenson's proposal — like Niebuhr's — is not without problems. Whereas in Niebuhr there seem to be tendencies toward a dualism of Christ and culture that Jenson rightly attempts to overcome, there seems to be in Jenson tendencies toward an equally problematical monism. Since theology has its life in conversations, such concerns may be raised as questions.

The first question concerns the mode of Christ's presence to the world that, as we have seen, is of crucial significance for a theology of culture. Is it theologically appropriate to focus the mode of God's presence to the world as sharply as Jenson seems to do it in some formulations on the presence of Christ in the church as the body of Christ, and more specifically on the bread and the cup in the Lord's Supper? The difficulty that Brenz and his followers experienced of not being able to provide a "really satisfactory statement of the difference between Christ's 'bodily' presence in the Eucharist and his 'bodily' presence elsewhere" is not only a theological embarrassment. It seems to come from their unwillingness to answer the question: "Is Christ only bodily present in the Lord's Supper?" with a straightforward "Yes," and the complementary question "Is Christ anywhere else bodily present than in the Lord's Supper?" with an equally straightforward "No." Jenson seems to be more confident than Brenz and company in responding to the first question with a decisive "Yes. " However, does the *sessio ad dextram,* the risen Son sitting at the right hand of the Father, occur only in the Lord's Supper? The danger of Jenson's position, as it appears to me now, is that it comes very close to the understanding of the church, the body of Christ, as an extension of incarnation, which, at least in some aspects, seems to be incompatible with the Reformers' emphasis on the church as *creatura verbi divini,* the creature of the divine Word. If Christology leads straight into ecclesiology via the theology of the sacraments, there is the danger that the question of Christ and culture is transformed into the question of the church and culture. One could also put the point in this way: Whereas Niebuhr is intent on relativizing the church through reference to the lordship of Christ, Jenson seems in danger of absolutizing the church by interpreting its relation to Christ as its identity with Christ's body.

The second question — and this is really the question of the fool carrying coals to Newcastle — concerns the Trinitarian framework of a theology of culture. Is it not the case that the emphasis on Christology must be within the framework of God's Trinitarian action so that Christ's person and work are theologically described in relation to creation, reconciliation, and the perfection of God's communion with his creation? To put it bluntly: Is heaven "simply" to be described "Christologically" or would a complete theological description require a Trinitarian interpretation? If so, should what applies to "heaven" not also be true for "the church" and "culture"? The understanding of the church could, for instance, not exclusively be based on the statement "You are the body of Christ" but would have to be supplemented by the, as Jenson himself says, "regularly paired 'You are the community of the Spirit.'"[56] The implications of such a Trinitarian contextualization of the problem of Christ and culture would seem to offer a resolution of the tension between transcendence (as emphasized by Niebuhr) and immanence (as emphasized by Jenson), since the doctrine of the Trinity is the Christian "approach" to the problem of transcendence and immanence.

56. Jenson, *Systematic Theology,* vol. I, p. 204.

The third question concerns an inner-Lutheran debate. Is the mode of God's presence to the world not to be interpreted through the doctrines of law and gospel and, even, through the doctrine of the two kingdoms? If Jenson is right (and I think he is) that we are wrong in thinking of theology as one "compartment" separated from other intellectual disciplines, because reflecting on "God and the world" is the Christian theological task, then these two doctrines come into play. Not because the law exercises an autonomous function apart from the gospel, and not because the kingdom to the left is somehow an independent realm as popular misconception has it, but because they indicate the patterns that God's universal Trinitarian agency takes in bringing an estranged humanity and a fallen creation into communion with himself.

Once we attempt to deal with Niebuhr's problem of Christ and culture through the insights Jenson's "You Wonder Where the Body Went" affords, the theological conversation must continue. This should not surprise us if we are the creatures of a God whose "being is specifiable as conversation."[57]

57. Jenson, *Essays in Theology of Culture*, p. 125.

Robert Jenson's Soteriology

GERHARD O. FORDE

In a good systematic theology, soteriology is more or less presupposed in everything that is said and done. That is to say, it is often more implicit than explicit. Yet that makes the task of doing it justice somewhat difficult. In the end I have decided simply to concentrate on what I have called three "phases" of Jenson's work where the discussion seems most concentrated; these phases seem to me to be determinative for the basic shape of the understanding of salvation.

Phase One: Encounter with Barth

Robert Jenson's soteriology is, at least in its earliest stages, a result of his critique, positive and negative, of the Christology and soteriology of Karl Barth. One might call it an extension, if not "a correction," of Barth's soteriology *and* Christology. The "and" is important because it seems to me that Jenson's work on this locus, coming off his study of Barth, is really more about the tradition called Christology than it is about soteriology. It is really more about the person of Christ than it is about the work of Christ. Or perhaps one might say, to put the best construction on the matter, that person and work coalesce in Jenson's thought. The person is the work and the work is the person. In so saying, however, we get ahead of ourselves. The point to be made at the outset is that Jenson's soteriology is the outcome of his wrestling with the particular set of problems he encounters in his reading of Barth. This means that Jenson's soteriology tends to be more implicit than explicit, and that makes for difficulty in ferreting out a full-blown view of the soteriology.

What is the root of this set of problems? Basically it is the age-old problem of eternity versus time. Given Barth's doctrine of election in which all are elect in Christ, the danger will always be present that eternity simply gobbles up time and so transfers the event of the cross from "earth to heaven," from time and actual happening to a timeless eternity where nothing really happens. The big question therefore is whether "for the gospel God's will and rule becomes Jesus Christ," or whether for Barth "Jesus Christ has become the eternal decree."[1]

Thus battle between time and eternity becomes the hallmark of Jenson's theology. There is a constant polemic throughout his work against the "timeless" God of the Greeks. Virtually every theological "sin" and false formulation can be traced to the intrusion of such timelessness into the theological scene. In soteriology this raises the question whether Jesus and his cross actually accomplish salvation here in time, or whether the saving deed is really "preaccomplished" by virtue of the divine decree in eternity.

Jenson's earliest reflections on matters soteriological come in his reservations about tendencies operative in Barth's reconstruction of the doctrine of predestination. The problem is the one we have already mentioned: the assertion that all that is comprehended in the pretemporal decree threatens the historical reality of the soteriological event. In the closing section of *Alpha and Omega,* his earliest book, Jenson sets forth his reactions to Barth, both positive and negative. These reactions are determinative for the subsequent development of Jenson's soteriology.

The first reaction is positive. Jenson begins by approving Barth's view of evil. Evil "is what it is in that God rejects it," and "exists exactly in that God rejects it."[2] Yet this entails for Jenson a rejection of the view that reconciliation is only God's reaction to human sin. Then eternity slips back into the picture. "If God's will to rescue and exalt us in Christ is really to be God's last secret, then it must be His eternal will as He is eternal. It cannot be merely his reacting to anything. The coming of Jesus Christ to sinful man is, as Barth says, its own sufficient reason."[3]

1. Robert W. Jenson, *Alpha and Omega* (New York: Thomas Nelson and Sons, 1963), p. 162.

2. Jenson, *Alpha and Omega,* p. 150.

3. Jenson, *Alpha and Omega,* p. 150

Nevertheless, this coming of Jesus Christ to sinful man is not to be understood as a mere stratagem on God's part. There is a real historical encounter between the opposing forces of wrath and love. This is not something generally available to ordinary human perception but is a matter of revelation. The world as we find ourselves living in it is disclosed to us by revelation as the opposing "old age" under the wrath of God. "The historical and natural forces which dominate our lives are revealed as *enemies* of God, and we as willing captives."[4] We are exposed by the cross as rebels seeking to eliminate God once and for all from our lives. Yet we and our world are, despite all, God's good creation. This is manifest by the very fact that it is revealed in the cross. The revelation *is* the joining of the battle and the promise of ultimate victory. In the cross God saves in that he does battle against us, condemns and rejects our rebellion, and thereby claims us as his own.

Yet in spite of criticism it is important to note that Jenson characterizes himself as "far too convinced of the necessity of Barth's thought and too impressed by what is to be learned from him"[5] to allow his critique of Barth to become an assault. Perhaps it is fair to say that Jenson approves the basic shape of Barth's reconstruction but cannot rid himself of his reservations. The problem continues to be whether one does justice to historical actuality by depicting the whole long history of God with his creation as though each step were taken "in order" to accomplish the next. Is the entire history "comprehended within a solution given in advance?" If so, creation and reconciliation collapse into each other. Reconciliation is already comprehended in creation, and nothing essential happens in our time.

Jenson continues to fear that Barth is in danger of making this move. Against this danger Jenson repeatedly asserts the place of the "nevertheless." Yes, the Son of Man goes as it is written, *nevertheless* woe to that man by whose hand he goes. The unity of creation and reconciliation is the unity of this one person in his history, and thus it cannot be determined in advance. It *occurs* in this person's life history.

There was a time when he was the Agent of Creation but not yet the Redeemer. That the Agent of Creation *is* the Reconciler is a unity that only happens in the event in which he *becomes* the Reconciler. It is a unity given in the overcoming, in the "nevertheless which is the history of the Cru-

4. Jenson, *Alpha and Omega,* p. 152.
5. Jenson, *Alpha and Omega,* p. 151.

cified and Risen."[6] All of this is necessary to accommodate the understanding of soteriology as lying in the decision of God. Jenson's approval of this fact is a key to his own soteriological starting point. Our salvation lies in a decision of God, the decision by which Jesus Christ lives as God for us. Karl Barth's understanding of this decision is in all essentials correct: It is its own basis. It carries its eternal validity within itself. So far as this decision in and of itself is concerned, even Barth's "supralapsarianism" is correct: God's love for sinners in Christ is not merely his accommodation to an unfortunate situation but the opening of a depth in God in which he loves and sacrifices himself for the sinner as sinner.

Grace is not a repair job. It is God's will and the basis of our whole existence.[7] Yet the carrying out of the will of God to be grace for us opens another will to us, his will to create us as creatures destined to participate in his life. It is his will to preserve and rule us to that end.

However, once again the note of the theology of the cross is sounded. Since this other will "becomes visible in reconciliation, in forgiveness, it appears to us as the judgment which it becomes to the creature who rejects it."[8] Once again the note of the theology of the cross is sounded. This "second" will of God "appears" to us as God's attack on our created lives, as a closing of the way to participation in his life. It appears as the rule of God in nature and history that carries the double secret of man's rebellion and God's rejection. Whereas the first will assures us that God is absolutely and eternally determined to reconcile sinful creatures with himself by sending his Son, and indeed directs all history to that goal, the direction of history and God's will is hidden by human rebellion and God's judgment. There is inescapable hiddenness here. "The Gospel does not *explain* the rule of history's hidden Lord."[9] One does not "see through" history in advance by means of a series of "in order thats." "The necessary connection of each event with the past is established when it occurs and by its occurring and not before."[10]

Jenson's polemic against timelessness is constant throughout. What he has done in his analysis of Barth's work, he says, "is to dissolve the 'in order that' with which supralapsarianism old and new ties together the ele-

6. Jenson, *Alpha and Omega,* pp. 155-56.

7. Jenson, *Alpha and Omega,* pp. 158-59.

8. Jenson, *Alpha and Omega,* p. 159.

9. Jenson, *Alpha and Omega,* p. 158.

10. Jenson, *Alpha and Omega,* p. 164.

ments of God's will and works."[11] Yet dissolving the "in order that" runs the risk of falling back into an infralapsarianism with its abstract deity or dividing reality into two kingdoms, one ruled by the gracious God and the other more like an angry demon. Jenson rejects both charges. What separates him from Barth, he maintains, is the one "drastic sentence" that insists that the unity of God's one eternal will is an event that occurred in time at the cross. Where Barth puts an "in order that," Jenson insists, there should stand the cross. The following passage sums up Jenson's soteriology as it emerges from its encounter with Barth:

> We must seek to describe God's will — its eternity undiminished — as an event in history, as the chronologically and geographically fixable event of the life of Jesus of Nazareth, the Christ. We wish to speak of God's decision and, in so doing, speak more unequivocally than Barth of the life of Jesus Christ in our history, of His life in created time and space. Jesus Christ is God's great decision about us, and not as an event in a "third" level between time and eternity. In *our* history God makes His *eternal* decision.[12]

That, in sum, is a brief statement of Jenson's soteriology to this point. The basic structure, I think we can say, is Barthian. The saving act is rooted in the divine election carried out in Christ Jesus, the Son of God. Salvation is not the result of an alteration in the divine will due to human sin. Rather it is God's carrying to perfection his eternal will in Jesus Christ. Even though the structure is Barthian, Jenson's objections are clear throughout. Barth's "solution" to the problem of election, Jenson insists, threatens to lose its hold on the actual historical event nature of the cross. Jesus Christ threatens simply to replace the eternal decree of Calvinism. God's will, Jenson insists to the contrary, must be described as an event in our history.

Yet how, one must ask at this juncture, does one escape the nonhistorical threat of the Barthian structure? Does proper dogmatic description do it? Does one not have to be aware that the very act of the description abstracts and removes the matter from time so that one ends by doing just what one did not intend to do? Must it not be recognized that the basic problem here is a hermeneutical one, that the "description" must drive

11. Jenson, *Alpha and Omega*, p. 160.
12. Jenson, *Alpha and Omega*, p. 163.

the preaching and that the words must be used so as to *do* the event to the hearer — words that put the old to death and raise the new? Without this hermeneutical turn attention will likely be concentrated on the *identity* and *being* of the "reconciler" rather than on his work. This results again in a strong pull away from history as well as the tendency to express the soteriological significance of Jesus in terms of participation in his *being* rather than in what he does to and for us. So it is only consequent that Jenson spends much of his remaining theological effort developing and expounding the doctrine of the Trinity. Already at the close of *Alpha and Omega* he says that we must follow Barth in developing a "christological ontology."[13] Yet Jenson is well aware of the problems involved. One must take care not to abstract from the actual history. Christ cannot be seen as the logos unchanged from all eternity. He, the eternal Word, *became flesh.* There is a progression. This progression of his life, moreover, "*is our being.*"[14] The suspicion that salvation comes by participation lies near at hand, and salvation by participation slides too easily into salvation by *gratia gratum faciens.*

Phase Two: Reformation

Jenson's most explicit treatment of traditional soteriological questions appears in his chapter on "Pneumatological Soteriology" in the *Christian Dogmatics.*[15] As the chapter title indicates, Jenson's soteriology here takes a turn in the direction of the doctrine of the Holy Spirit, particularly as he finds it in the Greek Fathers. Thus a theological preference becomes evident that persists through the remainder of Jenson's career. The Greek Fathers are to be preferred because they "conceptualized the creative relation of God to his faithful people in a specifically biblical way."[16] Even though his appropriation of St. Paul was the great blessing of Western theology, on the one hand, St. Augustine appears largely as the culprit who made a proper understanding of matters soteriological impossible, on the other hand. Whereas for the Eastern Fathers the operations of the triune God

13. Jenson, *Alpha and Omega,* p. 171.

14. Jenson, *Alpha and Omega,* p. 171. Italics added.

15. Robert W. Jenson, "Pneumatological Soteriology," in Carl E. Braaten and Robert W. Jenson, eds., *Christian Dogmatics,* vol. 2 (Philadelphia: Fortress Press, 1984), pp. 125-42.

16. Jenson, "Pneumatological Soteriology," p. 126.

were taken to be God's own reality among us, Augustine obscured the matter by making the persons functionally the same. Thus he had no way of explaining the saving relation between God and his creatures as did the Greek Fathers, who could speak of the Father and Son as being transformingly present in the Spirit.[17]

The result was that the theology of grace in the Latin West got trapped in the wrong system. God is conceived as a "substance" who acts causally on his creatures. Creatures are likewise "substances" who are to act in ways obedient to God (it is to be hoped!). The system therefore drives inexorably to the idea of cooperation in salvation. If one speaks as St. Thomas did in terms of willing, the only way a will can be authentically moved is by "co-willing." The question of cooperation always leaves the Christian in doubt about the sufficiency of such cooperation. The systematic problem inexorably becomes a pastoral problem.[18]

It was this "perversion," to use Jenson's own words, that necessitated the Reformation with its doctrine of justification by faith alone. The Reformation, Jenson says, was "a protest against a whole way of thinking about and proclaiming the faith, and against corresponding structures of medieval Western liturgies. . . ."[19] Luther's search was not just for God's effect on us but rather for God's own presence among us. This led, in Jenson's view, to a recovery of biblical and pre-Augustinian language of Spirit, and this brings about a turn to what Jenson calls *Pneumatological Soteriology.*

Pneumatological soteriology is about the proper use of language in theological discourse. The trouble with the usual discourse is that all attempts to *describe* the salvation process, no matter how correct, are nevertheless bound to destroy what they want to promote. The discourse inevitably shifts to the third person: "God freely forgives those who truly repent," and so forth. The description may be true but it leaves the hearer turned in to a self-wondering whether or not the repentance has been "truly" adequate to the job. The third-person discourse has created, according to Jenson, "an alienation of the third article, a transformation of the biblical discourse about God's Spirit into a stipulation of method for our spirituality."[20]

17. Jenson, "Pneumatological Soteriology," p. 126.
18. Jenson, "Pneumatological Soteriology," p. 127.
19. Jenson, "Pneumatological Soteriology," p. 129.
20. Jenson, "Pneumatological Soteriology," p. 128.

Jenson shifts the focus from mere description in the third person to actual doing of the salvific deed in present-tense, first-to-second-person proclamation and teaching. As such it sets itself forth as the doctrine of the Spirit, the one who "calls, gathers, enlightens, converts, justifies, renews, and unites with Christ." The third-person descriptive discourse must be turned into first-to-second-person address. Theology, that is, "must be done from the location of the preacher. . . . pneumatology must become hermeneutical reflection."[21] The upshot of this hermeneutical turn is the claim that the Reformation doctrine of justification is not just another attempt to be descriptively correct, not even an attempt to insist that all Christians must hold such a correct view. Rather, the Reformation doctrine ought to be viewed as hermeneutical instruction for preachers. It is best considered as a proposal of dogma for the church. Jenson supports his hermeneutical turn at this point by a careful analysis of Melanchthon's *Apology* to Article IV of the *Augsburg Confession.* Here Jenson lays out in most helpful fashion Melanchthon's fundamental hermeneutical distinction between law and promise. It is the great divide between the Lutheran Reformation and medieval hermeneutics. It determines the shape of one's soteriology as well as one's ethics. If hermeneutics are to be regarded as instruction for preachers, Jenson's exposition of the Apology is fundamental for that regard.

The turn to hermeneutics involves for Jenson at the same time a recasting of the doctrine of predestination, a doctrine vital to soteriology. The basic difficulty one encounters in the tradition is the problem of the two absolutes. The first absolute is the unconditional promise proclaimed in the gospel. The gospel promise, that is, is guaranteed by the immutable will of God. Without this absolute we would be lost. Yet this also entails immediately the second absolute, the absolute will of God in creation and in all events. If it happens, God in some way wills it. The first absolute is absolute by virtue of its known content — the gospel: God's promises will not fail. The second, however, is absolute by virtue of the absence of known content.

The relation between these two absolutes poses the theological problem. Mostly those of the tradition have backed off from the problem and taken refuge in semi-Pelagianism of some sort (election *ex intuitu fidei*, and so forth), which, as Jenson rightly observes, means the end of any seri-

21. Jenson, "Pneumatological Soteriology," p. 130.

ous doctrine of God.[22] To escape such fate Jenson first reclaims Barth's Christological move. Election is done through the proclamation of Jesus Christ, not abstractly by a God in eternity separating souls, like good potatoes from bad potatoes, apart from Trinitarian relations. Once again we encounter the ambiguity of the Barthian position. Does Christ descend into time to do the choosing or is he taken from us into eternity to take the place of Calvin's eternal decree?

Whereas in the earlier phase of Jenson's work he insisted that the cross must be set against the Barthian "in order that" he now moves to make Spirit discourse rather than Father or Son discourse the primary locus of his interpretation. The eternity of the moment of the divine choosing must be established by changing the prefix in predestination to "post-" rather than "pre-." That is, Christ *will* be Lord over all. Jenson parodies Barth: The Holy Spirit is the choosing God.[23]

This still leaves Jenson with the problem of the two absolutes — admittedly the most offensive problem of predestinarian reflection. How can the two absolutes (absolute love and mere absoluteness) be held together? The "solution" in Jenson's view is again in the turn to Spirit reflection. As long as reflection stays with the first two articles of the creed, one must seek some kind of synthesis between the two absolutes. One seeks to *explain* how the God of immutable love can will the terrors, evils, and disasters of creation and human perfidy. If, however, one thinks in terms of all three articles, one can abandon the attempt to synthesize and construct theodicies and look instead to the "postdestination" in the Spirit. The notion of Spirit, Jenson says, is precisely the synthesis between the two determinations. From the perspective of the gospel God's will is absolute because it is immutable love. From the perspective of the total picture God's will is absolute because it is absolutely undetermined: whatever happens, God wills it. Yet that means that for the time being God is hidden and faith is "a desperate conflict within an encompassing hope."[24]

22. Jenson, "Pneumatological Soteriology," p. 137.
23. Jenson, "Pneumatological Soteriology," p. 138.
24. Jenson, "Pneumatological Soteriology," p. 139.

Phase Three: Resurrection

"The project of the present work . . . remove[s] the Crucifixion from a kind of centrality it has sometimes occupied in theology. What the church in her self-identification has denoted by 'the gospel' is the message of the crucified one's resurrection. But much theology has proceeded as if the Crucifixion were itself the encompassing burden of the message. . . ."[25] It belongs to the great merit of Jenson's *Systematic Theology* that he gives such prominence to the resurrection. This is done most explicitly in the final section to concern us here, Jenson's brief but pithy chapter on crucifixion in volume I. The resurrection must be taken together with crucifixion as the necessary conclusion and bearer of the meaning, so to speak, of the narrative. The crucifixion is good only when it is dramatically linked with the resurrection (*ST* I, 190). The unity of the crucifixion and the resurrection is a narrative unity. Rather than a unity manufactured in the mills of abstraction, it is a dramatic unity, a unity of the narrative itself. On this basis Jenson criticizes previously popular theories of the atonement such as those of Anselm, Aulén, and Schleiermacher (*ST* I, 186-88). The narrative itself, including its integration into the Old Testament narrative, alone must carry the weight. The following paragraph fairly well "tells the story."

> The Gospel tells a powerful and biblically integrated story of the Crucifixion; this story is just so the story of God's act to bring us back to himself at his own cost, and of our being brought back. There is no other story behind or beyond it that is the real story of what God does to reconcile us, no story of mythic battles or of a deal between God and his Son or of our being moved to live reconciled lives. The Gospel's passion narrative is the authentic and entire account of God's reconciling action and our reconciliation, as events in his life and ours. Therefore what is first and principally required as the Crucifixion's right interpretation is for us to tell this story to one another and to God as a story about him and about ourselves. (*ST* I, 189)

25. Robert W. Jenson, *Systematic Theology,* vol. 1: *The Triune God* (Oxford: Oxford University Press, 1997), p. 179. Hereafter abbreviated *ST,* by volume and page. Italics in quotations are Jenson's.

Postscript

It is fitting, I think, to bring our exposition of Jenson's soteriology to a close here. It is fitting because we have at last arrived almost at the goal where all proper soteriology must end: with the telling of the story, the proclamation of the "naked narrative," stripped of protective abstractions. Jenson's systematic carries through Luther's insistence that the divine is manifest in and through the historical fate of the human Jesus and not outside or above or beyond it. This is a major systematic achievement. If it were carried out to the extent that it reached the pulpit and the altar of the church, it would be a blessing of major proportions.

We must also muster a few critical remarks. In spite of the excellence of Jenson's work, I find myself saying *on the whole*, "almost." Or perhaps I should say "too far." When one builds heavily on the attempt to erase the timelessness of God, one all too easily slips into the tendency to attempt explaining the timelessness away. One goes too far. The systematic threatens to "flatten out" once again into its own variation of a timeless scheme. One reiterates the rejection of timelessness, but nothing "timely" ever happens.

When Martin Luther issued his frightening dictum to Erasmus and stated that God, hidden in majesty, has not bound himself to his word but kept himself free over all things,[26] he was, I think, insisting on the impossibility of simply collapsing God into Jesus. True, not many have followed Luther on this, but it is a critical point ultimately for soteriology and contemporary theology as well. For Luther it springs from his realization that it is simply impossible to bring the "naked God" in his majesty to heel systematically. Indeed, God hidden in majesty actively removes or hides himself from the clutches of our control — our so-called "free choice." There is no solution to this problem in systematic theology or kindred theological disciplines for that matter. The only solution lies in the living proclamation in the present. Yet it must be a timely happening, an actual "break through," not just a systematic assertion that the faith it engenders will always live in the face of temptation.

Like his mentor Karl Barth, Jenson knows all this. On occasion he speaks of these things, but then in the name of the systematic theology he

26. Martin Luther, "The Bondage of the Will," in *Luther's Works*, vol. 33, ed. Philip Watson (1972), p. 140.

seems all too often to forget them, and the systematic theology fights within itself. In Luther's theology the attributes of divinity such as divine necessity, immutability, timelessness, impassibility, and so forth, function as masks of God in his hiddenness. That means that they function on the one hand as wrath, as attack on human pretense, and on the other hand ultimately as comfort, as backup for the proclamation. However, they never simply go away, and a systematic theology can't make them do so. They keep coming back to terrify "the conscience." So much ought to be obvious by now. Attempts to settle accounts with the immutability of God, for instance, are legion. Yet they never finally work, not for lack of erudition usually, but for failure to use the proper weapons.

Luther knew that no one can tear the mask from the face of the hidden God, but he also knew from the eschatological perspective that there was ultimate comfort in the divine names. They provide assurance that in spite of all apparent contingencies, the saving events — the baptism, supper, absolution, and so forth — are the immutable will of God, whatever the cost of such affirmations might be. "If God were not immutable," Luther asks, "who can believe his promises?"[27]

It would seem to me that Jenson's soteriology lacks something of the pathos that comes from a perception of faith's struggle with temptation, with the wrath of God, suffering and death. Soteriology in the New Testament sense has much to do with the death of the old being and the rebirth of the new. But the mention of that in Jenson is rather sparse. In a similar vein, some of the essential aspects of the narrative deserve more emphasis to give the story its clout. There is, for instance, the fact that "we did it," that his own and even finally God deserted him.

Luther's theology is our guide here. There is a frank recognition of a dialectic (for want of a better word), even a contradiction *(precisely because the passage between them is a matter of death and life)* in the predications of God. If one of the paired terms is erased, both are lost. The "mutability" of God in the Son gets its pathos from the fact that the one who won't change nevertheless does so because of the personal union and the *communicatio idiomatum.* The God who can't die nevertheless does so. If one simply erases the immutability systematically, the mutability flattens out to be self-evident. God threatens to become just a patsy who is enriched by sharing our

27. Ibid., 42.

misery. Again, sensitivity to all this is not absent from Jenson's systematic theology. A passage like the following, for instance, catches the eye.

> We may strive to free ourselves of pagan antiquity's metaphysical prejudice, according to which God is intrinsically impassible. But the religious impulse itself, without which we would not worry about God in the first place, will never desist from offense at God's self-presentation as a victim. God must be powerful and sweep all before him, else why do we need him?
>
> No one has seen so deeply here as Martin Luther. Faith is "the conviction of things not seen." Therefore, said Luther, that which is to be believed, God and his goodness, must be hidden. "And it cannot be more deeply hidden than under a contrary object. . . . Thus when God makes alive he does it by killing, when he justifies he does it by making guilty, when he takes into heaven he does it by sending to hell. . . ." God is hidden in the whole course of his history with us but he is doubly — and so salvifically — so hidden precisely as Jesus crucified, in whom are all the treasures of wisdom and knowledge, but hidden. . . ." It is just so that the "conviction" of things not seen must also be the "assurance" of what can only be hoped for. (*ST* I, 234)

Such words would bear a lot of contemplation just by themselves. Is only "pagan antiquity" caught in the trap of this metaphysical prejudice? How does this relate to the "religious impulse" that will never desist from the offense? Are we not all caught? Is this not precisely the reason God hides himself from us in the cross — that there is no "way through" except that the cross be "done" to us, suffering the darkness of the "why have you forsaken me"? This is to say, I expect, that although the movement to make the resurrection more prominent in soteriology is imperative, the cross cannot be left behind. Jenson's soteriology is a fine and important achievement but important questions remain.

Doctrine of Justification and Trinitarian Ontology

TUOMO MANNERMAA

The pleasant task given to me by the editor of the *Festschrift* for Robert Jenson is to view his *Systematic Theology* from the standpoint of a researcher into Luther.[1] My considerations are preliminary for two reasons. First, I have for four semesters given lectures on the first volume of this magnum opus, but I could attend to hardly more than a first reading of the newly published second volume. Second, the *maiestas materiae* in Jenson's work is so overwhelming that it takes an unusually long time to assimilate it. The reader has to be careful not to formulate precipitate assertions. Moreover, I still feel myself a student before this magnificent work.

Nor is it easy to characterize his theology with any specificity. Jenson will not have his systematic theology labeled as "Lutheran theology" (*ST* I, vii). He works out his theology in the context of the *one* church and in the anticipation of the *one* church. He himself asserts that some of his key positions are "reinventions of Orthodox wheels." In some questions he "espouses the Catholic side" (*ST* I, viii).

Yet he also admits that ". . . no one can escape being bent and limited by the division of the church and by his or her particular location in the

1. *Systematic Theology,* vol. I: *The Triune God* (Oxford: Oxford University Press, 1997), and *Systematic Theology,* vol. II, *The Works of God* (Oxford: Oxford University Press, 1999). Hereafter abbreviated *ST,* by volume and page. Italics in quotations are Jenson's unless otherwise noted.

landscape created by the divisions" (*ST* I, viii). Further, ". . . where typically Lutheran and Reformed positions diverge [he is] more likely to draw from the Lutheran side" (*ST* I, viii). Certainly Jenson says in the preface of the second volume of his system that his work can be an offense for the disciples of such theologians as Luther: "But in the time since, I have become more aware of how thoroughly this work dismembers its predecessors and uses the fragments in strange ways, and of the offense and puzzlement this can be for disciples of, say, Thomas or Barth or Palamas or Luther" (*ST* I, vi). As far as I can see, however, the most fundamental structure of Jenson's system bears a close affinity to the fundamental structure of Martin Luther's theology.

I shall take my point of departure from the critical side of Jenson's thought. One of the main themes in his work is his criticism of the *Denkform* of "Mediterranean antiquity." According to this false *Denkform*, eternity and time are contradictory realities. "The relation of eternity to time was grasped by mere negation" (*ST* I, 94). Jenson says that in this discourse, ". . . deity is a quality, which may be analyzed as immunity to time plus whatever are its necessary conditions" (*ST* I, 94). God was defined with time-denying predicates as "immutability" and, centrally, "impassibility," that is, immunity to suffering and temporal-historical contingency in general.

According to Jenson, the assimilation of this *Denkform* of Mediterranean antiquity has been a great disaster for the history of Christian theology. For him, the real presence of God in human history, his "historicity" and his "passibility," are decisive. It can be said that Jenson's own *Denkform* has very close relation indeed with the Lutheran maxim *finitum capax infiniti.*

For Jenson, as for Luther, the concrete reality of the historical Jesus and the whole narrative of God's history with mankind *(Heilsgeschichte)* are the foundation on which a theological ontology as Trinitarian ontology must be conceptualized. In other words, narrative proclamation, that is, the theology of the Word, and theological ontology as Trinitarian ontology join together in a relation of mutuality. Jenson says in his prolegomena: "What we have rushed into is thus the doctrine of Trinity, and our haste but reproduces that which took the church to this doctrine as her first deliberately defined dogma. The present, here much unclarified, point: to attend theologically to the resurrection of Jesus is to attend to the triune God. To attend to the gospel in its character as witness to a determinate reality is to worship in trinitarian specificity: in petition and praise to the Father with the Son in the Spirit. It is by failure intentionally to cast its theology in the space determined by these coordinates that much Protestant theology slips its object" (*ST* I, 13).

The reciprocity of the theology of Word and a theological (Trinitarian) ontology can be clearly seen, for example, in how Jenson combines the ancient catholic rule, *lex orandi lex credendi,* with the Reformation's rule (as he formulates it), *lex proclamandi lex credendi.*

According to the catholic principle, regularities of the church's communal life of prayer must govern the church's formulation of her belief. Central among historical instances of obedience to this rule is the development of a conceptually elaborated doctrine of Trinity with all its ontological implications. According to the Reformation's rule, theology must be understood "as critical reflection interior to the church's mission of proclamation" (*ST* I, 13). Theology must think out its issues in such a way that it guards the proclamation in its authenticity. It was precisely for this reason that the doctrine of justification was formulated to state the authenticity, the unique character of the proclamation, that is, "to state its *lex.*"

Both Trinitarian ontology and the doctrine of justification (or the theology of the Word) are valid and necessary. The *Reformation's* doctrine of justification and proclamation is only an explication of the *catholic* rule. "Reformation theology merely pointed to one relatively neglected aspect of the agreed situation . . ." (*ST* I, 13). The theology of the Word, in its core the doctrine of justification, is inseparably linked with a Trinitarian ontology.

Jenson's doctrine of justification (see *ST* II, 290-301) is, thus, situated primarily within the doctrine of the Holy Trinity: "What then is justification? It is the underived event of communal faithfulness *in* God, as this is set free by the Spirit and is actual in the reality of the incarnate Son. That we are justified means that this history is *not only God's but is made to be ours also*" (*ST* II, 301, italics mine). According to Jenson, the three doctrines of justification, "hermeneutical," "transformational," and "Pauline," all have a common referent, namely, a triune event: "For there indeed is one thing that the three doctrines of 'justification' jointly interpret. . . . Their common referent, it is here suggested, is a triune event, a mode of the divine persons' mutual life" (*ST* II, 300).

How is it possible for Jenson to define justification as a "triune event . . . that is made to be ours also"? What makes such a definition possible, I think, is that he formulates his solution *with the help of Luther's doctrine of justification.*

Characteristic of Luther's doctrine of justification is its consequent Christological and coterminously Trinitarian orientation. Christ himself is *both* God's favor *(favor),* that is, forgiveness of sins, *and* gift *(donum).* "Gift" here is understood as the ontic presence of God and of his divine nature together with all of its properties. In faith as such Christ is present both as *favor* and *donum.* In union with Christ the Christian has both forgiveness of sins and an actual participation in the divine nature and its properties: this participation occurs centrally in the divine light (which donates a new understanding) and in agape-love (which creates a new will). Jenson agrees with this doctrine.

As to the idea of Christ as gift *(donum),* Jenson says:

> As the soul is united with the gospel it hears, it is united with Christ whose word this gospel is, so that the two become one moral subject: "Faith . . . unites the soul with Christ, as bride with her bridegroom. From this marriage it follows . . . that Christ and the soul have everything together: what Christ has belongs to the believing soul and what the soul has belongs to Christ" (Luther, WA 1, 20, 25). This claim is not intended as rhetoric or trope but as a proposition about an ontic actuality. An unexpressed premise, clearly stated in other writings, radicalizes the traditional *theologoumenon:* God's moral predicates, communicated in his Word, are not different from God himself. Thus, when God in Christ forms us by his Word to the virtues displayed in it, He forms us to Himself; He, indeed, becomes the metaphysical form of the believers' "humanity," the defining shape that makes these entities human. (*ST* II, 295-96)

There is no doubt that Jenson follows Luther in his interpretation of Christ as gift *(donum)* received through faith. Faith is understood here as a real participation in God, and such participation occurs equally in the Holy Spirit as well as both in and with Christ. Justification from the perspective of *donum* is clearly a triune event, but this characterization does not yet capture the complete meaning of justification. Justification from the perspective of *favor Christi,* that is, from the perspective of forgiveness and of the abolition of the wrath of God, also has its foundation wholly in the triune life. Jenson treats this forensic side of justification not in reference to Luther but to Jonathan Edwards, though he asserts that Edwards agrees with Luther in this matter. Jenson says, "And we must here recur to the forensic quality of justification. We may relax our adherence to Luther and let Jonathan Edwards join him in drawing the fact: when the Father judges the believer and says that he or she is righteous, the Father is simply acting as a just judge who finds the facts — about the only moral subject that actually exists in the case, Christ in the believer and the believer in Christ" (*ST* II, 296).

In the theology of Luther, the presence of Christ *(inhabitatio Christi)* and the imputation of the merit of Christ are connected in quite the same way as disclosed in the quotation from Edwards above. The following texts of Luther link together into a coherent logical structure — *inhabitatio, deificatio, imputatio* — and the general Trinitarian context.

Luther treats first the generation of Christ from the Father, the incarnation, and the deification of man, going on to assert that God says that his favor rests on all that Christ is and does. Thus, you can see on one hand the favor of God and his whole heart in Christ, and, on the other hand, you can see Christ in the heart and in the favor of God. Both of them are in each other in the greatest profundity and highest sublimity. Further, because Christ, the beloved child, with all of his words and deeds is nevertheless yours, you are also certainly in the same favor in which God holds Christ. You are as deep in God's heart as is Christ, and God's favor, God's own heart, is just as deep in you as it is in Christ. You, God, and his beloved Son are entirely in you; and you are entirely in him, so that altogether you form one thing *(eyn ding):* God, Christ and you.[2]

2. "Als sihestu, das Got mit diesen worten Christum ynn sich zeucht und sich ynn Christum mit dem, das seyn wolgefallen sey ynn allem, was Christus thut, und widderumb mit den selbigen worten beyde sich selbs und Christum seynen lieben son ausschuttet uber uns und sich ynn uns geust und uns ynn sich zeucht, das er gantz und gar vermenschet wird und wyr gantz und gar vergottet werden. Wie so? Also, weyl Gott spricht, Es gefalle yhm wol, was Christus ist und thut. So furen dich die wort dahyn, das du Gotts wolgefallen und seyn gantz hertz ynn Christo sihest ynn allen seynen worten und wercken, und widderumb Christum sihest, ym hertzen und wolgefallen Gottes, und sind die beyde ynn eynander auffs aller tieffest und hohest, und kan dyr des keyns feylen, weyl Gott nicht liegen kan. Weytter, weyl denn Christus das liebe und angeneme kind ynn solchem wolgefallen und ym hertzen Gottes gefasset mit all seym reden und thun deyn ist und dyr damit dienet, wie er selbst sagt, so bistu gewislich auch ynn dem selbigen wolgefallen und eben so tieff ym hertzen Gotts als Christus und widderumb Gotts wolgefallen und hertz eben so tieff ynn dyr, als ynn Christo, das nu du und Gott

In this text the doctrine of justification with its central notions of favor and gift has clearly been understood within a Trinitarian framework, even though the pneumatology has not been made explicit. The favor of God rests on the believer because Christ, with all of his words and deeds, indwells the Christian, and God's favor rests on Christ. This conception means that both *favor Dei* and *donum Dei* are necessary, logical conditions for the understanding of justification. Therefore, Luther's doctrine of justification cannot be understood outside of the context of his Trinitarian ontology.[3] Jenson's thesis that all three doctrines of justification — the hermeneutical, the transformative, and the Pauline — have a triune event as their common referent is supported by Luther's conception.

I would not assert, however, that no differences obtain between Jenson's and Luther's doctrines of the Holy Trinity. Jenson holds a complicated ecumenical doctrine, whereas Luther's conception is clearly more Augustinian, for Luther emphasizes in the triune communion the unity of the one essence of God. Consequently, communion in the church is understood analogously as participation in the unity of the divine nature (2 Pet. 1:4), a unity in which all members of the church participate.[4] His differ-

---

sampt seynem lieben sone ynn dyr gantz und gar ist, un du gantz und gar ynn yhm bist, und alles mit eynander eyn ding ist, Gott, Christus und du" (Martin Luther, *W.A.* 20, 229.28-230.10).

3. See my study *Hat Luther eine trinitarische Ontologie? Luther und die trinitarische Tradition: Ökumenische und philosophische Perspektiven* (Erlangen, 1994), pp. 43-60.

4. Unity both in the triune and in the ecclesial communion can clearly be seen in the following passage from a sermon of Luther (1528), where he interprets John 17:21: "Da ruhret er abermal den hohen artickel von seiner gottheit, den wir droben ettlich mal gehandlet, und setzet sich und den Vater zum gleichnis und exempel zuverkleren, was er für eine einigkeit meine. Ich und du sind eines (wil er sagen) jnn einem gottlichen wesen und maiestet. Dem selbigem exempel nach sollen sie unternander auch eines sein und dasselbige also, das eben die selbige einigkeit jnn uns eines sey, das ist jnn mir und dir eingeleibet, summa, das sie alle eines und eitel eines sein jnn uns beiden, ja so gar ein kuche, das sie alles haben, was du und ich vermugen, also das wir auch mit genossen werden der Gottlichen natur, wie S. Petrus sagt. ii Petri i. Denn ob wol der Vater und Christus auff ein ander hoher unbegreifliche weise eines sind des gottlichen wesens halben, so haben wir doch solchs alles, das es unser ist und sein geniessen. . . . Summa, du kanst keinen Christen verachten, schmehen, verfolgen odder gewallt thun, noch widderumb ehren und wolthun, du hasts gott selbs gethan. . . . Denn Gott hatt es alles was er hat an den Herrn Christum gehenget, Christus aber an seine braut; so henget ein jglicher Christen an der selbigen als ein geliedmas, Und ist

ence from the Eastern doctrine, which takes its point of departure from a consideration of the three persons of the Godhead, is, thus, not as profound as could be supposed, for Luther understands the unity of the divine nature as the unity of the divine agape-love,[5] and love is a personal notion.

One need not analyze in more detail the differences and similarities between Luther's and Jenson's doctrines of the Trinity. One issue, I hope, has nevertheless become clear: for both of them the doctrine of justification can be understood only in the context of a Trinitarian ontology. Doctrines of justification have as their common referent "a triune event."

---

alles jnn einander geschlossen als eine keten und machet einen gantzen runden zirckel, ja einen lieblichen schonen krantz" (Martin Luther, *W.A.* 28, 183.26-184.34).

5. Unity of the Holy Spirit is agape-love as the nerve of the whole Christian religion: "Hoc enim est idem sapere, non sua quaerere sed quae aliorum, ut Ephe. 5. docet. Hic enim affectus spiritualis est nervus totius Christianae religionis, sine quo subsistere nequeat, quem alibi vocat unitatem spiritus . . . " (Martin Luther, *W.A.* 7, 484.6-19).

Robert W. Jenson's Theology of History

JEREMY IVE

I. Introduction

As a historian by training, and now a parish priest, coming, not least through reading Robert W. Jenson's many published (and some unpublished) writings, to see the importance of the doctrine of the Trinity, I am profoundly in his debt. My response to his work as it relates to the theology of history is a critique from the inside, of one committed to the same enterprise of promoting a radical reorientation of life and thought along Trinitarian lines: a disciple, like him, of the "Person of the Future."[1]

II. Jenson's Account of the Grand Narrative

Jenson's theology of history is based on the grand narrative of the gospel centered on the person of Jesus Christ.[2] From the accounts of creation

1. Full references are in my unpublished M.Phil. thesis "The God of Faith" (University of London, 1995). It will be cited below simply as "Ive." The thesis was completed before the publication of Jenson's *Systematic Theology*, vol. I: *The Triune God* (Oxford: Oxford University Press, 1997), and his *Systematic Theology*, vol. II, *The Works of God* (Oxford: Oxford University Press, 1999). Hereafter abbreviated *ST*, by volume and page. Italics in quotations are Jenson's unless otherwise noted.

2. Ive, p. 76. In this sense, it cuts across the modernist and the postmodernist accounts alike. The best overall account of the grand narrative as Jenson sees it is in his *Story and Promise: A Brief Theology of the Gospel about Jesus* (Philadelphia: Fortress Press, 1982).

on, the grand narrative is not a mythic account, with purely ontological, a-temporal claims, but rather a purposive entity with a history (*ST* II, 10-11, 14, 318-19).

Adam and Eve are those human participants in this history, called into being by God's address who respond appropriately in the vocative.[3] They are the first historical human beings to whom a mandate, (borrowing the convenient Chinese phrase) the "mandate of heaven," is given (*ST* II, 62-63). It is this mandate that constitutes a human polity (*ST* II, 82-83). This gives them both embodiment, which is more than physical but also ethical availability to one another,[4] and language, the possibility of future orientation. This mandate brings into being the first true human community. Humankind is "one diachronically extended community" that has a sinful character, and Adam and Eve "are compelled to posit a 'fall' of humankind, occurring within created time," since they were the first community of our ancestors who (consciously) disobeyed God (*ST* II, 150).

This human community is made possible in anticipation of the incarnation and is made identifiable as one human community by Jesus' life and death for all (*ST* II, 104). This is in turn possible only through the only true choice and determination: that of the triune God (*ST* II, 107). To draw on an insight of Jonathan Edwards: "precisely the work of *redemption* [Jenson's italics], just as it occurs in the actual event of Christ, is the purpose of creation" (*ST* II, 20). This is made possible by the tri-unity of God where those created as respondents in that communion can also be personal (*ST* II, 96). This community with one another gives space as the "*dramatic location*" of the persons of the Trinity (*ST* II, 98). The incarnation is thereby not simply a remedy but also the provision of the very conditions for participation in the divine community, according to God's intention (*ST* I, 72; II, 19). It is through the "dramatic coherence" of the life of the incarnate Son that our self-identity, as human beings, is possible (*ST* II, 319).

As Wolfhart Pannenberg also argues, the incarnation is in turn retro-

3. *ST* II, 58-61. Jenson sees Adam and Eve as historical figures, albeit within the context of a process of historical development, that is, within a particular hominid (Neolithic?) context. Certainly there would already have been death and indeed all the hazards of nature, but what characterizes Adam and Eve is not that they are the first humans as such, but rather the first leaders of the first human community clearly to receive and then reject the mandate of God.

4. *ST* II, 110; Ive, pp. 93-95.

spectively dependent on the resurrection:[5] "The Resurrection was the *executing* [Jenson's italics] of the triune God's unity with himself."[6] Jenson, like Karl Barth, sees human life as bounded necessarily by death. Death is not something introduced adventitiously through sin; it is intrinsic to the human condition (*ST* II, 75, 326-31). Jesus, by dying, accepts these conditions and is thus truly human, and the resurrection does not bypass this acceptance but rather raises it to the center of all reality: that at the heart of all things is the One who has died and is now risen (*ST* I, 219): "If there is such a God as the gospel presents, he is invested in historical particularity" (*ST* II, 117). The risen Jesus is thus seen to share the very identity of God himself.[7]

The identity of God in the person of the risen Jesus can be read both backward and forward from the event of the resurrection. It can be read back to the act of creation (*ST* II, 14, 68, 91). The defining event, above all, is the deliverance of the people of Israel from slavery in Egypt. The same God that redeems Israel is the One by whose power Jesus is raised from the dead.[8] There is a chain of connectedness in the prophetic witness that runs forward from the Exodus to that of the Christ event itself, culminating in the resurrection:[9] ". . . the Son appears as a narrative pattern of Israel's created human story before he can appear as an individual Israelite within that story" (*ST* I, 141). The resurrection is in turn brought forward to us by the witness of the apostles.[10] Scriptural witness, which is what this is, is not therefore, *pace* Rudolf Bultmann, simply to be understood as an existential appeal (*ST* I, 167-71; II, 309-11). It is rooted in God's concrete dealings with a historically particular people in the Hebrew Bible or Old Testament, and in the historical events that surround the resurrection of Jesus[11] and the community to which these give rise in the New Testament.[12]

5. Ive, p. 130.

6. Robert Jenson, *Unbaptized God: The Basic Flaw in Ecumenical Theology* (Philadelphia: Fortress Press, 1973), p. 140. See Ive, p. 55.

7. *ST* I, 47; II, 70-71, 132; Ive, p. 54.

8. *ST* I, 42-44, 49; Ive, pp. 49-51.

9. *ST* I, 63-71; II, 69-72; Ive, pp. 54-55.

10. Ive, pp. 89-91.

11. Although Jenson differs from Pannenberg in not seeing the resurrection as susceptible to straightforward historical investigation and empirical proof because the very discipline of historical research is too secularized for this to be possible (Ive, p. 83).

12. Ive, pp. 56-57.

The narrative needs to identify God in order to be the expression of the community with whom God has identified (*ST* I, 57-60): one cannot have the latter without the former. Jenson is committed to the use of historical-critical techniques, and indeed he sees them as part of the heritage of Martin Luther, in our taking Scripture seriously;[13] but this should be with a view to obtaining a fuller historical appreciation of the text rather than of evacuating it of any concrete reference and reducing it to mere proclamation. Far from the "eschatological" and the "historical" being contradictions, Jenson affirms that the resurrection (which for Bultmann is part of the "eschatological" content of the proclamation and therefore not "historical") is intrinsic to the narrative of Jesus — apart from the resurrection, there is nothing in the story of Jesus to ground faith.[14]

Thus, what forces Jenson's concern to preserve the historical concreteness of Scripture is his eschatological vision. The eschaton is not the vacuous sublimation of history in the eternal present, a view Jenson charges to Bultmann (*ST* I, 166), the early Barth,[15] and even Pannenberg (*ST* II, 310 n. 4). Rather, it is characterized by our encounter and identification with the risen Jesus. The future is to be known as that which is and can be centered on him (*ST* II, 317-19, 326). Jesus did not (*pace* Barth) rise into the eternal present, but into the future that awaits us of a new heaven and earth patterned according to the personality of the risen Jesus. Heaven is no more and no less than that future toward which the Spirit draws all creation and in which Jesus is located at the right hand of his Father (*ST* II, 123). Our expectation of his return is for a specific encounter toward which all history is heading and in relation to which history is being transformed. It will be *Jesus,* not Nero, Attila, Hitler or Stalin — or even Gandhi — in whose resurrection we shall share in a publicly experienceable way.[16] Our meeting with the risen Jesus will at once be the culmination of history and the possibility of a new narrative. The hoped-for One will have arrived, but his arrival will not thereby be the end of hoping (the antinomy

13. Ive, p. 91. Jenson describes historical research as "*secularized* repentance" ("An Hermeneutical Apology for Systematics," *dialog* 4 [Fall 1965]: 271).

14. *ST* I, 57-60. Although, as noted below, there is an ambiguity in that Jenson, like Bultmann, also has not escaped the tendency of portraying the death of Jesus as the *terminus ad quem* of his historical identifiability.

15. *ST* I, 170; II, 121, 135-38, 178 n. 53; Ive, p. 109.

16. Ive, pp. 54-55.

of hope)[17] but rather the experience of love in and through our inclusion in the life of the Trinity.

It is inclusion in the life of the Trinity that constitutes the church. Jenson refers with approval to Luther's suggestion that the church was founded in paradise with the original mandate to Adam and Eve (*ST* II, 76-77). He has a strong understanding of the church as the body of Jesus: as Jesus has gone into the future, the church constitutes his presence with us now. At the same time, the church is the messianic community brought about by the demonstration of the person of the Spirit.[18] At Pentecost, the Spirit opens a time for the church by descending eschatologically without yet "raising all the dead and ending this age" (*ST* II, 178-79). In baptism[19] and the Lord's Supper[20] Jesus is, according to Jenson's Lutheran understanding, physically present with us not by the inward piety of believers nor by the fiat of a priest, but by the sheer promise that the exercise of the mandates of those two sacraments realize.[21] The sacraments name and bear witness to the irreducible historicity of the gospel message: it is not a proposition or outcome that can derive from our situation but a historical given with which we are presented.[22] The *totus Christus* is that which in the beginning made sense of the rest of creation from the end, where Israel spoke from heaven "within which she was already in full possession of her destiny" (*ST* II, 159). The church thus exists in and by *anticipation* since it is only at the last day that the church can be gathered (*ST* II, 171-72). The beginning and end are one event to achieve "the sole object of eternal election . . . Jesus with his people, the *totus Christus*" (*ST* II, 175; see also 151). It is thus that Jesus, as the head, surrenders himself to the Father, and the church, as it comes to recognize its betrayal of Christ, becomes the *totus Christus* through its complicity in its sacrifice (*ST* I, 191-92). The church thus is enhypostatic in Christ.[23]

17. *ST* I, 220; II, 321; Ive, pp. 83-84. The antinomy of love is related (*ST* II, 333-34).

18. *ST* I, 189. As Metropolitan John Zizioulas puts it: "it is *instituted* by the Son and *constituted* by the Spirit" (*Being as Communion: Studies in Personhood and the Church* [Crestwood: St Vladimir's Seminary Press, 1985], p. 140).

19. *ST* II, 187-88, 195-97; Ive, pp. 99-100.

20. *ST* II, 185-86, 355; Ive, pp. 100-101.

21. Ive, pp. 98-99.

22. Ive, p. 62.

23. Ive, p. 89. This sits curiously with the notion of the church as betrayer, since Jenson sees Mary Jesus' mother as "the churchly actuality of this enhypostasis" ("An Attempt to Think about Mary," *dialog* 31.4 [Fall 1992]: 263).

The church therefore, as the body of Christ, constitutes within itself, by virtue of that identity as *totus Christus,* the new reality by which the whole universe is to be transformed. The church is not just the community of the saved but also the saving community through which God works redemptively in the world.[24]

The transformation of the universe, as the bringing of the future into the present, is distinctively the work of the Holy Spirit. Through the Spirit, God "*anticipates* his future and so possesses it. . . ." (*ST* II, 121). The Spirit is "the novelty of a genuine narrative," the One who brings about the resurrection, "the great occurrence of dramatic causality in God. . . ."[25] Liturgy is the expression of this work. Liturgy is to be contrasted with violence in that, unlike the latter, it is not the causal, externally defined impact of one monadic entity on another, but rather our inclusion into the life of a loving community.[26] The promise of the gospel is "inclusion in the triune community by virtue of union with Christ. . . ." (*ST* II, 311). The work of the Holy Spirit is what draws all things forward to their consummation.[27] The eschaton, or kingdom, will be characterized by beauty, or, as Jenson loves to note, by Jonathan Edwards's vision of perfect musical harmony into which the divine conversation finally resolves itself.[28] The final judgment brings God's people into "exact concert with the triune community and its righteousness" as this is defined by Christ's death and resurrection (*ST* II, 326; see also 300-301). Thus will the great eschatological transformation take place whereby the people of God will directly be Christ's availability for her members, and Christ will directly be our availability to one another.[29]

Here we need to retrace our steps and look again at the temporal framework within which Jenson sees this grand narrative unfold.

24. Ive, p. 89.

25. *ST* I, 160; Ive, pp. 131-34.

26. Ive, p. 96.

27. Ive, pp. 131-32.

28. Ive, pp. 97, 133.

29. *ST* II, 240. See also II, 355. This raises all the problems of the direct identification of the church as the *totus Christus,* since it is in danger, as is suggested below, of reducing Christ to the outcome of the historical process rather than being constitutive of it.

III. Time and the Temporality of God

Time for Jenson is not only the direction of the created order but part of the constitution of divine being itself, as he puts it, "the arrow of God's eternity, like the arrow of causal time, does not reverse itself" (*ST* I, 218). The plot of salvation history, which in turn culminates all human (and indeed nonhuman) history, is "the movement of divine life itself,"[30] or as he puts it still more radically, "God is the temporality of the world."[31] Further, God not only provides for us in his being the possibility of our being in time, he creates by making space for us in his being (*ST* II, 46-48). Jenson distinguishes between what he calls the "Augustinian" view of time, in which time is understood as the distention of consciousness: "real time," and the "Aristotelian" understanding in which time is the external relation of one material state of affairs with another: "imaginary time."[32] He suggests a resolution of the dichotomy between these two positions by the notion of conversation between the three Persons of the Trinity.[33]

Jenson's understanding of the Trinity is thoroughly temporal,[34] that is, he does not see time as incompatible with divinity but, on the contrary, as the way God is, as he puts it: "The specificity of the triune God is not that he is three, but that he occupies each role of time as a *persona dramatis*" (*ST* I, 89). The history of the world is enclosed in the triune being of

30. Ive, p. 134.

31. Robert Jenson, "The Triune God," in R. W. Jenson and C. E. Braaten, eds., *Christian Dogmatics,* vol. 1 (Philadelphia: Fortress Press, 1978), p. 168; Ive, p. 63.

32. *ST* II, 29-34. J. M. E. McTaggert argued that the determination of time with any sense of past, present, and future (which he called the "A-series") was not possible in any absolute, "de-tensed" sense (which he called the "B-series"). See John C. Yates, *The Timelessness of God* (Lanham, Md.: University Press of America, 1990), pp. 66-67.

33. *ST* II, 34-35. Robert Richard Russell has argued against an earlier statement of Jenson's position that he conflated the two understandings without sufficiently distinguishing them. "Is the Triune God the Basis for Physical Time?" *Center for Theology and Natural Sciences Bulletin* 11.1 (Winter 1991): 7-9.

34. In this he is far more consistent than Pannenberg, the theologian whom he otherwise is closest to in the structure of this theological system. Jenson charges Pannenberg with "historical-idealism" and that he, like Barth, finally reduces futurity to the eternal present ("Review of Pannenberg's *Systematic Theology,* vol. 2," *First Things* 53 [May 1995]: 60-62; *ST* II, 310 n. 4).

God. The created order comes into being and takes its direction through the divine conversation between the Father, Son, and Holy Spirit:[35] "God the Father is the sheer given of creation; God the Spirit is the perfecting Freedom that animates creation; God the Son is the mediator of creation" (*ST* II, 25, 45, 48). The Father as the past is bracketed with the Holy Spirit as the power of the future while the Son is the spacious present between them.[36]

The question may be asked: How can the great conversation, which makes time possible, take place if the persons themselves are elements in the temporal process? If a drama is to take place, the actors cannot themselves be the stage, or the stage properties, although they can define and shape it and make sense of the whole. Jenson has rejected Pannenberg's suggestion that the persons of the Trinity can be understood as persons in the sense of being three centers of consciousness. This moves him strongly to the Hegelian understanding of the Son as the "self" of the Father, and the Spirit as the process of unfolding consciousness. Certainly, the Western tradition brings with it the valuable insight of the persons of the Trinity as subsisting relations, but the danger is that the personhood of each of the three persons is obscured.[37] Ambiguities in both Jenson's Christology and pneumatology have implications for his theology of history.[38]

The ambiguity in Jenson's Christology consists in the fact that the Son is at once to be regarded as the bracket (in the God event) between the Father and the Spirit and as the One whose personality has universal significance as the ultimate lover.[39] It is in this sense that Jenson states that Christ as a participant in human history (as the One who, *sub specie resurrectionis,* is shown to be one of the Trinity) "is definitive for all participants" (*ST* I, 138). Jenson turns Augustine around, with the Son as the bond of love between the Father and the Spirit, rather than the Augustinian view of the Spirit as the bond between the Father and the Son. The incarnation, then, seen in the light of the resurrection, has a place-holding role: it marks out the boundary between the Father and the Spirit by constituting the distinct personality of the Son in the God-Man Jesus of Naza-

35. Robert Jenson, "Creation as a Triune Act," *Word and World* 2.1 (Winter 1982): 38-42.

36. *ST* I, 218-19; II, 25-28, 45-48, 173, 338-39, 347; Ive, pp. 124-25.

37. Ive, p. 131.

38. See Ive, pp. 144-45.

39. Ive, p. 82.

reth.[40] As Jenson puts it: "what identifies [the risen Jesus] to the Father in the triune life . . . is the life lived from Mary's womb to Golgotha."[41] Further: "The Son speaks the actuality, the givenness by the Father, of the purposiveness which the creature has by the Spirit . . . the Son has his own individual entity *within* created time." The implications for Jenson's theology of history are thereby to confine Jesus to the "evangelical events"[42] since it is by these that Jesus is identified as one "possessing a mother, a narratable story and a historically placeable executioner" (*ST* I, 201; see also 219). This then tends to play down his role in creation and, ironically, in the eschaton, because the eschaton then takes on a strange quality of déjà vu, almost a replay of the resurrection (*ST* II, 26-28; see also 318-19).

The ambiguity in Jenson's pneumatology arises from a conflation of the role of the Spirit with the state of affairs that the Spirit is bringing about.[43] This is certainly an ambiguity inherited from Karl Barth and, more profoundly, from Georg Hegel and, ultimately, Augustine. The identification of the Spirit with God's futurity tends to detract from the past or present work of the Spirit in the world, as well as from the Father and the Son in the future. The latter consideration tends also to blunt the force of Jenson's own solution to the antinomy of hope in terms of love (*ST* I, 220). As he strongly

40. A position that moves him toward Hegel, whose position is characterized by Douglas Farrow as an "inverted Eutychianism" ("Robert Jenson's *Systematic Theology*, Three Responses," *International Journal of Systematic Theology* 1.1 [March 1999]: 90).

41. *ST* I, 200; see also II, 61, 74, 99. The mention of Golgotha as the *terminus ad quem* for the identifiable life of Jesus is curious. It demonstrates a deep ambiguity in Jenson's attitude to the historicity of the resurrection. Jesus' identifiability is completed by his death, but he is at the same time the "risen One." The "recollectable Jesus" is the risen One, but Jenson then comments that he cannot, "after all, be quite congruent with the 'historical Jesus'" ("Once More the Jesus of History and the Christ of Faith," *dialog* 11 [Spring 1972]: 121; see Ive, p. 91, n. 436). Jenson "somewhat hesitantly" affirms the empty tomb (*ST* II, 201). The distinction between the "historical" aspect of Jesus (culminating in his death) and the "eschatological" character of the risen One still remains. The resurrection "liberates" Jesus from history (*ST* II, 181), but it is the Son's "whole life" from his conception by the Holy Spirit to his ascension that "in fact" founds the church (*ST* II, 178-83, 286-87), and Jenson affirms, *pace* Bultmann, that Jesus "in his full historical reality of birth, death and resurrection" is the Word of God (*ST* I, 171).

42. Robert Jenson, *The Triune Identity: God according to the Gospel* (Philadelphia: Fortress Press, 1982), pp. 106-7; Jenson, "The Triune God," p. 137; Ive, p. 64.

43. *ST* II, 347; Ive, p. 134.

emphasizes, it is in the person of Jesus as the "person of the future" that the final coincidence of love and freedom will be realized.[44] In this respect Jesus, as much as the Spirit, surely bears the distinctive character of futurity.

God cannot simply be identified with the historical process since that would be to divinize the historical process and ironically rob it of its transcendence. As the historical process is the succession of past, present, and future, by characterizing the persons of the Trinity as this succession (albeit with the primacy of the future over the past) Jenson runs precisely this risk.

IV. A Trinitarian Understanding of History

The identification of the persons of the Trinity with past, present, and future, which Jenson advances in a powerfully suggestive and systematic way cannot, for the considerations advanced above, finally do justice to the engagement of all three persons in the historical narrative over time. Nevertheless, it takes us a considerable way forward in our understanding of the engagement of God in the historical process. There is some point in identifying the Father with the past since that is where our calling comes from, and the Spirit with the future, since it is through the operation of the Spirit that things are taken forward, and Christ with the present, since that is where we encounter the truth and the coherence of the world; but it is a question of whether Jenson does not finally reduce the operation of the persons *to* the historical process itself.

The *whole* divine *perichoresis*, the making space for one another by all the persons of the Trinity, needs to be seen as running through history from beginning to end and cannot be reduced to it. Jenson's account of history falls at both these fences. First, by focusing on the temporal roles he limits our understanding of the engagement of all three persons universally at every point in the grand narrative. Second, there is a problem in that the transcendence of God's actions in history is always, in his account, in danger of being reduced to the historical process itself. Jenson avoids the latter problem by stressing the uniqueness of Jesus and the transcendent character of the resurrection, but these in turn create the new problem:

44. Robert Jenson, "Appeal to the Person of the Future," in R. W. Jenson and C. E. Braaten, eds., *The Futurist Option* (New York: Newman Press, 1970).

How does one relate the man of Nazareth to history from the beginning to the end, and not simply to the "evangelical events"? We can see the whole of history *sub specie resurrectionis* it is true, but that does not seem to express the full universality of the One through whom all things were made.

The rock to build on is what Jenson calls the "christological determination of all creation," a notion that he develops in the context of his exposition of Colossians 1.[45] It is in the fully human Jesus that the personality of God is known, and the personality of Jesus is none other than the personality of God.[46] As Jenson puts it: "nature does not subsist apart from [his] personality."[47] Further, as Jenson notes: "he is the *content* of the proclamation whose *power* is the Spirit and whose *source* is the Father" (*ST* I, 71). It is important that the Trinitarian relations themselves, understood in a mutual way,[48] provide the framework for this in order to avoid the pitfalls of falling into the dangers of Logos theology, which, as Jenson warns, move us to subordinationism.[49]

A historian needs to hold in tension the synchronic and diachronic, and both of these with a sense of ultimacy. In a similar way we can see in Jesus and the Spirit the relation of the coherence of all things with the dynamic, which means that things can truly be transformed as creation responds to the call of the Father. This makes sense of the distinct identities of the Son and the Spirit without reducing either to the futurity that, as has been suggested earlier, should consist of the operation of all three persons acting together. It also makes sense of the mutual interdependence of all three persons, which Jenson suggests very powerfully, and relates the economy of the Trinity directly to the inner-Trinitarian relations, without running the danger of directly reducing the Trinity *to* the historical process, as Jenson's strongly tensed approach is in danger of doing.

45. Jenson, "Creation as a Triune Act," p. 41. See *ST* I, 139.

46. This is the doctrine of the *enhypostasia,* a cognate of the terminology developed in the sixth century most specially by Leontius of Jerusalem (See P. R. Gray, *The Defence of Chalcedon in the East (451-533)* [Leiden: E. J. Brill, 1979]) and subsequently formalized by Maximus Confessor and John of Damascus. Jenson puts Maximus's insight as "Christ's human history happens because his divine history happens, and not vice versa" — but this needs to be thoroughly worked through (*ST* I, 138).

47. "The Holy Spirit," in *Christian Dogmatics,* vol. 2, p. 172.

48. See figs. 2 and 3 in Jenson, *The Triune Identity,* pp. 143, 147.

49. Jenson, *The Triune Identity,* chap. 3, pp. 53-102.

V. Conclusion

Jenson's temporal account of the Trinity offers an immense boost to our understanding of God's engagement with the world in the historical process. Resolutely, and one might say, unfashionably, he has consistently urged upon the church to take seriously the grand narrative that it has at its root centered on the resurrection of Jesus. This forces us not the least to take time and temporality seriously and to be open, as an embodied community, to the work of the Spirit as the power of the future.

The temporal account, which itself is so powerfully suggestive, is at the same time very problematical. By identifying the Persons of the Trinity as elements *within* the historical process rather than constitutive *of* it, there is a danger of reducing the Trinity *to* the historical process, as Hegel has done. The gap between Hegel and Jenson in this respect is the historical particularity of the risen Christ, but the fundamental problematic is the same.[50]

Drawing on insights of Jenson himself, an alternative path might be to take seriously the "christological determination of creation" within the framework of Trinitarian relations. Jesus as the "Person of the Future" is the one through whom all things were made and toward whom they are heading. The Father and the Spirit, as the givers of the ultimate and the historical, are coordinate with the Son. Through the coordinate relation, thus, of all three persons, our understanding of the irreducible transcendence of their joint operation in history from beginning to end is secured.

50. As Jenson puts it: "Hegel's only real fault was that he confused himself with the last judge; but that is quite a fault" (*The Knowledge of Things Hoped For: The Sense of Theological Discourse* [Oxford: Oxford University Press, 1969], p. 233 n. 327).

Is Pentecost a Peer of Easter? Scripture, Liturgy, and the *Proprium* of the Holy Spirit

ROBERT LOUIS WILKEN

In the first volume of his *Systematic Theology* Robert Jenson raises a question posed by Augustine of Hippo, whom he calls "Western theology's founder." In his work *On the Trinity* Augustine had discussed the vexing problem of how to understand John 4:24, "God is Spirit." Augustine knew, as other early Christian thinkers had known, that scriptural usage of the term "spirit" put certain difficulties in the way of the church's effort to work out a coherent and consistent understanding of the Holy Spirit. The term Spirit in the Scriptures can be used for "the triad as a whole" *(universaliter)* but is also used specifically *(proprie)* to refer to the Holy Spirit whom, he adds, we understand to be "not the triad but in the triad."[1]

Augustine's question, as Jenson knows well, cut to the very heart of the church's understanding of the triune God. In 393 as a young priest Augustine had been asked to give a series of talks explaining the creed before the African bishops gathered at Hippo. When he came to the third article on the Holy Spirit, he said that "commentators on the Scriptures," his description of theologians who had preceded him, had not discussed the Holy Spirit with the same thoroughness and care that they had given to the Father and the Son. The matter that needed most urgent attention was the

1. *De Trinitate* 5.11.12.

proprium of the Holy Spirit, the Spirit's distinctive character, that which set him apart from the Father and the Son.[2]

This topic has been approached in many ways, but when I read Jenson's *Systematic Theology* I was struck by his formulation of the question. First, he puts the question in Augustine's terms: "The problem," he writes, "is imposed by Scripture. The same Gospel in which the Spirit appears most explicitly as another" than the Son and the Father also contains the Bible's closest approach to a definition of the divine nature, that "God is Spirit. . . ." The problem is religiously important: "Is invocation of the Spirit anything distinctive over against invocation simply of God?" Second, Jenson adds: "Is Pentecost a peer of Easter or does it merely display a meaning that Easter would in any case have?"[3]

This question got me to thinking whether this way of putting the matter had echoes in Augustine, that is, whether the event of Pentecost had a place in Augustine's thinking about the Holy Spirit as the incarnation and resurrection had in his thinking about the Son. What follows then is an exploration of Augustine's discussion of the Holy Spirit at the end of book 15 of *De Trinitate* in light of Jenson's question. As we shall see, the inquiry led me to explore the relation between the Scriptures and the celebration of Pentecost in the liturgy, an approach to theology that is very much in a Jensonian mode.

Unlike the early Christian Pasch that was celebrated as an annual festival early in the church's history, the feast of Pentecost emerged only slowly. In the earliest sources the term Pentecost designated not a single feast day but the period of time after Easter, what Tertullian called "a most joyous space" for baptisms.[4] Basil of Caesarea, writing in the middle of the fourth century, said that the "entire season of Pentecost" is a reminder of the future resurrection.[5] Pentecost was viewed as a continuation of Easter and had no distinctive character of its own. Only in the fifth century does it emerge as a feast day in its own right.

In some ways the history of the feast of Pentecost can serve as a met-

2. *De Fide et Symbolo* 1.19.

3. Robert Jenson, *Systematic Theology,* vol. I: *The Triune God* (Oxford: Oxford University Press, 1997), p. 146. Hereafter abbreviated *ST,* by volume and page. Italics in quotations are Jenson's unless otherwise noted.

4. *De Baptismo* 19.2. For other reference see Francesca Cocchini, "L'Evoluzione Storico-Religiosa della Festa di Pentecoste," in *Rivista Biblica* 25 (1977): 316ff.

5. *De Spiritu Sancto* 27.66.

aphor for the development of the Christian doctrine of the Holy Spirit. Although the book of Acts makes the outpouring of the Holy Spirit on Pentecost a pivotal event in the formation of the church (Acts 2), and hence of the economy, the ordered pattern of God's revelation in history, discussion of the status and character of the Holy Spirit trailed behind the debate about the Son. The earliest creeds mention the Holy Spirit, but it was only at the end of the fourth century, at the council of Constantinople, that a full article on the Holy Spirit was added to the creed.

This feature of the church's teaching on the Holy Trinity was not lost on the Church Fathers. "Theology," says Gregory of Nazianzus, "reaches maturity by additions." In the Old Testament the Father was proclaimed openly but the Son "obscurely." The New Testament revealed the Son but only "gave us a glimpse of the deity of the Spirit." Only "now," by which he means the time of the church, when "the Spirit has taken up residence among us, does he give us a clearer manifestation of himself." To this he adds, acknowledging the audacity of his language, that it would have been imprudent when Father and Son had not been acknowledged to "burden us further with the Holy Spirit. . . ."[6] The truth arrives through time.

Gregory's arresting comment also suggests that the discussion of the Holy Spirit will proceed on somewhat different lines than the debate over the relation of the Son to the Father. Since it was through the "dwelling of the Holy Spirit among us" that his person and nature became clear, the theology of the Holy Spirit will be anchored in Christian experience, and in particular participation in the church's worship and sacraments: in baptism, in the calling down of the Holy Spirit in the great prayer over the bread and wine in the Eucharist, in the laying on of hands during the ordination of bishops, to name the most obvious rites. No doubt this was one reason why Gregory's dear friend Basil could write that if one does not confess the divinity of the Holy Spirit, one would "deny what was received at Baptism."[7] What was done was evidence of what was to be taught. *Lex orandi legem statuit credendi.*

Christianity was religiously Trinitarian before it was dogmatically Trinitarian. In his book *The Doctrine of the Trinity* the English theologian Leonard Hodgson wrote: "Christianity began as a trinitarian religion with a unitarian theology. The question at issue in the age of the fathers was

6. *Oration* 31.26.
7. *De Spiritu Sancto* 10.26.

whether the religion should transform the theology or the theology stifle the religion."[8] Nowhere is this dynamic of early Christian thought more evident than in the development of the doctrine of the Spirit.

Gregory says that the New Testament "manifests" the Son but only "gave us a glimpse of the Spirit." There is some exaggeration here, but his point is well taken. Although there are many references to the Holy Spirit in the New Testament, they offer no clear and unequivocal testimony to the Spirit's nature and character. The works are many, but it is not easy to discern what, if anything, is unique to them. As the Church Fathers knew well, within the New Testament the Spirit is most often presented as completing and perfecting the work of Christ. In one of the earliest extended discussions of the Holy Spirit in the early church, the Spirit is identified as the Spirit of the Son. "When we are enlightened by the Holy Spirit it is Christ who enlightens us," wrote Athanasius, and when we "drink of the Spirit we drink of Christ."[9] The offending text was 2 Corinthians 3:17: "Now the Lord is the Spirit." Was the expression "Holy Spirit" simply another way of depicting the work of Christ? Like John 4:24, this passage from 2 Corinthians complicated the exposition of the *proprium* of the Holy Spirit.

The ambiguity of the language of the Scriptures on the Holy Spirit presented early Christian thinkers with a particularly acute problem. The doctrine of the Spirit had to be constructed from the ground up using only the materials provided by the Scriptures. Of course one might say the same thing about the teaching on the Father and the Son, as the debates over the meaning of scriptural texts after Nicaea showed, but the Church Fathers knew that the teaching on the Holy Spirit was dependent on the Bible in a way that teaching on the Father and the Son was not. In his chapter on the Holy Spirit in book 1 of *First Principles,* Origen says that it is possible to gain some idea of God (i.e., the Father) from the "visible creation" and "from those things that the human mind instinctively perceives." He is thinking of Romans 1:20, "his invisible nature has been clearly perceived in the things that have been made." With respect to the Son, even some philosophers believe that all things were created by "the Word of God or

8. Leonard Hodgson, *The Doctrine of the Trinity* (New York: Charles Scribner's Sons, 1944), p. 103. Cited in *ST* I, 95 n. 37.

9. *Letter to Serapion* 1.19 (J. P. Migne, *Patrologia Graeca,* vol. 26, pp. 573-76; hereafter *PG*).

reason." But knowledge of the Holy Spirit, says Origen, is not given to us through creation or the workings of reason. For "only those who are versed in the law and the prophets or profess faith in Christ can have any notion of the existence of the Holy Spirit."[10]

Origen was not alone in this view. In the *Confessions* Augustine said that when he was reading the books of the Platonists, "God and his Word kept slipping in."[11] That is, it was possible to have some knowledge of the Father and the Son independently of the Scriptures. Yet, says Augustine, the "pages of the Platonic books have nothing to say . . . about the guarantee of your Holy Spirit."[12] Because there were no analogues in human experience or thought to the Holy Spirit, the existence of the Spirit could be known only through the Scriptures and the life of the church. Hence the discussion of the nature and character of the Spirit imposed constraints on Christian thinkers that were absent when speaking of the Father and the Son. The philosophical tradition would provide little guidance on this aspect of Christian doctrine.[13]

For these reasons it is not surprising that in the course of book 15 of *De Trinitate* when Augustine comes to the Holy Spirit he says twice that he intends to discuss the Holy Spirit *secundum Scripturas sanctas.*[14] Of course at

10. *On First Principles* 1.3.1. Origen, however, adds that we cannot know "higher and more divine teaching about the Son of God" except through the Scriptures.

11. *Confessions* 8.2.3.

12. *Confessions* 7.21.27. Nello Cipriani observes: "in nessun luogo Agostino afferma di aver trovato nei libri neoplatonici l'intera Trinita et in particolare lo Spirito Santo." He notes that in book 10 of the *City of God,* Augustine acknowledges that Porphyry knew the Father and the Son, but not the Holy Spirit (Nello Cipriani, "Le Fonti Cristiane della doctrina Trinitaria nei primi Dialoghi d. S. Agostino," *Augustinianum* 34 [1994]: 257).

13. There are of course some terms for the Spirit with philosophical overtones, particularly in Marius Victorinus. For example: "Adesto, sancte spiritus, patris et filii copula" (Hymn 1, "Adesto, lumen verum," line 3, in Marius Victorinus, *Traités Théologiques sur la Trinité,* ed. P. Henry and P. Hadot, Sources Chrétiennes 68 [Paris: Editions du Cerf, 1960], p. 620); "Tu, spiritus sancte, connexio es; connexio autem est quicquid connectit duo; /Ita ut connectas omnia, primo connectis duo;/ Esque ipsa tertia conplexio duorum atque ipsa conplexio nihil distans uno, unum cum facis duo; O beata trinitas" (Hymn 3, "Deus, Dominus, Sanctus spiritus, O beata trinitas," lines 242-47, in Victorinus, *Traités Théologiques sur la Trinité,* p. 650).

14. *De Trinitate* 15.27; 15.39. The literature on Augustine's doctrine is large. For summary discussion with up-to-date bibliography see Eugene Teselle, "Holy Spirit," in *Augustine Through the Ages: An Encyclopedia,* ed. Allan D. Fitzgerald, O.S.A. (Grand

the beginning of *De Trinitate* Augustine had said that his purpose was to "establish by the authority of the Holy Scriptures" what was to be believed,[15] and that "the aim of all the Catholic commentators" who had written on the Holy Trinity was to "teach according to the Scriptures."[16] Yet the appearance of the phrase *secundum Scripturas sanctas* twice in book 15 in the section on the Holy Spirit would suggest that any theologian who embarks on a discussion of the Holy Spirit will be occupied chiefly with expounding the Scriptures. Even a cursory look at the treatises on the Holy Spirit in the fourth century — Athanasius's letters to Serapion, the pages in Hilary's *De Trinitate,* the treatises of Ambrose and Didymus and Basil on the Holy Spirit, Gregory Nazianzus' theological oration on the Holy Spirit[17] — will bear this out. In these works the discussion is overwhelmingly exegetical.

However, when one looks at these treatises on the Holy Spirit more closely, it becomes apparent that there is scant agreement as to which passages from the Bible count as relevant and how they are to be brought together to form a theological unity. Some texts appear again and again, for example, 1 Corinthians 2:12, Galatians 4:4, and John 4:24, but it is difficult to discern a pattern in their exegesis. Interpretation required something more than expounding the words of passages that mention the Holy Spirit. For if the exposition of individual texts did not summon up the whole, what the Fathers called the *skopos,* the controlling conception of the matter at hand, they remained fallow and otiose. Yet in the case of the Holy Spirit it was precisely the whole, the Spirit's character and distinctive work, that was at issue. Though there is much citing of the Bible, and passages are marshaled to support theological arguments, the Fathers are less engaged in defending something than in searching for something. Only gradually and after they peered intently at the murkiness before them, does the goal of their quest come clear.[18]

Rapids: Eerdmans, 1999), pp. 434-37; also the articles by B. Studer in his two volumes of collected essays, *Dominus Salvator: Studien zur Christologie und Exegese der Kirchenväter* (Rome: Pontificio Ateneo S. Anselmo, 1992); Rowan Williams, "Sapientia and the Trinity: Reflections on de Trinitate," in B. Bruning, ed., *Collectanea Augustiniana,* vol. 1 (Leuven: Peeters, 1990), pp. 317-32.

15. *De Trinitate* 1.2.4.

16. *De Trinitate* 1.4.7.

17. *Oration* 31.

18. For survey of early Christian theology of the Holy Spirit see F. Court, "Trinität in der Schrift und Patristik," in *Handbuch der Dogmengeschichte,* vol. 2

Of course from the beginning certain theological claims had to be defended, and the earliest discussions focus on two questions: whether there is a Holy Spirit, and whether the Holy Spirit was a creature. In the chapter on the Holy Spirit in *First Principles* Origen cites a series of biblical texts, "take not thy holy Spirit from me" (Ps. 51:13), "receive the Holy Spirit" (John 20:22), "no one can say that Jesus is the Lord except in the Holy Spirit" (1 Cor. 12:3), to argue that the Scriptures bear witness to the existence of the Holy Spirit. Having established that there is a Holy Spirit, Origen then introduces a second series of texts to show that the Holy Spirit was not "made" or "created."[19]

Similarly in his letters to Serapion, Athanasius, responding to critics of the divinity of the Holy Spirit, does something similar, though at much greater length. Near the end of his letters he writes: "Therefore the Spirit is not a creature but is in God and of God." As in his great work *Contra Arianos,* Athanasius also deals with several texts that had been used by detractors of the Holy Spirit. One of these was Amos 4:13: "I am he that establishes thunder and creates spirit and declares unto men his Christ, forming the morning and the darkness, and mounting on the high places of the earth. The Lord God almighty is his name."[20] Here Athanasius faced a problem not unlike the one raised by the Arian interpretation of Proverbs 8:22, "The Lord created me the beginning of his ways." As he had had to demonstrate from the Scriptures that the Son was not "created," so now he had to show that the Holy Spirit was not "created." Consequently his reasoning moves along parallel lines: as the one who redeems cannot be in need of redemption, so the one who sanctifies cannot be from among those who are in need of sanctification. What is confessed in the creed about the Son is now applied to the Spirit: he is not a creature but is "one in essence with the Father."[21]

(Freiburg: Herder, 1988); P. Smulders, "Esprit Saint: Pères latins," in *Dictionnaire de la Spiritualité Ascétique et Mystique: Doctrine et Histoire,* ed. Marcel Viller et al. (Paris: G. Beauchesen 1937-), vol. 4, pp. 1272-83; Yves Congar, *I Believe in the Holy Spirit,* vol. 1 (New York: Seabury Press, 1983); Boris Bobrinskoy, *The Mystery of the Trinity: Trinitarian Experience and Vision in the Biblical and Patristic Tradition* (Crestwood, NY: St. Vladimir's Seminary Press, 1999).

19. *On First Principles* 1.3.2-3.

20. *Letters to Serapion* 4.2 (*PG* 26, 640).

21. *Letters to Serapion* 1.3 (*PG* 26, 536). Another troubling text was 1 Tim. 5:21, "In the presence of God and of Christ Jesus and of the elect angels I charge you to keep

It is not until one turns to the works of Hilary of Poitiers, Didymus the Blind, and Ambrose, that one has the sense that the interpretation of biblical passages on the Holy Spirit has moved to a deeper level. Hilary, for example, says that the question "whether the Holy Spirit exists" is not one that requires discussion. "He does exist," writes Hilary, "since he is given, received, and possessed."[22]

Hilary's reasoning is noteworthy. Unlike Origen who had brought forth biblical evidence to show that there is a Holy Spirit, Hilary takes that for granted and focuses on the distinctive characteristics of the Spirit, that he is given, received, and possessed. In support he marshals a series of texts from Paul, among which are the following: "Because you are sons, God has sent [= given] the Spirit of his Son into our hearts, crying, 'Abba Father!'" (Gal. 4:6); "Do not grieve the Holy Spirit of God in whom you were sealed [= received]" (Eph. 4:30); "We have received not the spirit of this world, but the Spirit which is from God, that we might know the things given us by God" (1 Cor. 2:12); "But you are not in the flesh, you are in the Spirit, if in fact the Spirit of God dwells [= is possessed] in you" (Rom. 8:9); and "If the Spirit of him who raised Jesus from the dead dwells [= is possessed] in you, he who raised Christ Jesus from the dead will give life to your mortal bodies through his Spirit which dwells in you" (Rom. 8:11).

After reciting this litany of Pauline texts Hilary concludes: "Since [the Holy Spirit] exists, and is given, and is possessed, and is of God, let his accusers be silent."[23] The Holy Spirit then can be called *donum fidelium*,

these rules without favor. . . ." Here the Holy Spirit is not explicitly mentioned and seems, according to some thinkers, to be counted with the angels, being himself the greatest in that category. Athanasius's task was to show that this passage did not teach that the Spirit was a creature, albeit angelic (esp. *Letters to Serapion* 1.3 [*PG* 26, 556]). Peter Widdicombe believes that there are hints in Athanasius that point in the direction of the Augustinian conception of the Spirit as the bond of love. "As the grace given is from the Father through the Son, so we can have no fellowship in the gift except in the Holy Spirit. For it is when we participate in him that we have the love of the Father and the grace of the Son and the fellowship of the Spirit himself" (esp. *Letters to Serapion* 1.30). The biblical texts are 1 Cor. 12:4-6 and 2 Cor. 13:13. Athanasius, however, speaks only of love flowing from God and drawing believers into fellowship, not love between Father, Son, and Spirit. See Peter Widdicombe, "Athanasius and the Making of the Doctrine of the Trinity," *Pro Ecclesia* 6 (1997): 472-73.

22. "Est enim quando quidem donatur, accipitur, obtinetur" (*De Trinitate* 2.29).

23. *De Trinitate* 2.29.

"the gift to the faithful."[24] Gift is a shorthand way of referring to being given, received, and possessed. Hilary has noticed something distinctive about the biblical language for the Holy Spirit, namely, that there is a field of terms in the Bible associated with the Spirit that variously depict being given and poured out, on the one hand, and being received or indwelling, on the other. That is, the "gift" is seen not only from the perspective of the giver, but also from that of the recipient. What is given enters into the life of the recipient and becomes his own, which in turn relates the recipient to the giver. Gift, as presented in the Scriptures, has built into it overtones of reciprocity and mutuality.

Surprisingly, and this is an indication of how unsystematic the exegesis is at this stage of development, Hilary does not cite the one text that was a pillar for Augustine's thinking, Romans 5:5: "God's love has been poured into our hearts through the Holy Spirit which has been given to us." Didymus the Blind, however, writing in the 380s, did cite Romans 5, *caritas Dei diffusa est in cordibus nostris,* and noted the importance of the term *diffundo* (pour out, diffuse) and cognates, as for example, "give" (Luke 11:13), in the biblical depiction of the Holy Spirit.[25] In this connection he also cited Joel 2:29 (= Acts 2:17): "I will pour out *(effundam)* my Spirit on all flesh." He also observed that "pour out" is a unique form of divine communication. When God sends an angel or some other creature, he does not say, "I will pour out my angel." This way of speaking, says Didymus, applies only to goods that are received "by participation," as in Romans 5:5: "the love of God has been poured into our hearts through the Holy Spirit which has been given to us."[26] The Holy Spirit is *capabilis,* "capable of being participated in," a term not used for human beings or angels, but only for "uncreated beings," says Didymus. When the Spirit is received, the recipients "have communion with him."[27] To be filled with the Holy Spirit, then, does not mean filling one thing with another, as one would fill a glass

24. *De Trinitate* 49.

25. *De Spiritu Sancto* 2.29. Didymus's treatise, written in Greek, comes to us only in a Latin translation by Jerome. Text edited by Louis Doutreleau, S.J., *Traité du Saint-Esprit: Didyme l'Aveugle,* Sources Chrétiennes 386 (Paris: Editions du Cerf, 1992).

26. *De Spiritu Sancto* 50. On Didymus see A. Heron, "The Holy Spirit in Origen and Didymus the Blind: A Shift in Perspective from the Third to the Fourth Century," in *Kerygma und Logos,* ed. A. M. Ritter (Göttingen: Vandenhoeck & Ruprecht, 1979), pp. 298-310.

27. *De Spiritu Sancto* 55.

with water; it means participate in. Because the Holy Spirit fills those who are able to receive *(capere)* wisdom and virtue, he is the "fullness of divine gifts" *(plenitudo munerum divinorum)*.[28]

Ambrose, who knew Didymus's treatise (Jerome said he plagiarized it), also highlights the language of giving or bestowing embedded in the term *effundo* (pour out) that occurs in Joel 2:28: "I will pour out *(effundam)* my Spirit."[29] He also cites the text that will be so influential in Augustine's thinking, "the love of God is poured out *(effundit)* in our hearts through the Holy Spirit," and interprets the term "pour out" to mean that the Holy Spirit is "gift."[30] In expounding this passage, however, Ambrose highlights a term in the text that Didymus did not, namely, "love." Romans 5:5, says Ambrose, shows that the Holy Spirit is the "dispenser and abundant fount of divine love."

When we turn to Augustine with this background before us, it is clear that many of the elements that will provide an exegetical direction for Augustine's teaching are in place: Spirit as "gift," "pouring out" as a distinctive term for the sending of the Spirit, "being filled" or "indwelling" for receiving the Spirit, the Holy Spirit as the "dispenser and abundant fount of love," and key texts such as Romans 5:5, to mention the most obvious. Furthermore, as in Ambrose, Didymus, and Hilary, what occupies Augustine's attention is the *proprium*, the distinctive character of the Holy Spirit. Yet a perceptible shift in focus is evident. In earlier thinkers the *proprium* of the Holy Spirit was discussed in relation to mankind; for Augustine the distinctiveness of the Holy Spirit is also discussed in relation to the Father and the Son. As he puts the question in book 5: "Was he already gift before there was anyone to give him to?"[31] In other words, does the term "gift" as a designation of the Holy Spirit only apply to the economy?[32]

Before turning to the discussion of the Holy Spirit in book 15, however, it is necessary to pause and consider some other factors that shape Augustine's thinking. Early in *De Trinitate* Augustine cites Galatians 4:4 to establish that there were two distinct "sendings" recorded in

28. *De Spiritu Sancto* 34.

29. Ambrose, *De Spiritu Sancto* 1.7.85. Ambrose echoes Didymus in saying that this form of expression cannot be used of an angel.

30. *De Spiritu Sancto* 1.5.66. The term "effundo" occurs three times in this passage.

31. *De Trinitate* 5.15.6.

32. *De Spiritu Sancto* 1.8.94.

the Scriptures, the sending of the Son and the sending of the Holy Spirit.[33] "But when the time had fully come, God sent forth his Son, born of a woman, born under the law, to redeem those who were under the law, so that we might receive adoption as sons. And because you are sons, God has sent the Spirit of his Son into our hearts, crying, 'Abba Father!'" (Gal. 4:4-5). This passage not only mentions the names used by the church in confessing God as triune, Father, Son, and Holy Spirit, but also states how the triune character of God is known, namely, through the "sending" of the Son and the "sending" of the Spirit. Sending, Augustine says, is characteristic of both the Son and Spirit, and only of the Son and Spirit. "The Father alone," says Augustine, "is nowhere said to have been sent."[34]

The Son was "sent" when he was born of the Blessed Virgin Mary. The "sending" of the Son refers to what took place as a result of the incarnation, including of course Christ's suffering, death, and resurrection. Indeed, as Hilary had shown, it was the historical event of the resurrection that is the basis for the Christian confession that Christ is God. It was only after the resurrection, he wrote, that the apostles knew that God was not a "solitary God."[35]

As the "sending" of the Son means that certain things took place, so also the "sending" of the Holy Spirit refers to what had taken place in history. "If the Son is said to have been sent in that he appeared outwardly in created bodily form while inwardly in uncreated spiritual form remaining always hidden from mortal eyes, then it is easy to understand how the Holy Spirit can also be said to have been sent." Augustine explains: "He was visibly displayed in a created guise which was made in time," either when he descended on our Lord himself "in bodily guise as a dove" (Matt. 3:16), or when ten days after his ascension "there came suddenly from heaven on the day of Pentecost a sound as of a violent gust bearing down, and there appeared to them divided tongues as of fire, which also settled upon each

33. Johannes Arnold, "Begriff und heilsökonomische Bedeutung der göttlichen Sendungen in Augustinus De Trinitate," *Recherches Augustiniennes* 25 (199l): 3-69. On the role of the Holy Spirit in the "sending" of the Son, that is, the incarnation, see the observations of Jacques Verhees, "Heiliger Geist und Inkarnation in der Theologie des Augustinus von Hippo," in *Revue des Etudes Augustiniennes* 22 (1976): 234-53.

34. *De Trinitate* 2.5.8.

35. *De Trinitate 7.12. On this point see Robert L. Wilken, Remembering the Christian Past* (Grand Rapids: Eerdmans, 1995), pp. 63-94.

one of them" (Acts 2:2).[36] The "sending of the Holy Spirit," says Augustine, has reference to an *operatio,* an "action visibly expressed and presented to mortal eyes." The purpose was that the "public manifestation of his coming in time" might stir the minds of men to his "hidden eternity which is always present."[37] Or in the words of the Orthodox theologian, Nikos Nissiotis, cited by Jenson, the coming of the Holy Spirit at Pentecost is "a new intervention of the Holy Trinity in time."[38]

Each sending, that of the Son and that of the Holy Spirit, is unique and has its own distinct character (which is to say that each sending is historical). Augustine is very precise here. The Son appeared as a human being and formed a bond between the flesh and the divine Word. The flesh of Christ is permanently united with the Word. The Holy Spirit, however, did not have such a relation to the material things in which he appeared. As Augustine puts it, the Holy Spirit did not make the dove (at Jesus' baptism) "blessed" (as in "blessed is the fruit of thy womb Jesus"), nor did the fire and wind at Pentecost become "blessed." He did not join these things to himself in an "everlasting union." Hence, though the dove is called the Spirit and the apostles spoke as the Spirit gave utterance, we cannot say that the Spirit is "God and dove" or "God and fire" as we say that the Son is "God and man." Nor does the use of "rock" for Christ in 1 Corinthians 10:4 offer a parallel, because the rock already existed and came to have a symbolic meaning. But the dove and fire "came suddenly into existence" to "signify something and then pass away."[39]

By Augustine's day Pentecost was a separate liturgical festival, and Augustine understood Pentecost as the celebration of an event that had taken place at a particular moment in space and time. We are celebrating, he says in a sermon preached on the day of Pentecost, "the solemnity of a day so holy, that today the Holy Spirit himself came."[40] Or: "This day that we are celebrating . . . is the one on which the Lord Jesus Christ, glorified after his Resurrection and glorified in the Ascension, sent the Holy Spirit."[41] The feast of Pentecost is an annual "feast" that recalls the "com-

36. *De Trinitate* 2.5.10.

37. *De Trinitate* 2.5.10.

38. Nikos Nissiotis, *Die Theologie der Ostkirche im ökumenischen Dialog* (Stuttgart: Evangelisches Verlagswerk, 1968), p. 74; *ST* I, 146 n. 3.

39. *De Trinitate* 2.6.11.

40. *Sermon* 270.1.

41. *Sermon* 271.1. See also *Sermon* 272b.1.

ing of the Holy Spirit," "something that happened once."[42] The Holy Spirit existed before Pentecost (e.g. Zacharias, father of John the Baptizer, was filled with the Holy Spirit), but at Pentecost "there was a kind of giving which had not happened before."[43]

Augustine also refers to the pouring out of the Holy Spirit in baptism, in the prayer over the gifts in the Eucharist, in the laying on of hands at the ordination of a bishop.[44] He also knew the creed with its separate article on the Holy Spirit. In his writings Augustine most often mentions the Apostles' Creed, but it is clear that he knew the Creed of Nicaea.[45] He mentions it explicitly only late in life,[46] but allusions to it are scattered throughout his writings, including *De Trinitate.*[47] The creed of the council of Constantinople in 381 without the anathemas and a fuller article on the Holy Spirit, however, was unknown in the West during Augustine's lifetime. Yet in his early exposition of the Apostles' Creed, *De Fide et Symbolo,* he has a lengthy exposition of the article, "I believe in the Holy Spirit."[48]

Because the sending of the Holy Spirit is distinct from the sending of the Son, as is evident in the festival of Pentecost or the calling down of the Spirit on the gifts during the anaphora, Augustine interprets the scriptural texts on the Holy Spirit to mean that the Spirit is not simply the Spirit of the Father or the Spirit of the Son but has a unique identity or *proprium.* This is most apparent in the pivotal discussion of 1 John 4:13 in *De Trinitate* 15.31. "In this we know that we abide in him and he in us, because he has given us

42. *Sermon* 267.1 and 169.1.

43. *Tractate on John* 32.6; also 52.8.

44. Ordination: *De Trinitate* 15.26.46; Baptism: *De Trinitate* 5.26.46; Eucharist: *De Trinitate* 3.4.10. On this topic see Cristina Simonelli, "La fede nella risurrezione di Cristo nel De Trinitate di Agostino" (Ph.D. dissertation, Augustinianum, Rome, 1999), pp. 133-42.

45. On this point see Basil Studer, "Augustin et la Foi de Nicée," in *Dominus Salvator,* pp. 371-77.

46. In *Contra Maximinum Arianum Libri* 2.14.3.

47. *De Trinitate* 15.14.23. See also *De Genesi ad litteram opus imperfectum* 1.2: "Deum patrem omnipotentem universam creaturam fecisse atque constituisse per Filium suum unigenitum, id est Sapientiam et Virtutem suam consubstantialem sibi et coaeternam, in unitate Spiritus sancti, et ipsius consubstantialis et coaeterni."

48. *De Fide et Symbolo* 9.19ff. Already in 393, when this discourse was delivered, Augustine noted that the key theological task was to identify the *proprium* of the Holy Spirit, "quo proprio fit ut eum neque Filium neque Patrem dicere possimus, sed tantum Spiritum sanctum."

of his Spirit" (1 John 4:13). Both Didymus and Ambrose had cited this passage to establish the unity of the Spirit with the Father and the Son. Didymus says that 1 John 4:13 (and other texts) demonstrate "that the substance of the Trinity is inseparable and indivisible."[49] Ambrose, citing the text from 1 John, says that it refers to the "unity" of the Holy Trinity.[50] Augustine, however, cites 1 John 4:13, not as a text on unity, but of differentiation, in the midst of a discussion of whether the Holy Spirit is properly called "love." Augustine had already argued that the term "spirit" (as in "God is Spirit" in John 4:24) can in a general sense refer to Father, Son, and Holy Spirit, but also in a particular sense refer specifically to the Holy Spirit.[51]

Now he proceeds to show that the term "love," which can be used of Father, Son, and Spirit, is used to refer specifically to the Holy Spirit. 1 John 4:13 reads: "By this we know that we abide *(manemus)* in him and he in us, because he has given us of his own Spirit." In this passage, says Augustine, the writer wanted to say something more plainly about the *proprium* of the Holy Spirit, namely, that it is the Holy Spirit "that makes us abide in God and him in us." In other words the text describes an activity that is distinctive to the Spirit, to make us abide in God. "But," says Augustine, "that is precisely what love does." For the goal of love is to bring one into fellowship with the beloved. If then love is the work of the Spirit, as is evident from Romans 5:5 (which Augustine cites once again), then it follows that the Holy Spirit is the "gift of God who is love."[52]

Interestingly his argument on the distinction between the general and particular sense of a term is supported not by a philosophical discussion but by an appeal to scriptural usage. Augustine shows that the term "law" is sometimes used to refer to the "books of the Old Testament" (as in 1 Cor. 14:21 and John 15:25), but sometimes to refer specifically to the law of Moses (as in Matt. 11:13). Just as the term "law" can be used "in a general sense" *(communiter)* to refer to the law and the prophets, so it can be used "particularly" *(proprie)* to mean the law of Moses.[53] A few paragraphs

49. *De Spiritu Sancto* 189-90.

50. *De Spiritu Sancto* 2.9.95.

51. *De Trinitate* 15.17.27.

52. *De Trinitate* 15.17.31.

53. *De Trinitate* 15.17.30. On this point see B. Studer, "Zur Pneumatologie des Augustinus von Hippo (*De Trinitate* 15,17,27-27,50)," in *Mysterium Caritatis: Studien zur Exegese und zur Trinitätslehre in der alten Kirche* (Rome: Pontificio Ateneo S. Anselmo, 1999), p. 321.

later he also appeals to scriptural usage to explain why "gift of the Holy Spirit" means simply "Holy Spirit." "Just as the 'body of the flesh' (in Col. 2:11) is nothing other than 'flesh,'" so the "gift of the Holy Spirit" is nothing other than the Holy Spirit. He is the gift of God in as much as he is given to those to whom he is given. In himself *(apud se)* he is God even if he is not given to anyone, because "he was God, coeternal with the Father and the Son, before he was given to anyone."[54]

The *proprium* of the Holy Spirit is expressed almost wholly in language of participation and mutuality. As we have seen, Augustine singles out the phrase "abide in him" in 1 John 4:13: "we abide in him because he has given us of his own Spirit." If the Holy Spirit causes us to "abide in God and [God] in us," then he is rightly called love. That is to say, the gift by its very nature is reciprocal, for it creates a communion between the one who receives and the giver. This is why the pairing of Romans 5:5 with 1 John 4:13 is so significant. The gift of the Spirit "enkindles love for God," that is, turns the recipient toward God. Yet this turning only takes place because love has its origin in God. "Man has no capacity to love God except from God."[55]

Augustine wants to say not only that the gift of the Holy Spirit creates a communion between God and the believer but also that the Spirit is the "communion" between Father and Son. There is "a good reason," he writes, "for distinctively calling him love." He drives the point home by yoking *communio* to *ambo* (both) in the phrase *communio amborum,* the bringing together of two into fellowship. Though the Holy Spirit is not "alone in being either holy or spirit, because the Father too is holy and the Son too is holy, and the Father too is spirit and the Son too is spirit . . . yet he is properly called the Holy Spirit, and with good reason. Because he is common to them both, he is called properly what they are called in common."[56]

At one level one might say that what makes this exegesis work is the conjunction of 1 John 4 with Romans 5, and that certainly is the case, for the two passages give Augustine the key words for his discussion — "poured out," which signifies "gift" and "love" — and he uses them for the

54. *De Trinitate* 15.19.36.

55. *De Trinitate* 15.27.31.

56. *De Trinitate* 15.19.37. See also *Sermon* 71.18: "Insinuatur nobis in Patre auctoritas, in Filio nativitas, in Spiritu sancto Patris Filiique communitas, in tribus aequalitas."

work of the Holy Spirit. Though both passages are cited in Didymus and Ambrose, each is used to make a different point. In Augustine they are brought in relation to each other. Yet what Augustine finds in these texts is not simply drawn from the words of the text. We are accustomed to think of exegesis as a matter of drawing out the meaning of a text by seeking to discover what the words in the text signify. In this view the interpreter begins with the words, that is, signs, and seeks to discover the *res*, the subject matter about which the text speaks, assuming that one can know what the text means by understanding the signs.

Yet one might say that the interpreter does not know what the words mean unless he already has some knowledge of the *res* to which they refer.[57] In our print-oriented culture we tend to think that what is written on the page (or the computer screen) is the word. However, the written word is only a sign for the spoken word, which is in turn a sign of the *res*. The better one knows the word and the thing to which it refers, the more likely one is able to pronounce it correctly, pronunciation being not simply a matter of vowels and consonants, but accent, emphasis, tone, hence of meaning.

In the same way the interpreter of the Bible does not come to the text without prior knowledge of the realities to which the text refers. How well one interprets the text depends not simply on how skilled one is in the language of the biblical writer or the literary genre of the work or on how well one knows the Bible's idiom, the history it portrays and assumes, or its leading ideas and themes. One's interpretation also depends on one's participation in the mysteries of the faith as known through the church's worship, creeds, and life. The meaning of the text is accessible only if one has prior knowledge of the reality to which the text refers, the thing itself of which the words are but signs. It is only when one knows a painting at first hand that the words of the art critic are satisfying. Having a painting described in words, or even looking at a picture of a painting, is not the same as seeing it for oneself. It is only by actually looking at the painting, having a sense of its size, observing the shades of color, studying the strokes of the brush or the thickness of the paint, peering closely at details, or standing back to grasp the whole that one can read what is said of the painting with

57. On the importance of the *res* in patristic exegesis, see the observations of Basil Studer, "Die patristische Exegese, eine Aktualisierung der Heiligen Schrift," in *Mysterium Caritatis*, pp. 113-16.

profit. In the same way it is only after one has visited a historic site that a guidebook comes to life.

What Augustine discovered in the biblical texts about the Holy Spirit did not come from the texts alone. In part what he said depended on how he related the several texts to each other and which ones are privileged. Terms and images of certain texts provided an interpretive key to the other texts, and it is only as the texts are brought into relation to one another, and the Bible as a whole, that their meaning becomes apparent. Yet there is something else at work here. Augustine knew what he was looking for. The Holy Spirit was not a religious idea or concept that was spun out of the mind. For Augustine the Holy Spirit was a living presence, a throbbing reality, known in history, by experience, in particular through the church's worship, and in the creed.

It is perhaps stretching the point to say that the entire discussion hangs on certain biblical words, but "pour out" *(effundo,* or *diffundo),* "gift" *(donum),* "abide in" *(manere),* "love" *(caritas),* provided the linguistic leverage that allowed Augustine to forge conceptual categories to speak about the *proprium* of the Holy Spirit. The term "poured out" as used both in the passages that speak of the "sending" of the Holy Spirit on mankind, for example, Joel 2:28, and in texts that speak about the Holy Spirit entering the hearts of the believer, for example, Romans 5:5, designated a distinctive kind of communication. When this term is linked with texts in which "give" is used in connection with the Spirit (diligently, even pedantically cited one by one in a long section in 15.33-35), it becomes clear how "gift" and "poured out" and "love" came to be seen as complementary, each expressing from a different perspective a distinctive activity. Note, for example, how they are yoked together in this passage near the very end of book 15: "As for the reason why he first gave *(daret)* the Holy Spirit. . . . I think it is because love *(caritas)* is poured out *(diffunditur)* in our hearts through this gift *(donum)*."

For Augustine, and other early Christian thinkers, the words of the Bible were vehicles of discovery, one word reminding them of other words in the Bible, each being illuminated by its juxtaposition with others. The words of the Bible not only inflamed the heart but also excited and provoked the mind. It was the words, not the ideas or concepts, of the Bible that worked on the imagination. Like tiny lenses that magnify, the Church Fathers allowed them to penetrate more deeply into the mysteries of the faith. As Christian thinkers struggled to find ways of defining the *proprium* of the Holy Spirit, words such as "poured out" and "gift" offered a place to start, a kind of conceptual scaffolding that could be used to construct the house of Christian doctrine. When Hilary said, the Spirit does exist "because he is given, received and possessed," he gave later thinkers a series of terms that would help give content to the biblical term "poured out." Augustine's unique contribution was to add another biblical word, "love," linking "abide" in 1 John 4:13 to "love" in Romans 5:5. By interpreting these two texts in tandem Augustine is able to see "gift" and "poured out" as designations of something that is received, hence possessed, which turns the recipient toward the giver. "So the love which is from God and is God is distinctively the Holy Spirit; through him the love of God is poured out in our hearts, and through it the whole triad dwells in us. This is the reason why it is most fitting that the Holy Spirit, since he is God, is also called the gift of God, and this gift is properly *(proprie)* understood to be nothing other than the love that brings us through *(perducit)* to God, without which no other gift of God whatsoever can bring us through to God."[58] In Rowan Williams's nice phrase, speaking of the inner Trinitarian relations: "*Sapientia* exists by being, quite simply, love in search of an object."[59]

On first reading, the extended exegetical discussion at the conclusion of book 15, the final book of *De Trinitate*, comes as a surprise. After all that has gone before, particularly the elaborate discussion of the image of the Trinity in the mind of man in the first part of book 15 and in previous books, the reversal of strategy is jarring. At the beginning of book 15 Augustine had said that he would be discussing the image of God in man by examining of the workings of the human mind. That is what he does for the first half of the book. Beginning with 15.27, however, the section on the Holy Spirit, Augustine's strategy changes and the argument becomes wholly exegetical. Now he moves from text to text and from word to word. He introduces no analogies from the human mind, he provides no discussion of the inner word in relation to spoken words, and he does not cite Virgil (as he had in 15.25). Instead he builds his argument by teasing out the meaning of words given in the Bible.

This returns me to where I began. Origen sensed in the early third century that the doctrine of the Holy Spirit posed a unique challenge for Christian thought. Augustine had echoed this view when he wrote the

58. *De Trinitate* 15.18.32.
59. Williams, "Sapientia and the Trinity," p. 328.

Confessions. Only when he came to write the *De Trinitate,* however, did he realize the truth of what he had said. Without the Scriptures he could say nothing on the Holy Spirit. Hence, when he finally brings his great work to a climax and seeks to fulfill his promise to the reader at the beginning of book 8 to discuss the Trinity "in a more inward manner" than he had in earlier books (which were largely concerned with the Scriptures), he found this was only possible with the Father and the Son. The doctrine of the Holy Spirit drove him back to the Scriptures and the words of revelation.

Yet when Augustine came to the Scriptures he did not come empty-handed. Not only did he have before him a dossier of texts examined by others, he was guided by the suggestions of earlier commentators, and he drew on his experience of the church's festivals, in particular Pentecost, and sacraments. I suppose that one might conclude from all this that Augustine's teaching on the Holy Spirit is evidence of the ancient truth that the Scriptures do not stand alone and are intelligible only in light of tradition. Yet that formula is too neat, too abstract, too intellectual. There is no tradition here with a capital T. Tradition is many-sided, and it worked on Augustine's mind in subtle and complex ways. What is most evident in the development of the doctrine of the Holy Spirit is the power of the biblical language, when read in the context of the church's life and worship, to fire the imagination and serve as an instrument of thought. Rather than limiting the discussion, the language of the Bible opened Augustine's thinking to new possibilities. One might say, with only a little exaggeration, that in the end it was the scriptural language that allowed him to make sense out of the philosophical categories he had elaborated earlier.

When I first read Jenson's discussion of the Trinity in volume one of his *Systematic Theology,* I was struck at how biblical it was and at the same time how Trinitarian. To some this may seem puzzling, but the reason is of course obvious. The Bible is a book about the triune God, and, as Jenson shows repeatedly in his writings, the God Christians worship and confess is identified by the narrative in the Bible. This narrative, as Augustine said in *De Trinitate* (citing Gal. 4:4-5), is marked by two signal events, two "sendings," the sending of the Son and the sending of the Holy Spirit. One does not of course need Augustine and other Church Fathers to grasp this point and to see its significance for the church's doctrine of the Holy Trinity. Yet it helps, and it surely has made a difference that Jenson read Augustine and many other Church Fathers all his life. His thinking has deep roots in the Fathers as well as in the Bible. It would seem then that the conclusion to this essay should be that if one wishes to be a theologian, one must read the Bible and the Church Fathers. Yet now that we have Jenson's *Systematic Theology,* that conclusion needs to be modified. If one wishes to be a theologian, one should also read Jenson.

Robert Jenson's Ecclesiology from a Roman Catholic Perspective

SUSAN K. WOOD

Robert Jenson's familiarity with Roman Catholic sources and, in many respects, strong Catholic sensibilities are particularly evident in his sacramental theology and ecclesiology. For instance, he goes beyond Martin Luther's argument for the real presence of Christ in the Eucharist and argues for a constructive interpretation of the Eucharist as an anamnestic sacrifice, presents a convincing case for the necessity of a teaching office in the church, and finds a place for a ministry of unity and communion in the office of Peter. In his communion ecclesiology, in particular, he heavily draws on *Lumen gentium* to explicate the relationship between the local churches and the universal church within this communion. In his identification of the church as the body of the risen Christ, however, he exceeds contemporary Roman Catholic thinking on the relationship between Christ and the church. Not a few theologians of the Reformation have found this last to be an intolerable assertion, mostly because of their conception of the church as a sinful institution. Roman Catholic ecclesiology now nuances this relationship through the category of sacrament.

Much in Jenson's ecclesiology strikes this reader as being neither singularly Protestant nor exclusively Roman Catholic, for it is an ecclesiology steeped in ecumenism and the churchly tradition. His discussion of the church as the people of God, the temple of the Spirit, and the body of Christ is a notable example of this inclusiveness. At times the silent dialogue partner is Judaism, particularly in his discussion of the church's relationship to Israel. This present reading of his ecclesiology from a Roman Catholic perspective will consequently highlight those areas where Jenson's Reformation heritage seems particularly evident or where questions arise from a Roman Catholic perspective.

The Placement of the Treatment of the Church within Jenson's Systematic Theology

Robert Jenson most clearly reveals himself to be a son of the Reformation in the place the word of God — here we may read "gospel" — takes with respect to the church within his systematic theology. Within its most practical self-understanding, the Roman Catholic communion does not tend to see itself as functionally gathered by the word. Although it acknowledges a ministry "word and sacrament," "word" tends to be subordinated to "sacrament" despite the teaching of Vatican II that among the responsibilities of a bishop, the preaching of the gospel has pride of place.[1] Notably, however, the absolute ground of Jenson's systematic theology is the biblical narrative. My own understanding of Jenson's enterprise was clarified as I saw it as an instance of the Lutheran principle of *sola scriptura.* This is not to say, however, that it is fundamentalist, dismissive of ecclesial dogmatic definitions, ignorant of centuries of theological dialogue, or neglectful of the church's liturgy. Quite the contrary. However, the biblical narrative becomes the *norma normans non normata* of critical judgment and interpretation of doctrine, theology, and ecclesial life. In Jenson's words, "God's grace occurs as *word,* as the address by which one person communicates him- or herself to others."[2] God's gifts are "bespoken to us," "the stuff of promise" (*ST* I, 13-14).

Jenson defines the mission of the church within this primacy given to the gospel, for the church is "to see to the speaking of the gospel, whether to the world as message of salvation or to God as appeal and praise" (*ST* I, 11). In his view "church" and "gospel" mutually determine each other (*ST* I, 5). In his view, "whether we are to say that God used the

1. *Lumen gentium,* 25.

2. Robert W. Jenson, *Systematic Theology,* vol. I: *The Triune God* (Oxford: Oxford University Press, 1997), p. 13. Hereafter abbreviated *ST,* by volume and page. Italics in quotations are Jenson's unless otherwise noted.

gospel to gather the church to himself, or that God provides the church to carry the gospel to the world, depends entirely on the direction of thought in a context" (*ST* I, 5).

Within Jenson's systematic theology, the church takes its place as one of God's gifts among the gifts of creation. Jenson places his treatment of the church in his second volume, organized according to the works of God *ad extra.* Consequently, it comes after volume I, which treats the Trinitarian God. It also comes after his discussion of creation and the creatures, and before eschatology. This placement of the church within the systematic theology argues for the church's identity as a "creature of the word," a theme very consistent with Reformation theology. Despite the placement of the section on the church, however, Jenson chooses to consider the church as God's intention, which is antecedent to the gospel, the goal of God's discourse being the community.[3] His treatment of the church elevates it beyond creaturely status. In this elevation, Jenson not only resonates with Roman Catholic ecclesiology; he exceeds it.

The Church as Body of the Risen Christ

Jenson identifies the church as a fourth dramatic person in the biblical narrative, the first three being the persons of the Trinity. The danger of identifying the church in this way is that it tends to place the church on the same plane as the other three persons. Jenson is not completely immune from this criticism, for he does closely identify the church as the body of the risen Christ.

Jenson seems to be addressing issues on several Reformation fronts here. One seems to be John Calvin's problem of location, but with a difference. Calvin's question, simply put, was how, if the risen Christ is at the right hand of the Father in heaven, he could simultaneously be in the Eucharist on the altar or identified with his body, the church. Jenson states clearly that Christ does not have to leave one location to be bodily present in another location, that the difference between God's being in heaven and his being on earth can only be a difference between styles of his presence

3. Robert W. Jenson, *Systematic Theology,* vol. II, *The Works of God* (Oxford: Oxford University Press, 1999), p. 168. Hereafter abbreviated *ST,* by volume and page. Italics in quotations are Jenson's unless otherwise noted.

(*ST* II, 254). His problem is not how the risen Christ can be simultaneously present in two places, but he does insist that a body has to be present some *place,* that is, in an identifiable location. He also interprets Paul as clearly thinking of the Lord "as in some sense visibly located in a heaven spatially related to the rest of creation; the only body of Christ to which Paul ever actually refers is not an entity in this heaven but the Eucharist's loaf and cup and the church assembled around them"(*ST* I, 204). Jenson could not be more explicit: "The church, according to Paul, is the risen body of Christ. She is this because the bread and cup in the congregation's midst is the very same body of Christ" (*ST* I, 205).

A second issue seems to be the Reformation problem of an invisible church, although Jenson summarily dismisses this possibility and states that no use of this concept will be made in his work (*ST* II, 174). This statement simply means that Jenson does not support the notion of an invisible church, for his argument constitutes a refutation of the concept. Thus he uses the concept to refute it. The church simply cannot be invisible if it is the body of Christ since bodies must occupy locations. However, then he argues that if Christ is not to be embodied, that is, reduced to pure spirit or embodied in a very thinned-out fashion, like a "spook," there must be a place, and this place is the Eucharist and the community of believers (*ST* I, 202ff.). Here Jenson succumbs to the presupposition that the body of the risen Lord occupies space and time in an analogous way to other bodies and must do so in order to be available to others. He consequently combines two arguments into one: the risen Christ must occupy space somewhere, and the risen Christ is the eucharistic sacrament and the church. The second argument is not necessarily consequent upon the first.

I concur that in the first letter to the Corinthians there is an identity between the risen Christ, the eucharistic body, and the body of believers. The Greek word *soma* bears all these connotations in this context. However, Jenson may not have completely shrugged off the Reformation problem of location. He comes close, but there is some ambivalence or at least a mixture of metaphorical, sacramental, and realistic language. For example, in the second volume he states: "Christ, as the second identity of God, is at the right hand of the Father and just so can find his Ego in a community of earthly creatures and have that community as his body" (*ST* II, 254). Here we have the mixed-language metaphor of sitting at the right hand and the realistic-sacramental language of a presence in a community of believers. Ironically, the category that offers a way out of the difficulty is the subject of the chapter — sacramentality. As deeply sympathetic as I am with Jenson's identification of the church as the risen body of Christ, I fear that he often makes this identification too directly. In his theology the church risks becoming a prolongation of the incarnation in a way that *Lumen gentium* attempted to avoid.

In all fairness to Jenson, there are a number of places in his text where he attempts to distinguish between the church and Christ. For example, he notes: "We may not so identify the risen Christ with the church as to be unable to refer distinctly to the one and then to the other. Protestants have for just this reason often feared such language as appears in the previous paragraphs" (*ST* II, 213). However, he attempts to address this by an analysis of subject-object relations borrowed from German idealism. For example, the church as community is the object-Christ available for the world and her own members. Yet, Christ is also subject over and against the church: "the church as association is objectively confronted within herself by the same Christ" (*ST* II, 213). However, the relationship is much more intrinsic than that, for Christ is also the "subject whose objectivity is the community" (*ST* II, 215). Here the church becomes Christ's "objective self." In this relationship the church becomes the visibility of the risen Christ, and we still have a very close identification between Christ and the church. I question whether subject-subject doesn't more accurately describe the relationship between Christ and the church. I suggest that an exploration of the sacramental character of the church might be a more satisfactory solution. It maintains a close relationship between Christ and the church; at the same time it distinguishes identities and avoids a disembodied spiritualism.

If Jenson were to use the category of sacrament in addition to those of "people," "temple," and "body," this would create a space, a difference, between the church and the risen Christ. Sacraments conceal as well as reveal. As he so well states, they point to a reality and contain a reality beyond themselves. The church is the sacramental presence of the risen Christ as the Eucharist is the sacramental presence of Christ. Historical presence is not the same as sacramental presence. They are two different modalities of being present. The category of sacrament tells us the manner in which Christ's body is present; it does not solve problems of location of that body. For example, even though sacramentality seems to offer a "localized" presence, that is, where the loaf and the cup are to be found, it is not that simple. For even though there are many altars, many cups, and many loaves, there is but one body.

The visible sign of the sacrament includes the institutional and social aspects of the church, that is, all that is manifest in history, located in space and time. The referent of the sign is the resurrected Christ. As with the incarnation, in the church there is the union of the divine and the human, the human being the manifestation and revelation of the divine. Henri de Lubac draws this analogy: "The church is here below the sacrament of Jesus Christ, as Jesus Christ himself is for us, in his humanity, the sacrament of God."[4] The human element becomes the manifestation and revelation of the divine. *Lumen gentium* expresses this relationship thus:

> This society, however, equipped with hierarchical structures, and the mystical body of Christ, a visible assembly and a spiritual community, an earthly church and a church enriched with heavenly gifts, must not be considered as two things, but as forming one complex reality comprising a human and a divine element. It is therefore by no mean analogy that it is likened to the mystery of the incarnate Word. For just as the assumed nature serves the divine Word as a living instrument of salvation inseparably joined with him, in a similar way the social structure of the church serves the Spirit who vivifies the church towards the growth of the body (see Eph. 4:16).[5]

Here the church is likened to the incarnate word; it is not equated with the incarnate word.

The concept of the church as the sacrament of Christ avoids too close an identification between Christ and the church. The concept of sacrament is able to express the unity between the sign and the referent of that sign at the same time that it maintains the distinction between sign and referent. It expresses the corporeality of the church and its relationship to the Eucharist, also a sacrament of the risen Christ.[6] Too close an identification between Christ and the church ignores the fact that the church has not fully arrived at the eschaton. The church is in a state of be-

4. Cited by Gustave Martelet, "De la sacramentalité propre à l'Eglise," *Nouvelle revue théologique* 95 (1973): 26.

5. *Lumen gentium,* 8. Translation from *Decrees of the Ecumenical Councils,* vol. 2: *Trent to Vatican II,* ed. Norman P. Tanner, S.J. (Washington, D.C.: Sheed & Ward and Georgetown University Press, 1990).

6. See Jenson's discussion of the relationship between the Eucharist and the church in *ST* II, 220.

coming, and its expression as sign is not fully complete. The presence of the risen Christ exceeds any sacramental instance of it, although we may say it is more intensively localized in its sacramental manifestation,[7] this sacramental manifestation being inclusive of both the Eucharist and the church.

The connection that Jenson draws between the Eucharist and the church, profoundly Augustinian in origin, retrieves a pre-twelfth-century theology whereby "the body of Christ received in the Eucharist, according to . . . recurring passages from Corinthians, is itself identical with the community it creates" (*ST* II, 221-22). Insofar as the interpretation of this remains within a sacramentally realistic rather than historically realistic context,[8] this is a profoundly "Catholic" interpretation that has yet to be fully integrated into contemporary Roman Catholic consciousness. In this Jenson provides a valuable contribution to Roman Catholic ecclesiology.

Mediating Ecclesial Institutions

Another issue in ecclesiology that can divide Protestants from Catholics is the role played by institutions in the church's life. As the time between the resurrection and the fulfillment stretched out, not only did the church find herself living in the continuity of a recognized tradition, she also had "to make arrangements for carrying out the self-identity so constituted into a future of her own," that is, she had to have "deliberate institutions that would be constitutive of her life" (*ST* I, 24). Jenson attempts to reject both the Catholic temptation to take these developments as unproblematic and the Protestant response to take them as illegitimate. In short, institutional development is both problematic and necessary for the life of the church. He states:

> No structures of historical continuity merely as such can assure the integrity of witness to reality that is other than the transmitting group. . . .

7. *The Constitution on the Sacred Liturgy,* 7.

8. This distinction does not deny that sacraments exist in history but is meant to distinguish between a sacramental mode of really existing from the historical mode of existing whereby the eating of Christ's body would cause pain to Christ's historical body. Yet "sacramental" has a heavier ontological density than the "merely symbolic" or "sign."

> Thus neither Scripture nor creed nor liturgy nor teaching office, nor yet their ensemble, can as historical structures guarantee the fidelity of our proclamation and prayer to the apostolic witness. Affirmation that the church is still the church pledges the certainty of a historical continuity that no structures of historical continuity can make certain. This affirmation therefore reaches beyond its immediate object to the faith that *God* uses the church's communal structures to preserve the gospel's temporal self-identity and so also the temporal self-identity of the gospel's community (*ST* I, 25).

Insofar as structures and institutions can be mediatory, so must they be instruments of the Spirit's work in the church.

The first "institution" of the church is the canon of Scriptures that is both "received" and formulated by the church. A second is the "instituted liturgy" as "a historical event that initiates a diachronically identifiable rite and mandates its repetition" (*ST* I, 34). Third are the dogmas as expressed in the creeds and conciliar statements of the church. These "institutions" largely concern texts, although the liturgy encompasses more than texts. They are institutions considered authoritative by Lutherans. Canon, liturgy, and creed are not possible, however, apart from an ecclesial authority that can authoritatively legislate and interpret. This brings Jenson to the necessity of a teaching office, a magisterium. Jenson argues for a magisterium from its necessity in order for Scripture and dogmatic texts to assert themselves. Son of the Reformation that he is, Jenson argues from the gospel to the necessity of a magisterium, thus arriving at a very Catholic concept from a principle of the Reformation all the while sensitive to the Protestant fear that "here is a circle that obviously could set the teaching office adrift to define the gospel as whatever pleases its momentary holders" (*ST* I, 40). This magisterium is a personal office. Citing Joseph Cardinal Ratzinger, he notes that ministerial succession is the necessary *personal* aspect of the church's total diachronic unity with the apostles.[9]

Within Jenson's systematic theology, ordained ministry is consequent upon the nature of the church as communion. His thoughts here are in strong accord with Roman Catholic teaching. The challenge is to convince his Protestant counterparts. The primary responsibility of ordained

9. *ST* I, 41. Referring to Joseph Cardinal Ratzinger, *Theologische Prinzipienlehre* (Munich: Erich Wewel, 1982), p. 256. This point is reiterated in *ST* II, 233.

ministry is to oversee the communion of the church in its diachronic and synchronic dimensions. Synchronically it "occupies the place in the eucharistic celebration from which this unity can be tended and where Christ is most clearly represented" (*ST* II, 232). Thus it is the responsibility of the ordained to preside over the eucharistic celebration. Diachronically, ordained ministry is in communion with the apostolic witness through its ability to say, "This is/is not the gospel." This is the function of a teaching office or magisterium.

Jenson's discussion of the office of communion is helpful to Roman Catholics and, I hope, will contribute to a rapprochement between Lutherans and Roman Catholics. What he does so well is to describe why apostolic succession has to reside in persons rather than in "legal perdurance or even agreement in formulated doctrine" (*ST* II, 233). He rightly argues that "a personal aspect is essential because the continuity in question is personal communion" (*ST* II, 233). He agrees with the Congregation for Doctrine and Faith that "churches lacking episcopal succession are 'wounded.'"[10] This was the term that caused much ecumenical consternation at the time it was uttered. A more contemporary and immediate reference is, of course, the recent failed agreement between the Episcopalians and the Evangelical Lutheran Church of America (ELCA) at the time of publication of Jenson's second volume.

Jenson attempts to bring Reformation ecclesiology closer to Roman Catholic ecclesiology by making a case for the local church being the diocese (*ST* II, 236). With this, he also reconciles the difference this asymmetry in theologies of the local church makes with respect to where the fullness of office resides, in the bishop or in the pastor, by noting that the bishop's office is definitively pastoral. Here the argumentation acknowledges the fullness within the bishop's office by essentially asserting that it serves the same function as a Lutheran pastor, that of shepherd. However, he also argues for the ecclesiality of the diocese by noting its character as "a certain miniature communion of communions," which mirrors the nature of the church it is. His theology of the local church raises no protests from the perspective of Roman Catholic ecclesiology, but it challenges the traditional Protestant view that "the church is the assembly of all believers

10. *ST* II, 242. Citing Congregation for the Doctrine of the Faith, *Letter to the Bishops of the Catholic Church on Some Aspects of the Church Understood as Communion,* 17.

among whom the Gospel is preached in its purity and the holy sacraments are administered according to the Gospel."[11] In both the argument for the ecclesiality of the local church and the fullness of office for the bishop, Lutherans must concede more to his theology than must Roman Catholics. Nevertheless, Jenson also challenges Roman Catholics to reform: "Dioceses must be demographically able to function as continuing if infrequent eucharistic assemblies," and "the work actually prescribed for bishops must be sacramental and instructional, and be administrative only in necessary consequence" (*ST* II, 241). He supports the historical monarchical episcopate but calls for a reform in its exercise so that the bishop may function less as a "branch manager" and more like a "shepherd."

Robert Jenson's ecclesiology is in profound sympathy with the Roman Catholic Church. Nevertheless, he remains a son of the Reformation. In a memorable address he gave at Saint John's University in Collegeville, Minnesota in March 1998, he described Protestants as pounding on the door of the Roman Catholic Church, saying: "Let us in! Let us in! We want to reform you!" My hope is that Robert Jenson's systematic theology will help move us closer to reconciliation.

11. *Augsburg Confession,* Article 7.

The Parlement of Foules and the Communion of Saints: Jenson's Appropriation of Patristic and Medieval Theology

A. N. WILLIAMS

'Now pes', quod Nature, 'I comaunde here!
For I have herde al youre opynyon,
And, in effecte, yet be we never the nere.'

The Parlement of Foules, 11.617-19

Robert Jenson has been known chiefly as a constructive theologian, and a rather combative one at that, who does not shrink from reprimand where he believes the prior theological tradition to have erred. From his earliest work, though, he has been deeply engaged with the classical tradition that he sometimes criticizes, and, on the whole, he has become more explicitly and deeply affirmative of it with the passing of time. The general rule describing his appropriation of pre-Reformation theology is that, with the exception of two loci, the Trinity and key elements of the doctrine of God, Jenson becomes increasingly sympathetic to and more deeply steeped in the prior tradition, so that his work falls into three periods corresponding almost exactly to the three decades in which he has published. In the first period, up to 1979, he engages the premodern tradition, but his appraisal of it is very mixed. The second period, from 1981 to 1989, is dominated by his work on the Trinity, time and divine impassibility, all points on which he believes the classical tradition to have wandered far from the biblical witness. In the most recent period, from 1991 onward, he does not reject the stance of his earlier work on the Trinity and doctrine of God but turns to issues pressing on the contemporary church, increasingly drawing on older theology and moving closer to the position of an idiosyncratic neo-Thomist. Thus while Jenson has always belonged as a disputant in the noisy "parlement of foules" that is the assemblage of patristic and medieval doctors of the church, with the passing years he has come to dispute less — and come closer to the "pes" (peace) that Nature requires of the fowls in Chaucer's poem.

The gradual movement toward Thomism begins in one of Jenson's earliest monographs, *The Knowledge of Things Hoped For,* which focuses on Origen and Thomas Aquinas. While Jenson criticizes the epistemology of both his predecessors, his choice of figures is augural, indicating how large a role both patristic and medieval theology will play in the later work. Jenson's treatment is appreciative, but he is also certain that Origen is heretical[1] and Aquinas is guilty of "epistemological works-righteousness."[2] Both Origen and Aquinas offer "hints of the directions in which to look,"[3] however, which in the context of this early book means a useful basis for constructive theology, and in the context of Jenson's later theology means an indication of where he himself will go as he becomes less a specifically Lutheran polemicist who sees medieval theology as the problem and more of a catholic one who sees the problem as contemporary, secularized Christianity.

The general character of Jenson's work in this period, though, reveals little interest in medieval theology, and the focus among patristic theologians is very much on Augustine, as in, for instance, *Visible Words,* Jenson's contribution to sacramental theology. The working assumption (as well as the title) of this early work is drawn from Augustine, and Jenson cites no other patristic theologian, though he draws extensively on early liturgies. The sacramental practice of the early church provides the baseline against which later theology and practice are largely measured (and often found

1. Robert Jenson, *The Knowledge of Things Hoped For: The Sense of Theological Discourse* (New York: Oxford University Press, 1969), p. 24.

2. Jenson, *Knowledge,* p. 94.

3. Jenson, *Knowledge,* p. 97.

wanting). Here, too, where Jenson is critical of the medieval church the critique often applies, as he acknowledges, to *all* later Western theology.[4]

In this period, we see also the first small indication of what will prove the exception to the general schema we have posited: Jenson's views on the Trinity. In a late essay of this period, "The Triunity of Truth" (dating from 1979), Jenson broaches the theme that will become the dominant preoccupation of the next decade and the area in which he will make his most original — though not necessarily his most significant — contribution. In this arena, Jenson is sharply critical of both the patristic and the medieval tradition, in part because he believes both to be the inheritors of a "Hellenic" culture that, in stressing divine impassibility, has denied the biblical inheritance, removed God from time, misconstrued the doctrine of the Trinity, and not had the good sense to agree with Martin Luther and Georg Hegel.[5] The later *Triune Identity* and "The Triune God" in *Christian Dogmatics*[6] will amplify the theme, never deviating from the original insight. If Jenson's Trinitarian theology often acknowledges the Cappadocians with appreciation, it nonetheless follows a theological line that is unmistakably modern.

The conclusions of "The Triunity of Truth," which in their rejection of divine impassibility and the immanent Trinity are so far from the spirit of both the Fathers and the medievals, nevertheless bear a further, and quite different, portent of the theology to come: Jenson's refusal to separate academic theology from the church's life of worship and the individual Christian's life of prayer. "There is no doing theology," he writes, "outside the context in which the matter of theology is present to us, that is, worship."[7] This conviction runs deeper in Jenson's theology than any other methodological principle, and it shows him at work not merely in the parlement of disputants but in the communion of the doctors of the church. Thus, in "Appeal to the Person of the Future" in *The Futurist Option*,[8] he cites no patristic or me-

4. See Robert Jenson, *Visible Words: The Interpretation and Practice of Christian Sacraments* (Philadelphia: Fortress Press, 1978), pp. 92, 170.

5. Robert Jenson, "The Triunity of Truth," in *Essays in Theology of Culture* (Grand Rapids: Eerdmans, 1995), pp. 91-94.

6. See Robert Jenson, *The Triune Identity: God According to the Gospel* (Philadelphia: Fortress Press, 1982); "The Triune God," in Carl E. Braaten and Robert W. Jenson, eds., *Christian Dogmatics* (Philadelphia: Fortress Press, 1984).

7. Jenson, *Essays*, p. 87.

8. Robert Jenson, "Appeal to the Person of the Future," in Carl E. Braaten and Robert W. Jenson, eds., *The Futurist Option* (New York: Newman Press, 1970).

dieval theology at all, but in considering prayer as a theological topic, he aligns himself with premodern theologians such as Origen, who deemed prayer a subject worthy of a theologian's attention.

For the next decade, though, Jenson's attention turned chiefly to the Trinity, and during this period his deepening connection to earlier theology is obscured by the veil of polemic against faulty assumptions of the classical tradition. In the two large treatments of the Trinity in this period, the highest praise he can give in *The Triune Identity* to the patristic tradition beyond the Cappadocians is that its "paradox Christology" makes a good-faith effort to assert both Jesus' true humanity and the "standard predicates of Hellenic theology,"[9] although in the slightly later contribution to the Lutheran dogmatics, he is willing to claim he stands in continuity with the medieval tradition, albeit the minority strain of it represented by Peter Lombard and Bonaventure, to which Karl Barth is also heir.[10] Jenson's reading of patristic Trinitarian theology is open to dispute, but nevertheless we see him here gingerly moving away from an approving Augustinianism and toward a view that, for all its unconventionality, concurs with one strand of the medieval tradition.

This trend of increasing appreciation appears even more clearly in essays in this period. Maintaining his approval of Augustine's notion of sacraments as visible words, Jenson declares in "Praying Animals" that he is operating with a Thomistic conception of the human person.[11] The slightly earlier "The Doctrine of Justification and the Practice of Counseling," however, reveals the complexity of Jenson's response to older theology. On one hand, he emphatically rejects the claim of one of his former seminary professors that God never violates human personality;[12] Jenson is surely accurate in maintaining that the doctrine of justification in the form in which it has been adopted by Lutherans indicates that God does just this.[13] Yet in this same essay, Jenson also declares his operative anthropology to be more indebted to Thomas Aquinas than Luther[14] and pronounces "the Eastern soteriology" (of theosis) to be "better than we have thought."[15] Most surpris-

9. Jenson, *The Triune Identity,* pp. 63-64.
10. Jenson, "The Triune God," pp. 84, 86 n. 2.
11. Jenson, *Essays,* p. 121.
12. Jenson, *Essays,* p. 109.
13. Jenson, *Essays,* p. 109.
14. Jenson, *Essays,* p. 111.
15. Jenson, *Essays,* p. 113.

ingly of all, given the preceding ringing affirmation of the doctrine on which Lutherans believe the church stands and falls, Jenson declares the medieval practice of penance to have been not nearly as bad as it was painted.[16] The developing theological stance is that of a catholic ecumenist, who simultaneously adopts medieval theology as he insists upon the rights of the Reformation.

The essays of this period offer another kind of foretaste of the work of the next decade as well: its concerns with aesthetics and worship. In "Beauty" (1986), Jenson begins from the lynchpin of Aquinas's aesthetic and proceeds to write: "Western history has gone on to teach another lesson as well: the experience of beauty does not survive the cessation of worship."[17] Without mentioning an Eastern theologian, Jenson recalls a key element of Eastern Orthodox self-understanding[18] and, in so doing, anticipates also an essay of the next decade where he tacitly rejects Aquinas's eucharistic theology, only to reach a conclusion that turns out to be this same Eastern one: "If [as Jenson wants to maintain] the space occupied by the sacramental elements is heaven, then the space the elements define around themselves is the gate of heaven, just as Orthodox theology, of course, has always said."[19]

In the latest decade of his works, the tendency to affirm pre-Reformation theology becomes increasingly pronounced. Now, even in the context of a discussion of time, Jenson readily acknowledges "my pseudo-Thomistic method,"[20] although again, his answer to the question of whether God has time is unquestionably modern. In the essays of this period, Jenson roots himself more and more deeply in the patristic and medieval world, his quarrels having been either adequately aired or superseded by the more immediately pressing problems of a post-Christian society and a secularized church. In "Hermeneutics and the Life of the Church," for example, Jenson finds a parallel between the early church's struggle against gnosticism and the issues of the day,[21] thus making common cause with Irenaeus. His advocacy of the

16. Jenson, *Essays,* p. 110.

17. Jenson, *Essays,* p. 148.

18. See Timothy Ware, *The Orthodox Church,* new ed. (London: Penguin, 1993), p. 264.

19. Jenson, "You Wonder Where the Body Went," in *Essays,* p. 222.

20. Jenson, "Does God Have Time?" in *Essays,* p. 198.

21. Robert Jenson, "Hermeneutics and the Life of the Church," in Carl E. Braaten and Robert W. Jenson, eds., *Reclaiming the Bible for the Church* (Grand Rapids: Eerdmans, 1995), pp. 95-97.

literal and narrative meaning of the Bible[22] runs against patristic (and, of course, medieval) practice inasmuch as it seems to rule out allegorical and spiritual meanings of the text, but Jenson believes himself at this point to be doing nothing other than commending Irenaeus's hermeneutical rules. Significantly, Jenson does not bother to quarrel with this allegorical tradition of exegesis: the common ground shared by the Fathers and those, like himself, who are concerned at the prevalent divorce between biblical studies and theology is evidently more important than the disputes of the sixteenth century. In insisting particularly that scripture is the *church's* to interpret,[23] Jenson acknowledges that it is not only what Irenaeus calls the Rule of Faith, but the theological tradition of the church since Irenaeus's time, which is normative for biblical exegesis.[24] Tradition has now been added to Scripture in the only way Aquinas, to name but one medieval example, would have countenanced it: not as an independent informant of the church's teaching, but as the matrix *within which* the church interprets Scripture.[25] In case anyone missed the radicalness of his suggestion, Jenson spells it out: "Rarely do we appreciate the rather drastic point here. There can be no churchly reading of Scripture that is not activated and guided by the church's teaching. . . . there can be no reading of the Bible that is not churchly."[26]

To note his increasingly explicit approval of pre-Reformation theology and theological method is not to suggest Jenson has somehow departed from his own tradition, but only that he has come to read it, as other prominent Lutherans have, in a new way. Thus, in "The Church as *Communio*," Jenson thinks with both Aquinas's theology of the Trinity and the Fathers' theology of salvation, sanctification, and consummation (i.e., theosis), finding in the two in tandem a theological basis for contemporary ecclesiology.[27] Yet in affirming *perichoresis* in God as providing a model for the church's *koinonia*,[28] Jenson roots himself not only in the past but in the future: his interest in the Christian tradition is not archaeological, but con-

22. Jenson, "Hermeneutics," p. 97.

23. Jenson, "Hermeneutics," pp. 97-98.

24. Jenson, "Hermeneutics," p. 98.

25. *Summa theologiae* I.1.8 ad 2.

26. Jenson, "Hermeneutics," p. 98.

27. Robert Jenson, "The Church as *Communio*," in Carl E. Braaten and Robert W. Jenson, eds., *The Catholicity of the Reformation* (Grand Rapids: Eerdmans, 1996), p. 3.

28. Jenson, "The Church as *Communio*," p. 3.

structive, urgently concerned that the church grow into the likeness of God's life, rather than into that of the secular corporation that modern churches of every stripe seem all too often to resemble.

The pattern we have been tracing shows itself perhaps most forcefully of all in a late essay, "Catechesis for Our Time" (1999),[29] in which Jenson refers to no pre-Reformation theologian by name, but where his vision is largely informed by the liturgical and catechetical practice of the early church. In the crisis of catechesis (or lack thereof) that Jenson sees facing Western churches in the late twentieth century, he finds a parallel to the pre-Constantinian church struggling to communicate a moral and theological vision radically different from that of the surrounding society. The wheel has turned, he seems to say, and in seeking commonality and direction for the future, we do well to look to the past.

The trends we have been tracing converge in what, even at this early juncture, we must deem Jenson's magnum opus, the *Systematic Theology.* He emphatically announces one of the central characteristics of his mode of engaging the Christian tradition in the preface to the first volume, where he defines theology as "the church's enterprise of thought"[30] and continues: "and the only church conceivably in question is the unique and unitary church of the creeds" (*ST* I, vii). By defining theology in this way, Jenson does three things: (1) he places his own theological endeavor within the context of a particular community; his theology could not, therefore, arise out of anything other than a dialogue with that community's history, its active recollection of its intellectual and spiritual past. (2) He privileges a particular period in the community's history, the patristic. (3) He states a reason for privileging that period, namely, that it was a period of unity. While the first of these points places Jenson in the company of the vast majority of Christian theologians, past and present, the second two distinguish him from precisely that vast majority. While Eastern Orthodox and Anglican theologians would agree that the patristic period has a normative character equaled by no other, Orthodox theologians would not grant Jenson's reason, which regards both East and West as doctrinally normative for an undivided church. The irony of Jenson's appro-

29. Robert Jenson, "Catechesis for Our Time," in Carl E. Braaten and Robert W. Jenson, eds., *Marks of the Body of Christ* (Grand Rapids: Eerdmans, 1999).

30. Robert Jenson, *Systematic Theology,* vol. I: *The Triune God* (Oxford: Oxford University Press, 1997), p. vii. Hereafter abbreviated *ST,* by volume and page.

priation of patristic and medieval theology is that he proposes to use precisely the theology from which division first emerged to heal division. His appropriation of pre-Reformation theology is thus central to his self-appointed and decisively ecumenical task in these two volumes.

If Jenson states this intention unambiguously in the preface, he does so in a gesture of good faith, for the pages that follow do indeed both seek an honest dialogue with the past and, for the most part, seek unity, Jenson's proclivity for occasional polemic notwithstanding. Where execution may differ from promise lies in what parts of the tradition Jenson himself claims to be most deeply indebted. In his view, his system is inescapably Western, despite its acknowledged dependence on Eastern Orthodoxy at key points (*ST* I, viii). The Western character of this theology is debatable, despite Jenson's frequent quarrels with Byzantium's greatest theologian, Gregory Palamas, for Jenson resorts frequently to two earlier Byzantine theologians, Maximus the Confessor and John Damascene. When, however, Jenson claims that on issues where the West is divided against itself he will most often espouse the catholic side (*ST* I, viii), he is indubitably correct. Indeed, given its heavy use of both the Greek Fathers and Augustine, as well as Aquinas himself, perhaps the most accurate label for the systematic theology is "neo-Thomistic."[31] These three strands, then, are those in the pre-Reformation tradition on which this theological system most deeply draws: the Greek Fathers (and let us specify: up to and including Damascene), Augustine, and Aquinas.

The trend of his earlier works — that where he diverges sharply from the tradition it will be in a tightly defined set of loci concerned with the Trinity and some of the classical attributes of God — continues to hold. In this context, he regards the West's Augustinian inheritance to be deeply flawed. Augustine, he charges, is responsible for the West's error of taking the Trinity's work *ad extra* to be undivided inasmuch as the works of the Three are indistinguishable, rather than because they are perfectly mutual (*ST* I, 113); thereby Augustine effectively empties the Trinity of any real distinctions in Jenson's view. This criticism of Augustine is quite common; what is less usual is the conclusion Jenson draws from it: if the term *person* has no real content, as Jenson takes Augustine to be saying, then "propositions about God's immanent triunity . . . cannot function in the life of the

31. The three theologians Aquinas cites most frequently are Denys, Augustine, and Damascene.

church or elsewhere in the system of theology" (*ST* I, 113). While one must surely concur that the doctrine of the Trinity ultimately becomes dysfunctional in theology and piety (*ST* I, 113), Jenson's desideratum is Augustine's own, for the treatise Jenson legitimately faults nevertheless evidences a unity of theology and spirituality that later Western theology has rarely attained. Ironically, Jenson approves that part of Augustine's Trinitarian thinking that has been most sharply criticized of all, the notion of "vestiges" of the Trinity in the human person.[32] Jenson, however, locates the precise point of similarity of the divine and human persons in divine self-transcendence, a point of Jensoniana created in dialogue with Augustine, rather than in repetition of the latter, which is methodologically just what Jenson promised he would do in the preface to volume I.

A similar relationship of contiguity and innovation prevails in Jenson's treatment of Thomas Aquinas on the procession of the Spirit. Reviewing the debate between East and West on this point, the *filioque*, Jenson chides Aquinas (and Augustine, on whom Aquinas draws in this regard) for depersonalizing the Father and the Son in the course of arguing that the Spirit proceeds from both (*ST* I, 149-51). Yet even as he acknowledges the validity of the East's objection at this point (as argued by Vladimir Lossky), Jenson also rebukes the East for its static portrait of the Trinity (*ST* I, 151-52). As Aquinas's problem turned out to revert, in Jenson's reading, to Augustine, so Lossky's problem reverts to Palamas, whose role in the Eastern tradition approximates that of Aquinas in the Roman Catholic tradition (*ST* I, 152-53). This sharply critical dialogue with Palamas is one of many scattered throughout both volumes, in the course of which the Byzantine theologian is presented in a starkly negative light. In parting company with Palamas, Jenson seems at odds with his own claim that his account of the Trinity is more Eastern than Western (*ST* I, 123); in fact, he is true to his first promise, that he would think in continuity with the church of the *creeds.* Accordingly, while he is largely hostile to the later Byzantine tradition, he is so because he believes it broke away from the theology of the Cappadocians. Jenson's doctrine of the Trinity is indeed patristic and Eastern, to the extent that it is indebted to any earlier theology, since it springs from dialogue with the Cappadocians. Where Jenson

32. Robert Jenson, *Systematic Theology,* vol. II: *The Works of God* (Oxford: Oxford University Press, 1999), p. 65 and n. 51. Hereafter abbreviated *ST,* by volume and page.

differs from later Byzantine theology, as well as from that of Augustine and Aquinas, he does so largely because he finds it static. Here again, we see the extent to which the conclusions he reached early in his career continue to hold sway — but as in the earlier work, these issues are the only ones where Jenson departs significantly from the pre-Reformation tradition.

This particular quarrel with Augustine and Aquinas is ironic for two reasons. The first is that one of the points on which Jenson seems to find both thinkers most helpful is with respect to divine will (cf. *ST* II, 22-23, 42). For both Augustine and Aquinas, however, the notion of divine will is intrinsically connected to their doctrines of the Trinity. Both thinkers attain to persuasiveness in Jenson's eyes on a point that precisely demonstrates the role of the Trinity in their respective works: the Trinity is not only inseparable from their systems as a whole but also the source of their most important theological insights. Whether or not Jenson believes this to be true, his affirmation of these earlier thinkers on divine will is consistent with his wish for his own theology: that it be both in dialogue with prior tradition and deeply informed by the doctrine of the Trinity.

Where Jenson does side unambiguously with the East is on the atonement. His frank acknowledgment that no single form of this doctrine has ever been universally accepted (*ST* I, 186) affords him a certain freedom to reject the Anselmian model, which many in the West seem to regard as dogma. Jenson rightly asserts that the Anselmian theory wreaks havoc on the doctrine of God and renders unnecessary the resurrection. The solution he arrives at — that the crucifixion manifests God's nature as compassionate and gracious and that the resurrection is the logical consequent to *this* divine nature (*ST* I, 189) — develops out of the Christology he has earlier affirmed. Since that Christology is Cyrillian and Maximian, Eastern in other words, so is Jenson's theory of the atonement.

Yet despite the Eastern basis for Jenson's understanding of the atonement, the governing rubric of his doctrine of creation is thoroughly Western: the identity of essence and existence in God and their distinction in creatures, a notion he borrows from Aquinas. While Jenson feels the need to give it a fuller, and specifically Trinitarian, explication (*ST* I, 214ff.), this distinction becomes as central to his theology as it was for Aquinas's. By the time Jenson arrives at the doctrine of creation proper, in volume II, he has found it necessary to employ the distinction in conjunction with another insight indispensable to Aquinas's theology: his doctrine of analogy. Both the identity of essence and existence and analogy are items of Tho-

mism Jenson dealt with previously; while he has consistently held the first in high regard, the second is arguably presented in the *Systematic Theology* in a more positive light than in *The Knowledge of Things Hoped For,* and this shift confirms the general trend toward Thomism. Jenson's use of these cornerstones of Thomistic theology is significant both because they lie at the heart of the system in the larger *Summa,* and because they have been notoriously misunderstood by a theologian Jenson holds in generally high regard. In implicitly rejecting Karl Barth's misreading of Aquinas on analogy, Jenson indeed takes the catholic side, though in no sense that rejects thinkers in the Reformation traditions when the latter are not engaged in misunderstanding.

Jenson draws further on two of his favored sources in his doctrine of creation, although not uncritically. As noted, one point where his theological passions overlap significantly with those of Augustine is in the preoccupation of both with the question of time. While Jenson regards Augustine's view as the product of both "profound insight and obvious muddle" (*ST* II, 31ff.), he nevertheless attributes one cornerstone of his doctrine of creation to his predecessor: the notion "that for God to have creatures is first and foremost to take time for them."[33] Likewise, Jenson exploits Aquinas's notion of God's presence to elucidate the sense in which the nonspatially defined Trinity might exist in relation to creatures who *are* in space (*ST* II, 48). Again, in making use of precisely these loci in the work of his predecessors, Jenson shows a fine instinct for their distinctive contributions to Christian theology, for however flawed Jenson may find Augustine's notion of time, the latter has been one of the few who recognized the theological import of the issue, and, like Jenson, one of the few to make reflection on time a central feature of a major work. Similarly, the notion of God's existing in us by presence and power effectively summarizes both the heart of Aquinas's doctrine of sanctification and his articulation of the mechanism by which God and humanity are to be united.

Thus we are brought to the border of the realm of Jenson's most significant continuity with Augustine, Aquinas, and the Greek patristic tradition: the doctrines of sanctification and the Christian life. On the first point Jenson cites, as is entirely appropriate, Irenaeus and Athanasius, both of whom stand within the great communion that is the patristic doc-

33. *ST* II, 29; thus Jenson's formulation; Augustine does not to my knowledge put it quite like that.

tors in affirming that the purpose and effect of the incarnation is the deification of humanity (*ST* II, 322ff.). Here, though, Jenson's only reference to the Western tradition is to Luther, not to Augustine or Aquinas. Nevertheless, the fact that participation in divine life pervades this work as Jenson's assumption of humanity's telos perhaps more than anything else suggests the contiguity of his thought with that of his forebears.

So, too, does his tendency to see that telos in contemplative terms, as a *vision* of God. While he is critical of two theologians who gave considerable thought to the nature of that vision (Aquinas and Palamas), Jenson's conclusion remains Thomistic: if we will see God, if we will know God, if we will be united to God, it is because of a specifically Trinitarian work in us. The fact that Jenson does not *think* this is what Aquinas is saying does not detract from the fact that the point he wishes to reach is precisely the Thomistic one.

If this communion of saints agrees on the *visio Dei* as the end of human life, so does it agree on the means, and here Jenson's likeness to the Fathers, both patristic and medieval, assumes its greatest proportions, though his debt is to the spirit rather than the letter. It is the fact that his concern for the explication of divine freedom and foreknowledge comes in the context of a discussion of prayer (*ST* II, 44); that his anthropology is founded on humanity's innate desire to see God (*ST* II, 65-66); that his hamartology defines sin as a function of the restless heart wearily seeking its repose in God (*ST* II, 145); that he views faith as humanity's true life (*ST* II, 68); that he frequently appeals to the liturgy as a starting point for theological reasoning (e.g., *ST* I, 34-35, 190; II, 322); that he regards icons not only as legitimate objects of Christian devotion but also of theological reflection (*ST* II, chap. 29) — in all these respects, and many more, Jenson manifests not only his assumption of the relevance of the data of the Christian life for theological reflection but also his concern for the vitality of that life. His theology is respectably, but never merely, academic. Here also Jenson shows himself to be in concert with an earlier tradition, one neither derailed by the agendas of the Enlightenment nor mesmerized by the apologetic requirements of "public" theology so-called, but which remembers that its task is the same as that of the liturgy: to praise God truly.

For all his rightful suspicion of the term "spirituality," Jenson does exactly what the Fathers, the Western medievals, and dare it be said, the Byzantines, do: he writes theology *out of* the church's life and practice of faith and, *therefore,* speaks to the church and not merely the parlement of theologians. It is this doxological character of his work, too, that often keeps it from falling into the theologian's besetting sin of forgetting, in the midst of attacking false talk about God, that singing God's praise is the theologian's first and prime vocation. Thus it is that Jenson can say at the beginning of his first volume: "At bottom, the chief thing to be done about the integrity of the church across time is to pray that *God* will indeed use the church's structures of historical continuity to establish and preserve it, and to believe that he answers this prayer. Much futile polemical theology will be spared on all sides when this is recognized without qualification" (*ST* I, 41). Here Jenson himself summarizes the trajectory of his theology: its concern for the integrity of the church; his conviction that theology is advanced not only by disputation, but by prayer; its thoroughgoing, though never uncritical, ecumenism; and, related to all these as both source and goal, Jenson's assumption that he, too, stands in the midst of the patristic and medieval doctors of the church. Perhaps, in the end, the driving force of all his theology has been not his inclination to quarrel with the best of the parlement but his own deeply held and theologically consequent belief in the communion of saints.

The Church as Polity? The Lutheran Context of Robert W. Jenson's Ecclesiology

DAVID S. YEAGO

I. Introduction

Central to the ecclesiology set forth in the second volume of Robert W. Jenson's *Systematic Theology*[1] is the description of the church as a polity. The point, it needs to be said immediately, is not that the church *has* a "polity" as that term is commonly used, for example, in courses on "church polity" for ordinands in North American seminaries, which survey a particular denomination's administrative and governmental structures. The disjunction between "the church" and "the church's polity" implicit in most such courses is in fact the antithesis of Jenson's point. His claim is not that the church *has* a polity but rather that the church *is* a polity: that is, in its theologically significant essence the church is a *people*, the bodily concrete and "historically actual" — though not always "unambiguously delineable" (*ST* II, 194) — assembly of those whom God is calling to live in shared anticipation of the final fulfillment.[2] A "polity" just is, for

1. Robert W. Jenson, *Systematic Theology*, vol. 2: *The Works of God* (Oxford: Oxford University Press, 1999). See also *Systematic Theology*, vol. 1: *The Triune God* (Oxford: Oxford University Press, 1997). Both hereafter abbreviated *ST*, by volume and page.

2. This is of course an abstract way of saying "those whom God has brought by way of baptism to the eucharistic table."

Jenson, a gathering joined in shared anticipation of a particular future; this is his gloss on Augustine's definition of a people as "the assembly of a multiplicity of rational beings, joined in an agreed sharing of the objects of their love."[3]

The identification of the church as a polity plays a crucial role in the systematic structure of the ecclesiology of *The Works of God.* Specifically, it is the key move in Jenson's effort to think through with "epistemic seriousness" the common threefold description of the church as "people of God, body of Christ, and temple of the Spirit" (*ST* II, 189-90). To treat this description with "epistemic seriousness" is to take it as something other than a sampling of "images" to be drawn on eclectically for various rhetorical purposes; it is to take it instead as having substantive conceptual content and therefore to raise seriously the question of the "conceptual links" between the three descriptive terms of which it is composed. Jenson's attempt to address this question occupies two full chapters in *The Works of God.*

In chapter 25, "The Polity of God," Jenson sets out "to bring 'people' and 'temple' together in the Augustinian teaching that the church is, literally and indeed paradigmatically, a 'polity'" (*ST* II, 190). To speak of a polity as a gathering joined in shared anticipation of a particular future is as much as to say that a polity is a people "united in a common *spirit*" (*ST* II, 204), since for Jenson, "spirit" is defined as the power in which the present is opened toward and anticipates futurity. To speak of the church as "temple of the Holy Spirit" is thus to claim that the "common spirit" of this people is *God's own* Spirit, the power by which God's own life is opened toward the infinite futurity proper to it. The future toward which the church lives is the endless unfolding of the mutual faithfulness of Jesus and the Father in blessing and life, and the Spirit is the agent of that specific infinitude.[4] To use Augustine's language, the church is a multitude united precisely by the Spirit's act drawing all together in expectation to anticipate the peace of the coming kingdom; and as such, the church is, as Jenson says, *literally* a polity.

3. Augustine, *City of God* 19.24: "Populus est coetus multitudinis rationalis, rerum quas diligit concordi communione sociatus." One of the surprises of *ST* II is the large role played in it by Augustine, after Jenson's repetition of his long-standing criticisms of Augustine's Trinitarian theology in the first volume. For the latter, cf. *ST* I, 110ff.

4. Here of course Jenson builds on the pneumatology of his first volume; cf. *ST* I, 146-61.

In chapter 26, "The Great Communion," Jenson goes on to explore the links between this account of the church as polity and the scriptural description of the church as "body of Christ." In drawing the many together to become one people in anticipation of the kingdom, the Spirit constitutes this people as the body of Christ. The future that the Spirit anticipates is nothing other than the life that the crucified Jesus lives before the Father. As the church is drawn into that future by the act of the Spirit, and so becomes a polity, the church at the same time becomes the concrete locus where Christ's life is present in and for the world.[5] That the church is the body of Christ is therefore no mere trope but a serious affirmation. The church is the locus of the identifiability and availability of Jesus Christ for others, just as we are all identifiable by and available to one another by virtue of our bodies. The church is at the same time interior to Christ's *self*-identification: "To the question, 'Who am I?' he answers, 'I am this community's head. I am the subject whose objectivity is this community. I am the one who died to gather them.'"[6]

On this account, therefore, it is precisely *as* a polity — a people joined in a common life animated by the expectation of God's kingdom — that the church is the body of Christ, and vice versa. An immediate implication of this is that it is precisely as a *public* phenomenon — an "outward," "bodily," and "visible" community — that the church is an eschatological reality, participating in the newness of the resurrection; likewise, insofar as the church bears eschatological predicates, it is precisely as a public phenomenon, as a polity, that it does so. Jenson's ecclesiology is thus massively opposed to any account of the social-political and eschatological aspects of the church's life as features located on different ontological planes, such that the "outward" life of the church as polity would be seen as only the vehicle or concomitant of a more fundamental "inward" and spiritual life. For Jenson, the church is "spiritual" precisely *as* "political," for the church-gathering act of the Spirit is precisely to form a multitude into a polity by drawing them toward a shared future.

Three further observations may round out this overview. First, as a

5. Here again, it is crucial to note, we are describing abstractly what occurs concretely in the celebration of the Eucharist.

6. *ST* II, 214-15. The great prooftext for this claim in the patristic and Reformation traditions, which Jenson does not cite in this context, is the stunning question with which the risen Jesus rebuked a persecutor of the infant church: "Saul, Saul, why are you persecuting *me?*" (Acts 9:4).

polity, the church is an ordered community whose common life has a distinctive institutional form. Because the church *is* a polity, it also has a "church polity" in the more usual sense, and this polity has a proper form distinctive to the church as the body of Christ. It is in this perspective that Jenson appropriates and develops the themes and arguments of recent ecumenical *communio*-ecclesiology: "The great principle of the church's polity . . . is that any level or organ of ecclesial actuality that can truly be called church must itself be constituted as communion and that these communions are in perichoretic communion with each other" (*ST* II, 223). The eschatological character of the church is therefore of decisive significance for the institutional form of the church's common life; *communio*-ecclesiology founds "a doctrine of church polity drawn from the nature of the church herself, rather than by imitation of the worldly collectives around her" (*ST* II, 223).

Second, the order of the church includes *governance:* "As a polity, the church has a government."[7] The governance of the church is likewise structured and institutionalized: it takes form in an *office,* or a complex of offices, whose symbolic and functional dimensions are alike shaped by the church's distinctive character as the "polity of God." Thus Jenson devotes a further chapter to the office of ministry, under the title, "The Office of Communion." The implication of the title is that the governance of the church is embedded in the eschatological *communio*-structure of the church and is formed by and for it: here too the church is *eschatologically ordered.*

Finally, Jenson has placed this whole ecclesiological structure into the context of the doctrine of creation. Augustine's notion of polity is first introduced in *The Works of God,* not in part VI, on the church, but in part V, entitled "The Creatures" (*ST* II, 76-85). There it figures in Jenson's account of the *imago dei,* the self-transcendence of the human creature from and toward God. Such self-transcendence, in which we both possess ourselves and go beyond ourselves into the future, is not, according to Jenson, simply the innate power of the individual human being. It is constituted in

7. *ST* II, 205. I am not sure that Jenson ever quite gives the grounds for this thesis. His account seems open, however, to an argument like that of the Thomist political philosopher Yves Simon, who maintains that "authority" is not simply a defense against wickedness but is necessary precisely to make possible the communal pursuit of the good in any community of finite agents, with or without sin. Thus governance is intrinsic to polity. See Yves Simon, *A General Theory of Authority* (Notre Dame, Ind.: Notre Dame University Press, 1980).

and through the exchange of word and response within the human community. Insofar as I am *addressed* and *summoned* to the future in speech addressed to me by others, my transcendence of myself is established. It is in this way that I am simultaneously granted a perspective on "myself" and allowed freedom from "myself" as a presently existing factor. Thus communal discourse that looks toward a future — *political* discourse — is constitutive of human personhood.

Under the conditions of sin, of course, this dependence of personhood on community means that disordered community grounds damaged and distorted personhood, selves *de*formed by the *libido dominandi* that animates Augustine's "earthly city," the *civitas terrena.* By contrast, the one community in which human existence comes to authentic fulfillment is the "heavenly polity" whose present anticipation is the church. The communal discourse of the church is centered in the *gospel,* which bestows the infinitude of the triune life and love as the future that we may together anticipate. In this way, the church is not only literally but also, as Jenson puts it, *paradigmatically* a polity. That is, it is in the church that the true significance of human community first comes into view, and the true fulfillment of human common life is anticipated.[8] Thus the significance of the church is not, for Jenson, located in any special "religious" sphere; rather, the church is central to an extended theological-political analysis of human community, its meaning and its imperilment, that runs through the length and breadth of *The Works of God.*

This overview has done no more than trace the surface of Jenson's ecclesiological argument, and it has done little or nothing to unfold its depth and richness. Nevertheless, it is perhaps sufficient in order to raise the issue to which I shall devote this essay: the question of the relationship of this ecclesiology to the *Lutheran* tradition in which Jenson was formed theologically, and with which his thought retains deep and complex bonds,

8. This is perhaps the point at which to acknowledge that the notion of "anticipation" is heavily freighted in this context and raises all sorts of questions that cannot be pursued here. For Jenson's own introduction of the term and initial account of it, cf. *ST* II, 171-72. As an ecclesiological category, it means to affirm that "the church is neither a realization of the new age nor an item of the old age. She is precisely an event *within the event* of the new age's advent" (171). Thus to speak of the church living in *anticipation* of the kingdom distinguishes the church from the kingdom while at the same time relating the church to the kingdom in an ontologically serious way. "For it is what creatures may anticipate from God that is their being" (172).

even as his conception of the task of systematic theology has evolved in a pronouncedly postdenominational, ecumenical direction.[9] For it is certainly the case that the ecclesiology sketched here, with its focus on the ordered, public community of the church and its refusal to separate the "eschatological church" from the church visible, stands in considerable tension, indeed outright opposition, to a well-known ecclesiological standpoint that has for several centuries been repeatedly proclaimed as properly and unconditionally "Lutheran."

A fairly typical example of this view may be cited from a standard work coedited by Jenson himself:

> Lutherans have never considered a specific church order necessary. They have defined the essence of Christianity in terms of proper understanding of the gospel of grace rather than in terms of community structures. . . . Their position is consistent with their theological insistence that grace alone is the rule of Christian existence before God and the world. Such an insistence rejects any notion that a specific empirical form of behavior or organization is necessary for the church, or that it would make the church "better" in any theologically significant way.[10]

Jenson could perhaps make room for a version of the first claim in this last sentence, that a specific form of common life is not "necessary" for the church; that is, on his own terms, he could say that a community may still be church despite considerable *dis*order in the form of its common life. Yet it is clear that he would have to reject the second claim, which implies that the whole outward ordering of the church's life is simply irrelevant to the church's theological identity. If no form of behavior or organization is theologically "better" than any other, then the identity of the church as eschatological community has no implications whatever for the ordering of its public, "visible" life together. The question of how the church is to live as a people out in the "empirical" world is classified as a nontheological question — or at least, as a question with no specifically *ecclesiological* shape. There would, on this view, be no norms of the church's outward communal life that are proper to the church as such,

9. On the ecumenical character of theology, cf. *ST* I, vii-ix.

10. Philip J. Hefner, "The Church," in Carl L. Braaten and Robert W. Jenson, eds., *Christian Dogmatics,* vol. 2 (Philadelphia: Fortress Press, 1984), p. 236.

proper to the church as an eschatological community, the community of salvation. This, as even the superficial sketch provided above must clearly show, Jenson must flatly repudiate.

What then can we say about Jenson's relationship to the Lutheran tradition that the above citation claims to represent? Indeed, we may stipulate that it *does* represent the Lutheran tradition in one sense, in that it does accurately reproduce the majority opinion of Lutheran systematicians, and the tenor of much Lutheran denominational rhetoric, over the past two centuries. Has Jenson then simply abandoned Lutheran perspectives altogether and allied himself, on this point at least, with an ecumenical power bloc responsive to Anglican, Roman Catholic, and Orthodox concerns and indifferent to the challenge of the Reformation?

The question is of more than merely academic interest. The Lutheran churches of the world are increasingly polarized, within and among themselves, precisely over fundamental issues in ecclesiology, and such tensions seem, at the time of this writing, to have brought to the brink of schism the Lutheran denomination within whose institutions Jenson himself passed his teaching career. Yet this is not a matter of concern only for Lutherans. It is a fair question, one that others too might want to pose to an intentionally *ecumenical* ecclesiology, whether it requires those who would receive it to repudiate so significant a Christian theological inheritance as that of the Protestant Reformation. Moreover, the question is *also* of properly academic interest, for Jenson's own roots in the Lutheran tradition are deep enough that the exploration of his relationship to that tradition must be an inescapable aspect of the exposition of his thought.[11]

In this essay, I want to suggest that Jenson's disagreement with the Lutheran *communis opinio de ecclesia* reflects not his alienation from the Lutheran tradition but his specific placement within a long, difficult, and complex history of Lutheran wrestling with the meaning of the church. To

11. Jenson was formed in Lutheran institutions, taught in a Lutheran denominational seminary for twenty years, and is coauthor of the textbook most commonly used for over twenty years in courses on the Lutheran Confessions in seminaries of the largest North American Lutheran denomination and its predecessor bodies. See Eric W. Gritsch and Robert W. Jenson, *Lutheranism: The Theological Movement and Its Confessional Writings* (Philadelphia: Fortress Press, 1976). The question of his relation to the Lutheran tradition is therefore of intrinsic importance to the interpretation of his thought.

make that claim, I shall first narrate some main lines of that history and suggest that Jenson's ecclesiology has a specific background in the German *Kirchenkampf* of the 1930s and the intra-Lutheran debates that surrounded it. Then I shall turn briefly to the Reformation itself and suggest that his work in this area can be read as taking up significant themes in the ecclesiology of the Lutheran Reformers that have been pushed to one side and widely forgotten in the subsequent history of Lutheranism.

My goal in all this is not to claim Jenson against his will as a denominational theologian, but to clarify the *ecumenical* significance of the way in which his thought addresses issues that are not unique to Lutherans, though they may take particularly acute form within the Lutheran tradition. Examining the Lutheran genealogy of Jenson's theology of the church will, I hope, bring into sharper focus its implications for a range of questions that continue to confront the ecumenical church with undiminished urgency, even at this millennial turn of the times.

II. Ecclesiological Developments in Modern Lutheranism

The Lutheran *communis opinio* that consigns the outward order of the church to theological irrelevance is a product of the nineteenth century; it represents the initially victorious side in a conflict over the church and its ministry in which Lutherans have been embroiled for nearly two centuries.[12] The background of this controversy is the complex legal, political, cultural, and theological history of the Lutheran churches of the Holy Roman Empire in the post-Reformation period, as well as the new situation introduced by the termination of the legal arrangements governing the relationship of these churches to state and society in 1803, when the Holy Roman Empire formally came to an end.[13] This legal change was of course also contemporary with far-reaching cultural and political changes that

12. For an overview of this controversy, albeit one not especially friendly to the concerns of this essay, cf. H. Fagerberg, "Amt VII. Von ca. 1600 bis zur Mitte des 19. Jahrhunderts," in Gerhard Krause and Gerhard Müller, eds., *Theologische Realenzyklopädie*, vol. 2 (Berlin and New York: de Gruyter, 1977-), pp. 574-93, esp. 586-90.

13. Politically, of course, the Holy Roman Empire had been a fiction for centuries; but legally, the provisions of the Peace of Augsburg and the Peace of Westphalia governed church-state relations in the principalities belonging technically to the Empire until 1803.

accompanied Germany's difficult, singular, sometimes brilliant but ultimately catastrophic engagement with social and intellectual modernity; and this too is very much in the background of Lutheran struggles over the church.

Two factors in the post-Reformation Lutheran history stand out as especially significant background to the ecclesiological developments of the nineteenth century: the so-called "church-government of the territorial princes" *(landesherrliches Kirchenregiment),* on the one hand, and the legacy of Pietism, on the other.

In his 1522 *Address to the German Nobility,* Martin Luther repudiated the centralization of church authority in Rome, which had been engineered half a millennium before in the so-called Gregorian Reforms, and called on the territorial princes to initiate necessary changes in ecclesial life and practice in the role of "emergency bishops." However, having cut ties with Rome, Lutheran churches largely succumbed to the fate that Roman centralization had been designed to ward off: they became dependencies of the princes. German Lutheranism emerged from the Reformation with the church absorbed into the state and under its direct authority to a degree unprecedented in Christian history.[14] One of the most perspicacious Lutherans of the last two centuries, the nineteenth-century Bavarian pastor-theologian Wilhelm Loehe, summed up the outcome:

> The defects and evils of the present constitutional form of the Protestant Church have so repressed the church and its growth — every eye can see this which wants to see — that the Lutheran Church in three hundred years has not been able to attain the form which would win her respect from the outside and make her capable of being for the world what her birth from the word of God and the call of the church to be a blessing alike demand. Living in a marriage with the state, the church was not happy; her husband ruled as lord of the household. A free unfolding of her glory, a development of her life and being, were unthinkable. It is to be sure the case that occasionally the husband was in a good mood, and allowed his partner a bit of latitude. One can also be thankful to him

14. On the radical innovation this involved, cf. Karlheinz Blaschke, "The Reformation and the Rise of the Territorial State," in James D. Tracy, ed., *Luther and the Modern State in Germany,* Sixteenth Century Essays and Studies, vol. 7 (Kirksville, Mo.: Sixteenth Century Journal, 1986), pp. 61-75, here pp. 66-68.

> that he did not make an even worse mess of things. But what is true still remains true — and as a whole the connection between state and church was an unhappy bad marriage.[15]

Lutheran Pietism arose in the context of this bad marriage and was in part a response to the disarray it had brought about in the Lutheran household. Pietism was a complex movement, about which there have been too many easy generalizations, but perhaps it can be said that it tended to presuppose the spiritual irrelevance of ecclesiastical structures, and to seek alternative, *ad hoc* ways of mobilizing the faithful for mission and mutual care. It has therefore been easy for Pietist thinking about the church to see only instrumental significance in its outward order of life, to regard the "organized church" as a means toward ends to which it remains external. Moreover, some Lutheran Pietists, though by no means all, grounded their relative indifference to the outward forms in dualist ontologies that stressed the inner life at the expense of all bodily, outward things.[16]

In the nineteenth century, these two inheritances came together, against the background of massive cultural and political change, and took programmatic form in theological theories that explicitly declared the visible church an essentially secular phenomenon. So, for example, the founder of modern Lutheran theological ethics, Adolf von Harless, wrote:

> . . . with the exception of the general will of order expressed in creation, the divinely appointed moral tendencies of nature, which support all

15. Wilhelm Loehe (1808-72), *Aphorismen über die neutestamentichen Ämter und ihr Verhältnis zur Gemeinde. Zur Verfassungsfrage der Kirche* (1849), in Wilhelm Loehe, *Gesammelte Werke* 5.1 (Neuendettelsau: Freimund, 1954), p. 320. Interestingly, Blaschke uses the same language: "The marriage with [the] territorial state, which the Lutheran church formed willy-nilly as an adaptation to prevailing conditions, brought it no blessings, for the territorial state became the stronger partner in the marriage" (Blaschke, "The Reformation," p. 75).

16. This was perhaps particularly true of the North German Pietists; cf. Erhard Peschke's account of "the spiritualistic coloring of the idea of the Spirit" in the theology of August Hermann Francke. See Erhard Peschke, *Studien zur Theologie August Hermann Franckes,* vol. 1 (Berlin: Evangelische Verlagsanstalt, 1964), p. 60. By contrast, it was a Schwabian Pietist, F. C. Oetinger, who formulated the great affirmation that "Embodiment is the goal of all God's ways" *(Leiblichkeit ist das Ende aller Wege Gottes).* However, this did not render the Schwabian Pietists notably more interested in the outward order of the church.

> human society, and from whence also take their rise the declarations of the apostle on the position and vocation of woman in the Christian church, nothing has validity for the external form of the ordering of the ecclesiastical community and its government, except the rule that we should *not* reckon such and such constitutions of the community and forms of government as the essence of the church, and that even in the ecclesiastical community we should not make them instead of the doctrine our care, and least of all should expect from constitution and government saving efficacy, but should only estimate their value according to the measure in which they so further and maintain external order, that thereby the sole dominion of Christ in word and sacrament is in nothing injured or impeded.[17]

In other words, for Harless, the only norms that apply to the ordering of the church are those of natural law and creation order; there is no communal form distinctive to the church as the community of salvation, the eschatological community. Harless's implied argument for this view is a resounding *non sequitur,* for there are surely alternatives besides those he conjures up, either trusting in the outward order of the church for salvation or declaring the visible church a merely secular realm. Moreover, one has to ask critically about the *content* of the "dominion of Christ in word and sacrament" when it is placed in *opposition* to communal order and governance. A dominion of Christ that cannot take form in the ordering of common life is just thereby prevented from being dominion *over* common life. Harless therefore implies that Christ does *not* rule in the outer, bodily world where communities gather and conduct their affairs, but only in the privacy of believing inwardness.

The outward, visible church community is thus related merely extrinsically to the eschatological reality of salvation, which takes form only in the inner life of the individual. The outward church is regarded as a sort of functional delivery system for the preaching and sacramental celebration through which Christ engages and renews the human heart. Such preaching and sacramental celebration are in a sense public occurrences, tied to the utterance of words and the performance of rites out in the visible, bodily world. Yet preaching and sacrament have themselves no direct

17. Adolf von Harless, *System of Christian Ethics,* 6th ed., trans. A. W. Morrison & William Findlay (Edinburgh, 1873), pp. 492-93.

public *effect.* Their outcome and telos are not anything that occur and abide and occupy their own space in the public world; they are rather an inward and private experience that wins public presence only in a secondary, indirect, and supremely ambiguous way.

This way of thinking about church and salvation has been remarkably persistent and influential in subsequent Lutheranism, uniting otherwise very different schools of thought. It codified and at the same time *legitimated* what was doubtless a long Lutheran experience that not much was to be expected from the consistories and privy councils that had charge of ecclesiastical life. It made it possible even so to affirm the *necessity* of the ecclesiastical institution as the requisite delivery system for the ministry of the word while focusing pastoral and theological attention elsewhere, on the inner life, the religious consciousness and its depths and heights of misery and rejoicing under the impress of law and gospel. In nineteenth- and twentieth-century North America, where construction of an ecclesiastical "delivery system" was in any case an inescapable and protracted task for immigrant Lutherans, it functioned for generations as a serviceable framework within which theological commitment and what used to be called "churchmanship" could be related to one another.

Nevertheless, these developments did not go unopposed in nineteenth-century German Lutheranism. Wilhelm Loehe, for example, attempted in a series of important works to describe the "apostolic life" of the Christian assembly, centered in the celebration of the Eucharist and encompassing mission, office, liturgy, and ethos in a distinctive *Gestalt;* against the grain of modernist hermeneutics but anticipating contemporary developments, he struggled to read the New Testament as a community-forming text whose proclamation seeks a *public* result, the building up of a new and sanctified people living together in a new way.[18] Other

18. For Loehe's understanding of sanctification as a public, communal phenomenon, see his major essay in liturgical theology, *Von den heiligen Personen, der heiligen Zeiten, der heiligen Weise, and dem heiligen Orte* (1859), in Loehe, *Gesammelte Werke* 3.1 (1951), pp. 523-601. In addition, along with his *Aphorismen über die neutestamentlichen Ämter,* cited above, see the remarkable "Catechism of the Apostolic Life" that formed part of his *Vorschlag zu einem Lutherischen Verein für apostolischen Leben, samt Entwurf eines Katechismus des apostolischen Lebens* (1848), in Loehe, *Gesammelte Werke* 5.1, pp. 213-52. According to the foreword to the *Aphorismen,* they and the "Catechism" were worked out together and grew out of the same insight: "Several years ago, the author was surprised to notice that so much stands in the Acts of the Apostles and

Lutherans of the same period expressed similar concerns.[19]

These figures tended to be in one way or another outsiders to the academic theological establishment;[20] in the academy the pattern represented by Harless became dominant. Loehe, whose work probably represents the most significant nineteenth-century alternative to the standard view, was honored as an exemplary pastor but dismissed as a theologian; his ecclesiological views were stigmatized with the charge of creeping Romanism. Thus was formed the Lutheran *communis opinio* to which we have referred.

By now, however, it may have become clear that the issues at stake in this specifically Lutheran history are by no means exclusively Lutheran issues. Indeed, Harless's removal of the order of the church from the dominion of Christ reproduces precisely a way of drawing lines between public and private that John Milbank and others have persuasively identified as characteristic of Western modernity as a whole: the outward, public realm is equated with the secular and placed under the sway of instrumental reason, while "religion" is relegated to the inwardness of the religious subject, all the while being praised as far too sublime and serious a matter to relate directly to the externalities of "mere" bodily common life in history.[21] Nor

---

the letters of the New Testament that concerns the organism and constitution of the congregations, which one usually reads past without noticing" (Loehe, *Gesammelte Werke* 5.1, p. 255).

19. Among the most colorful was the self-taught polymath, ferocious controversialist, and arch-reactionary Marburg theologian August Friedrich Christian Vilmar (1800-1868); see his provocative attack on mainstream nineteenth-century theology, *Die Theologie der Tatsachen wider die Theologie der Rhetorik* (1854). Vilmar's eccentricity and conservatism (which nonetheless rendered him a bitter opponent of the imperial ambitions of Prussia) made him easy to dismiss, but his *Streitschrift* is both incisive and profound in its diagnosis of the alienation of academic theology from the "realities" of ecclesial existence, centered in Christ's sacramental "real presence" and present action in the worshiping assembly, and the consequent reduction of theology to an empty "rhetoric" in which Christian language and symbolism, detached from the living ecclesial context, are manipulated to various arbitrary ends.

20. Thus in Friedrich Mildenberger's standard *Geschichte der deutschen evangelischen Theologie im 19. und 20. Jahrhundert* (Stuttgart: Kohlhammer, 1981), Loehe and Vilmar are passed over with a single mention (p. 189). Mildenberger is nonetheless informative on the ecclesiological issues in nineteenth-century Lutheranism and their relationship to twentieth-century developments (see pp. 185-200).

21. See the now classic analysis in John Milbank, *Theology and Social Theory: Beyond Secular Reason* (Oxford: Blackwell, 1990). See also Nicholas Lash, *The Beginning*

is it only Lutheran preachers who have come to regard the telos of public preaching as an event occurring within the private inwardness of the individual hearer. In a critical review of standard preaching guides in the contemporary North American mainline Protestant orbit, Charles Campbell writes:

> When preaching focuses on individual experience in this way, the Christian faith all too easily gets relegated to the private realm. The gospel becomes divorced from serious, radical public claims and from a concrete, public community of faith. . . . One reads the literature with the impression that, where the sermon is concerned, the church is simply a rather loose collection of individuals who share some similar experiences and participate in the event of oral communication. . . . In their focus on discrete individual Word-events, contemporary homileticians have neglected the intimate relationship between preaching, polity, and discipleship.[22]

In this perspective, the Lutheran struggle over the meaning of the church can be seen as a paradigmatic episode in which the issues at stake in the larger Christian confrontation with Western modernity came to bear in a specific way. This interpretation receives particularly poignant force when it is extended into the twentieth century, as we shall see.

III. Lutheran Ecclesiology in the German Church Struggle

Harless speaks of "the declarations of the apostle on the position and vocation of woman in the Christian church" as a prime example of the importance of natural law and creation order as norms of the outward order of the church. This may already give some clue to the fate of church order in this scheme, for after the cultural conflicts of recent years we rightly approach with suspicion any set of views on "the position and vocation of woman" that claim to have been simply read off "nature." In short, like all attempts to build on first-article norms defined *in isolation* from the sec-

---

and the End of "Religion" (Cambridge and New York: Cambridge University Press, 1996).

22. Charles Campbell, *Preaching Jesus: New Directions for Homiletics in Hans Frei's Postliberal Theology* (Grand Rapids: Eerdmans, 1997), pp. 143, 144, 145. The citation pulls together remarks spread over several pages in Campbell's text.

ond and third articles of the creed, this ecclesiology in the end surrenders the common life of the church to the strife of interests that dominates and divides the *civitas terrena*.[23]

This became clear in the most important subsequent ecclesiological debate within Lutheranism since the nineteenth century, which took place in the context of the German Church Struggle. When Martin Niemöller and the Pastors' Emergency League tried in 1933 to formulate a distinctively *churchly* response to the triumphant Nazi regime, one that would resist reduction to party politics, they unwittingly reopened the ecclesiological question, for this implied that there were distinctive norms governing the church's public shape and thus its relation to other public phenomena, such as the state. Subsequent research on the *Kirchenkampf*, understandably preoccupied with the Confessing Church's response or failure to respond to war and genocide, has not perhaps done full justice to the volume and intensity of the specifically *ecclesiological* controversy that ensued and that was focused on issues of order and governance and the relation of church and state.[24]

23. This is not to deny that there are first-article norms, only to question whether they can be grasped with any clarity in isolation from the second and third articles. Harless, the main originator of the idea of creation order in modern Lutheran ethics, was well aware of this, at least as regards the second article of the creed:

> The Christian has in Christ not only the Lord in the kingdom of grace, but also Him by whom and for whom all things were made. . . . Thus at the basis of all creatively established and historically maintained creature order, lies a primitive original world-plan, which has its root in Christ, whose real power mirrors itself in continual self-testimony in every form of human society, but which is only properly recognized and followed by those who are in Christ. Herein lies for the Christian the twofold necessity and justification: on the one hand, of looking upon nothing which is an ordinance of the creature as something standing out of connection with Christ; on the other hand, however, of regarding everything which in the same sphere of arrangement is subject to human regulation as needing to be referred to its divine center of union in Christ, and capable of such a reference, and appointed with a view to the same. (Harless, *System of Christian Ethics*, p. 424)

It may have been Harless's blindness to the public relevance of the *third* article of the creed, his refusal to see any special relation of the public community of the church and the form of its outward life to the destiny of creation in Christ, that prevented this line of thought from exercising any critical function in subsequent Lutheran ethics.

24. Or rather, it has viewed the volume and intensity of the ecclesiological con-

In this controversy, the pattern of thought we have identified in Harless was turned directly against the Confessing Church. Thus, for example, Emanuel Hirsch,[25] the most significant theological theorist of a Lutheran embrace of Nazism, states:

> The community in which authentic believing Christian existence is rooted is the hidden church of the Spirit, which is of a supra-historical type and not a particular earthly community of shared destiny,[26] established as a totality of life on its own over against other such communities. There can be no Christian worldview and no Christian order of life as the authentic *logos* and *nomos* of an earthly community of shared destiny. There is only a Christian influence, a Christian share in weaving the *logos* and *nomos* of earthly communities of shared destiny.[27]

Therefore, Hirsch implies, Confessing Church opposition to the "adjustment" *(Gleichschaltung)* of the church's order of life to the realities of the new Germany — for example, by the exclusion of "non-Aryans" from church office — is un-Lutheran: "The church as an ordered and institutional form does not have the task of placing its own churchly worldview

---

troversy with dismay: "Why were they arguing about *this* sort of stuff while the Jews were being destroyed?" Nothing can excuse the failure of the Confessing Church to say a clear word on behalf of the Jews; but the depth of that failure is only seen when we realize that its essence was not the refusal of a known duty but the widespread inability to *see* a duty. A theological evaluation of the Church Struggle needs to take seriously the possibility that in their engagement with ecclesiology the theologians of the Confessing Church were also asking, in effect, "How could we German Lutherans become a people capable of *seeing* what needs to be done now?"

25. On Hirsch, see Robert Erickson, *Theologians under Hitler: Gerhard Kittel, Paul Althaus, and Emanuel Hirsch* (New Haven: Yale University Press, 1985), pp. 120-97.

26. "Community of shared destiny" is the best I can do with Hirsch's *Schicksalsgemeinschaft,* a typical category of *volkisch* philosophy of history. A *Schicksalsgemeinschaft* is a community in which, by virtue of the bonds of common blood and shared historical experience, each member stands or falls with the others and all therefore share a common destiny.

27. Emanuel Hirsch, "Gottes Offenbarung in Gesetz und Evangelium. 20 Thesen," in K. D. Schmidt, ed., *Die Bekenntnisse und grundsätzlichen Äußerungen zur Kirchenfrage,* Band 3: *Das Jahr 1935* (Göttingen: Vandenhoeck and Ruprecht, 1936), pp. 37-40; here p. 39.

and order of life over against the *logos* and *nomos* of the earthly communities of shared destiny among which it stands."[28]

Hirsch was a Nazi extremist, albeit a brilliant one, but his position on this issue was *not* extreme in the German Lutheranism of the 1930s. The two Erlangen professors of systematic theology, Paul Althaus and Werner Elert, unlike Hirsch by no means unqualified ideological supporters of the regime,[29] and both renowned representatives of mainstream Lutheranism, made essentially the same moves in their substantial affirmation of *Gleichschaltung* in 1933:

> According to Reformation doctrine, as distinct from Roman Catholicism, the outward order of the church must correspond *not only to the universality of the gospel but also to the historical-national* (volkisch) *differentiation of Christian persons.* . . . Oneness in Christ is for the Lutheran Confessions no question of outward organization, but a question of faith.[30]

This corresponds precisely to a move made in the previous paragraph of their report, addressing the relationship of salvation in Christ to earthly bonds:

> All those who come to faith are, according to the witness of the apostle, one in Christ. In this union with Christ there is no distinction before God between Jew and non-Jew. *But the status of child of God; common to all Christians, does not abolish their biological and social differences,* but rather binds each one to the social location *(Stand)* in which he was called (1 Corinthians 7:20). The biological connection to a particular *Volk,* which as a matter of destiny we cannot evade, is to be acknowledged by Christians in their attitudes and in their deeds.[31]

28. Hirsch, "Gottes Offenbarung in Gesetz und Evangelium," p. 39.

29. On Paul Althaus, cf. Erickson, *Theologians under Hitler,* pp. 79-119.

30. Paul Althaus and Werner Elert, "Theologisches Gutachten über die Zulassung von Christen jüdischer Herkunft zu den Ämter der Deutschen Evangelischen Kirche," in K. D. Schmidt, ed., *Die Bekenntnisse und grundsätzlichen Äußerungen zur Kirchenfrage des Jahres 1933* (Göttingen: Vandenhoeck and Ruprecht, 1934), pp. 182-86, here p. 184 (italics in original). The Erlangen theological faculty had commissioned Althaus and Elert to compose a response to this issue on its behalf.

31. Althaus and Elert, "Theologisches Gutachten," p. 184. Italics in original.

In other words, eschatological redemption nowhere takes public form and has no public effect; it holds good only in a special sphere apart from the public, historical world in which "biological and social differences" hold undisturbed sway. So the authors can say:

> The church's confession of the saving significance of Baptism includes, for example, no judgment whether marriages between Germans and baptized Jews who believe in Christ are desirable or ill-advised. The question of the ethnic *(völkisch)* relationship between German nationality *(Deutschentum)* and Jewish nationality *(Judentum)* is a question of a biological-historical kind. It can only be answered by our *Volk*, as by every other, on the basis of its particular biological-historical situation.[32]

Here the concrete social relations between baptized Germans and baptized Jews are declared to be without any theological significance whatsoever; the whole question is a secular issue, to be resolved by "race-science" and nationalist politics. Baptism thus does not initiate one into any distinctively ordered communal space in which relations between persons might receive a new formation, but only into an ahistorical place "before God," which is to be marked off carefully from any location within earthly historical common life.

It is in this context that we must hear the resonant sentence with which Dietrich Bonhoeffer begins the chapter entitled "The Visible Community" in the famous work of 1937 known in English, perhaps misleadingly, as *The Cost of Discipleship*:[33] "The body of Christ takes up space on earth."[34] In deliberate opposition to standard modern Lutheran ecclesiologies, Bonhoeffer argues that the church, precisely in its eschatological

32. Althaus and Elert, "Theologisches Gutachten," p. 185.

33. Dietrich Bonhoeffer, *Nachfolge*, ed. Martin Kuske and Ilse Tödt (Munich: Kaiser, 1989). This book has been read, at least in English, primarily as a devotional study rather than as a theologically pointed *Streitschrift* addressing the issues of the Church Struggle. As a consequence, it has not been widely noticed that it is essentially an ecclesiology. The footnotes to the critical edition of *Nachfolge* by Kuske and Tödt make clear, moreover, how self-consciously Bonhoeffer in this chapter is both addressing the Church Struggle and engaging critically the inheritance of Lutheran modernism. Hopefully the forthcoming English translation of the critical edition will retain this apparatus.

34. Bonhoeffer, *Nachfolge*, p. 241.

newness as the body of Christ, claims for itself a distinct public presence, a structured social space of its own.

This ecclesial space has, according to Bonhoeffer, a threefold form: The church "takes up space on earth" first in its proclamation, therefore as "the community assembled around word and sacrament."[35] However, this proclaiming and worshiping assembly is internally differentiated and ordered, and its order "is of divine origin and nature."[36] It contains ministries of leadership and governance that it has not invented for itself but that have been placed within it by God. The precise form of these ministries is changeable in response to historical circumstance and need, but this implies no separability of institutional office and order from the spiritual reality of the church; on the contrary, "if its order is attacked from outside, then the visible form of the body of Christ itself is attacked."[37] As an ordered community, the church has its own public discourse, its own politics, at the center of which is concern for sound doctrine, authentic proclamation of the gospel by which the church lives.[38]

Yet proclamation and office do not suffice to describe the church's distinctive occupation of social space on earth. The word of proclamation calls men and women to a bodily fellowship with Jesus Christ that is sealed in the bodily fellowship-meal at the Lord's Table. The church thus not only claims space on earth liturgically and institutionally but also claims such space in the formation of the daily lives of its members, their bodily existence in the world. Here Bonhoeffer speaks provocatively of the distinctive *Lebensraum* of the visible community — the space needed for the shaping of new modes of engagement with "the things and goods of this life,"[39] as well as new modes of relationship among the church's members. In what must surely be intentional contradiction of the Althaus-Elert report, Bonhoeffer is especially insistent on the latter:

> . . . with Baptism the space of the communal life of the members of the body of Christ is opened up without reservation to every baptized person. . . . Whoever grants baptized brothers the gifts of salvation, but refuses them the gifts of earthly life, or knowingly leaves them in earthly

35. Bonhoeffer, *Nachfolge,* p. 245.
36. Bonhoeffer, *Nachfolge,* p. 245.
37. Bonhoeffer, *Nachfolge,* p. 246.
38. Bonhoeffer, *Nachfolge,* pp. 246-47.
39. Bonhoeffer, *Nachfolge,* p. 249.

> need and tribulation, despises the gift of salvation and becomes a liar. Whoever still listens to the voice of his blood, his nature, his sympathies and antipathies, there where the Holy Spirit has spoken, commits sin against the sacrament. Baptism into the body of Christ transforms not only the personal situation of the baptized with regard to salvation, but all his life-relations.[40]

Bonhoeffer's warning against the voices of blood and nature is a precise correction of Harless's appeal to "the divinely appointed moral tendencies of nature" as the sole norm for the ordering of the church. What makes the church's life normal is not the "voices" we hear within ourselves purporting to speak for blood and nature but the voice of the Holy Spirit, who speaks in baptism, more broadly through the word and the sacraments, now recognized not only as words of assurance to the individual conscience but also as structuring words that give distinctive form to a common life.[41] The church is not surrendered to the shaping given the fallen human world by such voices; it occupies its own space in the world, shaped and ordered by another voice, the voice of God that speaks in the gospel.

After the war, the question of the true lessons of the Church Struggle itself became a hotly contested issue in German Lutheran theology, and not every Confessing Church theologian saw the alternatives as Bonhoeffer had. In 1950 Gerhard Ebeling, a Bultmann-school theologian

40. Bonhoeffer, *Nachfolge,* 250-251. A full discussion of this chapter, which of course cannot be offered here, would have to continue with a close reading of Bonhoeffer's subsequent long and difficult discussion of Paul's admonitions regarding slavery, including an interpretation of 1 Cor. 7:20, the text to which Althaus and Elert appealed for their view that baptism is without public consequences (cf. *Nachfolge,* pp. 251ff.). Here, I believe, Bonhoeffer was engaged in careful and deliberate deception of the censors, hiding what is actually a provocative rebuttal of the Althaus-Elert position in a reassuring conservative Lutheran rhetoric.

41. We might indeed go a bit further, without leaving Bonhoeffer entirely behind. Nature as God's creation may indeed have "moral tendencies," but we shall not discover them by listening to the voices within us, which may represent nothing more than our "sympathies and antipathies," the clamor of our concupiscence. Only the speaking of the Spirit, which gives form to the church, enables us to see at all clearly what "tendency" has been divinely appointed for nature, precisely insofar as it fashions a community whose life together anticipates the final fulfillment for the sake of which all things were made.

with blameless Confessing Church credentials, published an influential essay that forcefully reasserted all the old modernist rules delineating public and private.[42] This essay, "The Significance of the Critical Historical Method for Church and Theology in Protestantism," is best known to students of hermeneutics, but it is far more than an innocently abstract discussion of biblical interpretation. Rather, it needs to be read as a brilliant exercise in theological and ecclesiastical polemics, directed explicitly against those in the Confessing Church who saw recent history as calling into question the heritage of Protestant modernism.

In deflecting this challenge, Ebeling's strategy is twofold. First, he focuses on what was doubtless the weak point in his opposition's armor, their still-fumbling attempts to formulate a postcritical theological hermeneutic. This did indeed sometimes lead Confessing Church pastors and theologians into an *anti*-critical rhetoric that was easy to ridicule. Second, and most important, he outflanks the moral and theological challenge of recent history by an appeal to the Reformation: the modernist rules are really the heritage of the Reformers, he insists, and those who question them betray the distinctively Protestant standpoint and lapse back into "Catholicism."

The underlying question in the hermeneutical debate, according to Ebeling, is that of "the ontological categories under which the event of revelation is to be comprehended."[43] The implication of the Reformation *sola fide,* he asserts, is that "the event of revelation," that is, the eschatological breakthrough accomplished once and for all in Christ, is present in the world only "in the word"; thus we encounter eschatological reality only in and as the experience of the word's meaningfulness, "the assurance of salvation that lies in the *pro me*."[44] This is in the nature of the case an inward presence, a presence located in the conscience of the individual. The Reformation view therefore stands in unbridgeable systematic antithesis to Catholicism, precisely because the latter views the eschatological as having *public* presence, embodied in doctrine, sacrament, and church.

This is the real theme of the essay: its central move is to brand as "Catholic" and therefore unacceptable any transgression of modernity's

42. See Gerhard Ebeling, "The Significance of the Critical Historical Method for Church and Theology in Protestantism," in *Word and Faith* (Philadelphia: Fortress, 1963), pp. 9-61.

43. Ebeling, "The Significance of the Critical Historical Method," p. 30.

44. Ebeling, "The Significance of the Critical Historical Method," pp. 35-36.

rules about the secularity of the public world. It is not only the idea of "holy scripture" that Ebeling wants to rule off-limits to the heirs of the Reformation, the idea of a textually embodied revelation that demands to be read in a special way, but likewise the very ideas of "holy sacraments" and "holy church." The Reformation, he insists, requires Protestants to agree with modern culture that the eschatological can never "take up space" in the public world and disrupt its uniform secularity; thus "a fundamentally different attitude to the spirit of the modern age" has come to constitute a new church-dividing difference separating Catholics and Protestants.[45]

By focusing his argument on biblical hermeneutics and the authority of the Reformation, Ebeling is able simply to ignore and exclude from consideration the ecclesial-political concerns that animated much of the uneasiness with theological modernism in the Confessing Church. That his arguments might have implications for concrete issues of the kind that stood between Bonhoeffer and the Althaus-Elert report is nowhere acknowledged. Ebeling's essay — as indeed the bulk of his theological work — operates in a political vacuum, in which the really burning questions theologians face are the significance of "modern critical scholarship" and the necessity of establishing their Protestant credentials by distinguishing themselves from "Catholicism."[46]

A Confessing Church theologian whose work after the war moved in a radically different direction was Robert Jenson's *Doktorvater,* the Heidelberg theologian Peter Brunner. Brunner's work transgressed Ebeling's boundaries in all directions;[47] most importantly for our purposes, he de-

45. Ebeling, "The Significance of the Critical Historical Method," pp. 49-51.

46. That only ten years earlier respectable theologians in Ebeling's own church were convinced that honoring the authority of modern critical scholarship meant deferring to Nazi "race-science" and that being Protestant rather than Catholic meant yielding to *volkisch* sensibilities in the matter of "non-Aryan" pastors is never allowed to emerge as a problem. The point is not that Ebeling held reprehensible views on these subjects; quite the opposite, so far as I know, was the case. Yet he defines the theological issues in such a way that such concerns are not even allowed to appear on the horizon.

47. On revelation and Scripture, see Bonhoeffer's interestingly "postcritical" essay "Die großen Taten Gottes und die historisch-kritische Vernunft," in Peter Brunner, ed., *Pro Ecclesia,* vol. 1 (Berlin and Hamburg: Lutherisches Verlagshaus, 1962), pp. 183-202. On the sacraments see his *Aus der Kraft des Werkes Christi. Zur Lehre von der Hl. Taufe und vom Hl. Abendmahl* (Munich: Evangelisches Pressuerband für Bayern, 1950).

veloped an ecclesiology centered in the eucharistic assembly as the *public* epiphany of the crucified and risen body of Christ in the world:

> Every Lord's Supper is — hidden under the veil of the end-time mystery — an epiphany of the sacrificial love of God in the sacrificed body of his Son, which is also the Spirit-worked *(pneumatisch)* body of his *ekklesia*. Thus every obedient performance of the *anamnesis* of Christ in the Supper realizes the glory of the Triune God on this earth and for us human beings. . . .[48]

Brunner's identification of the sacrificed body of Christ with the Spirit-worked body of the church implies that the eschatological presence is located precisely in the Spirit's gathering of a *community* centered in the eucharistic anamnesis. The glory of God is realized on this earth in the corporate celebration of the assembly, and so in the public actions of a bodily people. The eschatological new reality is present in the world as the assembly of a people, and thus, or so it would seem, as a "political" phenomenon in its own right.

Brunner does not draw back from this conclusion but develops it explicitly in reference to the doxological dimension of worship. The present epiphany of God's mercy in the crucified body of his Son, which culminates in the gift of Christ's body and blood in the eucharistic meal, calls forth the acclamation, the song, and the bodily *proskynêsis* of his people. Yet this liturgical acclamation of the triune God, for Brunner, has a distinctly and irreducibly political character:

> The people honors its king. The dominion of the Triune God is acknowledged in a binding way. . . . As the homage offered in the presence of a king is something altogether different from the expression of a mood or an enthusiasm, so these acclamations in worship are not a lyrical expression for an inner impulse; rather, they are comparable — in analogy with paying homage — to legally binding acts. They bind the

48. Peter Brunner, *Zur Lehre vom Gottesdienst der im Namen Jesu versammelten Gemeinde* (Hannover: Lutherisches Verlagshaus, 1993), p. 253. This work originally appeared in the first volume of Walter Blankenburg, ed., *Leiturgeia. Handbuch des evangelisches Gottesdienst* (Kassel: Johannes Stauda Verlag, 1954). An English version appeared as *Worship in the Name of Jesus,* trans. M. H. Bertram (St. Louis: Concordia, 1969); see p. 196 for the passage cited in the text.

> community to the dominion of this Lord. They are means of the epiphany of this dominion.[49]

Just so, says Brunner, "the worship of the heavenly city projects already into the worship of the pilgrim church," and in this insight "the relation of the *ekklesia* to the *polis*" — the earthly political community — "becomes clear."[50] The public worship of the church anticipates the promised future precisely insofar as what is promised is a *city*, an eschatological polity in which God exercises unopposed dominion and receives the undivided acclaim of his people.

> When the worship of the church comprises acclamation, hymn, and *proskynêsis* in their inner connectedness, it becomes an eschatological-apocalyptic event in which the future *polis* begins to delineate itself in a first outline in the struggling and suffering church.[51]

Therefore the presence of the eschatological in and through the church is itself public and political, intruding directly into the tensions and conflicts of human common life:

> Because these last things begin to occur in worship, it acquires an extraordinary public character, even if it occurs in the quietest corner of the world. World-empires could shatter on this glorification of the Triune God, this "adoration" of the Kyrios Jesus.[52]

Brunner is the least autobiographical of theologians, but it is impossible to miss the echoes of the Church Struggle in his extraordinary affirmation of the immediately political character of Christian worship:

49. Brunner, *Zur Lehre vom Gottesdienst*, p. 262; *Worship in the Name of Jesus*, p. 208.

50. Brunner, *Zur Lehre vom Gottesdienst*, p. 263; *Worship in the Name of Jesus*, p. 209. In a way that is not easy to translate, Brunner is invoking here the full range of connotation of the German word for worship, *Gottesdienst*, literally, "service of God."

51. Brunner, *Zur Lehre vom Gottesdienst*, p. 267; *Worship in the Name of Jesus*, p. 213.

52. Brunner, *Zur Lehre vom Gottesdienst*, p. 267; *Worship in the Name of Jesus*, p. 213.

> Until the Last Day, what takes place here in the liturgy will have its "political" consequences. Where the bearers of state power reach for God's glory and want to deck themselves in God's authority, then the liturgy of the church, without the least change in its order, by its sheer performance, will by inner necessity become a political declaration of war and an act of political struggle.[53]

Notice that Brunner does *not* say that worship has political effect insofar as it alters the inner attitudes and motivations of the worshipers and thus indirectly, by way of the inner disposition of believers, comes to exercise an influence on public life. On the contrary, the acclamation of God the Lord has its own public meaning and implications precisely as an outward, bodily act.[54] Nor does he call for the "politicization" of worship, the rhetorical manipulation of the worship setting to render it a more effective political motivator.[55] On the contrary, for Brunner, the bodily gathering of the worshiping church is itself already the anticipatory appearing of the heavenly *polis,* and as such already "by its sheer performance" a public and political reality.

The kinship between Jenson's ecclesiology and that of his teacher should be apparent, though the relationship also has its complexities: it is not my intention to collapse Jenson into Brunner.[56] Yet perhaps this rapid

53. Brunner, *Zur Lehre vom Gottesdienst,* p. 263; *Worship in the Name of Jesus,* p. 209.

54. In this regard, Brunner's discussion of *proskynêsis,* which he takes seriously in its original meaning as bodily prostration, and his associated account of the meaning of bodily gesture in worship, are of considerable significance precisely as regards the political significance of Christian worship. See Brunner, *Zur Lehre vom Gottesdienst,* pp. 265-66; *Worship in the Name of Jesus,* pp. 211-13.

55. On this, cf. Bernd Wannenwetsch, *Gottesdienst als Lebensform — Ethik für Christenbürger* (Stuttgart: Kohlhammer, 1997); the English translation is forthcoming. Wannenwetsch is one of several contemporary Lutheran theologians whose work is challenging the ecclesiological *communis opinio* in ways that take up the legacy of theologians such as Brunner. See also Reinhard Hütter, *Suffering Divine Things: Theology as Church Practice* (Grand Rapids: Eerdmans, 1999).

56. Just to indicate what seems to be one significant point of difference: both Jenson and Brunner insist that "body of Christ" is more than a mere "image" and indicates a genuine ontological identity between the *ekklesia* and the crucified and risen body of Jesus. Brunner however continues to speak of the church as the "epiphany" of the body of the risen Jesus, which also exists in another way "in heaven before God's throne" (*Zur Lehre vom Gottesdienst,* pp. 151ff.; *Worship in the Name of Je-*

and incomplete sketch of modern Lutheran ecclesiological struggles is sufficient to indicate the "Lutheran genealogy" of Jenson's account of the church. Though in *The Works of God* he has, for good reasons, taken contemporary ecumenical *communio*-ecclesiology rather than modern Lutheran history as the point of reference for his treatment of ecclesiology, his work nonetheless stands in a long and distinguished line of challenges from *within* the Lutheran tradition to dominant assumptions of Lutheran modernism, especially with regard to the church.

IV. Ecclesiology in the Lutheran Reformation

There remains the question about the relation of Jenson's ecclesiology, and that of the Lutheran counter tradition in which it stands, to the insight and teaching of the Lutheran Reformers. From Loehe through Brunner to Jenson himself, the charge of a "Romanizing" betrayal of the Reformation has consistently been raised against those who have questioned the modern Lutheran ecclesiological consensus.[57] While it is probably well to preserve a certain detachment in the face of such charges — Lutherans need sometimes to be reminded that agreement with Luther is not the *final* test of theological truth — it is nonetheless an issue worth pursuing. The accusation that the emerging ecumenical consensus about the church is antithetical to the Reformation is becoming a staple of the rhetoric of Protestant anti-ecumenism, and if the charge were true, it would indeed diminish the ecumenical plausibility of Jenson's work, as well as that of the ecumenical consensus with which he associates himself. I want to conclude

sus, pp. 72ff.). These two modes of being interpenetrate to the point that the church is present in heaven in the glorified body and also that what happens to the church on earth affects the glorified body of Jesus as it stands before the Father. Brunner nevertheless continues to distinguish these as *two* modes in which the risen body of the Lord exists. Jenson, however, regards a *distinct* mode of existence before God's throne as unnecessary, simply identifying "heaven" with the eucharistic assembly: "Heaven is where God takes space in his creation to be present to the whole of it; he does that in the church" (*ST* I, 206; cf. the whole discussion on pp. 194-206).

57. Bonhoeffer has been spared much of this by his aura of martyrdom, but even in his case, there has been a discernable uneasiness with *Nachfolge*, a sense that it is dangerously "Catholic," and a corresponding readiness to exaggerate the distance between that work and Bonhoeffer's later writing.

this paper, therefore, with some extremely brief and compressed thoughts on the shape of the ecclesiological problem in the Lutheran Reformation, particularly as it bears on the theological significance of the church's outward order.

It is often forgotten that Luther's early thought protested not only the exaltation of human powers through doctrines of merit but also *the domestication of the eschatological* in the Nominalist doctrine of grace. According to Gabriel Biel, at least as Luther read him, divine grace only enhances a relationship to God that human sinners can in principle achieve on their own: it only makes it possible to do more readily and consistently what we could do without it. As Luther saw it, grace is thereby drawn into the world subject to death and sin and is given a functional role in the kind of religion native to that world. What Luther wanted to insist was that God's grace is the *end* of that world, the death of that whole regime and the beginning of a new creation. Thus he accepted very strongly Augustine's identification of grace with the *ipsa præsentia Spiritus Dei,* the very presence of God's Spirit, poured out by the risen Jesus Christ to make all things new. This twin affirmation, that with grace we have to do with *God's own presence* and, furthermore, with God present *to put an end to the old aeon and initiate the new creation,* constitutes one of the deep structures of Luther's thought and of the early Lutheran outlook.

The implications of this for *ecclesiology* become clear when we recall the extensive secularization of the late-medieval Western church. Part of the tragedy of the Gregorian Reforms was that they worked well to preserve the independence of the church but not so well to maintain the distinctiveness of its corporate character. The late-medieval church in the West easily took on the aspect of one secular power alongside others and was then capable of actions and arrangements that accomplished the very absorption of the church into the world, a situation that the great Popes at the start of the millennium had struggled to avoid.

One could almost see this secularization as an illustration of the domestication of grace in Nominalist soteriology. As an account of historical causation, this would be grossly misleading, but it sheds light on the Reformation protest to look at the matter so, since Luther in fact came to his ecclesiological critique by way of his attack on Nominalist soteriology. The various strands in the Reformation's critical attitude to the late-medieval church may be seen as having their unity in an underlying rejection of any kind of domestication of the church in this age, any implicit or explicit understanding of the church as one more worldly kingdom, one more community adapted to the dominion of death and sin.

Such protest is perhaps inevitably double-edged; it can take two forms, not in themselves incompatible with one another, but capable of development in contradictory directions. One possibility is to insist, against institutionalism and secularization, that the true being of the church does not lie in the carapace of canon law and the outward trappings of power but in the communion of the Spirit that only faith can share and perceive. Classic here is Luther's pungent statement in the *Smalcald Articles:*

> We do not grant them [i.e., the papists] that they are the church, for they are not the church, and we will pay no attention to what they command or forbid in the name of the church. For thank God, a seven-year-old child knows what the church is, the holy believers and "sheep who hear the voice of their shepherd" (cf. John 10:3). For the children also pray, "I believe in one holy, Christian church." This holiness does not consist in surplices, long gowns, and other ceremonies of theirs, which they have invented without Holy Scripture, but in the word of God and true faith.[58]

In and of itself, this line of protest is not untraditional, nor is it incompatible with a second line, an insistence that a community whose true being is the eschatological *koinonia* of the Spirit must *take form in the world* in distinctive ways. There are also ways of pursuing the first strategy that lead toward a *separation* of the social reality of the church from the communion of the Spirit, and it is perhaps not difficult to see why these ways have in fact been extensively pursued in Lutheran history. Lutheranism's long dependence on the princes hindered any full development of the insight that the spiritual reality of the church gives the church's social embodiment a distinctive form; by the time the Pietists came on the scene it was easy for the outward structures of state-church Lutheranism to seem at best a series of obstacles to be negotiated, necessary perhaps to keep order but with no inner relation to the true spiritual

58. *Smalcald Articles,* part III, *The Church;* my translation from *Die Bekenntnisschriften der evangelisch-lutherischen Kirche,* 11th ed. (Göttingen: Vandenhoeck & Ruprecht, 1992), p. 460.

reality of the church, the union of hearts in faith, hope, and love. In the nineteenth-century doctrine of the secularity of the visible church, we can see these experiences hardening into theory and at the same time being harnessed to new uses in a modern context.

The irony is that in the end this line of development surrenders the church more drastically to secularity than the late-medieval prince-bishops ever dreamed of doing. By turning the *distinction* between the spiritual reality of the church and its social form into a *separation* or even an *opposition*, it permits the Spirit no purchase on the embodied world and allows no true epiphany of God's reign in the flesh-and-blood community of the faithful. The social reality of the church is handed over to the *civitas terrena* and its sterile power struggles, while salvation is reduced to inward support for the alienated individual self in its struggle to cope with existence. The wheel turns around, and Luther's heirs end where Luther began, with grace and the church alike domesticated within the world of death.

In order to suggest a different trajectory, it will be helpful to look briefly at the position of the Lutheran Reformers on certain concrete issues of church order. Here, I want to suggest, we see in the Reformation not the separation of the spiritual communion from the institutional framework but an insistence that the spiritual communion of the church find appropriate embodiment in distinctive practice and structure. From this perspective, an ecclesiological framework like Jenson's helps make sense of central Reformation concerns, and at the same time makes contact with the Reformers' own deepest assumptions about the eschatological being of the church.

An appropriate starting point is Article 28 of the *Augsburg Confession,* entitled *De potestate ecclesiastica,* "On Church Authority." While the history of its interpretation is complex, in the end Article 28 is an insurmountable obstacle to the claim that the visible church was for the early Lutherans a purely secular realm. On the contrary, its whole emphasis is that the authority exercised in the church must be clearly distinguished in kind from secular authority, even though the latter is also ordained by God.[59] Therefore at this critical point, in the mode of authority by which it

59. "Therefore these types of authority, the ecclesiastical and the civil, are not to be mixed up with one another" *(Non igitur commiscendae sunt potestates ecclesiastica et civilis),* Article 28, par. 12; *Die Bekenntnisschriften der evangelisch-lutherischen Kirche,* p. 122. On the interpretation of this article, see now Gunther Wenz's magisterial *Theologie der Bekenntnisschriften der evangelisch-lutherischen Kirche: eine historische*

is governed, the outward community of the church is clearly *not* subject only to norms of natural law and creation order; it is subject to norms distinctive to it as the community of salvation.

The historical context is, of course, the union of civil and ecclesiastical authority in the prince-bishops of the Empire; the Reformers did not demand that the bishops give up their secular offices but insisted that the two roles be clearly differentiated. The *potestas* proper to the church is that conferred by Christ when he sent forth the apostles to preach repentance and forgiveness of sins in his name:

> Our side holds that the authority of the keys or the authority of bishops according to the gospel is the authority or divine mandate to preach the gospel, to remit and retain sins, and to administer the sacraments. For with this mandate Christ sent forth the apostles: "*As the Father sent me, so I send you. Receive the Holy Spirit; whose sins you remit, they are remitted, whose sins you retain, they are retained*" (John 20:21-23). And in Mark 16: "*Go, preach the gospel to every creature.*"[60]

This is a different *kind* of authority than that of the civil regime. It does not merely order and defend bodily life but confers eschatological goods: "eternal things, eternal righteousness, the Holy Spirit, eternal life."[61] Yet church authority is nonetheless a genuine public authority entrusted to human beings in history and exercised by human beings in space and time. Thus the character of the church as the eschatological community calls for a special mode of authority embodied in distinctive forms of common life. It calls in fact for a singular *jurisdictio,* which refers to the concrete *mode of governance* in which *potestas* is exercised.

> Therefore, concerning the jurisdiction of bishops, it must be distinguished from political command *(imperium).* Thus according to the gospel, or, as they say, by divine right, this is the jurisdiction that belongs to bishops as bishops: to them is committed the ministry of the word and the sacraments, to remit sins, to reject doctrine contrary to the gos-

---

und systematische Einführung in das Konkordienbuch, vol. 2 (Berlin and New York: Walter de Gruyter, 1998), pp. 370-412.

60. *Augsburg Confession,* Article 28, 5-6; *Die Bekenntnisschriften,* p. 121.

61. *Augsburg Confession,* Article 28, 8; *Die Bekenntnisschriften,* pp. 121-22.

> pel, and to exclude the ungodly whose ungodliness is public from the communion of the church, without human coercion but by the word *(sine vi humana sed verbo)*.[62]

The form of jurisdiction proper to civil authority is imperium, the power to command backed by the threat of coercive force; the church has been granted no such armed imperium. The church has been given only the word, only the mandate to teach and admonish, to proclaim and warn. Even the *ultima ratio* of church discipline, excommunication, applies no violence to the body but is an attempt to address the heart: it is the church speaking God's law to the impenitent as bluntly and dramatically as possible.[63]

This distinction between civil imperium and ecclesiastical *jurisdictio* has a further context in late-medieval understandings of episcopal *potestas;* there had come to be a disjunction in medieval Latin theology and canon law between *potestas ordinis* and *potestas jurisdictionis,* which might be paraphrased as "pastoral-sacramental authority" and "authority for governance." This disjunction was not only used to render bishops dependent on the Roman See, which alone could grant jurisdiction, but as the presupposition for this it also made room for a quasi-autonomous juridical and institutional sphere in the church, only externally related to the sacramental life of the church, its life in the gospel.

This disjunction between pastoral-sacramental and juridical-institutional spheres is doubtless an important element in the background of the later theory that declares the visible church a purely secular realm. One claims the pastoral governance of souls for the gospel and leaves the governance of common life to the state ecclesiastical consistory, or perhaps in more recent times to management consultants. Whatever its practical effects may have been, the *theological* impetus of the Lutheran Reformation was in the opposite direction. In his defense of Article 28 in the *Apology of the Augsburg Confession,* Melanchthon refers approvingly to what he calls "the old division of *potestas* into *potestas ordinis* and *potestas jurisdictionis,*" but then he goes on to interpret that distinction thus:

62. *Augsburg Confession,* Article 28, 20-21; *Die Bekenntnisschriften,* pp. 123-24.

63. Thus the Reformers' rejection of the so-called "Great Ban" that joined civil penalties to excommunication. See Luther's *Smalcald Articles,* part III, *On the Ban:* "The Great Ban, as the Pope calls it, we regard as a pure worldly penalty, which has nothing to do with us ministers of the church" (*Die Bekenntnisschriften,* p. 456).

> A bishop has the *potestas ordinis,* that is, the ministry of word and sacrament, and has also the *potestas jurisdictionis,* that is, the authority to excommunicate those guilty of public crimes, and then to absolve them, if they are converted and seek absolution.[64]

Gunther Wenz has pointed out the significance of this focusing of *jurisdictio* on excommunication and reconciliation: as Melanchthon uses the distinction it no longer marks "the separation of two kinds of official authority" but rather "serves to bring out their inseparable connection with one another."

> . . . the traditional distinction of *potestas ordinis* and *potestas jurisdictionis* is taken up in [the *Apology*] only with the goal of developing the distinctive character of episcopal jurisdictional power in strict relation to the *potestas ordinis* and in this sense to define it as an authority which can only be used appropriately in the context of the tasks characteristic of the *potestas ordinis.*[65]

In other words, there is no *potestas* in the church besides that conferred by Christ when he commanded the apostles to baptize and make disciples of all nations. There is thus no authority in the church that is not pastoral and sacramental in essence. This does not mean that there is no *jurisdictio,* no real governance; it calls rather for a distinctive *mode* of governance. True governance in the church is not an autonomous juridical-institutional management task in a separate compartment from pastoral ministry; it grows out of pastoral-sacramental ministry and returns to it.

This same concern for the distinctiveness of the church's governance is at work, it should be noted, in early Lutheran thinking about *teaching authority.* The Lutheran Reformers by no means denied the existence of a teaching office in the church. Article 28 says explicitly that it belongs to episcopal jurisdiction *by divine right* "to reject doctrine contrary to the gospel." The concern of the Reformers was rather to understand the proper *character* of teaching authority within the communion of the church. Proper magisterium cannot be what the second-generation Lutheran Mar-

64. *Apology of the Augsburg Confession,* Article 28, 13; *Die Bekenntnisschriften,* p. 400.

65. Wenz, *Theologie der Bekenntnisschriften,* vol. 2, p. 379.

tin Chemnitz called "dictatorial" authority, a kind of doctrinal imperium exercised in a one-way relation of command and obedience between clergy and laity. On the contrary, as a recent ecumenical statement puts it:

> The jurisdiction of bishops is one consequence of the call they have received to lead their churches in an authentic "Amen"; it is not arbitrary power given to one person over the freedom of others. Within the working of the *sensus fidelium* there is a complementary relationship between the bishop and the rest of the community.[66]

This is much of what is at stake in the Lutheran doctrine of the common priesthood, which does not underwrite the *independence* of the religious individual but rather the *interdependence* of the members of one body. Teaching authority must be exercised *within* this interdependence of the members of the body in common dependence upon their head.

According to the Reformers, teaching authority that respects this interdependence, in which all have been anointed with one Spirit, will be exercised in a specific way: it will seek the assent of the faithful to its teaching by a substantive appeal to Holy Scripture as the church's shared norm of faith and life. As Chemnitz put it: ". . . the interpreter must show the reasons and bases of his interpretation so clearly and certainly that also others who themselves do not have the gift of interpretation may be able to understand and grasp them."[67] Authentic teaching authority thus seeks the "Amen" of the people of God by its intelligible appeal to the knowledge of God shared by all, in order to be confirmed as the judgment of the whole body in which the Spirit dwells.

In these various concrete ways the Lutheran Reformers insisted that the inner character of the church as spiritual *communio* demands a distinctive outward order of life with distinctive practices and forms. Underlying this insistence, early Lutherans also had in the background of their thinking elements of what might be called a fundamental ecclesiology, an account of the eschatological constitution of the church. For the most part received from Scripture, the Fathers, and the liturgy, these elements were

66. *The Gift of Authority: Authority in the Church III*, a statement by the Second Anglican–Roman Catholic International Commission (New York: Church Publishing, 1999), p. 27.

67. Martin Chemnitz, *Examination of the Council of Trent*, vol. 1, trans. Fred Kramer (St. Louis: Concordia, 1971), p. 216.

not worked out by the Lutheran Reformers in full-blown theoretical format but operate in the background as a framework of assumptions that conditions their thinking on particular issues more or less consistently but only occasionally comes visibly into view.

For Luther and other early Lutherans, the divine action that establishes the church is essentially sacramental: it is the act of God in, with, and under the signs especially of baptism and the Lord's Supper, as well the preaching of Christ. Thus outward practice and inner spiritual reality are inseparably connected; as Luther put it:

> Now that God has let his holy gospel go forth, he deals with us in two ways: on the one hand, outwardly, on the other hand, inwardly. Outwardly he deals with us through the oral word of the gospel and through bodily signs, such as Baptism and the Sacrament. Inwardly he deals with us through the Holy Spirit and faith along with other gifts. But all this in such measure and in such order that the outward elements should and must come first. And the inward things come afterwards and by means of the outward, for he has decided to give the inward element to no one except by means of the outward element. For he will give no one the Spirit or faith without the outward word and sign which he has instituted. . . .[68]

What God does in this sacramental action is to establish *koinonia*, joining the believer and Christ together in an intimacy for which we have no proper concepts, and at the same time joining all believers with one another in an equally inexpressible unity. Thus Luther wrote in his 1519 *Sermon on the Venerable Sacrament of the Holy True Body of Christ:*

> The significance or effect of this sacrament is the fellowship of all the saints. . . . Thus it is that Christ and all saints are one spiritual body, just as the inhabitants of a city are one community and body, each citizen being a member of the others and of the entire city. All the saints, therefore, are members of Christ and of the church, which is a spiritual and eternal city of God. . . . This fellowship consists in this, that all the spiritual possessions of Christ and his saints are shared with and become the common property of the person who receives this sacrament. Again, all

68. *Luthers Werke: Kritische Gesamtausgabe* (Weimar, 1883-), vol. 18, p. 136.

> sufferings and sins likewise become common property; and thus love kindles love in return and brings about unity. To stay with our crude material comparison, it is like a city where every citizen shares with all the others the city's name, honor, freedom, trade, customs, usages, help, support, protection, and the like, while at the same time each shares all the dangers of fire and flood, enemies and death, losses, taxes, and the like. For whoever would share the profits must also share in the costs, and always pay back love with love.[69]

Luther is clear that the political analogy is "crude"; he does not mean to *reduce* the unity of the body of Christ to the dimensions of civic allegiance.[70] He uses the analogy however precisely in order to make the point that, like the unity of citizens in a city, the spiritual unity of the church in Christ has *public* consequences, that it shapes a form of life in history.

The 1519 eucharistic tract thus concludes with a critique of the lay brotherhoods or *Gemeinschaften* that were a prominent feature of civic life

69. *Luther's Works: American Edition* (Philadelphia: Fortress Press; St. Louis: Concordia Presses, 1955-), vol. 35, pp. 51-52. Translation altered. For this important tract, and its relation to *communio*-ecclesiology, cf. Heinrich Holze, ed., *The Church as Communion: Lutheran Contributions to Ecclesiology* (Geneva: Lutheran World Federation, 1997), especially the essays by Alejandro Zorzin and Simo Peura. Peura's essay also appeared in German in *Der Heilige Geist: Ökumenische und reformatorische Untersuchungen,* Veröffentlichungen der Luther-Akademie e.V. Ratzeburg 25, ed. Joachim Heubach (Erlangen: Martin Luther Verlag, 1996), pp. 131-56; see there also the important *Korreferat* by Michael Root, pp. 157-68. Compare also the slightly older essay by Vilmos Vajta, "The Church as Spiritual-Sacramental *Communio* with Christ and His Saints in the Theology of Luther," in Peter Manns and Harding Meyer, eds., *Luther's Ecumenical Significance: An Interconfessional Consultation* (Philadelphia: Fortress Press, 1984), pp. 111-21.

70. One can see how Luther's understanding of the unity of the church outruns any *merely* civic unity in his 1520 tract, *Fourteen Consolations:* "Therefore, when I suffer, I do not suffer alone, but Christ and all Christians suffer with me, for Christ says, 'Whoever touches you, touches the apple of my eye' (Zechariah 2:8). Thus others bear my burden, and their strength is my strength. The faith of the church comes to the aid of my fearfulness; the chastity of others endures the temptation of my flesh; the fastings of others are my gain; the prayer of another pleads for me. . . . Consequently I can actually glory in the blessings of others as though they were my very own. They are truly mine when I am grateful and joyful with the others. It may be that I am base and ugly, while those I admire are fair and beautiful. By my love I make not only their blessings but their very selves my own" (*Luther's Works,* vol. 42, pp. 161-62).

in Luther's day. Luther insists that true *Gemeinschaft* is formed by the Eucharist, and that this has concrete social consequences: "If they desire to maintain a brotherhood, they should gather provisions and feed and serve a tableful or two of poor people, for the sake of God."[71] The "divine" and "heavenly" communion of all the faithful in Christ, grounded in baptism and Eucharist, is the criterion and formative principle of all true "brotherhood" and "community" in the outward life of the church:

> Now all other brotherhoods should be so conducted as to keep this first and noblest brotherhood constantly before their eyes and regard it alone as great. With all their works they should be seeking nothing for themselves; they should rather do them for God's sake, entreating God that he keep and prosper this Christian fellowship and brotherhood from day to day. Thus when a brotherhood is formed, they should let it be seen that the members are a jump ahead of others in rendering the Christian community some special service with their prayers, fastings, alms, and good works, and this not in order to seek selfish profit or reward, or to exclude others, but to serve as the free servants of the whole community of Christians.[72]

The Reformation views of authority and order mentioned above should be read against this background as concrete applications in particular "problem areas" of this vision of the church as spiritual-embodied *communio* in Christ. In each case, the goal of Luther and the early Lutheran movement was not to isolate the eschatological from the outward and bodily church but to ask how the communion of church could and should "take up space in the world" in a manner appropriate to its eschatological character as the body of Christ.

On this reading, therefore, the Lutheran tradition already contains elements of something like a "communion-ecclesiology" in its normative sources. These point toward a way of relating eschatological new being to the church's life in history that is richer and more differentiated, but also more disruptive of modernist protocols and proprieties, than the modern Lutheran ecclesiological consensus easily allows. Jenson's systematic reworking of ecumenical communion-ecclesiology could thus provide a

71. *Luther's Works,* vol. 35, pp. 68-69. Translation altered.
72. *Luther's Works,* vol. 35, p. 71. Translation altered.

strategic perspective within which these elements of Reformation concern might come more clearly into view and exercise a more profound influence than they have so far on either Lutheran thinking or the ecumenical discussion. In this way, moreover, Jenson at the same time offers a distinctive and promising approach to the whole issue of Christian presence in the world, which seems to be at the heart of the manifold problems of ecumenical reconciliation, missionary engagement, and catechetical and spiritual formation that confront the Christian churches throughout the world on the threshold of a new century.

Jenson in the Public Square: Thinking the Church

RICHARD JOHN NEUHAUS

Although Robert Jenson has not been reticent in delivering himself of trenchant judgments on public policy, politics, and the state of the culture, those specific judgments are not my chief interest here. What is noteworthy about Jenson relative to the public square — as about Jenson relative to everything else, one might add — is that he is always and relentlessly, some might say incorrigibly, Jenson the theologian. This is more than a matter of personal or professional disposition. Rather, in his thought and work, theology as the church's disciplined reflection on God is of necessity reflection on everything. The political and cultural realities of the public square have their own integrity and legitimate urgencies, but they are not understood until they are understood theologically. Jenson does not "do ethics." He is too preoccupied with thinking and living the life of the church. In the process, a lot gets done that others call ethics, cultural criticism, and even political philosophy. This insistence upon ecclesiastically embodied theology is evident throughout Jenson's writings and is exemplified with particular nicety in his *Essays in Theology of Culture* (1995).

Theology understood as the communal speaking of the God of Israel and of the church is, quite simply, about everything. Theology "must be either a universal and founding discipline or a delusion."[1] Because theology is

1. Robert W. Jenson, *Systematic Theology*, vol. I: *The Triune God* (Oxford: Oxford

about everything, it is necessarily public. The achievements attending modernity's distinction between public and private — and in the political realm those achievements should not be denigrated — have seduced Christians into collaborating with liberal secularists in confining the gospel to the sphere of privacy, the sphere of poetry, values, and individual preferences divorced from the "real world" of public deliberation and decision. Against that seduction, Jenson declares, "We are . . . called to say our piece about God in the open arena of all nations or not say it at all. And we are promised that the gates of hell will not at last prevail against this attempt."[2]

Over the many years of my reading Jenson in the context of our friendly conversation, I am impressed that for him it is the case, as it is not the case for most theologians, that his thought on ethics, politics, culture, and other aspects of the public square is not theology *ad extra,* as distinct from theology *ad intra.* The entirety of all that is is, if one may put it this way, *ad intra* to the life of God, the Father, Son, and Holy Spirit. The life of God, in turn, is the subject matter of the church's reflection called theology, which engages, without subsuming, the entirety of all that is. Of Jenson's many contributions to the church's thought, it may be agreed that his most suggestive proposals have to do with what is ordinarily called the doctrine of God, specifically the triune life of God, and, more specifically yet, the life of God as the story through time of the God of Israel — Father, Son, and Spirit — with the people he speaks into being. In this essay I do not deal directly with that constituting dimension of Jenson's thought since I expect it will be amply discussed elsewhere in the present book, but his construal of the life of the Holy Trinity is the necessary assumption in everything else that is to be said about "Jenson in the public square."

A Christian understanding of humanity is, according to Jenson, inescapably public, social, and historical. It is also assertively Christological. Part of the charm of Jenson's work is in the improbable coterie of teachers to whom he is devoted and on whom he so heavily draws. For instance, Karl Barth, Wolfhart Pannenberg, and Jonathan Edwards do not collaborate so constructively in any other theological project of which I am aware. (It should be mentioned that Jenson correctly sees more Barth in

University Press, 1997), p. 20. Hereafter abbreviated *ST,* by volume and page. Italics in quotations are Jenson's unless otherwise noted.

2. Robert W. Jenson, *Essays in Theology of Culture* (Grand Rapids: Eerdmans, 1995), p. 35.

Pannenberg than is generally recognized.) It is specifically with Barth that Jenson underscores the Christological basis of man as a social and political animal. It is in the Son, who *is* the human person Jesus, that we both receive our being from God and are directed to God through this fellow human. Therefore Jenson affirms Barth's assertion: "The humanity of every person consists in the determination of his being as being-together with the fellow-human." It follows that "a human without the fellow-human" is the very definition of the inhuman.[3]

Jenson's thinking, then, about the questions of the public square is not, so to speak, an add-on. It is not an annex to or an extension of his more "purely theological" reflection. Theology is not the "theory" of which ethics and cultural criticism are the "application." All that he says is theological through and through. It is from beginning to eschatological end about the Word by whom all creation came to be, is sustained, and will be fulfilled in glory. Humanity's response to God's speaking him into being is archtypically a response of prayer; we are praying animals and therefore essentially communal animals and therefore essentially political animals (*ST* II, 7). This line of thought is necessary to understand why Jenson's frequent juxtaposing of liturgy and politics is not merely eccentric. The history of the City of Man is riddled with announcements of a "new politics," but the only really new politics is the liturgy that anticipates the triumphant Feast of the Lamb. So it is that the church at prayer must ever be, short of the kingdom, both a sign of hope and a sign of contradiction to the politics of the City of Man.

Among the most succinct and winsome accounts of Jenson's thinking about the public square and our moment in it is his 1993 essay, "How the World Lost Its Story."[4] For the church to speak the gospel, says Jenson, is to speak a story with a promise; the "postmodern" world, having lost its story, cannot credit the promise. Jenson is appropriately skeptical of current talk about postmodernity, suggesting that most of what is called postmodernism is simply a matter of catching up with Friedrich Nietzsche, and then only the half of Nietzsche that is his nihilism, which is not really Nietzsche since it lacks the eschatology of the "superman" that is the promise of a story told in

3. Robert W. Jenson, *Systematic Theology*, vol. II: *The Works of God* (Oxford: Oxford University Press, 1999), p. 73. Hereafter abbreviated *ST*, by volume and page. Italics in quotations are Jenson's unless otherwise noted.

4. Robert W. Jenson, "How the World Lost Its Story," *First Things* 36 (October 1993): 19-24.

explicit antithesis to the Christian story. Moreover, what is today called postmodernism is the "modernism" of the arts at the turn of the twentieth century that was an explicit rejection of what Enlightenment and Romantic thought called "modern." At this point one might pause and note that Jenson is also unusual among contemporary theologians in his paying of such assiduous *theological* attention to the arts; one might also wonder why he has not developed more systematically an aesthetic theology, or theology of aesthetics, along the lines of, for instance, Balthasar. Yet perhaps it is enough to attend to the many things he has done, rather than to wonder about what he has not done and may still do.

We return to how the world lost its story. Jenson contends that modernity lived for a long time off the moral and intellectual capital that it did not renew and that is now running out, if it is not already exhausted. In her living and speaking the gospel, the church should now understand herself to be in a postmodern circumstance comparable to her earlier mission in a post-Hellenic and post-Roman-imperial circumstance. (It is not entirely clear, however, that a postmodern world is the same thing as a post-Christian world.) Modernity assumed that the world, and our lives in the world, could be understood as a "realistic narrative" (Hans Frei) along the lines of a dramatic account that fits the world as it really is. In other words, it assumed "that the world somehow 'has' its own true story, antecedent to, and enabling of, the stories we tell about ourselves in it." The assumed narrative of modernity was a secular cannibalizing of the biblical narrative. However, as is now evident in literature, the arts, philosophy, and almost everywhere else, that secularized narrative cannot be sustained since it was "the attempt to live in a universal story without a universal storyteller," namely, the God of Israel.

Not only in the so-called high culture but in everyday life on the street, in the classroom, and in the workplace, people live in a world depicted by Samuel Beckett "in which no stories can be true." Until fairly recently, it was expected that people thought their lives were part of a story and the church's business was to propose the gospel as the true and deep meaning of that story. No longer. What is the church in the postmodern circumstance to do? "The obvious answer is that if the church does not *find* her hearers antecedently inhabiting a narratable world, then the church must herself *be* that world." As was the case in the world of dying antiquity, this she does chiefly by enacting the true story in the community gathered by the Eucharist. "Protestantism has been modernity's specific form of Christianity," says

Jenson. Protestantism assumed that modernity had a story, that the action was "out there" in the world, and that the purpose of preaching, catechesis, and worship was to equip people to get with the action. Protestantism trimmed the Christian story to fit the story of modernity, which turned out to be no story at all apart from the Christian story, and therefore Jenson concludes of Protestantism, "Just so, its day is over."

As with the church's story, modernity's story came with a promise, and that promise was called progress. At least since the First World War, it has been impossible to articulate credibly that promise. Historical disappointment has been turned into principle. "Promises, in the postmodern world, are inauthentic simply because they are promises, because they commit a future that is not ours to commit." In the absence of a narrative world, the church must be that world, and so also in a culture that precludes promise "the church must herself be a communal world in which promises are made and kept." Here Jenson indicates, as he also does elsewhere, his debt to Stanley Hauerwas. With Jenson, however, the ethical is but one dimension; in fact, I am not sure he has a distinct category called "ethics." He accents the worshiping community of apocalyptic vision whose Eucharist anticipates the Banquet of the Lamb. The community is a community of seeing as well as hearing, a seeing that anticipates the beatific vision. Jenson writes:

> Protestantism supposed that folk in the civil society already envisioned glorious Fulfillment, and needed no specific churchly envisioning, and therefore Protestantism for the most part eliminated the images and even where it retained them forgot how to use them. Protestantism's reliance on the world was here too an illusion, but here too an illusion it got away with for modernity's time. That time is over.

"How The World Lost Its Story" concludes with the claim that the dying of modernity mandates new necessities — "necessities of concretion and density and vision laid upon the life of the church within herself." Such a conclusion may appear to belie what was said at the start of this essay. Does Jenson here not end up with a turn *ad intra,* a counsel that the church should abandon modernity's public square to its own devices and devote her energies to her own renewal? That suspicion, while sometimes invited by Jenson's language, is unwarranted. It fails to appreciate that, in Jenson's view, the life of the church is the enactment of the triune life of the universal storyteller and is, therefore, the carrier of the universal story that is the story of the world. An authentic turn to the church is, reflexively, a turn to the world. To understand any theological assertion by Jenson in a way that is not, at the same time, an assertion about the triune God is to misunderstand. In this he is a relentless revisionist. With this Trinitarian relentlessness, for instance, he indicts and recasts almost the entirety of ecumenical theology in *Unbaptized God*.[5] With the same relentlessness, he rescues Jonathan Edwards from those who get bogged down in conundrums about predestination because they mistake Edwards's God for the God of the Deists.[6] At every point of his enterprise, and no matter what the subject at hand, Jenson is exploring the life of the Trinity. It is perhaps not too much to say that, for Jenson, the doctrine of Trinity is the conceptual hardware that runs any software.

While he acknowledges his debt to Hauerwas, and frequently sounds Hauerwasian in his sweeping indictment of "liberalism," I believe there are some critical differences between the two. In Hauerwas's turn to the church, at least in his writings to date, the controlling concern is ethical, whereas with Jenson, as we have seen, the framework is always *theo*logical. To be sure, Hauerwas insists that his ethics is theological through and through, but, unlike Jenson, he has not to date provided a detailed display of the theological structuring of his ethics. (We may hope that will be done in the Gifford lectures on which he is currently working.) In addition, and although Hauerwas repudiates the term, many readers detect in his work a "sectarian" bent. This is not possible for Jenson since the life of the triune God encompasses all that is, and therefore that life explicitly articulated and enacted in the church is the story of all that is.

The church cannot speak her own story in isolation and is necessarily engaged by and therefore engaging the stories antecedent to, and sometimes antithetical to, her own. Jenson also praises highly the work of John Milbank, but if I understand Jenson's project, here, too, there are critical differences. Milbank and his party of "radical orthodoxy" repudiate not only the language of social theory but all discourses that are presumably alien to the Christian telling of reality. Jenson, I believe, is closer to the spirit of Terence: "I am a man: nothing human is alien to me." Of course

5. Robert W. Jenson, *Unbaptized God: The Basic Flaw in Ecumenical Theology* (Minneapolis: Fortress, 1992).

6. Robert W. Jenson, *America's Theologian: A Recommendation of Jonathan Edwards* (Oxford and New York: Oxford University Press, 1988).

that must be recast to say that nothing human is alien to the fellow human who is Jesus Christ, who is God, and therefore nothing human can be alien to those who call the fellow human Lord.

Thus Jenson on the distinction between philosophy and theology states:

> The relation is not symmetrical. Since the gospel is intrinsically a missionary message, and since Mediterranean antiquity was there before it was invaded by the gospel, Christianity is the intruder even in the civilization it co-created. Within the West, it is therefore possible to be a disciple of Socrates and not of the prophets or apostles, though it is not possible to be unaffected by them. So there will be "philosophers" who are not Christian theologians. But within Western civilization, and so within the theological enterprise located there, it is not possible to be a disciple of the apostles and not a disciple also of Socrates. Therefore the labels "philosophy" and "theology" cannot mark a real distinction. (*ST* II, 163)

This catholic (also upper case) sensibility marks Jenson's disposition toward all traditions of reflection, as well as cultural expressions and the political tasks of more rightly (i.e., less wrongly) ordering the City of Man. From Barth, Jenson has learned the indispensability of the Christian *Nein!* Yet that is only because other discourses have set themselves against the story of the God of Israel (in liberalism's case, falsely claiming "neutrality" to that story) because it is mistakenly viewed as a heteronomous threat, when in fact that story is an emphatic Yes to all that is human.

It is a frequent criticism of Hauerwas that it is difficult to the point of near impossibility to locate this church that, as he says in many provocative ways, does not *have* a Christian ethic but *is* the Christian ethic. Jenson, by way of contrast, is adamant that the church he would serve is located in space and time and marked by "concretion and density and vision." Jenson cannot settle for a church that is the abstract construction of theologians. One is reminded of Hilaire Belloc's description of Catholicism as "Not a theory but the thing itself. It."[7] Available candidates for being "It" would

7. On the church constructed by theologians see R. R. Reno's critique of Milbank and "radical orthodoxy," forthcoming in *First Things.* On Hilaire Belloc, see "Chesterton and the Thereness of It" in "The Public Square," *First Things* 97 (November 1999): 86.

seem to be Orthodox Christianity and Roman Catholicism. Although Jenson draws on the Orthodox theological tradition, Orthodoxy itself is so ecclesiastically fissiparous and removed from the Reformation-Enlightenment-Modernity milieu that claims his intellectual attention that his concentrated engagement with Catholicism — as one who is ecclesiastically situated in a Protestantism whose "day is over" — is perhaps inevitable.

Like Hauerwas, Jenson's chief word regarding the public square is ecclesiological. Unlike Hauerwas, Jenson's commitment to ecclesiological concretion requires careful attention to questions of liturgy, catechesis, dogma, magisterium, and other necessary aspects of the church not as theory but as the thing itself. Jenson's theological project is therefore in sustained dialogue with Catholic teaching and, to a lesser extent, Catholic life. In this connection, he has made many imaginative, if not always convincing, contributions. His primary audience continues to be the Protestantism of which he is part, and he strives impressively to demonstrate that the Catholic reality can be sympathetically understood and perhaps reconciled with his understanding of a Protestantism that, while perhaps nowhere existent in historical fact, is the Protestantism of Luther and Barth. Thus, for instance, he deals imaginatively, one might almost say heroically, with the Roman Catholic dogmas regarding Mary and the infallibility of popes and councils. His self-consciously strained and cautious suggestion that the Marian dogmas of sinlessness and bodily assumption might be postulated of any faithful child of Israel, and that what is said of papal infallibility might be said of any pastor in circumstances where error is countered by truth, is of considerable theological interest. At the same time, one may be permitted to think it probable that the popes in 1854 and 1950 and both Vatican councils had in mind a somewhat more singular reference to Mary and the bishop of Rome, respectively.[8]

A useful comparison may be made with the work of Pannenberg in this connection. Both thinkers insist upon the public reality of the church as the apostolically constituted bearer and proleptic enactment of the story of creation and its fulfillment in the kingdom of God. Both are Protestants who go as far as they believe they can, while remaining Protestants, to accommodate and, if possible, reconcile the claims of the Catholic Church. Pannenberg, however, operates with a much more rigorous — some might say constrictive — Enlightenment understanding of reason, including

8. On Marian dogmas see *ST* II, 203-4, and on papal infallibility, *ST* II, 243-44.

theological reason. Both bridle at the claim of Rome that dogmatic definitions are "irreformable." The term "irreformable" is perhaps unfortunate in view of the insistence of the Reformation, seconded by the Second Vatican Council's Constitution on the Church *(Lumen gentium),* that the church is always in need of reform. In place of "irreformable," one might better understand the Catholic claim as saying that dogmatic definitions cannot be negated or reversed.

In the light of Jenson's radical realism in the identification of Christ and his church — a realism that is luminously evident in his treatment of the sacraments — one is somewhat puzzled as to why he does not make a theological move with respect to infallibility along the lines suggested by John Henry Newman on the development of doctrine, a line of thought endorsed by magisterial Catholic teaching (see, e.g., *ST* II, 250ff.). In his famous essay on development, Newman wrote of the church's teaching:

> It seems in suspense which way to go; it wavers, and at length strikes out in one definite direction. In time it enters upon strange territory; points of controversy alter their bearing; parties rise and fall around it; dangers and hopes appear in new relations; and old principles reappear under new forms. It changes with them in order to remain the same. In a higher world it is otherwise, but here below to live is to change, and to be perfect is to have changed often.[9]

Of course it is true that Newman thought the definition of infallibility "inopportune," but he could and did comprehend it in his understanding of development. It is also true that some Catholic thinkers today would force a decision between saying that the church's teaching has changed and that it has developed. For Newman, as for authoritative Catholic teaching, that is a false choice. Change, in the ordinary sense of the word, is obvious and undeniable. The question is whether change is the change of discontinuity, correcting an error, or the change of continuity, developing a truth. Which kind of change is involved — remembering always that perfection will not be reached until we "know even as we are known" (1 Cor. 13:12) — can be informed but not finally decided by historical study, hermeneutical reflection,

9. John Henry Cardinal Newman, *An Essay on the Development of Doctrine,* Notre Dame Series in the Great Books (Notre Dame, Ind.: Notre Dame University Press, 1989), p. 40.

and rational analysis. The will is involved, as in the determination to think with the church *(sentire cum ecclesia),* as also faith is involved. Jenson writes, "Faith that the church is still the church is faith in the Spirit's presence and rule in and by the structures of the church's historical continuity. Indeed, even the church's recognition through the second century of who were and who were not apostles cannot be justified except by trust in the Spirit's leading" (*ST* I, 23-24).

At the same time, Jenson makes the unexceptionable point that "neither Scripture nor creed nor liturgy nor teaching office, nor yet their ensemble, can as historical structures guarantee the fidelity of our proclamation and prayer to the apostolic witness." Yet he can entertain a hypothetical and draw from it a conclusion that is in tension with, if not contradiction to, faith in the Spirit's rule of the continuing community. "If, for example," Jenson writes, "the decision of Nicaea that Christ is 'of one being with the Father' was false to the gospel, the gospel was thereby so perverted that there has since been no church extant to undo the error" (*ST* I, 17). The entertainment of such contrary to fact hypotheticals is perhaps necessary to maintaining that the very existence of the church is dependent upon theological constructs, a position that would seem to result inevitably in a church of theological speculation rather than the ecclesial "concretion and density and vision" made possible by Jenson's alternative proposition: "Faith that the church is still the church is faith in the Spirit's presence and rule in and by the structures of the church's historical continuity." That the judgment of what is or is not the church is a theologian's judgment does not spare it from being what Newman called "private judgment," and a church premised upon private judgment cannot, so it seems to me, bear the weight that Jenson would assign to it in the public square.

At the beginning of his systematic theology, Jenson contends that biblical, sacramental, and dogmatic authority is not possible apart from a teaching office, or what he does not hesitate to call a magisterium. He then adds, "To affirm this, we need not yet commit ourselves about a mandated or appropriate *location* of teaching authority" (*ST* I, 40). Some five hundred pages later, that teaching authority has been located in the bishop of Rome and the bishops in communion with him (or who will be in communion in a future united church), but, as I have suggested, it is not evident in what way it is a magisterium legitimately commanding adherence. An ecclesiology that is subject to hypothetical disqualifiers and dependent upon promissory notes drawn on a possible church of the future will not, I think, do the work that Jenson wants his ecclesiology to do. What I have called the radical realism of his sacramental theology (especially with respect to baptism and Eucharist) does not extend to what the Second Vatican Council calls the sacrament of the church.

Jenson pays assiduous and sympathetic attention to ecclesiological realities of worship, sacrament, catechesis, and teaching authority — and mainly as these are most fully and explicitly found in Catholicism. At the end of the day, however, it seems that Jenson is thinking the church. Speaking from a Protestantism whose "day is over," Jenson is in "true but imperfect communion" *(Unitatis Redintegratio)* with the ecclesial reality to which he devotes such careful attention but from which he remains a step removed in order, it seems, to maintain a critical distance. One might suggest, at the risk of presumption, that the fullness of critical participation is the mode of greater fruitfulness and accountability for one who is so clearly determined to be a theologian of the church.

Jenson does not do justice to his great theological contribution when he casts himself, as he frequently does, in the role of maverick. For instance: "Finally we may ask how it can be *true* that the church with her sacraments is the body of the risen Christ, the object as which this human person is there for us. The answer is very simple, though it overturns the whole inherited structure of Western thinking. . . . [F]or it to be true that the church gathered around her sacraments is Christ's body, all that is needed is that the risen Christ's personal self-understanding determine what is real, that is, that he be the *Logos* of God" (*ST* II, 214). That has a fine ring to it, but is it so very simple that the whole inherited structure of Western thinking, also as it is ecclesiastically embodied, should be overturned?

As a theologian Jenson declares himself to be, and typically shows himself to be, a servant of the inherited and received tradition of the church's reflection to which, as he says, the appropriate disposition is that of obedience as an inescapable component of faith. Yet when it comes to the admittedly unsatisfactory embodiment of the actual church inherited, he appears to hold back the commitment of full communion, reserving such commitment for a church that is an ideal form or future promise worthier of the great and true story that he tells about the God of Israel with his people. The question, then, is whether Jenson's church is not just another form of what Newman called the "paper church" of Anglo-Catholicism, a theologian's construct that is not answerable to the apostolically institutionalized inheritance that is inseparable from the narrative he tells. Jenson's astute and sympathetic critique of that inheritance is a valuable contribution, but one is left wondering what it is about the critique that demands the price of attenuated *communio,* and whether there is not at work here — however much Jenson may formally repudiate it — a very modern, and very Protestant, notion of freedom apart from and even pitted against obedience. The conceptual church of the theologian's construction cannot excommunicate. Jenson insists that the church must be able to excommunicate.

A church that is not a theory but the thing itself must be able to patrol its borders, which is to say the entrance and exit doors must be clearly marked; there must be an understood course of catechesis and initiation as well as a capacity for excommunication. Jenson writes: "[W]hen members so live as to disprove the church's missionary claim to the Spirit, the church *must* separate herself from them or be herself unfaithful. The practice of excommunication is thus an absolute if wrenching necessity: 'Let such a one be to you as a Gentile and a tax collector'" (*ST* II, 205-6). At the same time, Jenson's understanding of the border patrol is admirably informed by self-knowledge and pastoral sensibility. "My political or academic or economic foe and I forgive each other as we approach the table, but our situations outside the church may condemn us to need the same forgiveness again the next day; it is the shared cup itself that is our permanent peace" (*ST* II, 205). The church "strives to escape the *libido dominandi*" of the City of Man, but, short of the kingdom to come it is always a matter of striving. The giving of the "keys of the kingdom" to those who govern in the polity of the church is to be understood both in the context of eschatological expectation and in the context of coping with the "failing peace" in the church as it presently is (*ST* II, 205).

However provisional and inadequate the church's government may be, it must have enough "concretion and density and vision" to be clearly distinguished from the surrounding polities disordered by the *libido dominandi.* The reference to surrounding polities raises the question of whether it is appropriate to think of Jenson as "America's theologian." He certainly does not uncritically baptize the American experiment, and he is most emphatically no court prophet of a consoling civil religion, but then neither was Jonathan Edwards, whom Jenson calls "America's theologian." Of the relationship between church and culture, Jenson declares, "The Constantinian settlement is now manifestly at its very end."

> The church's present position, in the midst of her divorce proceedings from the culture, of course differs from that of the ancient church in a way that inevitably generates confusion: most of those who need catechesis to prepare for life in the church are already members and suppose themselves already qualified for her life. During the time in which the church and the culture are separating but not separated, this ambiguity cannot be avoided or denied. (*ST* II, 305)

In the context of that passage, it is clearly the culture that has initiated the divorce proceedings. Church and culture in America are "separating but not separated." The final divorce, if I understand Jenson, is not theologically or morally mandated; it simply seems to him inevitable, based on his reading of the culture's hostility to the community that lives the story of God. Jenson does not preclude, in principle, a reconfiguration of something like the Constantinian settlement. I agree substantively with almost every aspect of Jenson's critique of our culture, but I believe he sometimes tends to be excessively dour and even, if I may say so, resigned to the triumph of the counter stories or of the abolition of stories altogether. This is in part, no doubt, a matter of personal disposition and how one reads "the signs of the times." For instance, Jenson shares with most intellectuals what I believe is an exaggerated notion of the culture-determining power of the economy. He also seems resigned to the irreversibility of the moral incoherence and polity-destroying force of the "culture of death" that is evident in the acceptance of abortion — an acceptance that is, I think, more fragile and tentative than he suggests. Yet these are instances of Jenson's specific judgments that, as I said at the outset, are not the subject of this essay. In these judgments it may turn out, of course, that Jenson is right, but the story of God with His people is marked by radical contingency that opens also the proximate future to promise, including the promise of an American polity and culture less at enmity with the truth of the gospel.

So, is Robert Jenson America's theologian? Not in any exclusive sense, to be sure, but I think the answer is Yes. In the preface to the book on Edwards, Jenson writes, "I have exercised my reflection on him for many years now and have found that America has indeed an American theologian and that I am, for better and worse, an American Christian."[10] It fol-

10. Jenson, *America's Theologian,* p. viii.

lows that Jenson is an American Christian theologian. There is no doubt that he is God's theologian, which is to say the church's theologian, first. "I die the king's good servant, but God's first," said another Christian who understood the connections between story, promise, and obedience. Although Henry did not recognize it, Thomas More was the king's better servant precisely because he was God's servant first. Just so (if I may borrow Jenson's signature phrase) is Robert Jenson America's theologian.

Only Theology Overcomes Ethics;[1] or, What "Ethicists" Must Learn from Jenson

STANLEY HAUERWAS

I. How Theology Became Ethics in America

I have been asked to write on Robert Jenson's "ethics" — a straightforward request that should elicit a straightforward response. There is, however, one small problem. Jenson does not "do" ethics. "Ethics" is not listed in the "Index of Topics" in either volume of his *Systematic Theology.* To be sure Jenson, who seems to share my view that it is better to have views than not, declares himself often on matters that many might consider to be "ethics." Yet he does not seem to think his declarations about abortion or politics or how they are connected constitute "ethics." The one time Jenson uses the description "Christian ethics," he does so only to express doubt whether such a discipline is a good idea. He explains he learned from Edmund Santurri that "the vast apparatus of 'ethical inquiry' characteristic of late modern societies may be mostly a device to mask corruption" (*ST* II, 209).

Yet that Jenson refuses to "do" ethics is why his work is so important for those such as myself who bear the burden of being identified as "Chris-

1. I have obviously "borrowed" this title from John Milbank's essay, "Only Theology Overcomes Metaphysics," in his *The Word Made Strange: Theology, Language, and Culture* (Cambridge: Blackwell, 1997), pp. 36-52. Jenson has expressed great appreciation for Milbank's *Theology and Social Theory* in his *Systematic Theology,* vol. II: *The Works of God* (Oxford: Oxford University Press, 1999). Hereafter abbreviated *ST,* by volume and page. Italics in quotations are Jenson's.

tian ethicists." I do not particularly enjoy being known as a Christian ethicist because that description often seems to legitimate for many in the "field" of ethics the leaving behind of a kind of theology represented by Jenson. For example, I cannot remember any session of the annual meeting of the Society of Christian Ethics devoted to a work like Jenson's *Systematic Theology.* Christian ethicists think they should read philosophy, political theory, and/or social science, but theology it would seem is not really that important for ethics. Therefore, I cannot resist using this essay as an opportunity to argue why theology, and in particular the work of Jenson, is so important for ethics. However, before I do so I need, so to speak, to set the stage by suggesting why theology, particularly in America, became ethics and ethics became a form of reflection that could be done whether God exists or not.

Americans are often described as a practical people, and thus there is the presumption that Americans are more like the practical Romans than the theoretical Greeks. Americans allegedly are not attracted to metaphysical questions but want to know how to "get things done." It is not by accident that pragmatism, which many mistakenly associate with the view that the truth of a proposition is tested by whether it works, is America's most distinctive philosophical contribution. The undeniable metaphysical cast of Jenson's work, therefore, seems to put him at odds with the American penchant for making practical and ethical questions primary.

Of course the characterization of the "practical American" is overdrawn; but it is still the case that there is some truth, particularly when considering American church practice and theology, to the generalization that American Christians focus on results. The problem, however, with such a description of American theology is how such a characterization occludes the theory that has produced the allegedly practical character of American thought. No matter how the challenge of surviving as well as making a world out of the "American wilderness" may have contributed to American's practical orientation, in fact the emphasis on the practical or the ethical in American theology is the result of European philosophical developments. In short the experiential and practical character of Christian theology in America but indicates the profound influence of Immanuel Kant.

If you accept — as Kant taught American liberal theologians to accept — that Christian theology can no longer tell you anything about God or God's relation to God's creation, then all you have left is "ethics." Science, and in particular a science shaped by mechanistic metaphysical assumptions, was assumed to have epistemic privilege. Moreover, the political arrangements necessary to sustain a "pluralist" society were thought to require all strong religious convictions to be relegated to the private realm. As a result it was assumed that theological claims by their very nature cannot be considered to have public status. Theology in America became anthropology in an endeavor to sustain the assumption that our lives can have meaning in a causally determined world and/or to motivate our moral behavior. Protestant liberal theology may have been the brain child of German theologians, but it was destined to flourish in America.

It is not by accident, therefore, that theology, particularly in America, found it hard to resist becoming ethics. Of course I am not suggesting that theology ceased being a subject in university and seminary curriculums. Theology was and is still taught, particularly in seminaries, but even in seminaries theology is understood as "information" rather than a discipline on which our lives depend. Thus there is the increasing distinction in seminary curriculums between theoretical and practical/ministerial courses, and the correlative complaint by seminarians that the former lack relevance. Ironically, one of the results of the division between practical and theoretical courses in seminary curriculums has been lack of clarity about whether courses in ethics are "practical" or should be "practical."

In most mainline Protestant seminaries of the present day ethics is usually taught after students have had systematic theology. That order, I suspect, reflects the ongoing presumption that theology at best has become or is "theory" necessary to provide the background assumptions for our ethics. Such a presumption not only makes theology irrelevant but frees ethics from any serious theological engagement. Accordingly, theology and ethics have become increasingly understood as separate disciplines that alleviate the practitioners of each from any responsibility to read one another's work. That students can now do Ph.D. work in theology *or* ethics (which of course, has demanded development of journals and academic associations that serve each discipline) simply reinforces the presumption that theology and ethics represent two quite independent spheres of investigation.

Christian ethicists have also thought it important to distance themselves from theology in order to fulfill their assigned task of being agents, or at least theoreticians, of justice in a social order like America. If the moral principles necessary for addressing issues of income distribution, abortion, or war depend on theological claims, then it is assumed that the Christian ethicist would not be able to speak in or to the "public" realm. For many Christians, ethics names the attempt to develop natural law accounts or to draw on other nontheological sources of moral wisdom to make it possible for Christians to responsibly participate as well as be of service to the American democratic experiment. Conservative and liberal Christian ethicists, who often disagree about everything else, agree that some "third language" must be developed if Christians are to act in public.

My account of the relation of theology to ethics in America may exaggerate the alienation of these disciplines. There are no doubt individual theologians and ethicists whose work would require me to qualify the generalizations I have made about the relation between theology and ethics. Yet I am more than willing to stand by the general picture I have drawn not only because I think it is accurate, but also because it helps us understand better the significance of Jenson's work as a theologian. He has refused to let theology become "theory" by insisting that if we get our speech about God wrong, we cannot help but get our lives wrong. Accordingly he does not understand ethics as something we do after we have done systematic theology, but rather Jenson rightly maintains we are already doing "ethics" when we struggle to speak with exactness about God.

II. Why Jenson's Theology Is Ethics

Some may find the account I have given of how theology became ethics in America to be self-serving. I have been the one, not Jenson, who has waged an undeclared war against those who would do Christian ethics in a theologically minimalist fashion. Am I not simply using Jenson to carry forward my own agenda? The answer is: of course, I am using Jenson to advance the way I have tried to do Christian ethics, but I do not think I am "using him" in an illegitimate fashion. After all, at least one of the reasons I have felt I have had to work to reclaim the theological center of Christian ethics was due to what I have learned from reading Jenson. What I learned from Jenson is what I think he and I both learned from Karl Barth: God matters.

It may well also be self-serving for me to claim to represent the attempt to reclaim a theological center for Christian ethics — after all, Christian ethics has a theological center. Yet the theology that is at the center of Christian ethics is liberal Protestant theology. Even more than Jenson, I have aggressively attacked the liberal theological presuppositions that have shaped and continue to shape most of the work done in Christian ethics. To think one can be more aggressive than Jenson is surely, as we say in Texas, "to put on airs." Yet in this case my critique of Reinhold Niebuhr in itself has been sufficient to give me a much more negative reputation in the field of Christian ethics than Jenson can ever hope to achieve. Jenson, I suspect, has not thought it necessary to criticize representatives of Christian ethics because he felt no need to beat what he considered to be a dead horse. Unfortunately, in the world of Christian ethics that horse is anything but dead, a fact that, of course, is one of the reasons that Jenson's theology is not read by those who do Christian ethics. He is simply thought to be too theologically "conservative."

So if I am "using" Jenson to further my own agenda, it is an agenda I hope that Jenson will recognize as congruent with his own. He has even suggested that while his understanding of ethics is not to be "fathered" on me, my work has provided a template for his own thinking about ethics (*ST* II, 209). I hope he means by this that the way I do ethics is appropriately theological. Yet if that is the case, then it would be a mistake to begin an account of his ethics by looking at what he explicitly says about ethics — for example, in the second volume of his *Systematic Theology.* Rather, as I suggested above, we must begin with what he says about God.

According to Jenson "theology is thinking what to say to be saying the gospel."[2] To speak rightly of God requires training by the gospel because the God that is the beginning and end of our existence is "whoever raised Jesus from the dead, having before raised Israel from Egypt" (*ST* I, 63).Theology is, therefore, the ongoing activity of the church to explore the prescriptive grammar required by the presumption that to be known and to know the one God of all requires the acknowledgment that the God Christians worship is the decisive fact about all things. Thus, theology "must be either a universal and founding discipline or a delusion."[3]

2. Robert Jenson, *Systematic Theology,* vol. I: *The Triune God* (Oxford: Oxford University Press, 1997), p. 32. Hereafter abbreviated *ST,* by volume and page. Italics in quotations are Jenson's.

3. *ST* I, 20. Jenson praises Barth's attempt in the *Church Dogmatics* "to interpret all reality by the fact of Christ; indeed, it can be read as the first truly major system of Western metaphysics since the collapse of Hegelianism. One need not adopt all Barth's characteristic theologoumena to take the massive work as a model and challenge in this

"Universal" and "founding" does not mean for Jenson that theology is not subject to the same contingencies that shape any disciplined mode of inquiry. Theology cannot be timeless for no other reason (and it is the only reason that matters) than because the God that is the subject of Christian theology is not timeless. The God of Israel and Jesus, the God we find in Scripture, is a storied God. That we learn of God, or, more exactly, that we learn who God is through a narrative, is not accidental but rather indicative of God's nature. God's storied character expresses, as Thomas Aquinas maintained, that "God's act of being is constrained by no form other than itself" (*ST* I, 215). Accordingly, the biblical God's eternity is not immunity to time, but faithfulness. "God is not eternal in that he secures himself from time, but in that he is faithful to his commitments with time. At the great turning, Israel's God is eternal in that he is faithful to the death, and then yet again faithful" (*ST* I, 217).

That the gospel must have a history is but an expression of God's Trinitarian nature. The phrase

> "Father, Son, and Holy Spirit" is simultaneously a very compressed telling of the total narrative by which Scripture identifies God and a personal name for the God so specified; in it, name and narrative description not only appear together, as at the beginning of the Ten Commandments, but are identical. By virtue of this logic, the triune phrase offers itself as the unique name for the Christian God, and is then dogmatically mandated for that function by its constitutive place in the rite that establishes Christian identity. The church is the community and a Christian is someone who, when the identity of God is important, names him "Father, Son, and Holy Spirit." Those who do not or will not belong to some other community. (*ST* I, 46)

Christians, therefore, when they go to the "public," cannot avoid saying what they know to be true, namely, that no public can pretend to the truth that denies that God is Father, Son, and Holy Spirit. Christians will only be-

---

respect" (*ST* I, 21). In his *Essays in Theology of Culture* (Grand Rapids: Eerdmans, 1995), Jenson reflects on why his two theological heroes — Jonathan Edwards and Karl Barth — should both come from a different theological tradition than his own: "It is, I think, because both are ruthless in refusing to be confined within or protected by a special epistemological 'compartment' called 'theology'" (p. 222).

tray their non-Christian brothers and sisters if, in the name of reason or in the interest of securing societal peace, they act as if it matters not which god or no-god is worshiped.[4] Therefore Christians can never accept the presumption that the gospel bears the burden of proof when confronted by accounts of the "public" or "reason" that pretend theological neutrality. It may happen that God, as a particular culture has understood him, may withdraw from the public realm of that culture, making our communication about God as well as our rational knowledge of him broken and difficult.[5] Such a situation, however, should never tempt Christians to qualify our presumption that reason requires the right worship of God.

The loss of that presumption has tempted Christians to save religion by withdrawing it from the demands of reason into the safety of private experience or, in the interest of apologetics, to conflate humanistic gods with the Father, Son, and Holy Spirit. Yet if Christians have heard the gospel, they have all they need to understand that the very character of reason requires that they persist in speaking of God in public. Christians are a people who have heard a revelation that includes the name of a man called Pontius Pilate, "and of a God who will verify himself by judging the quick and the dead, that is, the entire public history of man. We are therefore called to say our piece about God in the open arena of all nations or not say it at all. And we are promised that the gates of hell will not at last prevail against this attempt."[6]

Ethics simply names the theological discipline necessary for Christians "to say our piece about God in the open arena of the nations." So understood, Christian ethical reflection does not belong uniquely to any of the loci of Christian theology. When Jenson does what looks like ethics, however, it is done as an aspect of his ecclesiology. That his ethics is placed in the context of his ecclesiology does not imply that the way Christians must live is peculiar to them, but rather reflects Jenson's conviction that ethical reflection is dependent on the politics through which a community discovers and chooses its future.[7]

4. Jenson quite rightly observes that the concept of reason is fundamentally an ethical concept involving a set of commands. Those commands are, he suggests, the two sides of the enterprise of becoming human — its task-character and its mutuality (*Essays in Theology of Culture,* p. 31).

5. Jenson, *Essays in Theology of Culture,* p. 35.

6. Jenson, *Essays in Theology of Culture,* p. 35.

7. Jenson, *Essays in Theology of Culture,* p. 141.

Politics names the "process of that mutual moral address by which God speaks to us to initiate and sustain humanity. The polity is nothing less than the public space in which God calls us to be human in that we call each other to come together in justice."[8] Such a politics is not a given nor can it be assumed. A collective of persons and a state apparatus do not constitute a politics. Absolute rulers may repress deliberation of what ought to be done, but they can sustain the attempt only for a time. An isolated tribal community may live with little awareness that they are reasoning morally until they are confronted by an outer world that presents challenges they cannot master. Indeed, Jenson now theologically judges the specifically modern societies that began with the great hope of the expansion of politics called democracy to be driven into a "neo-tribal" existence. "What Americans are likely now to call politics is in fact the functioning of an almost entirely depoliticized collectivity and state: the manipulation of a mass of petitioners and their interests by professional managers of affairs. If there is a functioning American polity, it is the very tight oligarchy of the federal judges" (*ST* II, 79-80).

If we are to understand Jenson's ethics, these remarks cannot be relegated to "his opinion" of the current state of American polity. Rather they reflect what can only be called his theological politics that is inseparable from his understanding of God's timefulness.[9] Augustine, according to Jenson, rightly maintained that the only polity that could satisfy the earthly polity's own definition of itself, a definition marked by and in time, is "that republic whose founder and governor is Christ." Augustine also rightly argued in this age that the only polity capable of fulfilling that condition was and is the church. Yet the implication is not that Christians are committed to theocracy, but rather that Christians should seek to live in a polity that allows us to serve one another through God's law.[10]

8. *ST* II, 79. Jenson's understanding of politics is but a development of his quite extraordinary account of the significance of conversation for God's identity as well as our identity. With his usual economy he puts the matter exactly, noting "I am who and what I am precisely in conversation with those who offer me my self" (*ST* II, 104).

9. For this use of "theological politics" in distinction to "political theology," see Arne Rasmusson, *The Church as Polis: From Political Theology to Theological Politics as Exemplified by Jürgen Moltmann and Stanley Hauerwas* (Notre Dame, Ind.: University of Notre Dame Press, 1995).

10. *ST* II, 81-82. In *Essays in Theology of Culture,* Jenson puts the matter this way: "right polity holds itself open to prophecy. Right polity will, as the traditional political

Yet that is exactly what has become impossible in America to the extent that America has become a sexually anarchical society (*ST* II, 91). Many, of course, will think Jenson is being overly moralistic to link questions of political legitimacy to sexual immorality. After all, we have been taught — that is, those of us who are good citizens of a liberal democracy — that sexual behavior is "private," that sex should not be legislated by law or become a political issue. Yet for Jenson any account of justice entails how our bodies are to be formed in order that sex does not become but another way we can terrorize each other. The very interconnections between the commands of the Decalogue are but a reminder that no society

> can subsist in which the generations turn against each other; in which vendetta has not been replaced by public organs of judgment and punishment; in which the forms by which sexuality is socialized, whatever these may be, are flouted; in which property, however defined, is not defended; in which false testimony is allowed to pervert judgment; or in which greed is an accepted motive of action.[11]

According to Jenson, the one instance (and it is not the only example) that makes clear that America is no longer "a people," even by the least rigorous of Augustine's definitions of what constitutes a public, is abortion. A society in which an unborn child can be legally killed on the sole

---

ethics of the church have always said, open and guard a space for the public speech and reception of the community's speakers of godly promise" (p. 142). Jenson I think is suggesting something close to Barth's contention that at a minimum a just society must allow for the free preaching of the gospel. Thus the very existence of the church is a significant sign that a polity has at least the beginnings of justice. The difficulty, of course, is whether the gospel the church preaches is the gospel.

11. *ST* II, 86. Some may well think that I must be reading Jenson's mail since I often seem to be saying what he has already said before I knew he had said it. I confess, however, that I did not know Jenson was going to develop the significance of the Ten Commandments in the second volume of the *Systematic Theology* when Will Willimon and I began our little Sunday School book, *The Truth About God: The Ten Commandments in Christian Life* (Nashville: Abingdon Press, 1999). In this little book we argue just as Jenson does that the commandments are not simply negative prohibitions but cohere by positive virtues shaped in and to the course of their history. So the history of Israel and the church provides the positive meaning of the commandments that is not apparent in the text — at least not apparent in the text if the text of the commandments is divorced from the narrative in which they are reported.

decision of the pregnant person can only be a "horde." "If unborn children are members of the human community, then allowing abortions to be performed on decision of the most interested party is a relapse to pure barbarism" (*ST* II, 87). Just to the extent the American people approve this result — and there is every indication that on the whole they do — they have abdicated the moral coherence necessary to be judged a politics.[12] Jenson does not think abortion is but an aberration in America, but rather an indication of the inevitable result of Enlightenment politics and economics. There was a time, perhaps, when the politics produced by the Enlightenment might have been thought to be a blessing, but it is now plain that if the gospel is true, the politics of liberalism must be false.[13]

That's a bleak enough judgment if we forget the good news is that Christians have an alternative to such a politics. The alternative is called church. The church is God's polity whose great character is peace, the "tranquility of order." The church is a government that strives through the

12. Jenson provides the following example: "Historicist nihilism manifests itself most democratically as sheer inability to reason ethically. I choose an instance that notably infests the academic, reminiscently 'liberal' community. A Minnesota poll recent as of this writing (1990) reported that most Minnesotans believe (1) that abortion is the taking of personal human life and (2) that folk should have 'the right' to abort as they freely choose. The evil to which I here call attention is not the number of abortions that *Wade vs. Roe* has produced, terrifying as this is. The subtler, more demonic evil appears in our ability simultaneously to entertain the two referenced opinions. The nihilism is the escape of 'choice' from community. It is freedom that consists in excuse from responsibility for the other and for the story line of my life so far, freedom that occurs on a horizon of sheer temporal sequentiality with no plot at all" (*Essays in Theology of Culture,* pp. 187-88).

13. Jenson, *Essays in Theology of Culture,* p. 133. While Jenson shares the moral and cultural concerns of many that identify themselves as neoconservatives, he is anything but one of them. He is not because he understands that capitalism is at the heart of the Enlightenment dream that produced America. Indeed the retreat into the "family" is exactly the strategy a capitalist economy desires so that the family becomes an end in itself rather than an institution in service to a common good. For example, he observes that those that would celebrate the lack of conscience of the market fail to see that the inevitable result is for the market to become a communal good in its own right in which the moral vacuum created by the market drains the community of moral and aesthetic substance (*ST* II, 315-16). For Jenson nothing indicates immorality more clearly than ugliness. To be sure, the inequities produced by capitalism are terrible, but finally the problem with economic and political life produced by capitalism is that they are so ugly. Thus I confess I was tempted to write on Jenson's ethics as an attempt to reinscribe the significance of beauty in the moral life.

practice of the commandments to escape the *libido dominandi,* which requires as well as makes possible that the church forswears all coercion. Yet because the church has this specific mission, it must discipline her borders, and thus when members live in a manner to disprove the church's missionary claim to the Spirit, "the church *must* separate herself from them or be herself unfaithful" (*ST* II, 204-5). Excommunication is the ultimate act of peace.

The commandments, therefore, work differently in the church than they work outside the church. Outside the church the commandments state conditions of a polity's perduring, but in the "specific communal history of Israel and the church they acquire positive meaning as descriptions of virtues. It is the gospel that is the agent of the specific history of God's people and so enables and shapes such meanings" (*ST* II, 207). It is the Eucharist above all that shapes the *habitus* of the church's speech so that, for example, it is not enough that the Christian people refrain from perjury. Because Christians are constituted by the fear and love of God, the command not to bear false witness means we are a polity whose "citizens have reason to attribute good to each other, because good is unconditionally and finally promised to the community we make together" (*ST* II, 207-8).

Because Jenson is a Lutheran, some might be tempted to hear echoes of the Lutheran two kingdoms doctrine in his account of the church and the church's relation to all that is not church. If anything, however, Jenson is closer to the Reformers than the Lutherans (at least in terms of their past stereotypes) in his understanding of the relation of law and gospel with the correlative presumptions concerning the relation of church to the world. Note that he does not ever assume that the "world" is condemned to live only in accordance with what is prohibited. All are created to live by God's good commands. Yet God has called the church to participate in his life so that our justification is "a mode of deification."[14] God and we share a history through which we become acquainted. Of course in this age the knowledge that comes from our friendship with God and one another can only be a "beginning and some increase," but even that beginning cannot help but mark us as the people God has made his own (*ST* II, 302).

A Christian, according to Jenson, is someone whose nation and polity is the church, so the "baptized person must be the only available para-

14. *ST* II, 296. Jenson's strong claims in this respect make me wonder if he is not, secretly to be sure, a Methodist.

digm of human personhood" (*ST* II, 289). To know what it means to be human comes from being made part of the church. In other words we do not know in general what it means to be human and then discover that being a Christian is but a further specification of that more general way of being. Rather, what it means to be human in general is an abstraction from the humanity God has made possible in Christ. This does not mean the church must necessarily be "sectarian," but given the context in which we now find ourselves, the church has been freed

> to be much more decisively and peculiarly Christian, more sectarian even, than it has lately been. Such a church might even be able to preach the gospel again: it might reclaim the omnipotence and universality of God, so long predicates of an inactive state-God, for its Christ. The church might become so specific as again to have a specific thing to say in and to the world, and so become again a messenger-community to the — in this instance, American — ecumene. It might become a messenger-community of God's future that is not bound to America, which if need be will come, both ultimately and penultimately, over America's dead body, and which can be hope also for America just when America can have little hope in itself.[15]

I have not tried to report on everything Jenson has said that might be considered his ethics but rather to suggest why his ethics is inseparable from his theology. Even that way of putting the matter may be misleading to the extent that the description "inseparable" may suggest that some-

15. Jenson, *Essays in Theology of Culture,* pp. 65-66. Jenson often makes clear that no matter how justified or beneficial the Constantinian settlement may have been, he thinks we are now well rid of the Christian accommodation to the state. The separation between the church and the culture that was once Christian is a long and drawn out affair that cannot help but create for Christians deep ambiguity. That churches are tempted to accommodate "seekers" or incompetent members is but the way to apostasy. In this time of "uncertain boundaries, the church must not dilute or estrange her sacramental culture but instead train would-be believers in its forms, not dispense from God's *torah* but instead reform would-be believers' moral structure, not succumb to theological relativism but teach would-be believers the doctrine of Trinity." In short the church now finds herself returned to a situation in which the catechumenate was born. Those who have inculcated the metaphysical mechanism and moral relativism of the alien culture that surrounds us cannot help but be initially shocked and puzzled by the church's life (*ST* II, 305).

thing like ethical judgments "follow from" his theology. More accurately Jenson helps us see why the Christian unwillingness to countenance abortion is inseparable from our worship of the Father, Son, and Holy Spirit and why seeing that helps us face the challenge of that world called America. If Jenson is right, and I certainly think he is, Christian ethics as well as our politics are not areas to be developed after we have done theology, but rather are constitutive of Christian speech whose form is first and foremost prayer.[16] That is why Jenson, given the account I provided above of how theology became ethics in America, cannot be "America's theologian." Rather, he is a church theologian.

III. A Question for Jenson

I noted above Jenson's kind acknowledgment of the influence my work has had on the way he has thought about ethics. The account I have given of his work, moreover, I hope indicates how much I have learned from him. However, in the second volume of his *Systematic Theology,* he directs a question to me to which I should respond. He observes rightly that those whom the gospel calls into the church are not without antecedent hopes and fears. The church shapes and is shaped historically and geographically by the permissions and prohibitions, the morality, it finds among those to whom it witnesses. Therefore "the moral history of the church is not, as it were, pure; it is not simply other than the moral history of the communities around it. The gospel takes its ethical form just as it *interprets* an antecedent morality of those who at a time and place are there to hear and speak it" (*ST* II, 210). Professing not to know, Jenson asks if I would agree with these observations.

To disagree with Jenson on these matters I think would be almost as silly as the young woman who was reported to have told Chesterton that

16. Jenson, I think, quite rightly refuses to locate human significance in any one attribute that allegedly distinguishes us from the animals. Rather, he maintains that our "specificity in comparison with the other animals is that we are the ones addressed by God's moral word and so enabled to respond — that we are called to *pray.* If we will, the odd creature of the sixth day can after all be classified: we are the praying animals" (*ST* II, 58-59). Such a view seems quite congruent with Alasdair Maclntyre's account in his *Dependent Rational Animals: Why Human Beings Need the Virtues* (Chicago: Open Court, 1999).

she had decided to "accept the world." Chesterton is alleged to have responded, "You had better." So, of course, I assume that the various ways Christians must learn to live are shaped by "antecedent moralities," not just because we cannot avoid being so shaped but because, given the content of the gospel, that is what we should expect. For example, Christians have debated when a marriage begins because different cultures have quite various markers to indicate when the promise the couple makes to God and one another of lifelong fidelity is "public." There is simply no substitute for the wise exploration of such matters by the wise: which is but another way of indicating the necessity of casuistry for any significant way of life.

If my position on these matters has been misunderstood, I suspect it is partly due to my polemic against those who use abstract notions of nature and grace to justify an account of natural law in the interest of underwriting the presumption that the way things are is the way things ought to be.[17] That, of course, is the Catholic version. The Calvinists, with the same intent and result, appeal to the doctrine of creation abstracted from the Trinity in order to suggest that a "morality" exists that can insure an *a priori* agreement between Christians and non-Christians sufficient to sustain joint support for policy formation in democracies. The difficulty is that both these ways of underwriting a "natural ethic" justify an "ethic" that then is alleged to be in principle congruent with the gospel. In contrast Jenson does not pretend to know how Christians will discover the limits or riches of the "antecedent moralities" they confront without considering their content.

I do not know if Jenson will find my brief response to his question adequate. I hope he will, however, because of the paragraph that follows his question. It reads:

> The gospel turns our antecedent hopes into real possibilities by interpreting them as hopes for a Kingdom that is indeed coming. Just so it also reinterprets them materially. So, to take a central and by now familiar instance, all humans hope for something that may be called peace.

17. Despairing of the overly abstract discussions of the relation of nature and grace, I have largely ignored addressing the question of their relation. However, for my attempt to address why an account of nature is theologically unavoidable, see my *Sanctify Them in the Truth: Holiness Exemplified* (Nashville: Abingdon Press, 1998), pp. 37-60.

> But most societies have interpreted peace as the success of violence — in the ideology of Western states, as a "security" to be established by "defense." Just so the hope for peace becomes itself the constant occasion of conflict. The gospel promises the actual advent of peace and invites us to its anticipation in the Eucharist. The gospel makes peace a possibility by telling us that we do not have to defend ourselves, since our lives are hid with God in Christ. Just so, the gospel interprets peace as what Christ brings, as the fruit of his self-surrender. (*ST* II, 210)

As a Christian committed to nonviolence I could not wish for a better account of why I think Christians are committed to disavow violence. Thus my question to Jenson: "When every thing is said and done, at the end of the day, your position would seem to commit you to nonviolence. Why, therefore, have you not made clear that Christians cannot kill, particularly in war, in the name of Christ?"[18] Of course that way of putting the matter may not be sufficiently nuanced. Jenson may well respond that he cannot imagine killing "in the name of Christ" but there may be other modes of killing that are justified. Such justifications no doubt must involve the "antecedent moralities" Christians encounter, but then the question must be asked on Jenson's own grounds how such a morality can be given authority if it divides the unity of the church made possible by the celebration of the Eucharist.[19]

In an essay "Violence as a Mode of Language," Jenson suggests that vi-

18. I have tried to suggest in this essay why ethicists must read Jenson, but I think there is one "ethicist" that Jenson needs to read: John Howard Yoder. Of course Jenson may well have read Yoder and see no reason he needs to engage his work, but if that is the case Jenson has made a mistake. For example, as rich as Jenson's Christological reflections are, I think he has not dealt sufficiently with Jesus' teachings. In that respect Jenson would find Yoder a wonderful resource for reflection on why and how Jesus the teacher (Jesus the prophet) and Jesus the crucified are necessarily understood as the one Word of God. Unfortunately Yoder's most systematic reflections on these topics are in his never published book, *Preface to Theology: Christology and Theological Method.* The contents of the *Preface* are his lectures in systematic theology at Associated Mennonite Biblical Seminary and can be obtained from Cokesbury Bookstore at the Divinity School, Duke University.

19. Jenson may think something like a just war position can be theoretically justified, but he certainly cannot think that the United States is a polity capable of conducting a just war. Thus, even if he is theoretically a just warrior, in fact he is a pacifist — at least in terms of his being a United States citizen.

olence is implicated in our most basic relations with one another, that is, in the very way "in which our bodies participate in our communication with each other."[20] Because our language creates a shared life that constitutes the attempts of our bodies to communicate with one another, such attempts often cannot help but be violent. As Jenson puts it, "Violence happens when I want to say something to you that really cannot be said to you, that you are not in a position to hear, and when yet I insist that you are going to hear it. When my words do not move you, and yet I determine that you are going to move, then we have violence."[21] That is why, according to Jenson, we ought to understand Martin Luther's account of the "sword," that is, the recognition that the agents of law are always the agents of violence, agents of the justified use of violence necessary to say "Let (this) violence cease."[22]

Yet Jenson thinks that we now confront a situation that Luther did not foresee. In America we have created a society that has so shaped its language that anything that is said cannot be said without involving violence. In other words America for Jenson names that politics in which the language of our relations with one another cannot help but lie. The words we use cannot honestly face reality as it is and at the same time freely indicate what might and must be. For example, as long as we describe our economy as a "free enterprise" system, it is impossible to begin to recognize the powers that possess us. Which leads Jenson to the conclusion that "given the language of the world we inhabit, which is a language of violence, the church too will be driven to speaking violently."[23]

Yet Jenson asks, "How can the church speak violently when as Christians we are constituted by the liturgical anticipation that celebrates God's peace?" He responds by suggesting that the body-aspect of our missionary message cannot help but

20. Jenson, *Essays in Theology of Culture,* p. 41. This essay was first published in the *Bulletin of Lutheran Theological Seminary* 51 (1971): 33-42.

21. Jenson, *Essays in Theology of Culture,* p. 44.

22. Jenson, *Essays in Theology of Culture,* p. 45.

23. Jenson, *Essays in Theology of Culture,* p. 47. This is the source of Jenson's challenge to my account of nonviolence in his "Review of Stanley Hauerwas' *After Christendom?" First Things* 25 (August/September 1992). I tried to respond to Jenson in an essay on John Milbank's work that can now be found in my book, *Wilderness Wanderings: Probing Twentieth-Century Theology and Philosophy* (Boulder, Co.: Westview Press, 1997), pp. 188-98.

> be a peculiar sort of violent liturgy. We are called to preach in the language of the world; this is now a language of violence. We are called to speak to a society that understands only violence, and to speak of the utter overthrowing of all that is. But we are called to be nonviolent. I suggest that the body-side of such a word will be *violent* action in contradiction of injustice and hate, that is, transformed into liturgy by being done uselessly, as *play.*[24]

As an example of how such a liturgy might look Jenson calls attention (surprising, he acknowledges, even himself) to the destruction of draft files by the Berrigan brothers and their friends.

If Jenson refrains from declaring himself clearly to be among those who must disavow war because he believes even the witness of nonviolence is implicated in violence, I can only say to him that we who are committed to nonviolence welcome just that challenge. We may want to explore with him whether and how the violence of language can be distinguished from other forms of violence such as war.[25] Yet that is exactly the kind of work we have been taught by Jenson we ought to expect to be required by any theology that speaks truthfully about and to the world. Such work turns out interestingly enough to be the same kind of activity that Jenson's question above asked if I were willing to undertake. I only hope this reveals why I think his theology is an ethic that no one who wants to be a Christian ethicist in our time can or should ignore.

24. Jenson, *Essays in Theology of Culture,* p. 48.

25. Indeed, Jenson's theology rightly stresses the analogical character of our descriptions, which includes, of course, violence. He, therefore, needs to provide examples for the disciplined use of the language of violence in order to prevent violence from describing anything and everything. I am indebted to Alex Sider for pointing this out to me. I am also indebted to Professor Reinhard Hütter and Richard Church for critically responding to this essay.

A Theology of the Political

GILBERT MEILAENDER

One of the very first articles I ever published after I had begun to teach was a piece titled "Understanding the Apathetic Citizen." It was published in the Autumn 1978 number of *dialog* (I never quite understood the lower case name), whose editor at that time was a man I had never met and about whom I knew relatively little: Robert W. Jenson. I suspect I knew him then as coauthor of *Lutheranism: The Theological Movement and Its Confessional Writings*[1] and as author of occasional pieces (brisk, provocative, and sometimes a bit esoteric) in *dialog.* I have come to know both him and his thought somewhat better since then, and, contemplating my topic for this essay, I found myself a little surprised that back in 1978 Jenson should have accepted an essay that, in truth, seeks not only to understand but even, in certain respects, to defend the apathetic citizen.

Jenson himself has not, of course, written primarily about politics. He is best known as an eminent systematic theologian, and his explorations into politics have taken chiefly the form of occasional pieces. It is from such pieces that we must unravel his theological vision of politics — and there is, I think, such a vision, consistently articulated. As will become clear, the author of "Understanding the Apathetic Citizen" is by no means prepared entirely to agree with that vision, but it is a sign of the power of Jenson's intellectual probing that, despite devoting himself primarily to other projects, his theology of the political can still demand our attention.

1. Eric W. Gritsch and Robert W. Jenson, *Lutheranism: The Theological Movement and Its Confessional Writings* (Philadelphia: Fortress Press, 1976).

I

Jenson writes as a Lutheran theologian, but I suspect that few who read his occasional pieces about the nature of politics would be inclined to classify him as such. He does not fit the stereotypical picture to which we are accustomed, a picture captured by H. Richard Niebuhr's "Christ and Culture in Paradox." We can begin then with Jenson as Lutheran.

In at least one place he was compelled by the nature of the task he had undertaken to say something quite specific about a Lutheran perspective on the political. In the study of Lutheranism that he and Eric Gritsch wrote, in which Gritsch for the most part authored the historical sections and Jenson the constructive, chapter 13 is titled, "Politics — Two Kingdoms?" Jenson's portion of this chapter provides a brief systematic analysis of the meaning and continued relevance of the political "doctrine" most often associated with Lutheranism: the two kingdoms.

His first move is to question the doctrine's continued relevance, to question, that is, whether it has any direct application to the political world in which we (Western Europeans and North Americans) live. Because two kingdoms doctrine was, Jenson says, basically about how to apportion political responsibility between rulers and ruled, its contemporary application — after revolutions in France and America establishing that, in some sense, we are simultaneously ruled *and* rulers because we share in sovereignty — can only be indirect. That is, if the distinction between the two kingdoms was intended to make clear who rightly exercised sovereignty and to rule out revolution against a legitimate sovereign by his subjects, our problem is now different. We must now try to figure out how to participate in political decision making while also being subject even to decisions we think are mistaken.

Jenson is surely correct that putting the matter this way — that is, democratizing sovereignty — radically restructures our attitude toward political authority. I doubt, though, that the apportionment of responsibility between ruler and ruled is really all that two kingdoms teaching was about. It also had to do with the peculiar nature of political authority — which always involves the use or implied threat of force and seeks the good of justice in public life. Insofar as this work is God's, it appears to contrast with the way the same God works in the gospel. These two ways by which God rules are also part of the two kingdoms concept, and we will return later to the significance of this fact.

In any case, if there can be no simple, direct application of two kingdoms doctrine to our political world, Lutherans must construct a new political ethic, understanding their inherited two kingdoms approach as "a historical expression of Lutheranism's call for radical faith, and of Lutheranism's basic ethical attitudes."[2] According to Jenson, this reconstructed political ethic will involve at least the following four points, which I summarize here with my own brief interpretive comments:

(1) The most fundamental political question is always, Who shall rule? Every community must answer this question, and in answering it, in effect, "confesses some God or other."[3] Different sovereigns are bound to make a difference in the structure of the community's shared life. Which is to say: there can really be no absolute separation between the religious and the political. Presumably, any community that in its shared life does not confess the true God is bound to have that life, even so, distorted in various ways. In any case, politics always invites and requires theological assessment.

(2) Because the political realm gives us opportunities for service to our neighbors (in both the everyday and the dominical sense), participation in it "is commanded by God." [4] Which is to say: no apathetic citizens allowed here!

(3) Although political action confesses some god or other and, if properly ordered, would confess the true God, even in the best of polities we will not always be able to provide an unambiguous account of what God is doing within that polity. For God's rule in history takes various forms, not all of them readily reconcilable with the love this true God has revealed in the Lord Jesus. "God's right hand will know what his left hand has been doing when both are stretched out to receive the fruit of his creation . . . ."[5] Which is to say: Jenson is quite

2. Gritsch and Jenson, *Lutheranism,* p. 184.

3. Gritsch and Jenson, *Lutheranism,* p. 185.

4. Gritsch and Jenson, *Lutheranism,* p. 185.

5. Gritsch and Jenson, *Lutheranism,* p. 185. I wonder about this formulation, unless it is meant to have a poetic flavor. It suggests a God whose unity will not just be known but, in fact, exist only at the end of time. Yet we want to be able to say, I think, that what God does with his left hand he does *for the sake* of what he does with the right — that his alien work is a work of love because even now it is ordered toward the kingdom.

alive to the concern I noted above. Two kingdoms doctrine is not, in fact, only about the relation of ruler and ruled. It is also about the seemingly antithetical ways in which God rules as sovereign.

(4) Even if we cannot offer any premature synthesis of God's seemingly antithetical ways of ruling within history, we can interpret what God does through his word of gospel and of law. Each word, though in different ways, opens to us the future. "The two modes of God's self-communication open creatures to God's future in very different ways; but it will be the same future."[6] Which is to say: Granting all the ambiguity noted in (3) above, Lutherans can still learn from Karl Barth. Law is finally the form of the gospel, and the God whose left hand rules our polities just is the God whose face of love has been revealed in Jesus.

Although Lutheranism has sometimes been charged with creating quietistic or apathetic citizens, that is certainly not Jenson's reading of the point of two kingdoms doctrine (at least in its early history). Its point, rather, is precisely that Christians are set free from self-concern in order that they may serve God and their neighbors whenever and wherever opportunity presents itself — including, of course, in the political realm. In fact, this was precisely the effect of the teaching in early Reformation history. "The two-kingdoms ethic was, in its time of authenticity, politically energizing and a guide for action; those who lived by it defied an empire, bent princes to their purposes, invented new forms of international alliance, mobilized public opinion for the first time in history, and even created new polities to suit."[7]

If Lutheranism's use of two kingdoms doctrine has, since that "time of authenticity," provided cover for political withdrawal, that is less its fault than ours. We are the ones who made it that. In fact, however, "Lutheranism could be uniquely advantaged" to offer greater political wisdom — and, especially, a more accurate understanding of the relation of the religious and the political. As Lutherans emphasize calling to serve both God and the neighbor even in the midst of moral uncertainty, they are (at least on Jenson's reading) confident that in their political work they serve the very same God who in love is committed to bring their work to its comple-

6. Gritsch and Jenson, *Lutheranism,* p. 186.
7. Gritsch and Jenson, *Lutheranism,* p. 186.

tion, and (serving that God) they are regularly reminded that he cannot be identified with any political institution. "Religious history is an oscillation between the idolatry of politics and disgusted withdrawal from them. Political history offers mostly a choice between polities that make themselves absolute for their citizens and modern polities that avoid this by altogether banishing faith from citizenship."[8] Lutherans should be able to understand the ambiguities that cause them to recoil from politics, for they know that "the *one* God rules through all powers but in *more than one mode*."[9] Lutherans should also be able to resist idolatrous temptations since they also know that this one God may not "be identified with the sovereignties through whom he rules."[10] One may wonder whether there is really anything uniquely Lutheran about two kingdoms doctrine so interpreted, but it may be none the worse for not being unique.

II

Against this theological background Jenson most often focuses his attention on politics in the United States, and his reading of American political history follows a brief story line that appears regularly in his writing.[11]

The Protestants who came to the new world were fleeing from wars of religion, but that in itself did not make them "liberals" committed to separating religion and politics. On the contrary, they came to the new world to do better — to found a new Zion, a city set on a hill. They were moved by a vision that was simultaneously political and religious — and that, in fact, is probably the source of their appeal for one like Jenson who is so committed to constructing a theology of the political. By the time of the "Founders," however, this quest for the holy state had been abandoned

8. Gritsch and Jenson, *Lutheranism,* p. 190.

9. Gritsch and Jenson, *Lutheranism,* p. 190.

10. Gritsch and Jenson, *Lutheranism,* p. 190.

11. I will draw this story from a number of places where it appears in more or less the same form — namely, from *Lutheranism* (esp. pp. 186-89), and from a number of occasional pieces now collected in Jenson's *Essays in Theology of Culture* (Grand Rapids: Eerdmans, 1995). The essays in which the basic story line appears are: "The Kingdom of America's God" (pp. 50-66); "Is There an Ordering Principle?" (pp. 67-75); "Faith and the Integrity of the Polity" (pp. 95-104); and "Toward a Christian Theory of the Public" (pp. 132-46).

by men such as Thomas Jefferson and James Madison. Their inheritance from the seventeenth century had been twofold: Chastened by the wars of religion, they were suspicious of "dogma"; impressed by the marvelous promise of Newtonian science, they hoped for a new science of politics that might enable them to construct a lasting republic.

The Founders themselves, therefore, abandoned the quest for the holy state, preferring the deist's god — that great Engineer whose laws of nature Isaac Newton had uncovered. Emulating that god, they sought to "construct a polity that by an exact arrangement of forces could — like a great mill — be at once stable in itself yet productive of civil goods."[12] In such a political community one set of interests is arranged to balance another, and, if all goes according to plan, a stable community is created, though the community as such can no longer think of itself as living by any shared vision of its meaning and purpose.

What can be the role of religion in such a state? Jenson's story does not suppose that, after such a founding, religion was immediately "privatized." What the movements of awakening and revival within nineteenth-century American evangelical religion did, rather, was turn from the quest for a holy state to an attempt to create a holy people within the state. Jenson can even describe this as "a sort of second public arena, alongside the political arena, missing only the specifically political function of direct public decision making."[13] It was within this second public space that movements such as abolitionism, prohibition, and the social gospel were generated.

> After the Revolution, it was decided to adjust the two [public arenas] by dividing the territory. The public sphere within which you will expect to find sovereignty was divided between the state, which worships the deist god (the reason that the state does not seem to worship is merely that the deist god does not take much worshiping), and a second public sphere of the great public activisms that have made so much of the history of the United States, where sovereignty rested in assemblies of right-thinking citizens, those willing to show up for the school board meetings, to attend athenaeum, to march around with signs in a righteous cause.[14]

12. Jenson, *Essays in Theology of Culture,* p. 134.
13. Jenson, *Essays in Theology of Culture,* p. 63.
14. Jenson, *Essays in Theology of Culture,* p. 102.

In Jenson's telling this is, we should note, an eminently theological story, connected with even larger themes that play an important role in his systematic theology proper. Just as his systematic theology is shaped in important ways by a contrast between the timeless, impassible god of classical philosophy and the time-filled and timely God of the Bible, so also is his reading of American political history. That deist god so influential in the scientific conception of politics that dominated the American founding is distant and uninvolved. The God of that "second public arena" is the active, involved God who generates the kind of passion necessary for transforming life.

These two public arenas exist in what Jenson characterizes as a symbiotic relationship. The polity itself — the first public arena where decisions about the direction of a community's life are ultimately made — cannot in fact get along without the passion and spirit provided by the second public arena. This becomes evident in moments of crisis, when "it has always drawn from the reservoir of evangelical religious hope."[15] The second public arena — the holy people within the holy state — is also dependent on the polity to provide space within which its passion and spirit can develop and take effect.

At the end of the twentieth century, however, "our present spiritual vacuity" results from the fact that this "great symbiosis seems to have exhausted itself."[16] Having abandoned the attempt to make the whole people holy, Protestants focused their attention on saving some individuals as a kind of leavening influence. Christianity retreated to the private sphere, acquiescing in the notion that that is its proper place.

> Deprived of identification with the state God, evangelical religion's God ceases to have power over outer reality. Religion becomes a "private affair." This dogma, often taken for American tradition, has in fact scarcely fifty years' standing among us. We no longer pray, "O Lord, succor the poor"; we pray instead, "O Lord, make us feel better toward the poor" — giving God as light tasks as possible.[17]

15. Jenson, *Essays in Theology of Culture,* p. 63.
16. Jenson, *Essays in Theology of Culture,* p. 64.
17. Jenson, *Essays in Theology of Culture,* p. 64.

The upshot of this story is that our politics can no longer be understood as an "event on the road to the eschatological event."[18]

III

I suspect that Jenson's telling of this story, though certainly a part of the truth, would need some complications added to it. Thus, for example, while an early modern political theorist such as Thomas Hobbes was certainly influenced by Galilean science and by the conception of the world as a mechanical system of bodies in motion explicable with geometrical precision, he was also, after all, the translator of Thucydides and, in certain respects, an heir of Augustinian and Reformed Christian thought, with its emphasis on the will. Likewise, the American Founders drew not just upon mechanistic notions taken from Newtonian science but also on classical thinkers (such as Polybius) who discussed the virtues of "mixed government." Madison, for example, spared no effort in his attempt to learn from the vices of past confederacies how a better one — in which factions could be controlled — might be created.[19]

These complexities are not unimportant, for they might make one less dismissive than Jenson tends to be of the kind of "individualism" present in early modern and American political history. For the moment, however, we can consider the more systematic reflections that he draws out of the story he has told. What is fundamental for his thinking is the claim that a polity of the sort the United States has become can have no true "common good." What is called the common good can be nothing more than a

18. Jenson, *Essays in Theology of Culture,* p. 139. So, at any rate, goes Jenson's version of the story. I do not think, though, that even on his own terms this can be strictly accurate. Insofar as what God does in the left hand he does for the sake of his right hand's work, and insofar as both hands do the work of the one God whose will is mercy and grace revealed in the Lord Jesus, it must be right to say that even the "alien" work of politics is a work of love aimed at preserving the world toward that kingdom which God builds in a different way. Yet such a connection between the two kingdoms does not seem sufficient to satisfy Jenson.

19. See, for example, the discussion in chapter 3 ("Founding") of Philip Abbott, *Political Thought in America* (Itasca, Ill.: F. E. Peacock, 1991); and W. H. Greenleaf, "Hobbes: The Problem of Interpretation," in Maurice Cranston and Richard S. Peters, eds., *Hobbes and Rousseau: A Collection of Critical Essays* (Garden City, N.Y.: Anchor Books, 1972), pp. 5-36.

balance of conflicting individual interests that enter the public arena as they receive *representation* by elected officials. This, in turn, means that citizens do not really participate in the political community as moral subjects. "I am a moral subject only if I *deliberate* whether it would be *good* that my needs be satisfied, given the cost of satisfying them."[20] I am not a moral subject simply because my individual interests are represented in the larger clash of interests.

Built into Jenson's position, therefore, is a certain understanding of what it means to be an *individual* and a certain understanding of *politics.* Jenson's attention over decades to the intricacies of Trinitarian dogma has led to a description of God in terms of a threefold mutual agency — of the *dramatis dei personae,* the "characters of the drama of God."[21] Influenced especially by the Cappadocians' adaptation of that one category of Aristotle's — relation — that was not easily compatible with a metaphysics of substance, Jenson has rigorously developed the notion of a "person" as a "subsistent relation." Within the inner life of the triune God the three "persons" are distinguished by "their mutual exchanges in the biblical dramatic narrative" (*ST* I, 119); and within this same God's work *ad extra* — the work of creation and redemption — there takes place what we must learn to describe as "a *mutually* single act" (*ST* I, 111).

Individual identity is established and lived only in relation. There are no isolated monads who first subsist and then enter into relations with other such monads.[22] Jenson himself seems prepared to put political flesh on these metaphysical bones. Thus, he notes with appreciation how Jonathan Edwards "elaborated an understanding of personhood in community

20. Jenson, *Essays in Theology of Culture,* p. 74.

21. Robert W. Jenson, *Systematic Theology,* vol. I: *The Triune God* (Oxford: Oxford University Press, 1997), p. 75. Hereafter abbreviated *ST,* by volume and page. Italics in quotations are Jenson's unless otherwise noted.

22. It would, I think, be possible to defend such a claim apart from appeals to the intricacies of Trinitarian theology. We might consider simply the manner in which human beings come into existence, already having biological attachment to a father and a mother. By contrast, we can note that, in order even to get his theory of civil society off the ground, Hobbes had to suppose otherwise: "Let us . . . consider men as if but even now sprung out of the earth, and suddenly, like mushrooms, come to full maturity, without all kind of engagement to each other" (*De Cive* 8.1). Wholly apart from larger theological claims, there is something false about such a picture, although the developments in new reproductive technologies may raise some baffling metaphysical questions for us.

that was in radical dissent from the normative Enlightenment's individualism and the theories of representative republicanism it developed. . . ."[23] Indeed, "what counts as an individual" may depend on the larger framework within which we place our being and action.[24]

The thrust of Jenson's position should, I trust, be clear: To think of individuals chiefly or solely as those whose interests are represented in public and who, after all interests have been set against each other and a balance generated, receive some acceptable level of goods and services is a debased notion of the person. It pictures our moral being as subsisting apart from our relation with fellow citizens and our freedom as simply freedom from communal involvement. By contrast the true political freedom that should concern us, the only kind that recognizes the individual as a moral being, is "free access to the community in *its* moral self-determination."[25] Or again: "I am a moral subject only if I *deliberate* whether it would be *good* that my needs be satisfied, given the cost of satisfying them."[26]

Closely related to such an understanding of the individual is an apposite definition of politics. "Politics is the whole process by which a community chooses what sort of community it will be in the future; politics is the process of communal moral choice."[27] The two concepts — individual and politics — fit together neatly: One becomes an individual in the most important sense, morally, only as one is a participant in this process of communal self-definition. The point of political participation is not to see to it that various interests — especially one's own — receive fair representation. The point, rather, is to share in the effort the community makes to define and shape its life. The common good is not some pool of goods that flows back in common upon all; the common good simply is that shared communal life of participation and deliberation.

This will mean in turn — though I think Jenson never squarely faces

23. Jenson, *Essays in Theology of Culture,* p. 139.

24. Jenson, *Essays in Theology of Culture,* p. 139. This may be a metaphysical truth, but, if so, it offers us the opportunity to recall that politics cannot live by such truth alone. There have been states all too eager to assume that "what counts as an individual" may depend on the larger health of the people. Jenson, of course, would abhor any such move, but it is a danger that lies near at hand here.

25. Jenson, *Essays in Theology of Culture,* p. 146.

26. Jenson, *Essays in Theology of Culture,* p. 74.

27. Jenson, *Essays in Theology of Culture,* p. 96.

the issue — that justice will no longer be the cardinal political good. We can see how this is the case, and see what Jenson means by the common good, if we think of the shared life within a family. There it is not a matter of interests being represented, of a balance of forces among these interests, until an outcome is generated. A family's life is not an attempt to see that each receives exactly the same in goods and services and no one is asked to make greater sacrifices than another. Rather, a family flourishes — and its "individual" members flourish in that relation that, at least in part, defines their being — only when all share in the common life without constant concern about whether they are receiving their "due."

Jenson's good polity would, in this respect, be more like a family than like the political communities in which we live. This family would be not patriarchal but egalitarian in its shared life. If our polities are "on the road to the eschatological event,"[28] we ought to think about how they may be shaped by the coming kingdom. That kingdom will be "constituted by Jesus' self-giving to all his members."[29] "Thus also," Jenson hastily[30] concludes, "the question of political hierarchy is settled: none will be closer to Messiah than others, whatever other distinctions may obtain; the forum in which the community lives its moral creativity will include all directly."[31]

This is a powerful view — and one with deep roots in Western political tradition. That same tradition might, however, give us pause. To suppose that what counts as an individual may depend upon the larger social context, or to picture the polity as analogous to a familial or fraternal community, has not often been conducive to individual liberty or to justice. Although Jenson's case — in terms of the story he tells — is regularly made in terms of American political history, in which Puritans are the most important theological players, it is actually very congruent with one strand of Luther's own vision. Thus, for example, in his catechisms Luther interprets political authority as a kind of parental authority. "Out of the authority of

28. Jenson, *Essays in Theology of Culture,* p. 139.

29. Jenson, *Essays in Theology of Culture,* p. 143.

30. The reasoning does seem too hasty here. How we get to direct political participation by all from the fact that, in the kingdom, all will be equally close to the kingdom's Lord is not at all clear to me. Here Jenson may have learned too well from Barth the art of quick political conclusion from biblical analogy: as in Barth's well-known rejection of secret diplomacy on the grounds that Christians are not to hide their light under a bushel.

31. Jenson, *Essays in Theology of Culture,* p. 143.

parents all other authority is derived and developed. . . . Thus all who are called masters stand in the place of parents and derive from them their power and authority to govern."[32] I suspect, however, that such an identification constitutes the soft underbelly of Lutheran political thought. It misses important truths about the political: that a polity must make justice the cardinal good in a way that a family does not, that individuals may not be thought of as "parts" of a larger political whole, and that force is essential to political but not to familial authority. Indeed, although Jenson wants to emphasize that "'Kingdom of God' is not a metaphor,"[33] we might recall that when the new Jerusalem comes down out of heaven in Revelation 21, the civic metaphor switches rapidly to a familial one: she is "prepared as a bride adorned for her husband." The eschatological vision is of a community in which not power but love rules.

If the "individuals" whose interests are represented and served within our polities are, in some ultimate sense, metaphysical fictions, these may be necessary fictions for those who are still *in via.* By viewing us as, to some extent, isolated individuals, states seek justice — which, though it is not love, we cannot live without. By exercising force they bear witness to their own penultimate status. The point of politics may, then, be less to offer us an intimation of the kingdom than to make room for other, smaller, intimations.[34] Although we can understand, therefore, why Jenson suggests that what our polity needs is "an increment of direct democracy,"[35] although he is an incisive and instructive critic of the flaws to which our political systems are heir, and although he is quite right to argue that no "liberal" polity can survive without drawing on religious resources that it cannot itself generate or sustain, there may also be reasons to suppose that I was not, in my callow youth, entirely mistaken to defend those apathetic citizens who fall so short of Jenson's ideal.

32. *The Large Catechism,* Part I: The Ten Commandments, in *The Book of Concord,* trans. and ed. Theodore G. Tappert (Philadelphia: Muhlenberg Press, 1959), p. 384.

33. Jenson, *Essays in Theology of Culture,* p. 140.

34. I have tried to sketch such a vision of politics in chapter 11 of *The Limits of Love* (University Park and London: The Pennsylvania State University Press, 1987).

Verba Visibilia: Robert Jenson on the Sacraments

GEOFFREY WAINWRIGHT

"The Wesleyan tradition," writes the Lutheran Robert Jenson toward the end of his *Systematic Theology,* "has appeared too little in this work, owing to my ignorance of it."[1] While I try not to engage in the pedagogical task in too heavy-handed a way, it will nevertheless be as a historically Methodist theologian that I seek to fulfill the editorial commission to "introduce, appreciate, and respond to" Jenson's "theological achievement" on the topic of sacraments.[2] In any case, however, the honorand and I, in our different ecclesial locations, have been exposed to many of the same ecumenical influences in theology: Karl Barth; the Roman Catholics who adumbrated, accompanied, and extended the Second Vatican Council, such as Henri de Lubac, Yves Congar, Joseph Ratzinger, and J.-M. R. Tillard (although again

1. Robert W. Jenson, *Systematic Theology,* vol. I: *The Triune God* (Oxford: Oxford University Press, 1997); *Systematic Theology,* vol. II: *The Works of God* (Oxford: Oxford University Press, 1999). Hereafter abbreviated *ST,* by volume and page. Italics in quotations are Jenson's unless otherwise noted. Here *ST* II, 332.

2. Jenson himself advised me that his "mature treatment" or "most of what I now have to say" on the sacraments can be found in *Systematic Theology.* Earlier one could look at Jenson's *Visible Words: The Interpretation and Practice of Christian Sacraments* (Philadelphia: Fortress Press, 1978), his contributions to the *Christian Dogmatics,* ed. Carl E. Braaten and himself (Philadelphia: Fortress Press, 1984), in particular vol. 2, pp. 289-389, and his own *Unbaptized God: The Basic Flaw in Ecumenical Theology* (Minneapolis: Fortress Press, 1992). I appreciated and responded to the last-named book in *Modern Theology* 10 (1994): 415-17.

"Balthasar is much too little cited in this work" because Jenson has "never been able to get sufficiently into his thinking" [*ST* II, 367]); and the Eastern Orthodox tradition as made accessible through such twentieth-century figures as Georges Florovsky, Vladimir Lossky, John Meyendorff, Alexander Schmemann, Nikos Nissiotis, Olivier Clément, and John Zizioulas. On the active side, I was closely involved in the production of Faith and Order's Lima text on *Baptism, Eucharist and Ministry* (quickly nicknamed "*BEM*"), which Jenson draws on — together with statements from some of the international bilateral dialogues — as part of the remarkable ecumenical convergence in sacramental theology and practice in the past fifty years. In his own Lutheran tradition, Jenson stands in the line of two mid-century systematicians at Heidelberg, where he studied: Peter Brunner and Edmund Schlink both combined dogmatic, liturgical, and ecumenical interests.

In what follows, my modest purpose — justified, I think, by Jenson's opening claim that his *Systematic Theology* was "deliberately done in anticipation of the one church" — will be to locate Jenson's sacramental teaching in relation to some ecumenical controversies and convergences on the sacraments. Jenson himself considers that, with regard to church and sacraments, there existed for his systematic work "a historical mandate to follow the lines of recent ecumenical discussion," by which he means the post–Vatican II "ecumenical dialogues with their theological enablers and commentators" (*ST* II, 168-69). As far as possible, I will avoid the more speculative — and problematic — dimensions of Jenson's Trinitarianism and metaphysics, although Jenson himself naturally sees an organic connection between the further reaches of his thought and his interpretation of the sacramental rites.

It should be recognized throughout that, in his treatment of church and sacraments in the *Systematic Theology*, Jenson has chosen to "consider the church in its own proper entity." That is to say, his direction of thought will be that "God uses the gospel to gather the church for himself," rather than the equally defensible, and indeed necessary, movement whereby "God provides the church to carry the gospel to the world" (*ST* II, 168).

Anticipated Eschatology

From her very founding, says Jenson, the church is "an event within the event of the new age's advent"; the church is "anticipated eschatology"

(Florovsky); the Church "sacramentally anticipates the Kingdom of God" (Meyendorff) (*ST* II, 171, 301). Anticipation is Jenson's key category for expressing the tension between what is "already now" the case since the resurrection of Christ and the pentecostal gift of the Spirit and what is "not yet" the case until Christ's delayed return at the end. "When the risen Christ in the audible and visible words of the church enforces the rule of God, the Kingdom occurs. But the church which both carries this sacramental presence and is established by it is nevertheless not yet the Kingdom herself" (*ST* II, 171). Sacrament is the mode suited by God to the present state of the church and the kingdom. Jenson makes this clearest with reference to the Eucharist: "The church-assembly is the body of Christ, that is, Christ available to the world and to her members, just in that the church gathers around objects distinct from herself, the bread and cup, which are the availability *to her* of the same Christ" (*ST* II, 213). Thus "the church now possesses her Lord sacramentally only, that is, actually and truly but still in faith and not by 'sight.' Indeed, the eschatological separation is constituted in the sacramental relations themselves: the church, community of disciples, is now the presence of Christ only in that within her that same Christ is present as an other than she, and there only as a sign signified by other signs" (*ST* II, 334). Most concisely: "It is because the Lord has come but nevertheless is yet to come that the church's life is sacramental" (*ST* II, 334).

The limitative use of "only" in some of those and other texts of similar theological sobriety betokens, I think, a caution indebted to the Lutheran *theologia crucis,* but there seems no doubt that Jenson has picked up in a qualified way that infusion of boldness and splendor which recent Western liturgical renewal has acquired from ecumenical contacts with Eastern Orthodoxy and its perhaps exaggerated sense of the liturgy as "heaven on earth." Thus Jenson can also write: "When the Eucharist is celebrated, Christ's promises of the Kingdom and of his presence in it are in fact fulfilled: even though the Kingdom is still future so long as we are not risen, each celebration is already a wedding feast" (*ST* II, 216). If (as Jenson says there) "anticipation is visible prophecy," then what are the implications for the *present* life and worship of the church when, in a later passage that takes off from the New Testament Apocalypse, Jenson moves "from propositions to poesy" in imagining "the great transformation"?

> There will be a universally encompassing liturgy, with the Father as the bishop enthroned in the apse and the apostles as the presbyters around

> him and the redeemed of all times as the congregation and the angel-driven creation as the organ and orchestra, and the tomb of all martyrs as the altar, and the Lamb visibly on the altar, and the Spirit as the Lamb's power and perception, and the music and drama and sights and aromas and touches of the liturgy as themselves the Life who is worshipped. Let us say: there will be a political community whose intimacy is such that from the vantage of this world it could only be called delirium but which just so will be perfectly ordered because the delirium's dynamism will be the perichoresis of the triune life. The opposition of "Dionysian" and "Apollonian" will be transcended! (*ST* II, 340)

Meanwhile, a Methodist familiar with the Wesleys' *Hymns on the Lord's Supper* (1745) may think of the hymn that opens the section on "the sacrament a pledge of heaven":

> Come, let us join with one accord
> Who share the Supper of the Lord,
> Our Lord and Master's praise to sing;
> Nourish'd on earth with living Bread,
> We now are at his Table fed,
> But wait to see our heavenly King;
> To see the great Invisible
> Without a sacramental veil,
> With all his robes of glory on,
> In rapt'rous joy and love and praise
> Him to behold with open face,
> High on his everlasting throne! . . .
>
> We soon the midnight cry shall hear,
> Arise, and meet the Bridegroom near,
> The marriage of the Lamb is come;
> Attended by his heavenly friends,
> The glorious King of saints descends
> To take his Bride in triumph home. . . .
>
> By faith and hope already there,
> Even now the marriage-feast we share,
> Even now we by the Lamb are fed;

Our Lord's celestial joy we prove,
Led by the Spirit of his love,
To springs of living comfort led. . . .

Less rapturously, *Baptism, Eucharist and Ministry* speaks of the Eucharist as "the foretaste of [Christ's] *parousia* and of the final kingdom," "the anticipation of the Supper of the Lamb."

Eucharistic Presence

Paragraph 13 of the eucharistic section of *Baptism, Eucharist and Ministry* states: "The Church confesses Christ's real, living and active presence in the eucharist"; and the commentary elaborates: "Many churches believe that by the words of Jesus and by the power of the Holy Spirit, the bread and wine of the eucharist become, in a real though mysterious manner, the body and blood of the risen Christ, i.e., of the living Christ present in all his fullness. Under the signs of bread and wine, the deepest reality is the total being of Christ who comes to us in order to feed us and transform our entire being. Some other churches, while affirming a real presence of Christ at the eucharist, do not link that presence so definitely with the signs of bread and wine. The decision remains for the churches whether this difference can be accommodated within the convergence formulated in the text."

Jenson's teaching on Christ's eucharistic presence is heavily dependent on his Cyrilline or even neo-Chalcedonian Christology, which he stretches so far as to endorse Martin Luther's doctrine of the ubiquity of Christ's humanity as implied in what the reformer learned from some of his own disciples, namely, that "Christ, the one divine-human *person* as whom his divinity and humanity have their only actual existence, is not delimited by space. Thus we are to locate the divine-human Christ where he directs us to find him, where he has 'defined' his presence."[3] Jenson formulates systematically thus: "The person of the risen Jesus occurs as one

3. *ST* II, 257. Jenson refers to "the so-called *Syngramma Suevicum,* a joint manifesto by Johannes Brenz and other young pastors, many of whom had been students at Heidelberg when Luther came there for the famous disputations," and to Luther's *Vom Abendmahl Christi: Bekenntnis* (*WA* 29.324-42) and *Disputatio de divinitate et humanitate Christi* of 1540 (*WA* 39.2.101-2).

identity of this [trinitarian] God, without whom indeed this God would neither create space nor transcend it. Thus the risen man Jesus not only transcends space. Therefore his total self is located in God and in creation, and in either only because also within the other. . . . Christ, as the second identity of God, is at the right hand of the Father and just so can" be present and embodied "for and in" the church (*ST* II, 254).

With this, Jenson contrasts sharply the Leonine version of Chalcedon, in whose wake the "standard Western Christology" does not allow to the "hypostatic union" a "mutual participation" of the two natures but only a "communion of attributes" that "does not include a role for the man Jesus in any defining attribute of deity" (*ST* II, 255; cf. 257 n. 44). It was such "inadequate Christology" that, according to Jenson, lay behind the eucharistic occasions of confessional division in the sixteenth century:

> Catholic scholasticism had taught and continued to teach that the identity of Christ's body with the eucharistic elements was sheerly "supernatural," that is, true in exception to everything otherwise true of bodies, his included [Thomas Aquinas, *Summa Theologiae,* iii.75.4]. This exception must nevertheless be predictable; as we participate in the eucharist we cannot be wondering whether this time it is happening. The miracle is guaranteed by a character of the church's ministry: God grants the ordained minister authority to say, "This is my body" and have it be true in that it is said [Aquinas, *Summa Theologiae,* iii.78.4-5; 82.1-3].
>
> Reformers in the line of John Calvin in effect substituted the faith of the individual for the power of the church. Thus according to Theodore Beza's classic teaching, the bread and cup in their eucharistic use as visible *signa,* together with the verbal promises of Scripture, bring the *res* of the Supper before the soul. The Spirit uses this presence to open the soul and create faith. And to faith, local separation is no more real than to the Spirit who creates it. Thus in the eucharist the believer is joined to Christ in heaven, body and soul. (*ST* II, 255-56)

Jenson allows that the shifts to which Catholics and Calvinists alike resorted in order to compensate for their Christological inadequacies may themselves rest on other doctrines that are both true and necessary, whether the special character or charism of the ordained ministry or the life-giving and faith-creating activity of the Holy Spirit (*ST* II, 257). In a footnote he states that he does "not regard the differences between Catholic, Calvinist, and Lutheran theologoumena" in accounting for Christ's eucharistic presence "as legitimately church-divisive." Only Huldrych Zwingli is dismissed for sticking by "Leo's rule" and drawing "the conclusion others repressed": "In his human nature," said Zwingli, Christ "is departed," and that is to abandon "real presence" (*ST* II, 256).

The *United Methodist Hymnal* of 1988 contains, as hymn 627, hymn 57 of the Wesleys' *Hymns on the Lord's Supper:*

> O the depth of love divine,
> Th'unfathomable grace!
> Who shall say how Bread and Wine
> God into man conveys?
> How the Bread his Flesh imparts,
> How the Wine transmits his Blood,
> Fills his faithful people's hearts
> With all the life of God!

The Wesleyan eucharistic hymn 81, "Jesus, we thus obey/Thy last and kindest word," figures as hymn 614 in the British Methodist *Hymns and Psalms* (1983) and concludes thus:

> He bids us drink and eat
> Imperishable food;
> He gives his Flesh to be our meat,
> And bids us drink his Blood.
> Whate'er the Almighty can
> To pardon'd sinners give,
> The fullness of our God made man
> We here with Christ receive.

Anamnetic Sacrifice

The biblical and patristic category of "anamnesis" became central to liturgical and sacramental theology in the twentieth century. The command of Jesus to "do this for the remembrance of me *(eis ten emen anamnesin)*" regained the dynamism and direction inherited from Old Testament Israel's "cultic memorial" *(zkr)*, whereby God's mercy and works were recalled in thanksgiving and petition for their extension and renewal. By Christ's own institution, says *Baptism, Eucharist, and Ministry,* "the eucharist is the memorial of the crucified and risen Christ, i.e. the living and effective sign of his sacrifice, accomplished once and for all on the cross and still operative on behalf of all humankind" (E5). "United with the Son, its great High Priest and Intercessor," the church "gratefully recalls God's mighty acts of redemption" and "beseeches God to give the benefits of these acts to every human being" (E8).

Jenson brings out the narrative content and the ecclesiastical location of the "meal-thanksgiving": the prayer rehearses the history of God with Israel to which Jesus now conclusively belongs and the sacrifice by which he sealed the "new covenant" of Israel's eschatological hope; the shared bread and cup embodies joint participation in the new covenant's sacrifice of praise and petition (*ST* II, 186, 216, 219-20). Jenson finds in the notion of "anamnetic sacrifice" the clue to overcoming the Catholic-Protestant controversy over the sacrificial character of the Eucharist.

In the face of some popular beliefs and even theological theories, the sixteenth-century Reformers "rightly insisted that the mass is *not* a repetition of Calvary and adds nothing to it" — and "to sustain that answer, most of the Reformation thought it had to deny altogether that the mass is a sacrifice of Christ." From the other side, Catholics, while acknowledging abuses and denying that Christ's past sacrifice is repeated or added to, "were rightly determined above all to maintain the hitherto universal recognition that the eucharist is indeed a sacrifice and that Christ is its content." "*Representatio*" was the term found in Thomas Aquinas (*Summa Theologiae* iii.79.7) and used by the Council of Trent to express the belief that in the church's sacrifice "the same Christ is immolated without the shedding of blood, who on the cross offered himself once and bloodily" (DS 1739-1743). Jenson considers that the notion of "representation" is now best interpreted through the recovery of the biblical understanding of "*anamnesis,*" whereby a liturgical memorial renders that "the eucharistic sacrifice is the sacramental presence of the sacrifice on the cross" (*ST* II, 217-19, 258-60, 266). Jenson twice quotes the explanation of the Anglican-Roman Catholic International Commission on *Eucharistic Doctrine* (1972) that *anamnesis* or *representatio* is "the making effective in the present of an event of the past" (*ST* II, 258, 266); he draws also on the Joint Lutheran-Roman Catholic Commission's *The Eucharist* (1978) to say that the crucified and risen Christ is sacramentally "present *as* the once-for-all sacrifice for the sins of the world" (*ST* II, 266).

Jenson displays both the eschatological and Trinitarian dimensions of the eucharistic sacrifice. "The risen Christ," he says, "now offers himself and his church, the *totus Christus,* to the Father. This offering anticipates his eschatological self-offering, when he will bring the church and all creation to the Father that God may be 'all in all'" (*ST* II, 253). "As the Son and the Spirit come forth from the Father, so their agency is toward the Father. Therefore the body of the Son and the temple of the Spirit is directed to the Father. . . . The church gathers with the Son and in the Spirit to petition and adore the Father. . . . Agitated by the Spirit and implicated, as the Son's created body, with all creation as it is made through and for the Son, the church's petition and praise represent before the Father the petition and praise of all creation. That is to say, the church's vocation before the Father is *priestly,* and her service before him *sacrificial*" (*ST* II, 227). Jenson's accompanying capsule description of the eucharistic anaphora as "Praise, *Anamnesis,* and *Epiclesis*" matches exactly *Baptism, Eucharist, and Ministry*'s structure of "Thanksgiving to the Father," "Memorial of Christ," and "Invocation of the Spirit," and his systematic reflections chime with *Baptism, Eucharist, and Ministry*'s doctrinal declaration that "it is the Father who is the primary origin and final fulfillment of the eucharistic event. The incarnate Son of God by and in whom it is accomplished is its living centre. The Holy Spirit is the immeasurable strength of love which makes it possible and continues to make it effective" (E14). That not all Lutherans readily accept such developments emerges from the frequent complaint in many of their official responses to the Lima text that *Baptism, Eucharist, and Ministry,* by preferring the name "Eucharist," gave all too much weight to the man-to-God movement in the Lord's Supper.

The British Methodist *Hymns and Psalms* contains, as number 554, hymn 125 from the Wesleys' *Hymns on the Lord's Supper:*

> O God of our forefathers, hear,
> And make thy faithful mercies known;
> To thee through Jesus we draw near,
> Thy suff'ring, well-belovèd Son,
> In whom thy smiling face we see,
> In whom thou art well-pleas'd with me.

With solemn faith we offer up,
And spread before thy glorious eyes,
That only ground of all our hope,
That precious, bleeding sacrifice,
Which brings thy grace on sinners down,
And pérfects all our souls in one.

Acceptance through his only name,
Forgiveness in his blood, we have;
But more abundant life we claim
Through him who died our souls to save,
To sanctify us by his blood,
And fill with all the life of God.

Father, behold thy dying Son,
And hear the blood that speaks above;
On us let all thy grace be shown,
Peace, righteousness, and joy, and love;
Thy kingdom come to ev'ry heart,
And all thou hast, and all thou art.

Communion Ecclesiology

Jenson regards "*communio*-ecclesiology" as "modern ecumenism's chief theological achievement, to which the present work hopes only to contribute a few items" (*ST* II, 221). In fact, the sixth part of his *Systematic Theology,* where the themes of church and sacraments are woven together, includes three chapters with the titles "The Great Communion" (which takes its cue from 1 Cor. 10:16-17 and 11:17-34, where *koinonia* in the eucharistic and in the ecclesial body of Christ are mutually implied), "The Office of Communion" (where the ministerial structures and functions in the church are treated), and "The Mysteries of Communion" (where "sacramental events" are viewed as embodying or enacting "our communion with God and with one another").

An important stimulus to contemporary communion ecclesiology came from an article in the mid 1950s by the Orthodox theologian Nicolas Afanassieff on the Eucharist as "the sacrament of assembly." The notion was developed by John Zizioulas in a number of writings that were eventually gathered into his *Being as Communion* (1985). On the Roman Catholic side, the foundations were laid by Yves Congar, and the teaching found what Jenson calls a "compendious systematic presentation" in J.-M. R. Tillard's *Église d'églises* (1987) (*ST* II, 221). Tillard, whom Jenson recognizes as "a chief architect of much ecumenical consensus," exercised a strong personal and substantial influence on several bilateral dialogues as well as in the Faith and Order Commission of the World Council of Churches. When many of the official responses to *Baptism, Eucharist, and Ministry* called for deeper study of the implied ecclesiology, it was to *koinonia* that the commission turned for a governing idea.[4]

As Jenson notes, "*ekklesia* in the New Testament — and notably in 1 Corinthians [1:1; 7:17; 12:28] — can denote a local fellowship, or all such fellowships as a class, or all such fellowships as one great fellowship." A strength of communion ecclesiology is "its insistence on the integrity and wholeness of local churches," which — in their place — simply are the church; but a lopsided stress at this point can lead to "a remarkable sort of backhanded congregationalism in some Orthodox thinkers and their Western disciples." For "if besides the plurality of local churches, which are each the one church, this one church is herself a singular universal church, then this too must be a communion, and indeed a 'communion of many communities,' established in eucharistic fellowship among them and in the fellowship of pastors, liturgies, and disciplines that sustain this" (*ST* II, 223-25).

With regard to the bonds of communion among local churches, Jenson's opinions may be noted on three matters that have been historically controversial, especially between Protestants and Catholics. First, Jenson sets great store by the existence from New Testament times of an ordained ministry to care for "diachronic concord with the apostles" and considers it "logically included in responsibility for the church's historically continuing consensus that those who bear it are responsible for their

4. See *Baptism, Eucharist and Ministry 1982-1990: Report on the Process and Responses,* Faith and Order Paper No. 149 (Geneva: World Council of Churches, 1990), pp. 147-51; *On the Way to Fuller Koinonia: Official Report of the Fifth World Conference on Faith and Order, Santiago de Compostela 1993,* Faith and Order Paper No. 166 (Geneva: World Council of Churches, 1994); *The Nature and Purpose of the Church: A Stage on the Way to a Common Statement,* Faith and Order Paper No. 181 (Geneva: World Council of Churches, 1998).

own successors." Taking up a hint from fellow Lutheran George Lindbeck, Jenson places episcopacy — as a specific form of office clearly described by Ignatius of Antioch — among those historically contingent institutions, like canon and creed, that *post eventum* can be considered "dramatically necessary in the church's history, not mechanically determined beforehand but nevertheless, once there, the very thing that had to happen." They are irreversible in the sense that "on them the church has bet her future self-identity," and the Spirit's guidance may retrospectively be presumed if what results fits "the gospel's vision of fulfillment." The question is: "Does the picture of the bishop among the people, with flanking presbyters and serving deacons, *harmonize* easily with Scripture's evocations of the Kingdom? Can we, for example, call up the Revelation's scenes of eternal worship and sketch Ignatius's vision into them? Surely we can, and very satisfyingly. We could perhaps devise a different picture that fit, but again that can no longer be the point." Synchronically, it is the *college* of bishops which manifests and safeguards the communion of the local churches (*ST* II, 228-42).

Second, in envisioning the various "levels" at and between which ecclesiastical communion should exist, Jenson appears to have in mind not only the local and the universal church with whatever appropriate intervening *geographical* units, but also what used to be called "confessional families" and now go by the name of "Christian world communions."[5] Thus his "communion of communions" bears the marks of the "reconciled diversity" that the Lutheran World Federation has favored over "organic union" as a model of church unity. It must be asked whether it is appropriate to have more than one bishop "in each place." Or to put the question more positively: what institutional structures might allow for the continuance of authentic liturgical, spiritual, theological, and disciplinary traditions — without the divisiveness that separate "denominations" have enshrined?

With that we approach, third, Jenson's reflections on a "universal pastorate" (*ST* II, 242-49). "It is clear," writes Jenson, "that the unity of the church cannot now be restored except with a universal pastor located at Rome." The case for Rome is more than pragmatic though not strictly irreversible: it resides chiefly in the notion of apostolic churches as having "a

5. This seems implied by the expression "confessional churches" in *ST* II, 225, 226, 233.

continuing communal charism," with Rome specially distinguished as "the place to which the Spirit led Peter and Paul, in the book of Acts the Spirit's two primary missionary instruments, for their final work and their own perfecting in martyrdom." Vatican I is interpreted benignly, and Cardinal Ratzinger is invoked for the notion that the Petrine teaching office "cannot be restricted only to the expression of an already established common opinion but must under certain circumstances take the initiative over against the confusion of a church without consensus."

If Methodism has anything worthwhile to say on matters of a communion ecclesiology going beyond the local church, it may be related to lessons offered by the mixed history of "the conference" as an exercise of "corporate *episkopē*"; to the possibilities of "the connection" as a pattern for wider ecclesial networks; and to the vision of a separate denominational family mutating into what Albert Outler called "an evangelical order within the church catholic." In its Nairobi report, *Towards a Statement on the Church* (1986), the Joint Commission between the Roman Catholic Church and the World Methodist Council, declared it "not inconceivable that at some future date in a restored unity, Roman Catholic and Methodist bishops might be linked in one episcopal college, and that the whole body would recognize some kind of effective leadership and primacy in the bishop of Rome. In that case Methodists might justify such an acceptance on different grounds from those that now prevail in the Roman Catholic Church."

Baptismal Election

"The one sole object of eternal election," writes Jenson, "is Jesus with his people, the *totus Christus.* Augustine taught, with his elegant precision: 'just as this One is predestined, to be our head, so we many are predestined, to be his members.' What must be clearer than it is even in Augustine's aphorism is that these two choosings are only one event in God." The requisite clarity has been provided by Karl Barth: "According to Barth's insight, the dialectic of election and rejection is first to be construed not between human individuals, and so abstractly, but as the inner dialectic of the one person's, Jesus Christ's, story. As man he is elect, as God self-reprobate; but just so, within a proper Christology, he is reprobate and elect also as the man he is. Thus the dialectic of election and rejection is historical and so has *direction:* rejection is there always and only for the sake of election. Indeed, in that God in Christ takes our rejection on himself, it can no longer be our rejection, only Christ's. Christ is the accepted rejected one, and we who would have been rejected will be accepted in him" (*ST* II, 175-76).

"God's history with us," Jenson continues, "is one integral act of sovereignty, comprehended as his decision to reconcile us with himself in Christ Jesus. The existence and specific membership of the community are predestined in this decision, with the 'pre' appropriate to the biblical God." That last remark gets spelled out thus: "A right doctrine of individual predestination is precisely a doctrine about what happens to and for individuals when they encounter Christ in his gospel: that the judgment they hear then is nothing less than God's eternal act of decision. Baptism *is* the Father's giving of sheep to the Son's fold" (*ST* II, 178).

In Jenson it appears extraordinarily difficult to fail salvation, though not quite impossible. While at times he shares the neo-Lutheran stress on "performative language" that makes it seem sufficient to come within earshot of the gospel, he can also allow that "the gospel may not find faith" (*ST* II, 302). If "lack of faith cannot make the washing an ineffective sign," yet there may be "baptized persons who do not live by their baptism" and so perhaps, like unbelievers or those not (yet) brought into the church, "have not completed the history from reprobation to election" (*ST* II, 252, 360, 178 [cf. 364]). Like Barth, Jenson inclines strongly toward a final universalism but stops just short. With Isaac Dorner, one of his favorite oddball nineteenth-century Lutherans ("eccentrics," "outsiders"), Jenson contemplates the annihilation of the ungodly (*ST* II, 365).

In a way that allowed baptism itself to be understood as more than the punctiliar act with water, *Baptism, Eucharist, and Ministry* declared that "baptism is both God's gift and our human response to that gift. It looks forward towards a growth into the measure of the stature of the fullness of Christ (Eph. 4:13). The necessity of faith for the reception of the salvation embodied and set forth in baptism is acknowledged by all churches. Personal commitment is necessary for responsible membership in the body of Christ" (B8). Some Lutheran responses feared that this was undermining the efficacy of baptism itself, especially as administered to infants; but good Lutherans recognize with Luther and with Jenson that "the Christian has enough in baptism for his life's study and practice."[6]

6. *ST* II, 297, quoting Luther's *Large Catechism*, Baptism 41.

Methodists inherit from Wesley's preaching the sense that reliance on the regeneration sacramentally effected in baptism is a "broken reed" in the absence of the living faith that marks the filial awareness and obedient conduct of those who have received new birth as God's sons and daughters. Methodists also continue to be impressed by the position taken by Wesley in the face of the doctrines of predestination and perseverance taught by the Calvinists of his day: the promises of the covenant, in a Wesleyan understanding, are conditional. In both these matters, Methodists offend Lutherans accustomed to the "*baptizatus sum*" and the more recently fashionable terminology concerning the "unconditionality" of the gospel.

Numerical Flexibility

According to Jenson, "the profusion of the church's mysteries is historically rather than systematically determined and so can be captured by no merely conceptual structure." Not only systematically but dogmatically, Jenson appears to take a relaxed attitude toward the confessionally controversial question of the number of the church's sacraments: "there is no necessary dogmatic dissensus here" (*ST* II, 260-61).

While he devotes most attention to baptism, Eucharist, and ordination, Jenson also discusses confirmation (which is "one part of baptism's third- and fourth-century dramatic whole, gone off on its own"), penance (biblically needed for the discipline of the church as well as for a reconciliation "accomplished by an absolution directly on God's behalf"), healing (as "embodied prayer for the sick," "bodily disaster [being] a chief sign of creation's alienation from God's intention for it"), and marriage ("in its intrinsic intimacy and permanence, the chief created analogue of the Lord's relation to his people"). As further ecclesial mysteries Jenson reckons the name of God ("whether JHWH or Father, Son and Holy Spirit"), prayer ("especially the Our Father"), and "the departed saints' prayer for us" (*ST* II, 260-69, 368). In a chapter on "the Word and the icons," a sacramental consistency is attached by Jenson also to the reading of the Scripture and the proclamation of the gospel as well as to images that appropriately render Jesus and his story.

For Jenson, in contrast with "much of the tradition," "hearing" rather than "seeing" is the "paradigm of knowing": this is grounded in a metaphysic of "being as being mentioned" rather than "being as appearing." Eschatologically, "the redeemed will not cease to be created by the address of God," and insofar as their hearing will be "an immediate and fulfilled apprehension," it will be a "seeing," "the immediate presence that in created time we call sight" (*ST* II, 345; cf. 286).

In its Rio de Janeiro report, *The Word of Life: A Statement on Revelation and Faith* (1996), the Methodist-Roman Catholic dialogue affirms that "baptism, received once, and holy communion, received regularly in the Church's liturgical festivals, are at the heart of the life of holiness to which the faithful are called." The difference is noted that "while they are the two biblical sacraments recognized by the Methodist tradition, the Catholic tradition regards other holy actions of the church as also sacraments of the Gospel instituted by the Saviour: in them also God's grace reaches the faithful in keeping with some of the acts and words of Jesus to which the New Testament bears witness." After brief descriptions from the Catholic side of confirmation, reconciliation, anointing of the sick, marriage, and orders, the text continues:

> Although Methodists do not recognize these rites as sacraments of the Gospel, they too affirm the active presence of the Holy Spirit in the life of the faithful, the necessity of repentance for sins, the power of prayer for healing, the holiness of marriage, and the enablement by the Spirit of those who are called and ordained for the tasks of ministry.
>
> Catholics and Methodists both recognize other "means of grace" than those they count as sacraments. These include public and private prayer, the reading of Scripture, the singing of hymns, fasting, and what Methodists refer to as "Christian conversation." In the same category one may reckon the traditional works of mercy, such as visiting the sick and serving the poor. As the faithful meet the image of Christ in their neighbour, they acquire and develop a sense of the pervading sacramentality of the life of faith.

Conclusion

In *Unbaptized God* Jenson argued that the failure of the churches to attain ecumenical closure on several contested matters of faith and order was due to an inadequate doctrine of God. In keeping with a long and continuing ambition of his, he proposed to complete the "baptism" — in the name of Jesus crucified and risen — of the static and impassible deity that is the cultural inheritance from Greek metaphysics. I would rather speak of the perennial and ubiquitous need for postbaptismal catechesis in the church. Such has been met, in the second half of the twentieth century, by the remarkable "rediscovery of the Trinity," which liturgical and sacramental theology has both drawn on and contributed to.[7] Jenson has played his part in this through his stress on the historical character of God's self-revelation and redemptive work, although my preference would be to understand the divine sovereignty over time in a way that did not appear to make temporality constitutive of God. I agree with the Robert Jenson of the *Systematic Theology,* however, that some diversities, at least in metaphysics and theologoumena, need not, and therefore should not, be church-divisive — provided they do not thwart the worshiping assembly in its obedience to Christ's command to "do this" with trust in his promise of the great transformation that has already begun to be accomplished in the Spirit as earnest of the end.

7. See Geoffrey Wainwright, "The Ecumenical Rediscovery of the Trinity," *One in Christ* 34 (1998): 95-124.

Eschatology and Mission in the Theology of Robert Jenson

CARL E. BRAATEN

This essay will explore the treatment of eschatology, with particular attention to the systematic place of mission, in Robert Jenson's theological writings. Although there is no chapter on "the mission of the church" in the two volumes of his *Systematic Theology,* the missionary idea is integral to the eschatological structure of Jenson's theology. The biblical God is a missionary God; the gospel is a missionary address to the nations; the church is founded by the mission mandate of the risen Lord.

Ernst Troeltsch said at the end of the nineteenth century: "The bureau of eschatology is mostly closed nowadays."[1] At the beginning of the twentieth century Albert Schweitzer and Johannes Weiss opened a new chapter in the history of theology by demonstrating that Christianity began as an eschatological faith. The central idea of Jesus' message was the "good news of the kingdom of God." In the preaching of Jesus the kingdom of God was not thought of as an inner-worldly process of development leading to a better world through social reform, as taught by the theology of the Social Gospel Movement. The kingdom of God is rather, according to Schweitzer and Weiss, the power of God's own absolute future breaking in suddenly upon the present world, not the result of the progressive and cumulative good works of moral striving.

1. Quoted by Ludwig Widenmann, *Mission und Eschatologie* (Paderborn: Bonifacius, 1965), p. 11.

The generation of theologians after Schweitzer developed a variety of eschatological theologies. Karl Barth, Rudolf Bultmann, and Paul Tillich all made eschatology the starting point of their understanding of Christian faith and the mission of the church. Jenson's theology follows in the same line, but with a major qualification. He faults the school of dialectical theology for its neglect of the futurist orientation of biblical eschatology. In this respect his criticism is akin to that of his contemporaries, Wolfhart Pannenberg and Jürgen Moltmann. Jenson accepts Pannenberg's summary judgment: "Barth and similarly Bultmann related the Bible's futurist eschatology to the present by concentrating on the reality of God which is its constituting heart. But in the process they stripped it of its specific temporal structure, its drive toward future fulfillment."[2] Dialectical theology had an eschatology with no describable future contents. The future was reduced to futuricity, and eternity was equated with timelessness.

Jenson's eschatology is a theology of promise. The idea of promise forms the spine of his book *Story and Promise.* The biblical concept of promise points to God's future for fulfillment. This future is already present and at work in Jesus' ministry and destiny, his cross and resurrection. That is the good news of the kingdom of God. Jenson's futurist eschatology is the engine that drives his theology of mission. If the kingdom of God would already have arrived in the fullness of its power and glory on earth, there would have been no need for the church and its mission in world history. The element of "not yet" keeps the church on the way to the world proclaiming a message of hope for salvation. Present and future aspects of God's kingdom are present in the message of Jesus and the earliest Christian missionary proclamation. The Christian mission is the means by which the gospel of God's coming kingdom announces a future of fulfillment not only for the church but for the world.

Jenson's theology exhibits the closest possible connection between eschatological faith and missionary practice. We will show this to be true with respect to four major themes: the task of theology, the identity of God, the purpose of the church, and the meaning of eschatology. All of these themes are linked to the controlling theme of Jenson's entire theol-

2. R. W. Jenson, *Systematic Theology,* vol. I: *The Triune God* (Oxford: Oxford University Press, 1997); *Systematic Theology,* vol. II, *The Works of God* (Oxford: Oxford University Press, 1999). Hereafter abbreviated *ST,* by volume and page. Italics in quotations are Jenson's unless otherwise noted. Here, *ST* I, 309-10.

ogy, the confession of Jesus as the risen Lord. The resurrection of Jesus is an eschatological event. Without it there would be no need for Christian theology; there would be no Christianity. We would not know who God is — the God of the gospel. Without the appearances of the risen Christ, there would be no church, for the starting point of the church is the commissioning and sending activity of the post-Easter Jesus. The resurrection gives to Christian hope its definitive ground and content. Christian eschatology is not a mere replication of the eschatological ideas and apocalyptic dreams that can be found in the Old Testament and later Jewish writings.

I. The Task of Theology

Martin Kähler coined the saying, "Mission is the mother of all Christian theology." I think Jenson would agree and I will show why. The "Prolegomena" of Jenson's *Systematic Theology* contains a section entitled, "What Systematic Theology Is About." It acknowledges that various kinds of discourse may be called "theology." The word is often stretched to cover all sorts of religious reflection. However, Jenson uses the word "theology" in a very precise sense. Theology is the thinking of the church in the service of its gospel mission. He writes: "Theology is the thinking internal to the task of speaking the gospel. . . . The church's specific enterprise of thought is devoted to the question, How shall we get it across, in language, with signs other than linguistic . . . or by other behavior of our community, that Jesus is risen and what that means?" (*ST* I, 5).

"'He is risen' was — and is — the gospel."[3] The task of Christian theology is to reflect critically about the practices appropriate to the church, if it is to act on its belief that this proposition is true. "The church has a mission: to see to the speaking of the gospel, whether to the world as message of salvation or to God as appeal and praise" (*ST* I, 11). To the question whether theology is a "speculative" or "practical" discipline, Jenson prefers the Reformation answer: theology is a *habitus practicus,* a practical discipline. This was a conscious decision over against the medieval scholastic notion of theology as a speculative enterprise. The work of theology "must

3. R. W. Jenson, *God After God* (New York: The Bobbs-Merrill Company, 1969), p. 157.

always examine the church's verbal and other practice, and its own guidance of that practice, with the question, Does this teaching or other practice further or hinder the saying of the gospel?" (*ST* I, 11).

It is salutary for theology to realize that it has a definite object for its reflection. Theologians do not have to rummage around inside their guts to discover religious feelings or spiritual experiences to bring to expression. To cite a striking example of such a problematic approach Jenson quotes J. C. K. von Hofmann's influential statement: "I, the Christian, am the object of knowledge for me, the theologian" (*ST* I, 12). Doing theology as reflection on one's religious or Christian experience was the pattern of nineteenth-century Protestant theology in the line of Friedrich Schleiermacher. Jenson accepts Karl Barth's criticism of this approach; it turns theology into anthropology, away from God and the works of God to the human person and subjective states of mind or feeling.

The gospel cannot be equated with any set of religious experiences or moral values. The gospel is a witness to something that really happened — the resurrection of Jesus. Theologians are people "who take the gospel for the object of their reflection" (*ST* I, 11). Must a theologian be a believer? The question has been seriously debated. Medieval and Protestant scholastic theology held that theology was made up of "mixed articles," some of which could be held as true without being a believer, such as, there is a God, that God is One, all-powerful, and so forth. There could be a *theologia irregenitorum* — theology of the unregenerate — a body of truths that forms the first part of Christian theology. Jenson thinks, following Barth, that this is a mistaken way, and one that is indeed treacherous for Christian theology. The unbaptized elements, the truths that pagans and Christians supposedly share alike, provided the foundations on which the whole edifice of Christian theology was built. Since they were supposedly "natural" and "rational," the mixed articles of natural theology became the judge of the special articles of divine revelation. They occupied a large and privileged place in the prolegomena of both Protestant and Catholic dogmatics. Jenson refers to them as "systematically pompous prolegomena" (*ST* I, 11).There are no such mixed articles in Jenson's prolegomena. Absolutely everything — not only in the prolegomena but throughout the systematics — finds its place and derives its meaning from its relation to the gospel, the good news that Jesus lives and reigns beyond the grave. When this news is passed along from one generation to another, it creates a history of hearing and speaking the gospel. Everyone receives the gospel through this history of transmission, and thus in a more amplified sense, "theology is reflection internal to the act of tradition, to the turn from hearing something to speaking it. Theology is an act of interpretation: it begins with a received word and issues in a new word essentially related to the old word. Theology's question is always: In that we have heard and seen such-and-such discourse as gospel, what shall we now say and do that gospel may again be spoken?" (*ST* I, 14).

Jenson's answer to the question, "What is theology?" fits the missionary situation. Every missionary knows that evangelization is more than translating the Bible into a new language and placing it in the hands of people who do not yet believe. Proclaiming the gospel is more than repeating what has been heard and said before. The gospel must speak to the real hopes and fears of the people to be addressed, otherwise it will sail over their heads. Nor is the gospel spoken into a vacuum. In the missionary situation the gospel will always encounter a people with an antecedent religion of their own. It will find itself in a competitive situation. Theology is necessary to attend to the traffic that goes back and forth between the good news and the old religion. "In that the gospel is a message and Christianity therefore a missionary community, Christian understanding of God or humanity or destiny always emerges by the reinterpretation of some antecedent religious and theological understanding. People do not first invoke eternity when the gospel mission penetrates their temporal or geographical space" (*ST* I, 16).

Just because the God of Christian discourse is bound up with the story of Jesus and his resurrection, theological statements are eschatological. "A theological statement is therefore true if it in some way tells the story of Jesus Christ as the story of the end, and so the meaning, of our lives."[4] John Hick invented the phrase, "eschatological verification." Jenson accepts the phrase but, as one can readily expect, means something quite different than Hick had in mind.[5] The difference is Christological. When Christians confess that Jesus is Lord, they are saying that Jesus will make the final decision about their future, and that, of course, will prove to be true only at the end. Faith is the act of counting on it to be true even before it happens.

4. R. W. Jenson, *The Knowledge of Things Hoped For* (Oxford: Oxford University Press, 1969), p. 155.

5. Jenson, *The Knowledge of Things Hoped For,* p. 148.

II. The Identity of God

The resurrection of Jesus not only gives rise to the church and its mission; it also identifies who God is. When Christians talk about God, they have specifically in mind the "One who raised the Lord Jesus from the dead." To support this identification of God by the resurrection of Jesus, Jenson quotes a number of passages from Romans, 1 and 2 Corinthians, Galatians, Colossians, and 1 Peter. Yet in the history of Christian theology, I dare say, this is a Jensonian *novum*. Not even Walther Kunneth or Wolfhart Pannenberg — for whom the resurrection of Jesus is the criterion of all Christian truth — hinged the *identity* of God on the reality of Jesus' resurrection from the dead. I am more than happy to associate myself with this aspect of Jenson's doctrine of God. I think this is because when I was writing my book, *The Future of God*, Jenson was writing two of his books, *The Knowledge of Things Hoped For* (1968) and *God After God* (1969). We worried a lot at that time about how best to answer the "death of God" theologians who had assumed the initiative in American theology. A few sentences from my book formulate our common conviction that God defined himself in Jesus' resurrection. "The resurrection was an act by which God identified himself with the cause of Jesus, vindicating Jesus' claim to represent the future of God in his earthly ministry. . . . Our knowledge of God's final self-definition, the future of Jesus' own cause, and our mission of hope in the world are grounded in the resurrection of Jesus."[6]

It is important to add that for Jenson the Christian understanding of the identity of God as the agent who raised Jesus beyond death into lasting life presupposes Israel's answer to the same question, "Who is God?" For Israel God is "whoever rescued us from Egypt." In Christian faith they are the same God: the One who rescued Israel from Egypt is none other than the One who raised Jesus the Israelite from the dead (*ST* I, 44). Jenson puts the matter as succinctly as language will allow: God is what happens with Jesus. We cannot speak of the God of the gospel without speaking of Jesus. Is Jesus God? To say "yes" could be misleading. It might suggest that we already know who God is apart from Jesus, and then in recognizing something divine in him, we feel justified in calling him God. Jenson prefers to

6. Carl E. Braaten, *The Future of God* (New York: Harper & Row, 1969), pp. 73, 75.

say that God "is" Jesus, so that in identifying the latter we simultaneously identify the former.[7]

It has been the fate of many great theologians to have their career punctuated by important shifts of emphasis. The early Barth is contrasted with the later Barth, and even the latest Barth; the early Tillich with the later Tillich; and so forth. Not so with Jenson! His first systematic theology, *Story and Promise*, already made the moves we find in his latest opus, the two volumes of *Systematic Theology*. Already then, Jenson wrote, "The first great self-identification of Jahve was 'God is whoever got us out of Egypt.'" Yet that identification remained ambiguous until it could face and overcome the challenge of death. The new self-identification of God occurred in the resurrection of Jesus. "What was done in Israel's history, culminating in Jesus' resurrection, was that God worked out his self-identification."[8]

What does the self-identification of God in the resurrection of Jesus have to do with the doctrine of the Trinity, the construction of which has been the consuming passion of Jenson in these latter years? He has written as much on the Trinity as perhaps any contemporary theologian. Yet here too the resurrection of Jesus as eschatological event is the nexus for his understanding of the triune identity of God.

When the early missionaries preached the gospel to the Greeks, they did not simply repeat the names of God in the Old Testament. Their new way of naming God mentioned the Lord Jesus in the same breath. Most commonly in the apostolic witness God is "the Father of our Lord Jesus Christ" (*ST* I, 45). Here is the narrative origin of the Trinitarian naming of God as "Father, Son, and Holy Spirit." In Christian usage this is the proper name of God. This name acquired definitive status when Jesus commissioned his disciples to go and make disciples of all nations, baptizing and teaching "in the name of the Father and of the Son and of the Holy Spirit" (Matt. 28:19).

There is no God beyond the God of his temporal revelation in the person of Jesus. Jenson adopts and works with Rahner's Rule: The economic and the immanent Trinity are one and the same. Yet that was also Luther's radical insight; we do not come closer to the real God by rising

7. R. W. Jenson, *The Triune Identity* (Philadelphia: Fortress Press, 1982), p. 22.
8. R. W. Jenson, *Story and Promise* (Philadelphia: Fortress Press, 1973), p. 41.

above his temporal revelation, above his humanity in the life, death, and resurrection of Jesus Christ.[9]

III. The Purpose of the Church

The Trinitarian doctrine of God is reflected *ad extra* in the structure of the church's historical existence. Jenson writes: "The Christian missionary lives in the trinitarian time-pattern. Blown onward by the Spirit, he serves the Lord to carry out the promises of the Father. And he does not mitigate the tension of this situation, that is, he does not compromise these instances in any timeless unity."[10]

How did the church come into existence? Jenson appropriates a saying of Alfred Loisy as exactly the truth, "Jesus announced the kingdom, but it was the church that came" (quoted in *ST* I, 24 n. 6; II, 170). History did not come to an end, eschatological expectation went unfulfilled; instead, the Parousia was delayed, and the Spirit entered into the breach and empowered the early witnesses of the risen Lord to undertake the mission of the gospel to Jews and Gentiles. J. C. Hoekendijk was fond of saying: The church does not have a mission; the church is mission.[11] Jenson has his own way of making the same claim: "At the very beginning there was no difference between the church and its mission; the first gatherings of believers were gatherings of missionaries."[12] The mission was eschatology in the process of realizing itself. The earliest believers were messengers of the kingdom.

It soon became clear to the apostles that the eschatological message of the resurrection of Jesus could not be confined to the people of Israel. Israel herself believed that if her God were the one true God, the creator of the universe, he must be the God of all peoples, and that his salvation must somehow reach and embrace them. Again, it was the resurrection of Jesus, understood as an eschatological event, that opened the mission to all the Gentiles. The worldwide preaching of the gospel was carried out under the

9. Jenson, *The Triune Identity,* p. 27.

10. Jenson, *The Triune Identity,* p. 31.

11. In his book, *The Church Inside Out* (Philadelphia: Westminster Press, 1966), J. C. Hoekendijk criticized the centripetal tendencies in traditional views about the church, which made the mission an afterthought.

12. Jenson, *The Triune Identity,* p. 29.

authority of the risen Christ, who promised to be with his missionary people "to the close of the age." Israel's mission finds its fulfillment in the resurrection of Jesus as the beginning of the end and in the universal mission to the nations in the power of the Spirit.

The church has now existed two millennia since the coming of Christ. Yet, she is still looking forward to the coming of Christ. One of the more interesting locutions in Jenson's ecclesiology is: "The church is . . . an eschatological detour" (*ST* II, 171). What does this mean? It means that the church is not yet the kingdom of God. He rejects the notion of "realized eschatology" (*ST* II, 171). He prefers the language of Georges Florovsky, "The church is 'anticipated eschatology'" (*ST* II, 171). This idea seems to capture what Wolfhart Pannenberg means by "proleptic eschatology." It means that the kingdom is really present in Jesus, in his person, words and deeds, without ceasing to be future with respect to the church and the world.

The mission command of the risen Lord is to make disciples, baptize, and teach in the name of the "Father, Son, and Holy Spirit." Jenson places his doctrine of the sacraments within the framework of the eschatological mission of the gospel to the nations. Baptism is the missionary sacrament par excellence. It signifies a conversion from the old eon that is passing away to the new age that is dawning with the coming of Christ. It introduces new believers into a community centered in the worship of the triune God and committed to carry on the mission of making disciples, baptizing, and teaching.

Baptism is the church's initiation, the church's act to incorporate new members into herself. Christianity is a missionary faith: those who believe that Jesus is indeed risen are sent across history and geography to tell this gospel-news to the world. Those whom the mission brings to "repentance," whom it turns from old religion or irreligion to new faith, are just so brought into the new community of the church, the community of those who are in the one direction newly and differently turned toward God and are in the other direction sent in their turn on the mission. . . . When the church's mission holds its proper place in the church's consciousness, baptism will rank as what Luther called it, "the royal sacrament."[13]

13. R. W. Jenson, *A Large Catechism* (Delhi, N.Y.: An ALPB Publication, 1991), p. 46.

The church is not in the business of promoting religion. Religion in fact is the chief competitor of the gospel the church is called to proclaim. Those most strongly committed to a given religion are often most deaf to the gospel. To shake people loose from the worship of idols or other gods is the most difficult task of evangelism.

IV. The Meaning of Eschatology

Christian eschatology took shape on two fronts. On the first front it inherited from Israel the basic elements of its own answer to the realities of sin and death, and the problem of evil in the world. Israel expanded its own experience of salvation as the chosen people into a cosmic narrative of the creation and redemption of the world. Israel's story of salvation included the belief that God will appoint and anoint a special agent, a messiah, to accomplish his purpose. Christianity began as a radical revision of Jewish eschatological hope in its primitive confession that Jesus is indeed the long-awaited messiah. Jesus is the bringer of a new age, a new covenant, a new commandment, and a new mission of God to all the nations. Israel looked to the future for salvation; Christianity split that future into two parts. The future has already arrived in part with the coming of Christ; the rest will come at the end of history, when the kingdom of Christ is handed over to the Father.

Every Christian theology must somehow deal with the fact that Christianity began as an eschatological revision of Israel's messianic hope. Karl Barth stated in his Romans commentary: "Christianity that is not entirely and altogether eschatology has entirely and altogether nothing to do with Christ."[14] But what kind of eschatology? It might not be an exaggeration to say that the chief concern and contribution of Jenson's theology is to get eschatology right. What is the relation between eschatology and history, between eternity and time, and between the three tenses of time? Jenson is not afraid to perform a high-wire act of speculative metaphysical reflections on these topics.

There are historical and nonhistorical types of eschatology. Jenson's is radically historical. There are history-oriented eschatologies whose

14. Karl Barth, *The Epistle to the Romans,* trans. Edwyn C. Hoskyns (Oxford: Oxford University Press, 1933), p. 314.

prime category is the past, others whose center of gravity is the future. Jenson has taken the futurist option. The reason, I think, is twofold. As we have already indicated Jenson broke with the dialectical theology because in voiding the future it was untrue to the New Testament. The other reason is that a future-less eschatology does not correspond to the historical nature of human existence.

Jenson agrees with Bultmann's hermeneutical principle that we always approach a text with a prior interest. We bring a question to the text inquiring after its possible meaning for our existence. If this is so, we must ask what bearing the text has on our future. Jenson writes: "To question a text historically means to question it with reference to my own future — that is, with reference to the decision the text may call upon me to make. To question a text theologically is to question it about my final future, about what is to come of my life. . . . There must be a conclusion to my story if the occurrences of my life are to be a story at all. . . . Therefore the question about God is the presupposition of all historical questioning; and all historical questioning is implicitly the God-question."[15]

The decisive point in Christian eschatology is that the answer to the question about God as the end and meaning of life is given in Jesus' resurrection as the promise of our own future and the conclusion of the story of human life. In spelling out the logic of theological language we find the closest possible fit between the resurrection of Jesus as eschatological event and God as the future and fulfillment of all history and human life.

Jenson follows the tradition of dogmatic theology in placing his chapter on eschatology at the end. The chapter is relatively brief, and rightly so, because eschatology has formed the spinal column of the entire systematics project from start to finish. Often students tremble when they broach the subject of eschatology because the silliest things have been concocted under that rubric. Eschatology has proved to be the most unstable part of Christian doctrine. At this point Jenson's last chapter might well become one of the most useful teaching texts. Not only does it deliver eschatology from the wild cuckooland of fanciful and useless speculations à la Hal Lindsey and the like, but it provides the right starting point and set of criteria for making eschatological statements essential to Christian faith.

The right starting point is to ask the question: "What does the gospel

15. Jenson, *The Knowledge of Things Hoped For,* pp. 165-66.

promise?" (*ST* II, 311). The category of promise is the key to biblical eschatology; it is also the theme a different facet of which is explored in each of eleven chapters of Jenson's little systematic theology, *Story and Promise*, a favorite of many of his fans and by now a virtual classic of basic Christian teachings.

Well, what does the gospel promise? The answer to that question is what we mean by eschatology. The gospel promises that the outcome of history, the combined story of all persons, communities, nations, and even the entire cosmos, will be fundamentally different because Jesus lives, rules, and will come again to judge all the living and the dead (*ST* II, 310). So far any child in Sunday School would be able to understand that. But different in what respect? The plot thickens. The ultimate promise of the gospel is deification. That is a polysyllabic concept unheard of in the ordinary catechesis of Catholic and Protestant Christianity. Yet it looms large in the latest phase of Jenson's contribution to a full development of eschatological theology. Here East meets West. Jenson has been a serious student of the Eastern Fathers. He has also been more receptive than most other Western theologians to the contemporary rediscovery of the theology of Eastern Orthodoxy and its ecumenical significance. He quotes Basil the Great who says that in the end the Spirit will bring about "endless joy in the presence of God, becoming like God, and . . . becoming God" (*ST* II, 311). A thousand assertions of the like can be found in the writings of the Eastern Fathers. More interesting and also more controversial is Jenson's appeal to Luther in support of the idea of deification. He has expressed himself in full agreement with the recent Finnish Luther-interpretation of Tuomo Mannermaa and his disciples.[16] Here is a Luther-quote cited by Jenson: "Our shame is great, that we were the devil's children. But the honor is much greater, that we are children of God. For what greater fame and pride could we have . . . than to be called the children of the Highest and to have all he is and has?" Jenson takes this as an ontological assertion. The gift of final salvation is to be in union with Christ, and thus included into the life of the triune God, to participate in the glory of the life of the Trinity without ceasing to be finite creatures.

If we wish to create eschatological scenarios of the future with explicit content, beyond talk about union with Christ and entering into the

16. See Carl E. Braaten and Robert W. Jenson, eds., *Union with Christ: The New Finnish Interpretation of Luther* (Grand Rapids: Eerdmans, 1998).

life of the triune God, we are tempted to let our imaginations run riot in the field of biblical apocalyptic imagery and poetic symbolism. The notion of a chronological sequence of events piling up at the end of history is ruled out because it diverts attention from Christ as the sole object of Christian hope. The entire Christian hope for the future is directed to Christ. He is the one and only way of entry into the life of the triune God. There is no other way.

In contrast to the pluralistic theology of religions Jenson holds that if people of other religions attain salvation, this is bound to happen the same way as for Christians, by incorporation into Christ. "If followers of other religions enter the Kingdom proposed by the gospel, this is not because they have arrived at the salvations proposed by their religions" (*ST* II, 363). The only way of salvation is through the gospel. This does not rule out the possibility that people outside the church, people who have not heard the gospel, may be saved. Only God in the power of his freedom knows how this could come about, and as for us, Jenson writes, "it would be entirely useless to make guesses" (*ST* II, 364).

How can we talk about the eschatological future since it lies above and beyond the realm of human experience and empirical verification? How can we set limits to what the imagination might wish to project about the future outcome and final destiny of all things? How is it possible to have a Christian doctrine of "last things"? Jenson writes, "There are several limiting controls" (*ST* II, 317). The first is the doctrine of the Trinity. "No vision of fulfillment can be true if what it depicts could not fit into that life" (*ST* II, 317) — the life of the triune God. The second one is the vision of the kingdom of God, which tells of God's coming to perfect his rule over his creation. "No eschatological vision, therefore, can be appropriate that does not begin and end with God and his purposes for the community of creatures" (*ST* II, 318). The third control is the Ten Commandments, which stipulate God's intentions for the human community. In summing up what kind of eschatological vision will then result from observing these controls, Jenson comes up with a single word, "love." "'Love' is the New Testament's and the church's single word for the future the gospel holds out, whether for this age or for the End. It could not be otherwise. The Spirit is the agent of love in the triune life, and the Spirit is the agent of eschatological perfection. Therefore love must be the summary reality of all that blessed creatures can have in God" (*ST* II, 319).

Jenson stakes out a position on most of the disputed questions in the history of biblical interpretation and dogmatic teaching on the "last things." What is the final judgment? Will personal consciousness survive death in the resurrected state of being? Will only believers be resurrected on the last day, or will there be a general resurrection including everyone? How should we interpret the final advent of Christ? How can we achieve the final goal of deification without ceasing to be finite creatures? What is the appropriate way to conceive of eternal life? Why is the symbol of the immortality of the soul a distortion of the biblical symbol of the resurrection of the body? What about universal salvation? Will all be saved in the end? *Tolle lege!* Take up Jenson's two volumes and read, if you are looking for answers to these and many other questions.

I will conclude this essay with a word about the way Jenson concludes his two volumes of systematic theology. The section is simply entitled, "Telos." It is half a page in length. In the end God will be all in all. Yet Jenson says more than that. He ended his first volume, reflecting on the beauty of God, with the statement: "God is a great fugue" (*ST* I, 236). Now he ends volume two on the same note: "The last word to be said about God's triune being is that he 'is a great fugue'. . . . The end is music" (*ST* II, 369). Beautiful!

Bibliography

COMPILED BY JEREMY G. A. IVE

1. Books by R. W. Jenson

Alpha and Omega: A Study in the Theology of Karl Barth. New York: Thomas Nelson, 1963.

America's Theologian: A Recommendation of Jonathan Edwards. Oxford: Oxford University Press, 1988.

Essays in Theology and Culture. Grand Rapids: Eerdmans, 1995.

God after God: The God of the Past and the God of the Future Seen in the Work of Karl Barth. Indianapolis and New York: Bobbs-Merrill, 1969.

The Knowledge of Things Hoped For. Oxford: Oxford University Press, 1969.

A Religion against Itself. Richmond: John Knox, 1967.

Story and Promise: A Brief Theology of the Gospel about Jesus. Philadelphia: Fortress Press, 1973.

Systematic Theology, volume 1: *The Triune God.* New York: Oxford University Press, 1997.

Systematic Theology, volume 2: *The Works of God.* New York: Oxford University Press, 1999.

The Triune Identity: God according to the Gospel. Philadelphia: Fortress Press, 1982.

Unbaptized God: The Basic Flaw in Ecumenical Theology. Minneapolis: Fortress Press, 1992.

Visible Words: The Interpretation and Practice of the Christian Sacraments. Philadelphia: Fortress Press, 1978.

[with Carl E. Braaten] *The Futurist Option.* New York: Newman Press, 1970.

[edited] *Christian Dogmatics,* 2 volumes. Philadelphia: Fortress Press, 1984.

[edited, with Carl E. Braaten] *The Catholicity of the Reformation.* Grand Rapids: Eerdmans, 1996.

[edited, with Carl E. Braaten] *Either/Or: The Gospel or Neopaganism.* Grand Rapids: Eerdmans, 1995.

[edited, with Carl E. Braaten] *A Map of Twentieth Century Theology: Readings from Karl Barth to Radical Pluralism.* Minneapolis: Fortress Press, 1995.

[edited, with Carl E. Braaten] *Marks of the Body of Christ.* Grand Rapids: Eerdmans, 1999.

[edited, with Carl E. Braaten] *Reclaiming the Bible for the Church.* Edinburgh: T. & T. Clark, 1996.

[edited, with Carl E. Braaten] *Sin, Death, and the Devil.* Grand Rapids: Eerdmans, 1999.

[edited, with Carl E. Braaten] *The Two Cities of God: The Church's Responsibility for the Earthly City.* Grand Rapids: Eerdmans, 1997.

[with Eric Gritsch] *Lutheranism: The Theological Movement and Its Writings.* Philadelphia: Fortress Press, 1976.

2. Articles by R. W. Jenson

"About Dialog, and the Church, and Some Bits of the Theological Biography of Robert W. Jenson." *dialog* 11 (Autumn 1969): 272-78.

"Aspekte der Christologie in einer pluralistischen Gesellschaft." In *Christsein in einer pluralistischen Gesellschaft,* pp. 113-17. Ed. Hans Schulze and Hans Schwarz. 1971.

"Apostolicity in the Gospel." In *Lutheran-Episcopal Dialog: A Progress Report,* pp. 49-61. Ed. P. Day and P. D. Opsahl. St. Louis: Concordia Publishing House, 1972.

"Appeal to the Person of the Future." In R. W. Jenson and C. E. Braaten, *The Futurist Option,* pp. 147-58. New York: Newman Press, 1970. [Reprint of "Some Platitudes About Prayer." *dialog* 9 (Winter 1970): 61-66.]

"An Attempt to Think about *Mary.*" *dialog* 31, no. 4 (Fall 1992): 259-64.

"Beauty." *dialog* 25 (Feb. 1986): 250-54.

"The Body of God's Presence: A Trinitarian Theory." In *Creation, Christ and Culture.* Festschrift for T. F. Torrance. Ed. R. W. A. McKinney. Edinburgh: T. & T. Clark, 1976.

"A Call to Faithfulness." *dialog* 30 (Spring 1991).

"Can American Community Sustain Itself without Common Faith?" *dialog* 15 (Fall 1976): 270-78.

"Can Deterrence Be Justified as a Lesser Evil?" (Debate with Paul Hinlicky). *Currents in Theology and Mission* 12 (October 1985): 261-76.

"Can a Text Defend Itself? An Essay *de Inspiratione Scripturae.*" *dialog* 28 (Autumn 1989): 251-56.

"The Christian Doctrine of God." In *Keeping the Faith: Essays to Mark the Centenary of Lux Mundi,* pp. 25-53. Ed. Geoffrey Wainwright. London: SPCK, 1985.

"Christ-dogma and Christ-image." *dialog* 2 (Spring 1963): 146-51.

"The Church and Mass Electronic Media: The Hermeneutic Problem." *Religious Education* 82, no. 2 (Spring 1987): 278-84.

"The Church as Communion: A Catholic-Lutheran Dialogue-Consensus-Statement Dreamed in the Night." *Pro Ecclesia* 4, no. 1 (Winter 1995): 68-78.

"Concerning and Illustrating New Orders for the Eucharist" [Pan-Lutheran Liturgical Commission]. *dialog* 10 (Winter 1971): 68-72.

"Creation as a Triune Act." *Word and World* 2 (Winter 1982): 34-42.

"A Dead Issue Revisited." *Lutheran Quarterly* 14 (February 1962): 53-56.

"The Division of the Moral Person." In *Encounters with Luther,* vol. 1, pp. 259-67. Ed. Eric Gritsch. Gettysburg: Institute for Luther Studies, 1980. [Discussion, pp. 268-71.]

"Does God Have Time? The Doctrine of the Trinity and the Concept of Time in the Physical Sciences." *Centre for Theology and the Natural Sciences Bulletin* 11 (Winter 1991): 1-6. [Reply by R. J. Russell, pp. 7-19.]

"The Doxological Concept of History in the Theology of Peter Brunner." In *Zur Auferbauung Des Liebes Christi: Festgabe für Professor D. Peter Brunner,* pp. 181-96. Ed. Edmund Schlink and Albrecht Peters. N.p.: Johannes Stauda-Verlag, 1965.

"The Elusive Bottom Lines." *dialog* 29 (Spring 1990): 111-18.

"Eschatological Politics and Political Eschatology." In R. W. Jenson and C. E. Braaten, *The Futurist Option,* pp. 93-106. New York: Newman Press, 1970. [Reprinted from *dialog* 8 (Autumn 1969): 272-78.]

"Eucharist: Its Relative Necessity, Specific Warrants and Traditional Order." *dialog* (Spring 1975): 122-33.
"The Evil as Person." *Lutheran Theological Seminary Bulletin* 69, no. 1 (Winter 1989): 33-42. [Discussion, pp. 40-42.]
"The Eye, the Ear and Lutheranism." *dialog* 29 (Summer 1990): 174-77.
"Faithfulness." *dialog* 14 (Winter 1975): 38-41.
"The Father He . . . ." In *Speaking the Christian God: The Holy Trinity and the Challenge of Feminism,* pp. 95-109. Ed. Alvin F. Kimel. Grand Rapids: Eerdmans; Leominster: Gracewing, 1992.
"Film, Preaching and Meaning." In *Celluloid and Symbols,* pp. 41-49. Ed. John C. Cooper and Carl Skrade. Philadelphia: Fortress Press, 1970.
"The Futurist Option of Speaking of God." *The Lutheran Quarterly* 21, no. 1 (February 1969): 17-25. [Also published in Martin Marty and Dean Pearman, eds., *New Theology,* no. 7. New York: Macmillan, 1970.]
"The God Question." *Lutheran Forum* 26, no. 4 (November 1992): 46-50. [Reply by M. H. Madson, pp. 51-54.]
"God, Space and Architecture." In R. W. Jenson and C. E. Braaten, *The Futurist Option,* pp. 165-73. New York: Newman Press, 1970. [Originally in *Response.*]
"Gott als Antwort." *Evangelische Theologie* 26, no. 7 (1966): 368-78. [Reprinted in Jorg Schagarda, ed., *Philosophische Theologie in Schaten des Nihilismus,* pp. 146-59. 1971.]
"The Hauerwas Project." *Modern Theology* 8, no. 3 (July 1992): 287-95.
"An Hermeneutical Apology for Systematics." *dialog* 4 (Fall 1965): 268-74.
"The Holy Spirit." In *Christian Dogmatics,* vol. 2, pp. 105-85. Ed. R. W. Jenson. Philadelphia: Fortress Press, 1984.
"Jesus, Father, Spirit: The Logic of the Doctrine of the Trinity." *dialog* 26, no. 4 (Fall 1987): 245-49.
"Jesus in the Trinity: Wolfhart Pannenberg's Christology and Doctrine of the Trinity." In *The Theology of Wolfhart Pannenberg: Twelve American Critiques with an Autobiographical Essay and Response,* pp. 188-206. Ed. Carl E. Braaten. Minneapolis: Regent, 1988.
"Justification as a Triune Event." *Modern Theology* 11 (October 1995): 421-27.
"Karl Barth." In *The Modern Theologians,* volume 1, pp. 23-49. Ed. D. F. Ford. Oxford: Oxford University Press, 1989.
"The Kingdom of America's God." *dialog* 15 (Winter 1976): 12-20. [Also in

Sidney F. Ahlstrom, ed., *Religion and the Dilemma of Nationhood.* Minneapolis: Lutheran Church in America, 1976.]

"Die Kontinuitaet von Alien and Neuem Testament als Problem für Kirche und Theologie Heute." In *Hoffnung ohen Illusion,* pp. 88-103. Ed. Helmutt Zeddies. 1970.

"Language and Time." *Response* 8 (1966): 75-80.

"A Lenten Sermon" [Mark 6:14-29]. *dialog* 21 (Summer 1982): 229-30.

"Liberating Truth and Liberal Education." *Lutheran Quarterly* 13, no. 3 (August 1961): 211-17.

"Liturgy of the Holy Spirit." *Lutheran Quarterly* 26, no. 2 (1974): 189-203.

"Lutheran Conditions for Communion in Holy Things." In *Lutheran-Episcopal Dialogue: A Progress Report,* pp. 127-38. Ed. P. Day and P. D. Opsahl. St. Louis: Concordia Publishing House, 1972. [Also in *Concordia Theological Monthly* 43 (November 1972): 687-92.]

"The Mandate and Promise of Baptism." *Interpretation* 30, no. 3 (July 1976): 271-85.

"Marriage and Ministry." *Lutheran Forum* 31 (Winter 1997): 20-22.

"Mr. Edwards' Affections." *dialog* 24 (Summer 1985): 169-70.

"The Modernity of Lutheranism." In *Encounters with Luther,* volume 1, pp. 90-97. Ed. Eric Gritsch. Gettysburg: Institute for Luther Studies, 1980. [Discussion, pp. 98-103.]

"Modernity's Undermining of Its Own Foundations," *Trinity Seminary Review* 18 (Summer 1996): 5-12.

"Odysseus, Ulysses and the Wanderer" [with John C. Bale]. *dialog* 3 (Summer 1964): 179-84.

"On Becoming Man: Some Aspects." In R. W. Jenson and C. E. Braaten, *The Futurist Option,* pp. 107-20. New York: Newman Press, 1970.

"On Hegemonic Discourse." *First Things* 45 (August/September 1994).

"On Infant Baptism." *dialog* 8 (Summer 1969): 214-16.

"On Infant Communion Again." *Lutheran Forum* 30 (Winter 1996): 18.

"On the ELCA's Ecumenical Choices." *dialog* 35 (Summer 1996): 222-23.

"On the Problem(s) of Scriptural Authority." *Interpretation* 31 (July 1977): 237-50.

"On Recognising the Augsburg Confession." In *The Role of the Augsburg Confession: Catholic and Lutheran Views.* Ed. Joseph A. Burgess. Philadelphia: Fortress, 1980.

"On the 'Joint Declaration' of the LWF and the RC Church on the Doctrine of Justification" [editorial]. *Pro Ecclesia* 5 (Spring 1996): 137-41.

"On Renewing of the Mind: Reflections on the Calling of Christian Intellectuals." *The Cresset* 6, no. 4 (February 1988): 10-16.

"Once More the Jesus of History and the Christ of Faith." *dialog* 11 (Spring 1972): 118-24.

"Orpheus, the Buttonmaker and 'Real Community.'" *dialog* 10 (Winter 1971): 33-38.

"The Praying Animal." *Zygon* 18 (Summer 1983): 311-25.

"The Preacher, the Text and Certain Dogmas." *dialog* 21 (Spring 1982): 107-13.

"Proclamation Without Metaphysics." *dialog* 1 (Autumn 1962): 22-29.

"A 'Protestant Constructive Response' to Christian Unbelief." In *American Apostasy: The Triumph of Other Gospels,* pp. 56-74. Ed. Richard John Neuhaus. Grand Rapids: Eerdmans, 1989. [Discussion, "The Story of an Encounter," ed. Paul Stallsworth, pp. 80-84, 98, 102, 121-27.]

"Psalm 32." *Interpretation* 33 (April 1979): 172-76.

"A Quick Correction." Views and Counter-Views, *dialog* 30 (Summer 1990): 247.

"Rechtfertigung and Ecclesiologie" [Lecture delivered to the conference of the joint RC-Lutheran Study Commission, "Kirche and Rechtfertigung," Ecumenical Institute, Bossy, March 10-14, 1996]. *Kerygma und Dogma* 42 (July 1996): 42.

"Religious Pluralism, Christology and Barth." *dialog* 20 (Winter 1982): 31-38.

"The Religious Power of Scripture." *Scottish Journal of Theology* 1 (1999): 89-105.

"Reply to Peters on 'Sacrifice.'" *dialog* 24 (Fall 1985): 299-300.

"Response" [to H. Paul Santmire's review of *A Religion Against Itself*]. *dialog* 7 (Summer 1968): 229-30.

"Response" [to J. E. Smith on Karl Barth]. *Union Seminary Review* 28, no. 1 (Fall 1972): 31-34.

"Response to Aardahl." Views and Counter-Views, *dialog* 29 (Summer 1990): 223.

"Response to Marshall." Views and Counter-Views, *dialog* 29 (Spring 1990): 142.

"The Sacraments." Part 2 of R. W. Jenson and H. Schwartz, "The Means of

Grace." In *Christian Dogmatics,* vol. 2, pp. 291-388. Ed. R. W. Jenson. Philadelphia: Fortress Press, 1984.

"A Sermon Preached in the Chapel of Gettysburg Seminary" [Genesis 4:1-16]. *dialog* 19 (Spring 1980): 141-43.

"A Sermon Preached during the Summer of 1976 to a Flourishing Congregation in a Small Western Pennsylvania Town" [on Lamentations 3:22-33]. *dialog* 16 (Summer 1977): 255-56.

"Simplistic Thoughts about the Authority of Scripture." *Word and World,* supplement 1 (1992): 181-90.

"The 'Sorry' State of the Lutherans." *dialog* 22 (Fall 1988): 280-83.

"Story and Promise in Pastoral Care." *Pastoral Psychology* 26 (Winter 1977): 113-23.

"Thanks to Yeago." *dialog* 31 (Winter 1992): 23.

"Theosis." *dialog* 32, no. 2 (Spring 1993): 108-12.

"Three Identities of One Action." *Scottish Journal of Theology* 6 (December 1975): 1-15.

"Toward a Christian Theory of the Public." *dialog* 23 (Summer 1984): 191-97.

"Toward an Understanding of 'Is Risen.'" *dialog* 19 (Winter 1990): 31-36.

"'*Triplex Usus*' of Worldly Learning." *Lutheran Quarterly* 14 (May 1962): 121-25.

"The Triune God." In *Christian Dogmatics,* volume 1, pp. 83-191. Ed. R. W. Jenson. Philadelphia: Fortress Press, 1984.

"The Triunity of Truth." In Jenson, *Essays in the Theology of Culture* [v.s.], pp. 84-94.

"Violence as a Mode of Language." In *Encounters with Luther,* volume 1, pp. 37-50. Ed. Eric Gritsch. Gettysburg: Institute for Luther Studies, 1980.

"What Academic Difference Would the Gospel Make?" *dialog* 18 (Winter 1977): 24-27.

"What Did Forde Mean?" Views and Counter-Views, *dialog* 30 (Summer 1991): 247.

"What Difference Post-Modernity Makes for the Church." *Trinity Seminary Review* 18 (Winter 1997): 83-92.

"What If the Document on Justification Were Adopted?" *Pro Ecclesia* 6, no. 1 (Winter 1997): 99-105.

"What Is Salvation?" *dialog* 12 (Summer 1973): 197-205.

"Wilhelm Dilthey and a Background Problematic of Theology." *Lutheran Quarterly* 15 (August 1963): 212-22.
"Worship as Drama." In R. W. Jenson and C. E. Braaten, *The Futurist Option*, pp. 159-60. New York: Newman Press, 1970. [Originally in *Janus.*]
"Worship as Word and Tone." In R. W. Jenson and C. E. Braaten, *The Futurist Option*, pp. 175-83. New York: Newman Press, 1970.
"You Wonder Where the Spirit Went." *Pro Ecclesia* 2, no. 3 (Summer 1993): 296-304.

3. Editorials by R. W. Jenson (in Chronological Order)

"Vietnam: A Comment." *dialog* 5 (Spring 1966): 84-85.
"The America of the Inaugural." *dialog* 8 (Spring 1969): 84-85.
"Dr Strangelove on TV." *dialog* 8 (Autumn 1969): 245.
"Vietnamization Means War." *dialog* 10 (Spring 1971): 90-91.
"When Is a Conspiracy?" *dialog* 10 (Spring 1971): 91-92.
"The Pentagon Papers and the Technocrats." *dialog* 10 (Autumn 1971): 247-48.
"The Plot Not to Kidnap Kissinger." *dialog* 11 (Spring 1972): 88.
"Preus' Statement: Its Heresy and Foolishness." *dialog* 11 (Summer 1972): 164-65.
"LCA, Centralization, Gospel Authority and the Lutheran Clergy Association." *dialog* 11 (Spring 1972): 88-89.
"Ezekiel — Notes from an Editor Abroad." *dialog* 12 (Spring 1973): 88-89.
"Remember Watergate." *dialog* 12 (Autumn 1973): 249-50.
"Alger Undone — A Theological Parable." *dialog* 13 (Autumn 1974): 245-46.
"Managers at Baltimore" [LCA Convention]. *dialog* 13 (Autumn 1974): 249-50.
"Nixon and Homo Americanus." *dialog* 13 (Winter 1974): 6-7.
"Missouri and the Existential Fear of Change." *dialog* 14 (Autumn 1975): 247-50.
"A Jeremiad from the New Editor." *dialog* 14 (Winter 1975): 4-6.
"An Ironic Bicentennial." *dialog* 14 (Winter 1975): 10-11.
"The Wages of Covetousness." *dialog* 15 (Spring 1976): 100-101.
"You Shall Not Kill." *dialog* 15 (Summer 1976): 164-65.
"The Quinlan Case." *dialog* 15 (Summer 1976): 168.

"The Quinlan (and Other) Cases." *dialog* 15 (Winter 1976): 6.
"Remember the Sabbath Day." *dialog* (Spring 1977): 85-86.
"Commandment 1½." *dialog* 16 (Summer 1977): 165-66.
"Preaching and the Blackout." *dialog* 16 (Autumn 1977): 244-45.
"Carter and Homo Americanus." *dialog* (Winter 1977): 8.
"About This Issue" [Abortion]. *dialog* 17 (Spring 1978): 84-85.
"Male and Female." *dialog* 17 (Summer 1978): 164-66.
"The Last Book" [*Lutheran Book of Worship*]. *dialog* 17 (Autumn 1978): 247.
"Once More for Lutheran Union." *dialog* 17 (Autumn 1978): 246.
"The LCA Convention." *dialog* 17 (Autumn 1978): 249.
"Justice in Palestine." *dialog* 18 (Spring 1979): 85-86.
"On the Coming, Bigger Church." *dialog* 18 (Summer 1979): 166-67.
"T[hree] M[ile] I[sland]." *dialog* 18 (Summer 1979): 167-68.
"Once, Some Years Ago, the Editor Was Accused of Attacking Only Republican Presidents." *dialog* 18 (Autumn 1979): 244-45.
"Communion Malpractices." *dialog* 18 (Winter 1979): 4-6.
"In This Issue [The Church and the Liberal Arts], plus . . . ." *dialog* 19 (Spring 1980): 84-85.
"Belated re Kueng." *dialog* 19 (Spring 1980): 86-87.
"On Returning from the DDR to the American Campaign." *dialog* 21 (Summer 1980): 164-65.
"The LCA Convention." *dialog* 19 (Autumn 1980): 245-47.
"A Modest Proposal [re: non-sexist language]." *dialog* 20 (Spring 1981): 85-86.
"El Salvador." *dialog* 20 (Summer 1981): 184-85.
"Duplication Forever" [against the Lutheran merger]. *dialog* 20 (Autumn 1981): 266-67.
"Unity and Polity" [Lutheran Unity Study Materials]. *dialog* 20 (Winter 1981): 6-7.
"Back to the Barricades!" [nuclear deterrence]. *dialog* 21 (Spring 1982): 85-86.
"Twentieth Anniversary." *dialog* 21 (Summer 1982): 164-66.
"1982." *dialog* 21 (Autumn 1982): 244-45.
"What's That Again?" *dialog* 21 (Winter 1982): 4.
"On Communicidal Hatters." *dialog* 22 (Summer 1983): 166-67.
"Central America." *dialog* 22 (Autumn 1983): 244-45.

"The U.S. Lutheran-Roman Dialog on Justification." *dialog* 23 (Spring 1984): 84-85.

"About These Years." *dialog* 23 (Summer 1984): 164-66.

"Modest Proposals II [on the role of ordained clergy in the new Lutheran church]." *dialog* 23 (Autumn 1984): 286-87.

"The Inclusive Lectionary." *dialog* 23 (Winter 1984): 4-6.

"The Pastor Roth Case." *dialog* 24 (Spring 1985): 85-86.

"On the Decadence of American Politics." *dialog* 24 (Winter 1985): 6-7.

"Stop the [Lutheran] Merger." *dialog* 25 (Summer 1986): 162-63.

"One, New, Inclusive, Lutheran Church." *dialog* 25 (Winter 1986): 2-3.

"The Good Americans." *dialog* 26 (Summer 1987): 163-64.

"Who Do You Say That I Am?" *dialog* 26 (Summer 1987): 164-65.

"Now What?" [Lutheran merger]. *dialog* 26 (Winter 1987): 6.

"The Vatican, Father Curren and Us." *dialog* 26 (Winter 1987): 7-8.

"The Loss of the Word." *dialog* 27 (Autumn 1988): 248-49.

"Churchly Honor and Judge Bork." *dialog* 27 (Winter 1988): 2-3.

"The Parties against Democracy." *dialog* 27 (Winter 1988): 3.

"Charter for a Corinthian Mission." *dialog* 28 (Spring 1989): 82-83.

"Reflections from an Editor on Sabbatical Abroad." *dialog* 27 (Summer 1989): 163-64.

"On Lutheranism and Cozy Ecumenism." *dialog* 28 (Autumn 1989): 242-43.

"What Now?" [1991 ECLA Assembly]. *dialog* 29 (Autumn 1990): 245-46.

"How Long?" *dialog* 29 (Winter 1990): 4-5.

"Whatever Sort of Juice Are They Stewing up There in St. Anthony Park?" [Lutheran-Episcopal Dialog III]. *dialog* 30 (Spring 1991): 85-86.

"Reflections on a Burst of Patriotism" [Gulf War]. *dialog* 30 (Spring 1991): 88-89.

"Say It Ain't So Herb [Chilstrom]." *dialog* 30 (Autumn 1991): 264.

"So Why Did Braaten Do It?" *dialog* 30 (Autumn 1991): 262-63.

"A Sad Chiasmus." *dialog* 30 (Autumn 1991): 266.

"What Ails Lutheranism?" *dialog* 30 (Winter 1991): 3-4.

"Response to Philadelphia." *dialog* 31 (Spring 1992): 155-56.

"The Lima Text." *dialog* 22 (Winter 1993): 5-7.

"Some Contentious Aspects of Communion" [Roman Catholic response to ARCIC I]. *Pro Ecclesia* 2, no. 2 (Spring 1993): 133-36.

"An Inclusive St. Patrick's Day in New York." *Pro Ecclesia* 2, no. 2 (Spring 1993): 137-38.

"An Orthodox/Reformation Consensus." *Pro Ecclesia* 2, no. 4 (Fall 1993): 400-403.

"The Youth and Age of Theological Journals." *Pro Ecclesia* 3, no. 1 (Winter 1994): 22-23.

"Death in Vitro." *Pro Ecclesia* 4 (Winter 1995): 13-15.

"On the 'Joint Declaration of the Lutheran World Federation and the Roman Catholic Church on the Doctrine of Justification.'" *Pro Ecclesia* 5 (Spring 1996): 137-41.

"The American People." *First Things* 92 (April 1997): 12-13.

"On the Vatican's 'Official Response' to the Joint Declaration on Justification." *Pro Ecclesia* 7 (Fall 1998): 401-4.

Index